**The Poetics
of Empire
in the Indies**

PENN STATE STUDIES
in ROMANCE LITERATURES

Editors

Frederick A. de Armas   Alan E. Knight

Refiguring the Hero:
From Peasant to Noble in
Lope de Vega and Calderón
by Dian Fox

Don Juan and the Point of Honor:
Seduction, Patriarchal Society,
and Literary Tradition
by James Mandrell

Narratives of Desire:
Nineteenth-Century Spanish
Fiction by Women
by Lou Charnon-Deutsch

Garcilaso de la Vega and the
Italian Renaissance
by Daniel L. Heiple

Allegories of Kingship:
Calderón and the
Anti-Machiavellian Tradition
by Stephen Rupp

Acts of Fiction:
Resistance and Resolution
from Sade to Baudelaire
by Scott Carpenter

Grotesque Purgatory:
A Study of Cervantes's *Don
Quixote*, Part II
by Henry W. Sullivan

Spanish Comedies and Historical
Contexts in the 1620s
by William R. Blue

The Cultural Politics of *Tel Quel*:
Literature and the Left in the
Wake of Engagement
by Danielle Marx-Scouras

Madrid 1900:
The Capital as Cradle of
Literature and Culture
by Michael Ugarte

Ideologies of History in the
Spanish Golden Age
by Anthony J. Cascardi

Medieval Spanish Epic:
Mythic Roots and Ritual Language
by Thomas Montgomery

Unfinished Revolutions:
Legacies of Upheaval in Modern
French Culture
*edited by Robert T. Denommé and
Roland H. Simon*

Stages of Desire:
The Mythological Tradition in
Classical and Contemporary
Spanish Theater
by Michael Kidd

Fictions of the Feminine in the
Nineteenth-Century Spanish Press
by Lou Charnon-Deutsch

The Novels and Plays of
Eduardo Manet:
An Adventure in Multiculturalism
by Phyllis Zatlin

Fernando de Rojas and the
Renaissance Vision:
Phantasm, Melancholy, and
Didacticism in *Celestina*
by Ricardo Castells

James Nicolopulos

The Poetics of Empire in the Indies

Prophecy and Imitation
in
La Araucana and *Os Lusíadas*

The Pennsylvania State University Press
University Park, Pennsylvania

Publication of this book has been aided by a grant from The Program for Cultural Cooperation Between Spain's Ministry of Culture and United States' Universities.

Library of Congress Cataloging-in-Publication Data

Nicolopulos, James.
   The poetics of empire in the Indies : prophecy and imitation in La araucana and Os lusíadas / James Nicolopulos.
      p.   cm. — (Penn State series in Romance literature)
   Includes bibliographical references and index.
   ISBN 0–271–01990–5 (cloth : alk. paper)
   1. Ercilla y Zúñiga, Alonso de, 1533–1594. Araucana. 2. Camões, Luís de, 1524?–1580. Lusíadas. 3. Imitation in literature.
4. Prophecy in literature. I. Title. II. Series.
PQ6389.A23N53 2000
861'.3—dc21   99-42052
                                                                                              CIP

Copyright © 2000 The Pennsylvania State University
All rights reserved
Printed in the United States of America
Published by The Pennsylvania State University Press,
University Park, PA 16802-1003

It is the policy of The Pennsylvania State University Press to use acid-free paper for the first printing of all clothbound books. Publications on uncoated stock satisfy the minimum requirements of American National Standard for Information Sciences—Permanence of Paper for Printed Library Materials, ANSI Z39.48–1992.

*To my parents, Thomas J. and Sara L. Nicolopulos,
without whose early stimulus toward
reading literature—especially Homer—
this book would have been inconceivable.*

Contents

	Preface	ix
	Introduction	1
1	"Con que ilustrar pudiese más su historia": The Crisis of Imitation in the *Araucana*	21
2	Ercilla's Eclectic Web of Epic Prophecy	65
3	Ercilla's Literary Necromancy: Shades of Lucan and Juan de Mena in Fitón's Cave	119
4	The Light of *Lusíadas* in Fitón's Cave: Inscribing Imperial Rivalry in Magic Crystals	175
5	Plotting Imperial Rivalry: The *Mapaemundi* of the *Lusíadas* and the *Araucana*	221
	Notes	271
	Works Cited	307
	Index	319

Preface

The Iberian navigations and ultramarine conquests of the fifteenth and sixteenth centuries brought forth a newfound, exotic flowering from the hoary trunk of the tradition of the learned, heroic narrative poem: the so-called epics of the Indies. In these poems the hallowed occidental practice of *imitatio* (a method of composition predicated on the imitation of model texts) was confronted with the difficult task of "making sense" of the encounter of Europeans with new, non-Western physical and cultural realities. Poetic imitation, far from serving as mere digressive ornament in otherwise "historical" narratives, played a key role in the construction of a new "poetics" of imperialist expansion that had, for the first time in occidental experience, truly global repercussions.

The central hypothesis of this book is that the application of a coherent theory of imitation to the two foremost epics of the Indies reveals long-ignored dimensions of this novel poetics of empire "in action," as it were. In particular, this approach allows us to recover the general outlines of how aesthetically encoded messages elaborated through imitation strive for interpellative dominance on ideological, dynastic, and even economic fields of contention vital to the imperialist and colonialist enterprises of the age. In order to demonstrate this hypothesis, in the present study I focus on a pair of works that undisputably have been considered the two most successful long narrative poems—both commercially and artistically—of the so-called Golden Age of Iberian letters, as well as the two most outstanding and innovative examples of the newly minted epic of the Indies.

The groundwork for this study begins with an analysis of imitation in *La Araucana*, a heroic poem of thirty-seven cantos published serially in three parts (1569, 1578, 1589) by its author, the Castilian courtier-soldier-poet Alonso de Ercilla y Zúñiga (1533–94). Meticulous delving into the imitative strata underlying Ercilla's elaboration of the venerable theme of encomiastic prophecy—a motif central to imperialist epic from at least the time of Virgil's *Aeneid*—reveals compelling evidence of a poetic, ideological, and dynastic rivalry with the "other" most well-known epic of the Indies. *Os Lusíadas* (1572), a verse epic in ten cantos by the celebrated Portuguese poet Luis de Camoens (1524–80)—himself also a sometime courtier and longtime soldier by profession—has been compared often enough to *La Araucana*. Nonetheless, the constitutive relationship between the two poems seems to have been forgotten since the seventeenth century despite a number of fairly obvious generic affinities between the two works.

In no small measure the attraction for readers of *La Araucana* and *Os Lusíadas* can be attributed to the skill with which their respective authors combine the venerable discursive resources of the occidental tradition of learned heroic verse with novel subject matter and geographic theaters of action. Both Ercilla and Camoens sing of sixteenth-century Iberian ultramarine imperialist expansion into spaces of the globe that had been either totally undreamt of or that had constituted semifabulous "oneiric horizons" up until very recently before the two poets set out to proffer their own models for the "modern" renovation of what was still the most prestigious of all narrative genres. It has long been recognized that the various articulations of the imitation of prestigious literary models inform, configure, and determine much of sixteenth-century Iberian poetic practice in both the Old World and the New. Furthermore, few would deny that both Ercilla and Camoens rely heavily on imitation to mediate the alterity of their subject matter; nonetheless, a persistent, Post-Romantic tendency to deprecate the artistic value of imitation on the one hand, and on the other, to assign privileged status to the verifiable, historical elements in these poems, can perhaps be held responsible for the failure to discern the dialogic contours and connections of the poetics of empire in *La Araucana* and *Os Lusíadas*.

This is not to suggest, of course, that there has been a dearth of studies of imitation in the two poems. Almost all of these, however, at least up until quite recently, have concentrated exclusively on the identification and filiation of supposed sources, analogues, or both for the particular elaboration of given topics or passages. Furthermore, because most of these studies have been conducted on the premise that imitation is a fairly straightforward and one-dimensional practice, their authors have failed to descry the vital rivalry and dialogue between the two works that a more theoretically coherent approach reveals. The purpose of this book, then, is to offer a rectification of this case of critical myopia in regard to two of the most thoroughly studied long narrative poems in the Iberian tradition as an argument for the utility of a more nuanced appreciation of Renaissance practices of imitation, even in the newly reconstituted field of colonial studies. It is my contention that only through such an approach will we achieve a more comprehensive exploration of the poetics of empire in the Indies.

In order to further the achievement of this goal, I have marshaled my analyses and attendant arguments into an Introduction and five chapters. In the Introduction I review some of the issues raised by Ercilla's choice of genre and the consequent implications for the intrusion of poetic imitation into his fundamentally historiographical subject matter. In particular, I focus on how the issue of imitation has influenced ongoing debates about the representation of the Amerindian Other in the poem. This in turn leads to a discussion of the current state of imitation studies and the possible relevance of various approaches for analysis of the phenomenon in the context of the long narrative, rather than lyric, poem.

Once this groundwork for the section on theoretical approaches to imitation in Chapter 1 has been laid out, I reprise briefly the issues related to the processes and circumstances involved in the composition of the *Araucana*. This leads into a capsule overview of the critical reception of the poem, particularly in regard to the theme of prophecy and Ercilla's change of tack between Parts I (1569) and II (1578). Overall, the principal function of the Introduction is to prepare the ground for the central issues examined in Chapter 1.

In Chapter 1, I demonstrate that there is a noticeable change in course between Parts I and II of the *Araucana*. Part I, published in 1569, ends as it begins, focused exclusively on the war in Arauco. Ercilla engages in imitation of models, but does so eclectically, dissimulating his subtexts, and seems to be striving for an impression of firsthand reportage. Although there are isolated incidents of supernatural apparitions and prophecies, they are brief, incidental, and disjointed. They in no way constitute an integral part of a web of prophecy in the mold established by the *Aeneid* and consolidated by the *Orlando Furioso*, the two most influential and prestigious long narrative poems at the time Ercilla was writing. In contrast, Part II of the *Araucana*, first published in 1578, is carefully crafted around a web of prophecy that serves to highlight imitation of identifiable models, as well as to connect the action at the colonial periphery to the grand scheme of empire at the metropolitan center.

In the final section of the same chapter, I also propose certain theoretical criteria and a terminology for approaching the question of imitation, which is the key to unlocking the secret of the sea-change in the trajectory of the *Araucana* between 1569 and 1578. In my discussion of imitation, I establish that there is a fundamental difference, from the point of view of interpretation, between dissimulative imitation that seeks to disguise the poet's borrowings and imitation that advertises its relation to a specific subtext. Furthermore, imitation that deliberately calls attention to the model may take a variety of postures relative to that model. Among these are a reverential, or to use Greene's term, a reproductive, stance that seeks to re-create the subtext as closely possible. As I indicate in my discussion of Juan de Mena's imitation of the witch passage of *Pharsalia* 6 (in Chapter 3), this type of sacramental imitation often amounts to little more than translation when the model is inscribed in a different language from that of the imitation. In addition to presenting this reproductive approach to the model, however, the skillful poet disposes of various degrees of transformative imitation. In regard to these last, I make a fundamental distinction between other types of competitive imitation and what Greene calls necromantic imitation, where anachronism imposes a problematic gulf between the target text and the imitation. A successful necromantic imitation, as I demonstrate at length in Chapter 3, "revives" the ancient, "dead" model text, and makes it sing again in a new way, with renewed relevance for the cultural and linguistic circumstances of its own times. Often, such a resuscitation also involves an important dimension of rivalry, where the imitator, in addition to reviving the prior text, attempts to supplant it with his or her own. Not all cases of poetic rivalry expressed in imitation, however, are confined to circumstances where the problem of anachronism plays a major mediating role. I examine one such example in detail in Chapter 3 as well: Lucan's imitation of Ovid's witch scene. Returning to the final section of Chapter 1, I explain there why I reserve the term *emulation* for the description of this type of rivalry in which the poet clearly announces his subtext, and then subjects it to various transformations in an attempt to supplant it with his own version. The fundamental distinction is that in the case of what I call emulation, the target text is in no way dead or in need of revival in order to function in the *mundus significans* of the emulator; on the contrary, it must be surpassed on its own terms. As I explain in Chapters 4 and 5, it is in terms of emulation that we must examine Ercilla's *aleph* and *mapamundi*. Finally, it is important to bear in mind that these imitative practices, in general, had been refined by Petrarch and the Petrarchists and definitively assimilated into Iberian poetics by Garcilaso. I insist at some length on the significance of Garcilaso as a model for Ercilla, not only in terms of specific textual imitations, but even more important, as presenting a paradigm of imitative practice. It is crucial to bear in mind here that Camoens, too, is a consummate Petrarchist/Garcilasist, perhaps the most skillful and successful of the Iberian poets of his generation, a group that includes Ercilla.

In Chapter 2, I demonstrate how Ercilla weaves his web of prophecies in the manner of the *Aeneid* and the *Orlando Furioso*. Ercilla constructs this prophetic structure out of an essentially eclectic mosaic of imitations, borrowing from a variety of sources, and tends to dissimulate his debts to Virgil and Ariosto, among others, and to foreground his imitations of Lucan, Juan de Mena, and Garcilaso. This self-created "genealogy" of imitation clearly corresponds to a fierce sense of Iberian identity and a systematic program of Castilianization of his epic—within the norms of imitative practice established by Garcilaso—on the part of Ercilla. In the final section of Chapter 2, I show how Ercilla combines a direct textual imitation of Garcilaso with an emulation of Garcilaso's highly transformative imitative technique in the description of the powers of the wizard Fitón.

I elucidate Ercilla's most outstanding exercise in this Garcilasist, necromantic approach to imitation in Chapter 3. Ercilla's depiction of the chamber of magical substances is the most unequivocal example of the necromantic imitation and emulation that so characterize Part II of the *Araucana*, in contrast to the dissimulative imitation of Part I. Ercilla focuses on his Iberian predecessors in this passage and reveals an intense spirit of competition and a burning desire to supplant his forerunners in the tradition of the Spanish epic. As I point out in the concluding remarks of that chapter, understanding the depth, complexity, and ferocity of the competitive impulse in Ercilla's poetic practice is the necessary prerequisite for comprehending the visions in Fitón's cave and, ultimately, the different tack in the course of the *Araucana* that becomes evident with the publication of Part II in 1578.

Bracketed by his two most aggressively announced imitations of prestigious models—the list of substances and the conjuration of the infernal powers—Ercilla introduces the reader to the wizard's globe and to the first of the visions it displays. As I demonstrate in Chapter 4, Fitón's orb is no garden-variety magic mirror of the type found in the *Seven Sages of Rome*, and all of its subsequent manifestations, but rather a true *aleph*, or representation of the visualization of the Neoplatonic Intelligible All. Furthermore, both Ercilla's first and second séances with the Araucanian enchanter's magic crystal correspond to the respective appearances of a glowing globe representing the aleph in the *Lusíadas*. Camoens, of course, published his poem in 1572, six years before the appearance of Part II of the *Araucana* in 1578, making it certain that Ercilla had ample time to become acquainted with the Portuguese poem before publishing the second part of his own. As I point out, Manuel de Faria e Sousa, a seventeenth-century critic steeped in imitative practice and not blinded by the prejudices of Romanticism, clearly recognized Ercilla's *globo* as an imitation of the mantic spheres of the *Lusíadas*.

Furthermore, I demonstrate that Ercilla's aleph is not a simple, reproductive imitation of Camoens's prophetic globes. On the contrary, Ercilla effects a subtle transformation, reducing the highly philosophical conception of Camoens's *globos* back somewhat toward the idea of an optical instrument. This mutation corresponds to Ercilla's strategy of emulation. To have surpassed Camoens's poetic realization of the aleph would probably have been beyond Ercilla's powers in any case, but the field where the Castilian poet is most anxious to outdo his Portuguese contemporary and rival is that of the glories of their respective empires. To this end, Ercilla creates a recognizable, but not slavishly exact, imitation of Camoens's medium of imperialist prophecy—the aleph—in order to draw the reader's attention to the superiority of the content of the visions he proffers in contrast with those presented by the Portuguese poet.

In the first vision, Ercilla counterpoises the unity and transcendence of the Battle of Lepanto to the glorious, but somewhat diffuse, review offered by Camoens of some fifty years of seaborne military expansion in the East. It is the second vision in the aleph, however, that holds the real key to Ercilla's rivalry with Camoens. The Portuguese poet takes the topos of the literary mapamundi, a locus originally incorporated into the epic in poems celebrating the first European conquest of the cultural Other, Alexander of Macedon's triumph over the Persian Empire and march into India, poems themselves composed in the context of the crusades of the twelfth century—important precursors of the sixteenth-century Iberian overseas enterprise—and molds this topos into the culminating vision of his own celebration of overseas imperialism. As I have indicated, several points in the elaboration of the *mapaemundi* of the *Lusíadas* would particularly have affronted Ercilla's intense Castilian pride and would have been taken as a challenge to the dynasty that he served. The most serious of these, aside from the whole question of Portuguese independence from Castile, was the issue of the colonial control and exploitation of the Spice Islands.

Thus it is with the poetic gauntlet flung down in the mapaemundi of the *Lusíadas* in mind that Ercilla sets out to construct his own mapamundi. As I demonstrate in Chapter 5, section 5.4, there is a long list of correspondences between Ercilla's mapamundi and those of Camoens. In every case, Ercilla responds to the challenge of his Portuguese rival in some discernible and significant manner. Thus his response to Camoens's treatment of the sources of the Nile or the decline of Rome, for instance, is largely poetic, in the sense that Ercilla attempts to surpass his rival's poetic presentation of the *materia*. On the other hand, Ercilla also makes a much more overtly political response to Camoens's celebration of Portuguese independence, implicitly denying just that in his presentation of Lisbon and Coimbra as cities of Hispania. The same is even more true in the key question of Magellan's voyage and the "ownership" of the Moluccas. Above all, Ercilla seeks to surpass Camoens in the universality and grandeur of his mapamundi.

Nonetheless, it would be very easy to dismiss the points of correspondence between the mapaemundi of the *Lusíadas* and the *Araucana* as simply features inherent in the topos. Would not any sixteenth-century poet have sung of the sources of the Nile, fabled Meroë, the decline of Rome, and Magellan's discovery of the straits, to mention only a few of the coincidences between the two poems? Ercilla, after all, is not crude in his emulation, and he does not directly assault his rival, although the implications are clear enough for the competent reader. It is really not so surprising that for several centuries, critics steeped in the cult of originality and the perspectives of Romanticism should have failed to see the significance of the correspondences between Ercilla's and Camoens's mapaemundi, and this in spite of the fact that many have come very close to the mark. José Toribio Medina, for instance, cites the passage on Magellan from the *Lusíadas* in his note on the corresponding place in the *Araucana*, but without drawing any conclusions (Ercilla, *Araucana*, ed. Medina, 4:383). María Rosa Lida de Malkiel observes, correctly, that both Ercilla and Camoens are in some way imitating Juan de Mena in their respective mapaemundi (*Juan de Mena*, 32, 492), yet the great Argentine critic takes this notion no further. In fact, as Ercilla intended it to be, it is the presentation of the mapamundi in the second vision seen in the aleph, precisely as Camoens has framed his geographical prophecy, that confirms beyond a doubt that Ercilla wrote his mapamundi in a direct spirit of rivalry with Camoens. Of course, it is this realization that strips away the veils and permits us to perceive the emerging outlines of a new poetics of empire in the Indies.

Finally, this note would be incomplete if I did not take the opportunity to mention at least a few of the many, many people whose patient readings, kind advice, and generous support have made it possible for me to "bring this ship into a safe harbor" at last. First of all, I owe a tremendous debt to José Durand, who first introduced me to the wonders of Fitón's cave; as well as Arthur Askins, who played an analogous role for me with the complex world of the *Lusíadas*; and to Gustavo Costa and Louise George Clubb, who did the same for me with Ariosto. Without the patience and intelligent readings and commentaries of Emilie Bergmann and Ignacio Navarrete, the basic research would never have found its way into written form. For subsequent readings and acutely helpful comments I am equally indebted to Anne Cruz, Fred de Armas, and especially, Elizabeth B. Davis. Nor should I overlook the patient willingness to read and comment on the part of my colleagues Naomi Lindstrom and Vance Holloway. Finally, those who know me will appreciate that it is no mere formula or hyperbole to say that this project would never have reached completion without the untiring and unquenchable love and support of my wife, Christina Barber-Nicolopulos.

Introduction

On a cold night in late August 1557, a young Spanish officer lay awake within the damp fortifications that he and his comrades had hastily erected near Penco on the shores of the Bay of Concepción in what is now the South American country of Chile. If we are to believe what he tells us, it was not only physical discomfort and anxiety about the imminent assault by the warlike Amerindian inhabitants that kept him from sleep, but also an almost obsessive preoccupation with preserving the memory of his experiences in writing (*Araucana* 17.34–35). Alonso de Ercilla y Zúñiga (1533–94), for that was the young nobleman's name, like so many of his fellow countrymen who took part in the conquest of what were still being called the "western Indies," seems to have been particularly sensible of the extraordinary nature of the enterprise in which he was taking part.

Indeed, it has been observed often enough that there is an acute consciousness of participating in events of "epic" proportions that is evident in the eyewitness reports and chronicles of the conquest written by Ercilla's near contemporaries such as Bernal Díaz del Castillo or Alvar Núñez Cabeza de Vaca, to name only two of the best known. In contrast to these others, however, Ercilla was the first to formulate his account explicitly as a long heroic poem—*La Araucana* (1569, 1578, 1589, 1597)—rather than as a historiographical prose narrative. This choice of form was laden with implications and consequences that were not only to make Ercilla's poem the earliest, most successful, and most widely read literary portrayal of the conquest, but also to transform the *Araucana* into a highly problematic representation of that momentous encounter that still arouses readers' interest as well as often contentious critical debate.

One such consequence can be seen in the way in which Ercilla was to frame his tale of that night in 1557 and the attack that he was to help repel the following morning. By the time the poet came to write the version of the assault that first appeared in print in 1578, the military action itself still was described with a high degree of historical accuracy, almost as if in a chronicle, with one salient exception. The incursion by Tucapel—one of Ercilla's most memorable Amerindian characters—into the fort and his subsequent escape are clearly based upon classical and Renaissance literary models, as is Tucapel himself (*Araucana* 19.31–34, 51–52, 20.7–17; Murrin 98, 101).

Dwarfing the echoes of Virgil and Ariosto suggested by the Tucapel sequence, however, are two highly developed, extensive episodes that effectively bracket the fighting in and around the fort at Penco. In his narration of the night following the assault, Ercilla spins a tale of his encounter with an indigenous woman that permits him to intercalate a lengthy, quasi-pastoral, amorous fiction into his otherwise grim account of colonial warfare. Probably spun out of material inspired by models as diverse as Statius and Ariosto, the literary rather than historical provenance of the episode is patent to the competent reader (Schwartz Lerner 620–23).

The poet's rendering of the preceding night, and what ostensibly occurred to him as he lay awake torn between anxiety about impending danger and preoccupation with committing his experiences to verse, betrays an even more obvious debt to the dictates of literary tradition. With an unmistakable reminiscence of key, initial passages of Juan de Mena's fifteenth-century (c. 1444), protoimperialist, visionary allegory, the *Laberinto de Fortuna* (*copla* 13ff.), Ercilla the narrator-protagonist is rapt away to the heights of an Andean Parnassus by the allegorical goddess Bellona (*Araucana* 17.38ff.). This device permits the poet to introduce an encomium of his sovereign and intended reader, Philip II, as well as a "noble" European battle—Saint Quentin—that will counterbalance the cruelly unequal struggle in the remote wilds of Chile in much the same way as the following amorous interlude serves to ameliorate the savagery of the slaughter wrought by the Spaniard's firearms in the ditch before the fort at Penco (Lagos 174–78).

All three of these filterings of Ercilla's war experiences through literary allusions represent examples of the imitation of prestigious models that was so fundamental to the poetics of his time. Although this practice was made virtually obligatory by the writer's choice of form—the long narrative poem grounded in the complementary traditions of learned epic and Renaissance verse romance—it can hardly be comprehended as a simple and easily defined set of imperatives. Formal *imitatio* could operate on a variety of planes, ranging from the lexical reminiscence at the level of the individual verse all the way to the major structural design of the narrative architecture of the entire poem.

Thus, for instance, the first line of Ercilla's reworking of the visionary encounter with Bellona is itself an almost exact lexical recollection of a verse from the Castilian poet Garcilaso de la Vega's *Egloga II* (v. 537), although the episode as a whole has been borrowed from Juan de Mena's *Laberinto de Fortuna* (Ercilla, *La Araucana*, ed. Lerner, 507 n. 69). At the other end of the spectrum, it is apparent to the competent reader that Ercilla employs the Bellona passage for an additional purpose that transcends the obvious contrivance that permits the intercalation of the battle of Saint Quentin in northern France into the New World ambit of his poem. Before Encilla's awakening to the action at Penco, his dream vision continues on to an encounter with a mysterious woman in white—yet another reminiscence of the vatic *machina* of Mena's *Laberinto de Fortuna* (*copla* 20ff.)—who initiates what will become a web of interlinked prophecies that provides the underlying structure of the key, central section of the *Araucana*. It is through this web of prophecy that Ercilla's poem most closely approximates the arch-model of learned imperialist epic, Virgil's *Aeneid* (c. 19 B.C.); it also opens the discursive space where the *Araucana* can engage directly in a competitive dialogue with its most illustrious contemporary and rival for the laurels as master Iberian poem of ultramarine imperial enterprise in the Indies, this rival being *Os Lusíadas*, first published in 1572, by the Portuguese Petrarchist poet Luis Vaz de Camoens (1524–80).

Because the theme of prophecy provides the most salient and ample ground for the confluence of the consecrated practice of imitation, on the one hand, and poetic as well as political rivalry, on the other, it is the central focus of this book. Prophecy in the European learned heroic poem, from at least the time of the *Aeneid*, had established itself as the thematic medium most decisively employed for the elaboration of dynastic encomium, and through that device, for the construction of political and ideological legitimacy. It is largely due to this role of prophecy and its centrality to learned epic that the long heroic poem became inextricably coterminous with a set of cultural practices explicitly concerned with the legitimization/subversion of authority. The textual authority created within the poem itself is conventionally understood to extend to the "text" of society and to sustain or subvert a concrete, specific political authority. That this is accomplished through the vatic, quasi-sacral medium of poetry invests the legitimated authority with a glow of overtly mythic power that is simply not available to the secular construct of history. Furthermore, because the epic was recognized as the most prestigious and exalted form of literary expression, it became the indispensable emblem of a successful *translatio studii*, itself seen as the seal and confirmation of the *translatio imperii*—the ultimate signifier of "legitimate" authority.[1]

Central to the elaboration of the dynamics of authority in the learned epic poem is the practice of *imitatio*. By engaging in the deliberate imitation of prestigious models, the poet invokes their potency and seeks to infuse his own work with their power. Frequently, the imitating poet not only strives to appropriate the power of the model, but also to surpass or supplant the imitated texts with his own versions of the rendered topoi. The competitive and transformative dimensions of *imitatio* extend not only to the imitation of models whose aura of authority is amplified by distance in time, but also to rivalry between contemporaries.

Imitatio, as noted in the case of the Bellona passage of the *Araucana*, embraces a vast range of distinct practices and approaches and can be put to a great variety of uses. The identification of sources and analogues, while essential to the study of imitation, only begins to lay the groundwork for the productive elucidation of the constitutive roles that different approaches to *imitatio* may play in a given text. Only systematic analysis based on the theories of imitation as formulated by writers steeped in the tradition of *imitatio*, combined with careful evaluation of the actual practice of imitative poets, can fully illuminate the labyrinth of subtexts and their uses that underlies the learned poetry of the Iberian Imperial Age. In the chapters that follow, the reader will find the elaboration of just such an approach and its application to the praxis of imitation in the *Araucana* and, to a lesser but corollary extent, in the *Lusíadas*.

A coherent analysis of this type would certainly have been useful at any time since critics steeped in the prejudices of Romanticism began to deprecate and misread the more obvious cases of imitation in these poems. Nonetheless, perhaps the very real advances in critical methodology and increased sophistication of current readings and debates themselves have produced a situation in which a systematic study of the actual practice of imitation in the flagship epics of the Indies is more imperative than ever.

Much recent criticism of the *Araucana*, for instance, has concentrated on questions revolving around the representation of the Amerindian "Other" in the poem. Virtually all of these readings make some reference to the role of imitation in the realization of the major indigenous characters. Nonetheless, although the impact of literary models is often posited as a major factor in the analyses proposed, the practice of imitation itself is usually referred to only cursorily in passing, as if it were a one-dimensional and generally well-understood discursive resource. It is as if the urgency of the ideological stakes involved in the debates over the portrayal of the Other has left neither sufficient time nor space for a conscientious appraisal of the actual workings of imitation in the *Araucana*. This oversight is itself fraught with some perhaps unintended implications, and has produced influential categorizations of the poem that might tend to distort or obscure its significance among the cultural productions of the conquest and for colonial society.

Although there may be differing interpretations of the implications, it is generally agreed that one of the results—and not a few would go so far as to say the purposes—of the construction of the Amerindian characters in accordance with European literary models is the mediation of their otherness. Beatriz Pastor, for instance, maintains that Ercilla systematically represents the major indigenous protagonists of the poem in accord with the codes of medieval chivalry (*Discursos*, 369).[2] According to Pastor, this chivalric mythification derives from a strategy on Ercilla's part intended to "humanize" the Araucanians. By representing their violence as honorable and valorous, the poet would transform them from the brutish savages depicted by so many European texts into noble beings in harmony with their environment in the eyes of European readers (388–91).

David Quint is in basic agreement with Pastor about the essentially medieval chivalric values with which Ercilla imbues his Amerindian protagonists (*Epic and Empire*, 175). Nonetheless, Quint—who stands out among critics of the *Araucana* for the breadth and sophistication of his acquaintance with imitation—discovers the principal models for most characters and episodes in classical epic poetry, principally the *Aeneid* and the so-called Silver Latin poet Lucan's *Pharsalia* (c. A.D. 65).³ In fact, Quint reads the poem as a tantalizingly unresolved tug-of-war between these two epic subtexts, in which the Virgilian paradigm represents a triumphalist celebration of the Spanish enterprise of conquest and the Lucanian a counterdiscourse or "epic of the losers" commemorating the resistance of the Araucanians. Although Quint acknowledges the dynamic tension between the two, he posits a definite "tilt" in favor of Lucan and the Amerindians (158–59). To this extent, Quint goes even further than Pastor in reading the construction of the Other through imitation in the *Araucana* as not only an attempt to represent the antagonist as worthy of a truly "epic" struggle, but also as an indicator of an active sympathy with that resistance as well.

Not all readers of the *Araucana* are as sanguine as Quint or Pastor in their intepretation of the purposes and effects of literary models in the portrayal of Amerindians in the poem. Rolena Adorno, for one, although she coincides with Pastor in proposing that Ercilla "superimposed the world of medieval chivalry on the Araucanian warriors . . . because he needed a language of common reference with his readers," sees this process through a much darker eye ("Literary Production," 17). Adorno notes that a relatively large number of heroic poems on New World themes were published, and some, like the *Araucana*, met with considerable success, while more sober ethnographic studies based on direct observation and representation of Amerindian cultural practices unmediated by literary models were frequently suppressed. For Adorno, this indicates that while "ethnographically correct" portrayals were seen as truly subversive, and hence dangerous to the structures of power, the filtering of the indigenous world through epic models allowed the conquerors to control readers' reactions "in advance" and, furthermore, to impose an imperialist teleology that would inevitably uphold the ideology of domination (6).⁴ The "dissolving into fiction" of the realities of the conquest thus becomes a mechanism for rendering that often horrifying and always controversial process palatable to the society that was engaged in carrying it out (18–19).

Since Adorno published her thoughts on the question, a number of other critics have developed her line of analysis. Among the most persuasive and influential has been Francisco Javier Cevallos. Cevallos argues for a drastic reappraisal of Ercilla's representation of the Amerindian, and consequently, of the conquest itself. Cevallos insists on the contradiction between the portrayal of the anonymous mass of Araucanians and the idealized Amerindian heroes in the poem. He concludes that the idealization of the individually characterized heroic protagonists—which is to say their construction according to literary models—is primarily intended to elevate these characters to an adequate status as worthy adversaries of the Spaniards (1, 17). Nonetheless, he sustains and develops Adorno's contention that this should be read as nothing more than a conventional device that not only permits, but virtually guarantees, their eventual defeat and humiliation by the Spaniards' putatively superior civilization (5–7). Not only does Cevallos postulate that all of this is driven by epic convention—which is to say by the dictates of imitation—but it also leads him to conclude: "It is only after establishing the literary nature of the text that we may turn to a discussion of *La Araucana* for what it is—a Spanish poem of the European Renaissance" (17).

As the reader of the present book will discover, I concur wholeheartedly with Cevallos's concluding statement—if not necessarily with all of his preceding argument—and it is primarily in the light of the European epic tradition that I examine the issues of imitation and prophecy in the *Araucana*. Nonetheless, it is essential that such a sweeping appraisal be couched in a judicious appreciation of the overall contexts of the production and reception of Ercilla's poem and its progeny. There are all too many who, for ideological or other motives, would seize eagerly upon such an assessment as ammunition to help justify a considerable marginalization in status of the *Araucana* in the canon of colonial Spanish American literature, if not its complete elimination. It is precisely because such a categorization, taken out of context, has the potential to encourage such drastic, and to my mind misconstrued, initiatives, that the systematic analysis of the actual practice of imitation in Ercilla's poem is of more cogency than ever before.

That this crucial recourse of Renaissance writing has been given such short shrift up until now in the analysis of the long narrative poems of the conquest is not in itself that surprising. Despite the fact that the various articulations of *imitatio* revolve at the center of sixteenth-century Iberian poetic practice in both the Old World and the New, this crucial discursive resource has only begun to be studied with the aid of a coherent theoretical framework in the field of Iberian poetry. Moreover, while some work has proved to be extremely valuable, until very recently it has almost all focused on lyric poetry, especially the phenomenon of Petrarchism.[5]

Thus Anne J. Cruz, for instance, has paved the way for the present study with her *Imitación y transformación: el petrarquismo en la poesía de Boscán y Garcilaso de la Vega*. Cruz erects a highly serviceable theoretical scaffolding from a combination of cogent insights on imitative practice by both Renaissance theorists of *imitatio* and the foremost twentieth-century analysts of imitation and rivalry, including Harold Bloom, George W. Pigman III, and Thomas Greene. The approaches suggested by Cruz's work are of particular relevance for the study of the learned poems of exploration and conquest because she brings her theoretical apparatus into focus on the crucial genesis of the imperialist poetics of sixteenth-century Iberia at the hands of Juan Boscán and Garcilaso de la Vega.

Another student of Garcilaso, Mary Barnard, has made the point that Renaissance imitation must be analyzed as a variant of what late twentieth-century criticism classifies as intertextuality, or as she puts it, "the act of writing by which a text emerges as a product of prior texts" (316). Barnard explicitly rejects Roland Barthes's limitation of the term to the anonymous, inchoate, and ultimately untraceable reproduction of prior texts. She does, however, find some support for her use of the terminology in the work of Julia Kristeva, and encounters even more similarities between Renaissance ideas of emulation and rivalry and those of Bloom (316 n. 1). Nonetheless, Barnard cautions that Bloom's concept of the poet's emulative strategies as ultimately an attempt not only to surpass the model text(s) but also to "seem self-begotten" must be tempered by recognition of the reverence for "authority" found in even the most audacious and ambitious Renaissance poets (317).

Ignacio Navarrete is in basic agreement with Barnard's caveat about the application of Bloom's ideas to sixteenth- and seventeenth-century Iberian poets, but nonetheless finds his critical vocabulary useful for two principal reasons. First, his critical terminology has "passed into common use," and second, "Bloom's theory of poetic agon resonates," on the one hand with what George Pigman calls "eristic imitation" or "emulatio," and on the other with Bakhtin's explorations of the "relation between imitation and polyphony" (*Orphans*, 33–34). Navarrete's essentially heuristic use of Bloom's ideas has been the most successful attempt to date to incorporate late twentieth-century theories of intertextuality into the study of Renaissance imitation. Nevertheless, while Navarrete's contextualization of Spanish Petrarchism in the historical and social development of Iberian imperialism has been fundamental to the essential thesis of this book, I have preferred to center my own theoretical framework on the formulations of Renaissance writers themselves, as well as specialists in the field of Renaissance poetics such as Pigman and Greene. This having been said, I must express my general agreement that Renaissance imitation should be included in the overall study of intertextuality, albeit as a very special case.

An important factor in my choices in this regard has been the work of Alicia de Colombí-Monguió, who brings considerable erudition informed by a keen understanding of Renaissance theories of imitation to her studies of the Petrarchist idiom as practiced by colonial poets of the late sixteenth and early seventeenth centuries. Colombí-Monguió, quite rightly I believe, urges caution in the wholesale application of Post-Romantic literary theory—especially the ideas of Bloom—to the praxis of Renaissance poets (*Petrarquismo*, 138–40). In addition to her very precise treatment of theoretical concepts, Colombí-Monguió's work is invaluable for illuminating the key role of Petrarchist poetics, with its attendant emphasis on strategies of imitation, in the establishment of the privileged discourse of the European colonizers of the New World.

Finally, it is important to reiterate that Cruz, Barnard, Navarrete, and Colombí-Monguió have concentrated on the uses of imitation in lyric poetry. As Thomas Greene points out, the study of *imitatio* in the long narrative poem is fraught with special difficulties (*Light*, 50). Nonetheless, despite the problems noted by Greene, a systematic analysis grounded in a clear understanding of the modalities of *imitatio* proves itself to be essential for the illumination of heretofore opaque colonialist/imperialist dimensions of the sixteenth-century long narrative poems of exploration and conquest. However, because the subject is truly vast—due to the extent and number of the poems involved—the present study focuses on the crucial—for the colonialist/imperialist epic—intertwining of prophecy, empire, and imitation in the *Araucana*.[6]

In this relatively restricted context, the reader will discover at least one incontrovertible example of the light that a coherent theoretical approach to imitation can shed on the first explicitly literary narrative representations of Europe's sixteenth-century ultramarine navigations and conquests. Illuminating the pathways of imitation in the *Araucana* reveals a previously unremarked dynamic relationship with the most illustrious of all sixteenth-century Iberian imperialist epic poems, the *Lusíadas*, and leads to an appreciation of how poetic and imperialist rivalry drives a major change in the course of the *Araucana* that has frequently been misread.

The *Araucana* and the *Lusíadas*, of course, are the two most celebrated Iberian—Spanish and Portuguese, respectively—long narrative poems of the Imperial Age. Significantly, because both poems are primarily concerned with the extension of empire beyond the familiar confines of Europe, both must confront the challenge of integrating actions on the colonial periphery with the perspective of the metropolitan center. In both poems, the device of prophecy, expressed through the medium of Petrarchist/Garcilasist *imitatio*, plays a fundamental role in how this challenge is met. In the case of the *Araucana*, however, the narrative and imitative strategies adopted by the poet to accomplish this end have been consistently misunderstood by generations of critics who have shared an underlying antipathy to the poetics of *imitatio*. Because the *Araucana*, as the premier epic poem of the conquest of the New World, is the central focus of this study, it is appropriate here to review briefly some of the basic problems presented by the circumstances of the poem's composition and publication, as well as mutations in its critical reception over the centuries since its verses were forged in the fires of the European colonization of America.

Raised in the court of Charles V, educated as a page in the retinue of the future king Philip II, it is probable that the young Alonso de Ercilla already harbored ambitions as a poet before taking ship for the New World in 1555 (Medina, *Vida*, 31–36). Ercilla spent the years 1557 through 1559 soldiering in an obscure and inconclusive colonial police action (Medina, *Vida*, 38–81). That, at least, is what the nasty little war at the ends of the earth—the Arauco region of what is now Chile—would have seemed to Ercilla's European contemporaries had not the young aristocrat written and published the *Araucana*. Ercilla's long narrative poem spins this struggle waged against the Amerindian inhabitants of the remotest corner of Philip II's empire into an epic treatment of the Iberian imperialist enterprise on a worldwide scale.

Although Ercilla began the composition of his poem while still engaged in the campaign against the Araucanians and continued to work on the project during his four remaining years in America, the *Araucana* was still taking shape when the poet returned to Spain in 1563. As Marcos A. Morínigo has pointed out, it is likely that the fame of the yet unpublished poem spread among both courtiers and veterans of the wars in Chile while the work was still in progress (Ercilla, *La Araucana*, ed. Morínigo and Lerner, 1:47–48). In any case, Ercilla published Part I of the *Araucana* in 1569, asserting in the prologue that he did so at the urging of a number of his former companions-in-arms (1:48, 121). Part I of the *Araucana*, comprising the first fifteen cantos of the poem, contains very little of what Morínigo calls the "Diario de la guerra" that Ercilla had written during his actual participation in the war between 1557 and 1559, however (1:47, 59–60). On the contrary, in Part I of the *Araucana*, Ercilla relates the origins of the war and the major events that occurred prior to his own arrival in Chile. The putatively testimonial role of the poet only begins at *Araucana* 12.76, dominates *Araucana* 13, is absent from *Araucana* 14, and finally returns in the description of the stormy voyage from Peru to Chile that concludes Part I of the *Araucana* (15.56–83).

Some nine years after the appearance of Part I, Ercilla published Part II of the *Araucana* in 1578. Part II, comprehending cantos 16 through 29, commences with the conclusion of the storm passage that had begun in the closing section of *Araucana* 15, and the poet-protagonist's personal arrival in the theater of direct operations against the Araucanian resistance (*Araucana* 16). Although Ercilla at this point begins to weave text from what Morínigo calls his "War Diary"—the verses recounting the poet's own experiences in the Arauco campaign—into the fabric of his poem in Part II, this testimonial material occupies less than a third of the 7,742 lines that make up Part II of the *Araucana*. In fact, slightly more than five thousand verses are dedicated to either amorous episodes that cleave closely to established literary conventions or a carefully developed scheme of prophecy and the marvelous that the poet uses to introduce the Old World victories of Saint Quentin and Lepanto, as well as a mapamundi celebrating the Spanish Empire, into the colonial ambit of his poem (Ercilla, *La Araucana*, ed. Morínigo and Lerner, 1:53).[7] It is in the elaboration of what I have called the web of prophecy that spans Part II of the *Araucana* that Ercilla attempts to bind the main action of the poem, which occurs on the colonial periphery, to the grand sweep of empire as perceived from the metropolitan center. Furthermore, it is precisely here in the heart of his poem that Ercilla engages in the most intense, and ostentatiously announced, imitation of prestigious models. This intensification of *imitatio* in Part II of the *Araucana*, inextricably bound up with issues of both poetic and imperial rivalry, is the principal focus of this book.

In 1589, some eleven years after the publication of Part II, Ercilla published Part III of the *Araucana*. In Part III, the poet presents the remaining testimonial material—according to Morínigo about half of the original total of the "War Diary"—reflecting his experiences in Chile (1:60). Into this he interweaves his defense of the virtue of Carthaginian Dido, certainly to achieve variety and to ennoble the tone of his poem, but also in order to reinforce the implicit critique of the type of amorous fiction associated with Italian epic that characterizes his treatment of the theme throughout the *Araucana* (32.43–33.54).[8] The poem then draws to a somewhat enigmatic close with Philip II's seizure of the crown of Portugal, a historical event that had occurred in 1580. The tone and approach of Part III are noticeably different from those of both Parts I and II, probably reflecting both the poet's advancing age and his disillusionment over his failure to achieve a brilliant career as courtier and diplomat (1:60–61).

The first complete edition, containing all three parts of the poem, appeared in 1590 (Ercilla, *La Araucana*, ed. Medina, 4:19–21). In 1597, three years after the poet's death, the edition of the *Araucana* that has subsequently been reprinted as the definitive version of the poem was published, probably under the direction of Ercilla's widow (4:25–28). This edition of 1597 contains a number of modifications of that of 1589–90, the most important of which is the addition of 832 verses describing Ercilla's journey to the southernmost regions of Chile.[9] Although this posthumously added material forms the "natural" conclusion to Ercilla's "War Diary" recounting his personal involvement in events in Chile (Ercilla, *La Araucana*, ed. Morínigo and Lerner, 1:61), the general tone is quite somber, in keeping with the overall air of bitterness and pessimism that pervades Part III of the *Araucana*. As Morínigo observes, Part III, as published both before and after the author's death, gives the impression that Ercilla, mortally dispirited by personal tragedy and failure at court, simply wishes to bring his poem to an end and be done with it once and for all. Certainly, Ercilla does not contribute the same enthusiasm and polish, so evident in Part II, to his exercises in *imitatio* in Part III (1:60–61).

Ercilla's ambivalence about the colonial project becomes most evident in Part III of the *Araucana*, perhaps especially so in the case of the frustrated utopianism of the posthumously added journey to the south. Significantly, it is this section that forms the principal basis of some criticism of the poem that seeks to portray Ercilla as the paradigm of a decentering of the discourse of the conqueror brought about by inherent ideological inconsistencies in the enterprise itself (e.g., Pastor, "Silence," 154–57). Ercilla, like Camoens, certainly adopts a critical stance in regard to many of the actions of his fellow countrymen, and this basically reformist outlook is for the most part consistent with his status as a king's man who cannot entirely conceal his disdain for the unbridled greed and ambition of the general run of *conquistadores* who hoped to carve out vast estates and rise abruptly in social class in the New World (Durand 113–17).

Although it has become fashionable to characterize the discourse of the conquerors as a "monologue" (Pastor, "Silence," 158), this is at best a misleading simplification. The voices of those involved in the colonial enterprise are many and are often raised loudly one against the other. In regard to Ercilla, José Durand, in his article "El chapetón Ercilla y la honra araucana," has made a convincing case for situating the poet in the context of the struggle between the early conquerors "on the make" in the New World and the imperial functionaries and bureaucrats who followed. Furthermore, although there are valuable insights to be gained by focusing on the disruption or destabilization evident in the discourse of the conquest, a great deal of at least equal importance will be overlooked if the essentially idealist affirmation of empire is dismissed out of hand as conventional or superficial. It is in precisely such a spirit of celebration that Ercilla, nearing the apogee of his success and still far from the disillusionment that pervades Part III, plunges enthusiastically into both poetic and imperial rivalry through the medium of Petrarchist/Garcilasist *imitatio* in Part II of the *Araucana*.

If Ercilla betrays a different approach to his subject in Part II of the *Araucana* in comparison with Part III, there is an equally, or perhaps even more, important difference with respect to Part I. Published in 1569, a full six years after Ercilla's return to Spain, Part I shows every sign of having been conceived as a relatively true-to-life account of the war in Chile. Ercilla explicitly rejects many standard features of both the classical epic in the mold of the *Aeneid* and the Italian *romanzi* exemplified by the *Orlando furioso* in his introductory remarks and in his execution throughout Part I of the narrative. The poet repeatedly insists on the historicity of his account, and goes to great lengths to dissimulate the specific subtexts of his imitations of established epic loci (see Chapter 1). Prophecy and the supernatural are of only incidental importance, and Ercilla introduces these elements gingerly, insulating them with disclaimers of various kinds. Even in the context of the supernatural, where *imitatio* would be most at home, Ercilla seems to go out of his way to avoid ostentatious imitation.[10] His primary concern seems to be the construction of verisimilitude and the impression of historicity. In the same spirit, there is no attempt to link the events in Arauco to the larger scheme of empire.

Part II of the *Araucana*, on the other hand, represents a drastic shift in approach. The events of the war in Arauco are carefully interwoven and balanced with material that is proper to either classical epic or the *romanzi*, or both. Furthermore, this is accomplished through the medium of intensified, advertised imitation of prestigious models. Foremost among the imitative passages of Part II are the episodes that the poet spins into a web of prophecy intended to elevate the subject of the poem and that serves to bind the colonial to the metropolitan on an epic scale (Concha 38–49). These include Ercilla's dream vision of the goddess Bellona, who sweeps the poet to an Andean Parnassus from which he views the battle of Saint Quentin in northern France (*Araucana* 17.39–18.28), the continuation of the dream, in which the white-clad goddess Reason prepares the poet for his encounter with the indigenous enchanter Fitón (*Araucana* 18.29–74), and finally, the poet's two visits to the mantic cavern of the Araucanian mage (*Araucana* 23.24–24.98, 26.40–27.54).[11] It is in Fitón's cave that the prophetic structure of Part II comes to full fruition, and the poet is vouchsafed, first with a vision of the battle of Lepanto in the far-off Adriatic (*Araucana* 23.83–95)—occurring almost fifteen years in the future relative to the fictive time of Ercilla's narration—and then with a detailed tour through a mapamundi that exalts the Spanish Empire, particularly showcasing its extension and wealth in the New World (*Araucana* 27.5–54). Ercilla underlines the importance of these visions seen in the wizard Fitón's magic globe by surrounding and introducing them with his most ambitious imitations of prestigious subtexts. The visions themselves, as will be seen in Chapters 4 and 5 of this study, correspond to rival prophetic visions presented in similar circumstances by Ercilla's principal competitor in the field of the Iberian epic, Camoens. Although the prophetic machinery, and the prophecies themselves, have little enough to do explicitly with the war in Arauco, taken as a whole, they are crucial to establishing the truly colonial nature of the *Araucana*. Like all power in a colonial society, the ultimate source of authority emanates from the metropolitan center, and by introducing, on the wings of prophecy, these links with the grand scheme of empire, Ercilla strives to imbue the dirty, obscure war on the remotest periphery with a transcendence that he believes worthy of the valor displayed by the combatants on both sides.

As Morínigo points out, perhaps the best indicator of success in the case of a sixteenth-century work such as the *Araucana* is the number of editions printed in relatively close proximity to the initial publication of the text (Ercilla, *La Araucana*, ed. Morínigo and Lerner, 1:61). If the four editions of Part I that were published between 1569 and 1578 are indicative of a more-than-modest success (1:61), a supposition bolstered by direct testimony (Medina, *Vida*, 99–100), the six editions of Part II, either alone or in conjunction with Part I (Ercilla, *La Araucana*, ed. Medina, 4:8–17), published between 1578 and 1586, go far to support the conclusion that the intensified imitation and metropolitan resonances so prominent in Part II of the *Araucana* did nothing to impede the growing popularity of Ercilla's poem.[12] In fact, it is shortly after the publication of Part II that the *Araucana* begins to figure in literary manuals as a model of epic verse, and that praise of the poem begins to appear in the works of other authors, including Cervantes (*La Galatea*, Book 6, 2:191; Ercilla, *La Araucana*, ed. Morínigo and Lerner, 1:62). In these references there is no hint of any objection to the supernatural and Old World episodes, with their attendant, foregrounded *imitatio*, that are so central to Part II of the *Araucana*. In an age that understood both epic and imitation, the relevance and merits of Ercilla's web of prophecy and its attendant emulation of and rivalry with both ancient and contemporary poetic models required no justification.

This positive reception suffered an abrupt change, however, in the nineteenth century, with the rise of the aesthetic biases and value judgments associated with Romanticism.[13] Manuel José Quintana, writing in 1833, set the parameters for more than a century of criticism of the *Araucana* (Alegría 3). Among Quintana's more enduring and severe appraisals of the nonhistorical material of Part II is the oft-repeated opinion that the battles of Saint Quentin and Lepanto, along with the mapamundi, constitute major defects in the poem, being "absolutamente extraños y aun incompatibles con el argumento" (Quintana 162).[14] Marcelino Menéndez Pelayo, whose influence on subsequent criticism cannot be exaggerated, basically echoes Quintana's observation, adding that Ercilla's effort to tie the colonial action of his poem to the metropolitan ambit compares unfavorably with that of Camoens (Menéndez Pelayo 2:222).[15] This type of attitude crystallizes with Ramón Menéndez Pidal, and his insistence on the strict historicity (*verismo*) of the Spanish epic in contrast with the freer poetic licence (*verosimilismo*) of other European traditions. Menéndez Pidal, however, excuses the cave of Fitón on the ground that it is merely one of a few scattered episodes that reflect popular superstitions. Furthermore, its presence is excusable because it is an imitation of Lucan, whom Menéndez Pidal also considers a Spaniard—because, albeit a scion of a noble Roman family, he was born in Cordova—and whose supposedly realistic approach to the supernatural Menéndez Pidal counterpoises to the mythological and fantastic apparatus of such poets as Virgil (*Españoles*, 203–5).[16] Nor are the peninsular Spanish critics alone in propagating these views.

Andrés Bello, writing in 1841, opines that although fantastic and supernatural episodes may have been licit in poems treating the relatively distant past such as Balbuena's *Bernardo* or Tasso's *Gerusalemne*, they are totally out of place in such a rigorously historical poem as the *Araucana*. Bello caps this thought with the remark, "Así es que el episodio postizo del mago Fitón es una de las cosas que se leen con menos placer en la *Araucana*" (359). Bello's words did not fall on deaf ears, and Abraham König, who published his edition of the *Araucana* "for the use of the Chileans" in 1888, simply excised the offending episodes.

By the middle of the following century, however, Fernando Alegría feels free to scorn König's edition as "desprovisto de todo valor" and specifically criticizes his excision of the supernatural and European episodes of Part II (12 n. 14). Alegría defends the "máquina" surrounding the visits to Fitón's cave as imaginative and necessary to relieve the monotony of the constant narration of warlike deeds (44–45). It was only in 1969, however, that another Chilean critic, Jaime Concha, was to remind readers of the original importance in the structure of the *Araucana* of the web of prophecy in Part II and the related battles of Saint Quentin and Lepanto. Concha highlights the encomiastic function of these episodes and insists on their vital importance in binding the colonial sphere of action to the metropolitan march of empire (38–49). For Concha, far from being distracting and irrelevant digressions, the visions of the European battles and the mapamundi are fundamental expressions of the dynamic unity of the poem, essential for its epic totalization and universality (49). Concha's analysis has now become incorporated into much of the subsequent criticism of the *Araucana* (e.g., Lagos 158; Vidal 77–78).

Nonetheless, despite the acuity of Concha's reading of these passages, the underlying dimensions of poetic and imperial rivalry that drive the shift in direction and approach so evident in Part II of the *Araucana*, and that especially determine the shape taken by the prophetic episodes used to link the colonial with the metropolitan spheres of the poem, have remained unelucidated. It is necessary to first bring the light of a coherent theoretical approach to the issue of *imitatio* in the first two parts of the *Araucana* before the outlines of the rivalry that motivates these episodes can be traced clearly in the tangle of dissimulated and foregrounded imitation that forms the fabric of Ercilla's prophecies and their accompanying visions. A careful reading grounded in a systematic taxonomy of *imitatio* reveals, at the very heart of Ercilla's prophetic structure in Part II, a close textual imitation of the *machinae* that introduce the two culminating prophecies of the *Lusíadas* of Camoens—the poem with which the *Araucana* is still almost inevitably compared. The content of the two prophecies seen in Fitón's globe corresponds to the two final prophecies of the *Lusíadas*, not as textual imitations as in the case of the *globos* themselves, but rather as rival visions of imperial grandeur. Thus careful study of imitation in Part II of the *Araucana* strips away the veils that since the seventeenth century have obscured the central engine of an intense imperialist, colonialist, and poetic rivalry that drives the often disputed and misunderstood change in approach between Parts I and II of the *Araucana*. The understanding of this long-forgotten rivalry requires a detailed elucidation of Renaissance approaches to *imitatio*, and particularly the evolution of Ercilla's praxis from before the appearance of his celebrated rival's poem to after the competition represented by the *Lusíadas* challenged his role as the premier Iberian epic poet.

Central to this argument is the dramatic shift in Ercilla's stance in regard to imitation that is registered between Part I of the *Araucana*, published three years before the appearance of the *Lusíadas* in 1572, and Part II, published six years after the Portuguese poem had begun to dazzle Iberian readers of Ercilla's class and inclination. Consequently, Chapter 1 of my study opens with an examinion of a striking example of the transformation in Ercilla's imitative praxis. Ercilla leaves the reader in suspense at the end of Part I. The poet breaks off his narration in the middle of a furious storm at sea, his ship in imminent danger of foundering. The tempest is, of course, one of the most venerable loci of the tradition and poses a challenge to any poet who would enter the lists of contention for epic preeminence. In the first half of the storm, as recounted in Part I, Ercilla has recourse to many of the standard features of the locus, but exerts himself to dissimulate his imitations and give the impression of verisimilitude. Above all, there is no attempt to single out or challenge any particular subtext.[17] In the continuation of the storm in Part II, however, Ercilla explicitly calls the reader's attention to the three most famous storms of the classical tradition. I read this as an announcement of the heightened and foregrounded imitation that will characterize Part II of the *Araucana*. Precisely because the storm represents Ercilla's most ambitious attempt at imitation in Part I, it makes the most cogent contrast with the imitations of Part II.

The problems posed by the storm lead inevitably to an analysis of Ercilla's overall change in approach between 1569 and 1578. This in turn suggests the necessity of outlining a coherent theoretical approach to *imitatio*. In the concluding sections of Chapter 1, the reader will find a brief survey of Renaissance and twentieth-century theories of imitation and the parameters that guide my analysis in the following chapters. Chapter 2 is devoted to tracing the general outlines of Ercilla's web of prophecy in Part II of the *Araucana*. The Castilian poet weaves this web out of variegated strands of eclectic imitations that are intended to create a specifically Iberian genealogy of model texts that will advance Ercilla's claim to primacy in the peninsular epic. Of special importance in this initiative is the foregrounded imitation of Garcilaso, also a principal model for Camoens's poetic practice.

Ercilla places his most ambitious exercise in Garcilasist imitation in the cave of Fitón. Because of the fundamental importance of this highly transformative and competitive essay in imitation for the appreciation of Ercilla's approach to *imitatio* in general, and rivalry in particular, Chapter 3 is devoted to a detailed analysis of Ercilla's imitative strategies in the episode of the Araucanian enchanter's grotto. Thomas

Greene's metaphor of necromancy for the transformative revival of model texts across the abyss of linguistic and cultural change proves to be fundamental for the explication of Ercilla's multilayered imitative praxis in these passages, the most overtly advertised imitations of the *Araucana*. The application of Greene's distinction between "sacramental" or "reproductive" imitation, and the transformative resuscitation of long-dead verses, which Greene characterizes as "necromancy," reveals the fiercely competitive initiative that drives Ercilla's necromantic revival of model texts taken from his "Spanish" forerunners Lucan and Juan de Mena.

Once the keenness of Ercilla's competitive impulse has been established, and the strategies that are characteristic of his imitative practice have been identified, it is possible to undertake the analysis of his key imitation of Camoens in the mantic globe that occupies the center of Fitón's cave. Chapter 4 examines the tradition of the all-seeing globe or mirror and demonstrates exactly how Fitón's globe is intended to remind the reader of the prophetic spheres of the final canto of the *Lusíadas*. The concluding section of the chapter focuses on a comparison of the first visions seen in the corresponding orbs of the *Araucana* and the *Lusíadas*, and delineates the imperialist rivalry that underlies their elaboration.

The most transcendent moment of rivalry, however, is reserved for the second vision in the respective globes. These are the competing, colonialist mapaemundi of the two poems. Chapter 5 traces the development of the integration of the mapamundi into the epic poem and demonstrates that this locus has deep roots in the earliest attempts at colonial enterprise beyond the familiar confines of Europe. A detailed comparison of the mapaemundi of the *Araucana* and the *Lusíadas* reveals that a specifically colonialist, imperialist rivalry underlies and motivates the intensified imitation and prophetic structure of Part II of the *Araucana*. Additionally, the appreciation of this rivalry does much to illumine Ercilla's otherwise enigmatic choice of the seizing of the crown of Portugal for the conclusion of his poem.

My book, then, is not intended to be an exhaustive study of either the *Araucana* or the *Lusíadas*, but rather a demonstration of the utility of a coherent theoretical approach to imitation in the study of colonial epic poetry. As I make clear in the pages that follow, a lucid understanding of imitative practice informed by classical, Renaissance, and twentieth-century theoretical formulations of *imitatio* can reveal vital dimensions of the long narrative poems of exploration and conquest. These texts are the first explicitly literary representations of the encounter between Europe and its Others, and often play a crucial role in the establishment of the cultural and ideological edifice of the emerging colonial societies.

Especially in light of initiatives to diminish the relevance of such poems as the *Araucana* to New World colonial cultural production, it is well to remember the importance that Ercilla's poem had for early colonial readers. As Irving Leonard has demonstrated through his research on the New World book trade, the *Araucana* seems to have been by far the most popular literary item on colonial readers' shopping lists. Not coincidentally, perhaps, Camoens's *Lusíadas* was not far behind. The *Araucana* itself seems to have been the most widely disseminated and read representation of the conquest among the colonizers themselves (Leonard 119–20, 164, 224). Furthermore, analysis of imitations and responses to Ercilla's representation of the New World through the lens of established literary models demonstrates that the poem played a constitutive role in vital political and ideological colonial debates, especially on the crucial topic of the nature and capacities of the conquered Amerindian peoples.[18] Thus, I am convinced that the patience necessary to unravel the tangled fabric of imitation in these poems will be rewarded by insights that will illuminate not only the aesthetic appreciation of the texts, but also their more profound cultural and ideological resonances in the problematic foundation of the colonial societies of the New World.

1

"Con que ilustrar pudiese más su historia"

The Crisis of Imitation in the *Araucana*

1.1. The Storm

A furious storm batters the little Spanish squadron sailing down the coast of Chile as Part I of the *Araucana* (1569) comes to an end—but not a conclusion—engulfed in a cloud of desperation and suspense. Alonso de Ercilla, who had ample firsthand experience of sea travel in the sixteenth century, describes the storm with a wealth of detailed nautical terminology and an insistence on his personal witness that belie the set-piece tempest of literary convention. Nonetheless, from Homer's *Odyssey* on, the violent storm has figured among the most durable and oft-repeated loci of the learned epic poem in the occidental tradition (Morford 20–21). It would be unrealistic to expect the storm that concludes *Araucana* 15 to betray no filiation with its literary antecedents. Just as Ercilla incorporates other standard topics of the literary epic—for instance, the council of war (*Araucana* 2.8–38) and the celebratory games (*Araucana* 10.11–11.30)—into Part I of the *Araucana* without highlighting a specific model, he follows the general contours of the literary storm at the end of *Araucana* 15 in a manner that dissimulates rather than calls special attention to the literary provenance of many of its constitutive elements.[1]

Significantly, however, Ercilla resumes his narration of the storm at the beginning of Part II (1578) with specific references to the three most celebrated storm scenes of Greek and Latin literature. This is but the first harbinger of the far denser and more extensively developed poetic *imitatio* that will characterize Parts II and III (1589) of the *Araucana*. This intensification of direct allusion to prestigious literary models is particularly evident in the prophetic, supernatural episodes of Part II that Ercilla uses to introduce the Old World Spanish victories of Saint Quentin and Lepanto, as well as a visionary mapamundi, into the center of his poem—pivotal sections of the *Araucana* that have often been ignored or misread.

My principal purpose in this study is to elucidate the tightly interwoven skeins of imitation and prophecy that radiate from the cave of the Araucanian enchanter Fitón at the hub of Part II and to explain why Ercilla chose to spin these into the web of his poem in Parts II and III after having explicitly rejected any theme but a "true" account of the war in Chile in Part I. It is my thesis that a proper understanding of Ercilla's approach to poetic imitation and rivalry will illuminate this sea change in the course of the *Araucana*. Thus, while it is not my intention here to make a detailed analysis of Ercilla's storm, a few examples of his description of the tempest from Parts I and II will illustrate my point.

Most of the major features of the classical epic storm are already present in *Odyssey* 5 and *Odyssey* 12, but the topic was subsequently developed by a number of Latin poets, notably Virgil, Ovid, and Seneca, before achieving its definitive form in Lucan's *Pharsalia* (Morford 21–22, 26, 32–33, 36). Partly because Lucan's storms (especially those in *Pharsalia* 5 and 9) represent the culmination of the classical tradition, after which nothing new is really added until the sixteenth century, it is often assumed that Ercilla modeled his great storm on those of the *Pharsalia* (e.g., Janik 100). Even a cursory examination of the first half of Ercilla's storm—that found in *Araucana* 15.67–83 at the end of Part I—reveals the inadequacy of this widely, and uncritically, accepted opinion.

One of Lucan's most distinctive contributions to the epic storm was the inclusion of the portents that herald the onset of the tempest, on the whole borrowed from Virgil's *Georgics* 1.351–514 where the weather signs have nothing to do with either the sea or epic (Morford 38). The authority acquired by this particular element of the locus after Lucan can be appreciated if we recall that Juan de Mena felt it appropriate to preface the swamping of the ship of the Count of Niebla in his *Laberinto de Fortuna* (*coplas* 163–73) with an imitation of Lucan's weather omens in spite of the fact that no storm was involved at all (Lida de Malkiel, *Juan de Mena*, 64–65).[2]

Significantly, there is no trace of Lucan's "reddening moon" (*Pharsalia* 5.549) or other signs that augur foul weather whatsoever in Ercilla's storm, neither in the prelude (*Araucana* 13.34–40; 15.56–60, 65–66) nor in the tempest itself. On the contrary, Ercilla prepares his reader for the storm with a fairly realistic account of the rough sailing conditions encountered on the voyage from Ciudad de los Reyes (Lima) to Arica in northern Chile (*Araucana* 13.34–40, 15.56–60), adorned, it is true, with some classical flourishes more proper to the central passages of the storm description (*Araucana* 15.58–59).

In fact, Ercilla opens his rendering of the main body of the storm with a conflation of recollections of the urtext of literary tempests. Odysseus disentangled himself from Calypso's embrace and sailed away for seventeen days with a fair wind before Poseidon blasted him with wind and wave on the eighteenth (*Odyssey* 5.278–79; Gonçalo Pérez, fol. 115r), and later the wily Greek recounts that after waiting out the winds for six days, Zeus smote him and his crew with a furious storm after setting sail in a calm on the seventh day (*Odyssey* 12.391; Gonçalo Pérez, fol. 272r).[3] Likewise, the little Spanish fleet skimmed along calm seas before a favorable wind for six days before encountering the darkening sky and blasting wind seven days out of Coquimbo (*Araucana* 15.67). Ercilla combines the definite span of days of smooth sailing from Homer's first storm with the mythic number seven from the second.[4] Yet the allusion to the ultimate model of all classical literary storms is haunting but fugitive, for it is unclear, in fact, whether the similarities are deliberate or simply the results of jumbled recollections and inchoate reminiscences. Quite clear, on the other hand, is the total absence of a loudly announced, unmistakable reference to a single, privileged model.

The rest of the storm in Part I continues in much the same vein. Many elements of the literary storm are present, but it is the locus in general rather than any specific model that suggests itself to the informed reader. Ercilla, on the contrary, strives to shore up his authority as a genuine witness of the storm by confiding to the reader that he can only give testimony about the fate of the ship in which he himself was present (*Araucana* 15.69). Even more striking, however, is the density and detail of up-to-date nautical jargon.

From Homer on, the destruction in the rigging wrought by the storm formed an important part of the locus (Morford 21; *Odyssey* 5.313–18, 12.407–14). Virgil alludes briefly to the desperate cries of the sailors, mixed with the roaring of the wind in the rigging (*Aeneid* 1.87). Ovid expands magnificently on the possibilities suggested by Virgil and, as the wind rises, has the steersman cry out orders to the crew. Two of these frantic commands are reproduced in direct speech: "Lower the top yards right away!" (Ardua iamdudum demittite cornua); "reef the sail tightly to the spars!" (et antemnis totum subnectite velum) (*Metamorphoses* 11.482–83). Ovid goes on to describe the confused, frantic activity of the sailors and the despair of the pilot, so overwhelmed by the tumult and pandemonium that he "himself is in terror and admits that he does not know how the vessel stands, nor what either to order or forbid" (*Metamorphoses* 11.492–93).[5]

Neither Seneca nor his nephew Lucan would add anything to Ovid's detail in this regard (cf. *Agamemnon* 503–9; *Pharsalia* 5.593–96, 5.638–53, 9.324–29). Nowhere do they avail themselves of Ovid's vivid use of direct speech, and the nautical terminology is what we could expect of Roman aristocrats with little direct experience of sea travel.[6] All three of these Roman authors, in fact, employ poetic metonymies more frequently than specific nautical terms, especially to describe the hull and sails. The rigging is almost always referred to generically as *rudentes*, the mast is *malus*, and the spars are *antemnae*. Ovid is unique in introducing anything as specific as *ardua cornua* for top yards.

Thus, we are fleetingly reminded of Ovid when Ercilla has the pilot cry out, "¡Larga la triça en vanda!" (*Araucana* 15.70g). The despair of the "gran piloto . . . / que no sabe mandar de atribulado" (*Araucana* 15.80cd) recalls the similar quandry of Ovid's "ratis rector" (*Metamorphoses* 11.492–93). The continued use of direct speech (especially *Araucana* 15.80–81), however, illustrating the confusion with the cries of sailors and passengers, and the torrent of precise, authentic sixteenth-century nautical terms soon dispels any lingering phantasm of the literary storm. The flavor of authenticity provided by such exhortations as "¡Amayna la mayor! ¡hiça trinquete!" (*Araucana* 15.72b), where each sail is referred to by its proper name, and the proliferation of exact terms for rigging such as "la escota," "la braça," "el chafaldete," (*Araucana* 15.72*f*), and such specific terms for spars as the Americanism "mangle" for the precise type of tree trunk used as a mast (*Araucana* 15.75*c*), have seduced many critics into forgetting the literary provenance of Ercilla's storm entirely (e.g., Alegría 47).

In contrast to *Araucana* 15 where Ercilla has gone to great lengths to dissimulate his models, when the poet picks up the storm again at the beginning of Part II in *Araucana* 16, he loses little time in making direct, explicit reference to the literary substrata underlying his tempest:

> No la varca de Amiclas asaltada
> fue del viento y del mar con tal porfia
> que aunque de leños frágiles armada
> el peso y ser del mundo sostenía,
> Ni la naue de Vlixes, ni la armada
> que de Troya escapó el último día,
> vieron con tal furor el viento ayrado,
> ni el remouido mar tan leuantado.
>
> (*Araucana* 16.10)

Here we have, in fact, the three most well-known and prestigious literary storms of the epic tradition. As I have indicated above, the reference to the "nave de Ulises" (*Araucana* 16.10*e*) is no hollow, perfunctory nod to a Homer known only by reputation. There is every reason to believe that Ercilla would have known at least the first thirteen books of the *Odyssey* through Gonçalo Pérez's translation of 1550, and he gives concrete evidence of this in the opening stanza of his own storm description (*Araucana* 15.67). As classical scholar M. P. O. Morford has pointed out, the two storms of the *Odyssey* contain most of the essential elements and set the tone for all subsequent renditions of the locus (20–21). But where Ercilla has dissimulated even the most "authoritative" aspect of his imitation of models by scrambling together features of the storms of *Odyssey* 5 and *Odyssey* 12 in Part I, here in Part II he is deliberately drawing attention to his knowledge of the urtext of literary storms. Much the same can be said for "la armada / que de Troya escapó" (*Araucana* 16.10*ef*), an unmistakable allusion to the storm of *Aeneid* 1.34–158. As Morford indicates, Virgil's reworking of the Homeric motif became "by far the most important single influence on the writing of his successors—indeed, not one of the set-piece storms of the silver age can be considered without reference to him" (26). A close analysis of Ercilla's storm would reveal a great debt to Virgil, but to make the present point, it is only necessary to remark that, again, where previously, in Part I, the debt is disguised, here it is explicitly laid bare.

Regardless of the precedence of Homer and Virgil in the tradition, however, Ercilla correctly begins the tribute to his models by giving pride of place to the most important for his own purpose. The "barca de Amiclas" refers to Lucan's most flamboyantly realized storm, where Julius Caesar prevails upon the humble boatman, Amyclas, to ferry him over to Italy in spite of the dangers of the sea (*Pharsalia* 5.504–677). Lucan's storm descriptions represent the culmination of the locus in classical letters, and the storm of *Pharsalia* 5 is "the most elaborate and closest to the traditional literary storm" (Morford 37). Ercilla is no more in debt to this grand flourish of Silver Latin rhetoric for the details of his tempest than he is to Homer, Virgil, or Ovid; nonetheless, the storm that beset Caesar and Amylcas has a special resonance for the denoument of the perils suffered by the little Spanish fleet in Chilean waters. As Morford points out, Lucan uses the storm in *Pharsalia* 5 to underline the fact that Caesar is Fortune's favorite (30, 37–38). Significantly, Ercilla concludes the storm off the coast of Chile by bringing the fleet to a safe landfall with the comment:

> Pero el mar embidioso embrauecido,
> y el importuno viento rebramando,
> el vagel acometen con ruydo,
> en vano, aunque se esfuerçan porfiando:
> Que la fortuna de Phelipe asido,
> a jorro le lleuaua remolcando,
> sobre las altas olas espumosas,
> aun de anegar los Cielos desseosas.
>
> (*Araucana* 16.16)[7]

Thus, just as Caesar's braving of the sea, despite the portents explicated by Amyclas, is proof of his *audacia*, and his "miraculous" survival from the hyperbolic fury of the tempest is emblematic of his triumph in the Civil War (Morford 30), the little Spanish fleet's safe passage through the storm-tossed southern seas is linked to the imperial fortunes of the sovereign, King Philip II.

The reader familiar with David Quint's provocative book, *Epic and*

Empire, might well object here that Quint argues for a reading of Lucan's Amyclas episode that makes an association with the imperial fortunes of Philip II quite problematic. According to Quint, Lucan purposely opposes the capricious aspect of random chance to the epic teleology of empire, and thus reduces the victors to the same level of "nonnarrability" as the losers (*Epic and Empire*, 137–40). Quint's elucidation of the *Aeneid* is masterful, and his analysis of the *Pharsalia* often insightful; nonetheless, his reading of Lucan is much more in tune with the disillusionment of our own age, and perhaps that of Lucan himself, than with the temper of the Iberian sixteenth century. I find no indication in the commentaries and readings of Lucan during Ercilla's time that the deeply subversive aspect of the Latin poet was fully appreciated. Isaías Lerner, in a cogent article, lends support to my interpretation, remarking that Juan Luis Vives, in tracts published in the 1520s and 1530s, highly recommended Lucan in the education of young aristocrats precisely because of his "veracity" and the "solaz espiritual" that could be found in his work ("Ercilla y Lucano," 684–85). Perhaps the courtly context of scholarship alone would go a long way to explain this apparent "misreading" of Lucan.

Thus I think it far more likely that both the poet and his contemporaries would have read the reference to Amyclas in the following sense: saved from the perils of the sea by the grace of its far-off master's privileged status as Fortune's equal—like Julius Caesar before the decisive battle of Pharsalia—the battered Spanish squadron is swept into the protection of a little bay where a new menace awaits it (*Araucana* 16.18–19). The indigenous inhabitants are warlike (*Araucana* 16.20), and upon seeing the arrival of the broken ships, the hastily armed islanders stream down to the seashore, bent on the destruction of the storm-weary intruders (*Araucana* 16.21). As a handful of Spaniards prepares to meet this new threat under very unfavorable conditions (*Araucana* 16.23), the wind suddenly drops and

> cayó vn rayo de súbito boluiendo,
> en viua llama aquel nubloso belo,
> Y en forma de lagarto discurriendo,
> se vio hender vna cometa el Cielo,
> el mar bramó, y la tierra resentida,
> del gran pesso gimió como oprimida.
>
> (*Araucana* 16.24c–h)

> Cortó súbito allí vn temor elado,
> la fuerça a los turbados naturales,
> por siniestro pronóstico tomado,
> de su ruyna, y venideros males,
> Viendo aquel mouimiento deususado,
> y los prodigios tristes y señales,
> que su destrozo y pérdida anunciauan,
> ya perpetua opressión amenazauan.
>
> (*Araucana* 16.25)

The indigenous warriors drop their arms and flee in panic (*Araucana* 16.26). The Spaniards are then able to communicate the purpose of their coming to the terrified islanders: they are to be corrected for "breaking faith" with the "Sacred Sacrament" and the emperor (*Araucana* 16.29–30).

We have here a harbinger indeed of the new direction of Part II of the *Araucana* in comparison with Part I. The destiny of the metropolitan center is conspicuously interwoven with the otherwise insignificant police action on the colonial periphery through the complementary media of supernatural portents and the explicit foregrounding of prestigious literary models. Philip's mastery of Fortune is compared implicitly with that of Caesar, and the prophecy of colonial dominion is sealed by fire from the heavens. It comes as no surprise, then, that in Part II of the *Araucana* the tale of the war in Chile is intertwined with the two greatest Old World triumphs of sixteenth-century imperial Spain. What is more, this interweaving of apparently diverse materials is accomplished through the agency of a web of prophecy elaborated through specifically ostentatious, rather than dissimulative, poetic imitation.

1.2. Ercilla's Change of Tack

In order to fully appreciate the magnitude of this "sea change" in the *Araucana*, it is necessary to briefly recall Ercilla's statements of his own program in Part I. In the Prologue to the 1569 edition, Ercilla states that his poem is a "true history" (hystoria verdadera) and concerned with "affairs of war" (cosas de guerra).[8] Furthermore, he makes it clear that the war with the Araucanians, and above all, the heroism of these indigenous defenders of their liberty, is the exclusive theme of his poem. Thus he felt moved to write because many of his comrades-in-arms encouraged him, mindful lest memory of their deeds be lost to posterity. He is concerned, as well, that the magnitude of the exploits he has witnessed will be ignored, misjudged, or undervalued because of the remoteness and obscurity of the theater of operations (Morínigo and Lerner, ed. 1:121). There is nothing in the prologue to suggest that anything other than a factually accurate account of the colonial police action in which he personally took part will enter into his narrative scope; nor is there any hint of a proposal to link the actions on the colonial periphery to the grand scheme of empire as seen from the metropolitan center.

The initial indications of the prologue are successively reinforced throughout the text of Part I. The opening stanzas, with their explicit recollection and rejection of the Italian *romanzi* in the style of Boiardo and Ariosto, set the tone in no uncertain terms:

> No las damas, amor, no gentilezas
> De caualleros canto enamorados
> Ni las muestras, regalos y ternezas
> De amorosos affectos y cuydados,
> Mas el valor, los hechos, las proezas
> De aquellos Españoles esforçados,
> Que a la ceruiz de Arauco no domada
> Pusieron duro yugo por la espada.
>
> (*Araucana* 1.1)

This can be taken as implying a return to the relative austerity of Virgil's "I sing of deeds of arms and a courageous man" (arma virumque cano) (*Aeneid* 1.1) in counterpoint to the decadent amplitude of Ariosto's "Le donne, i cavallier, l'arme, gli amori, / le cortesie, l'audaci imprese io canto" (I sing of ladies, knights, deeds of arms, amours, / courtesies, and daring exploits) (*Orlando furioso* 1.1*ab*).[9] In fact, however, Ercilla sets his limits even more strictly than Virgil, whose "vir," after all, permits the poet to introduce love, fatherhood, and many other things implied in the life of a man beyond the strictly delimited field of the profession of arms. On the contrary, Ercilla has explicitly rejected love and has narrowly defined his subject as "el valor, los hechos, las proezas" (*Araucana* 1.1*e*). The exclusive homage to Mars at the expense of Venus is amplified in the following stanza:

> Cosas diré también harto notables
> De gentes que a ningún Rey obedecen.
> Temerarias empresas memorables
> Que celebrarse con razón merecen.
> Raras industrias, términos loables
> Que más los Españoles engrandecen
> Pues no es el vencedor más estimado
> De aquello en que el vencido es reputado.
>
> (*Araucana* 1.2)

Here again, not only is warlike activity the exclusive theme, but moreover, only those bellicose deeds carried out in the confined context of Arauco are included. Nor are love and courtly dalliance the only possible deviations that have been strictly excluded. Ercilla implicitly banishes the fantastic, especially chivalresque fiction in the style of the *libros de caballerías*—known to the more censorious of his contemporaries as "books of lies"—with the further statement, "Es relación sin corromper sacada / De la verdad, cortada a su medida" (*Araucana* 1.3*ef*). This last recalls the similar pronouncement by Ercilla's contemporary and fellow courtier Luis Zapata, in the prologue to his *Carlo famoso* of 1566, that his poem will cleave so closely to the truth that "a ningún historiador en prosa daré la ventaja" (fol. Aiii r). Unlike Zapata, however, Ercilla seems to disdain the possible admissibility of "cuentos fabulosos," authorized by their use by ancient poets, as legitimate ornaments to an otherwise historical poem (Zapata, fol. Aii v), and leaves himself no room to maneuver with his bald assertion that all will be "relación sin corromper sacada / de la verdad" (*Araucana* 1.3*ef*). Ercilla underlines this last by assuring his intended reader, King Philip II himself, that his poet bears personal witness to much of what he will sing: "Dad orejas señor a lo que digo / Que soy de parte dello buen testigo" (*Araucana* 1.5*gh*). Indeed, at this point the credulous reader might well be seduced into the belief that Ercilla intends to deliver up a rigorously *verista* rhymed chronicle of colonial war as he gives over his pen to the "furor de Marte" (*Araucana* 1.5*f*).

Nonetheless, as often occurs in sixteenth- and seventeenth-century letters, the program expressed in the prologue and introductory passages is not always strictly adhered to throughout the following text.

Unlike his contemporary Lope de Vega, for instance (Bataillon, "*La desdicha,*" 395), Ercilla does not deliberately set out to flout the principles laid down in his prologue. On the contrary, he is scrupulous about calling attention to his doubts and his ultimate surrender to temptation, as the poet of the *Araucana* finds it tiresome to steer closely the course he has set for himself well before he reaches the end of Part I. True to his brave beginning, Ercilla dedicates the bulk of his first fifteen cantos to the war between Spaniards and Indians in Chile, but in the last three cantos of Part I the poet begins to repent of his rigorous rejection of Venus in favor of Mars.

First, without any preamble or excuses, Ercilla slips the tender, amorous interlude of the indigenous lovers Lautaro and Guacolda into his narration of the war (*Araucana* 13.41*gh*–14.15). Although this is the first such scene in the poem, the reader is barely aware of the poet's faltering resolve because Guacolda's premonitory dream, her lover's confident reassurances, and the inevitable shock of Lautaro's sudden death in the first fury of the Spanish surprise attack all fit seamlessly into the narrative warp and woof of martial events. In fact, as Georgina Sabat-Rivers has pointed out, Lautaro's inattention to duty and unsoldierly abandon to passion mark the nadir of what has been a steady decline in the quality of his character as a commander ever since his introduction into the action in *Araucana* 3.33–49 (116–17). The night of lovemaking that induces the Araucanian chieftain to strip off his armor, and hence expose himself to the fatal shaft during the predawn assault is thus a necessary, constitutive element in the narration of the war and fundamentally different from the amorous episodes of Part II (Pittarello 250–51). Nonetheless, Ercilla demonstrates in his exordium to *Araucana* 15 that he is conscious of a potential conflict with his initial program as set out in the beginning stanzas of the poem:

¿Qué cosa puede auer sin amor buena?
¿Que verso sin amor dará contento?
¿Dónde jamás se ha visto rica vena
Que no tenga de amor el nascimiento?
No se puede llamar materia llena
la que de amor no tiene el fundamento,
los contentos, los gustos, los cuydados
Son, si no son de amor, como pintados.

(*Araucana* 15.1)

It is as if creeping guilt over the trespass committed by his seeking a fleetingly sensuous respite from the clamor of arms in the bivouac of Lautaro and Guacolda has finally caught up with the poet and forced a confession.

Ercilla continues the public airing of his dilemma in the following stanzas. It is clear that at this stage of the unfolding of the poem, he poses the questions of variety versus monotony and unremittant war versus the uplifting virtues of love in terms of imitation of prestigious models:

> Amor de un juycio rústico y grossero
> Rompe la dura y áspera corteza,
> Produze ingenio y gusto verdadero
> y pone qualquier cosa en más fineza,
> Dante, Ariosto, Petrarca y el Ibero
> amor los truxo a tanta delgadeza
> que la lengua más rica y más copiosa,
> Si no trata de amor es desgustosa.
>
> *(Araucana* 15.2)

Nonetheless, Ercilla conceives of his original program in terms that impede following the smoother, more delightful path blazed by the Italian masters and their Iberian pupil, Ercilla's idol Garcilaso. Although imitation of these illustrious models would solve the problem of monotony, Ercilla feels constrained by his commitment to provide a strictly historically accurate account of the war. The poet wrestles with his dilemma, outlining the options for the further course of his poem:

> Quíselo aquí dejar considerado
> Ser escritura larga y trabajosa,
> Por yr a la verdad tan arrimado,
> y auer de tratar siempre de vna cosa:
> que no ay tan dulce estilo y delicado,
> Ni pluma tan cortada y sonorosa
> que en un largo discurso no se estrague,
> Ni gusto que un manjar no lo empalague.
>
> *(Araucana* 15.4)

> Que si a mi discreción dado me fuera
> Salir al campo, y escoger las flores,
> Quiçá el cansado gusto remouiera
> La vsada variedad de los sabores:
> pues como otros han hecho, yo pudiera
> entretejer mil fábulas y amores:
> mas ya que tan adentro estoy metido,
> hauré de proseguir lo prometido.
>
> (*Araucana* 15.5)

He is fairly confident in his powers as a poet, and opines that he could spice up his martial narrative as well as Ariosto or any of the "others" if only he had chosen a less rigorous path at the beginning. As things stand, he is restricted to the type of dissimulative imitation of models pursued throughout Part I.

Furthermore, he must rely for variety on the type of narrative device that rotates around his little exordium here. Following the lead of Boiardo and Ariosto, Ercilla has left the two bloodstained champions, Rengo and Andrea, with their weapons suspended in midstrike at the end of canto 14. The little divagation on the seductive attractions of love and the rigors of historical epic serves very nicely to whet the reader's appetite for the resumption of the duel at *Araucana* 15.6.[10] The tension is obviously not resolved, however, as Ercilla brings Part I to a close with the most elaborately, densely imitative passage of the first fifteen cantos—the storm discussed at the opening of this chapter. Yet, as I have indicated, even here Ercilla is careful to disguise the literary as opposed to historical antecedents of his description in order to preserve the maximum illusion of verisimilitude.

Again, in the prologue to Part II, which first appeared in 1578, Ercilla communicates his anxiety over the monotony of his warlike material:

> Por auer prometido de proseguir esta historia, no con poca difficultad y pesadumbre, la he continuado, y aunque esta segunda parte de la *Araucana* no muestre el trabajo que me cueste: todavía quien la leyere podrá considerar el que se aurá pasado en escreuir dos libros de materia tan aspera, y de poca variedad, pues desde el principio hasta el fin, no contiene sino vna misma cosa, y auer de caminar siempre, por el rigor de vna verdad tan

desierta y estéril: paréceme que no aurá gusto que no canse de seguirme: assí temeroso de esto, quisiera mil vezes mezclar algunas cosas differentes, pero acordé de no mudar de estilo, porque lo q*ue* digo se me tomasse en descuento de las faltas que el libro lleua, auctorizándole con escreuir en él: El alto principio que el Rey nuestro señor dio a sus obras, con el assalto y entrada de Sanquintín, por auernos dado otro aquel mesmo día los Araucanos en el fuerte de la Concepción. Assi mismo trato el rompimiento de la batalla Naval, que el señor Don Iuan de Austria venció en Lepanto, y no es poco atreuimiento querer poner dos cosas tan grandes, en lugar tan humilde, pero todo lo merecen los Araucanos. (Prologue [Cossin, 1578])

This very brief, and largely veiled, acknowledgment of the profound change of course in Part II is more revealing for what it dissembles than for what it purports to declare. To begin with, Ercilla insists, as in the prologue to Part I, on the work he has invested in the poem. The poet's concern that the reader might not be aware of the "trabajo que me cueste" is, in part, formulaic and conventional; on the other hand, especially in Part II, it is probable that Ercilla wishes to call attention discreetly to the far more ostentatious imitation of prestigious models with which he has adorned his poetic rendering of the "harsh and rugged truth" without undermining his original claim to authority on the basis of absolute versimilitude. Indeed, he attributes the magnitude of his challenge to "auer de caminar siempre por el rigor de vna verdad tan desierta y estéril."

Nonetheless, Ercilla explains, he dares not depart too far from his initial program in search of variety. Thus he will seek to relieve the monotony without "changing his style." This seems to mean that he will continue to sing of war, historically accurate war at that, but he will broaden his scope beyond the confines of Arauco. He goes on to clarify: he will remedy the faults of his poor subject by introducing the European victories of Saint Quentin and Lepanto, although such exalted events may seem out of place in such humble surroundings. The valor of the Araucanians, however, is worthy of even such great company (Prologue [Cossin, 1578]). Here, at least, Ercilla does not dissemble. He is announcing his intention to ennoble explicitly his account of the obscure police action at the ends of the earth by interweaving it with the two greatest victories of the metropolitan, imperial center.

This confession of a change in plan is not complete, however. While Ercilla does warn the reader that the original program of an account limited to the war in Chile has been broadened to include war in Europe, he does not mention that this will require the implementation of all the machinery of supernatural prophecy with its attendant imitation of prestigious models in the epic tradition. Still less does Ercilla advise the reader that this will be accomplished through the medium of intensified imitation that deliberately calls attention to, and invites comparison with, specific models within that tradition. In fact, Ercilla comes much closer to revealing the true dimensions of his project when his Araucanian guide, Guaticolo, explains that it has been prophetically revealed that in Fitón's cave the poet will be made privy to "estraños casos dignos de memoria / con que ilustrar pudiesse más su historia" (*Araucana* 23.61gh). "Ilustrar" is a verb that is often used by Ercilla's contemporaries to describe the practice and goal of imitation. This is made especially explicit by Du Bellay and Ronsard (Py 15, 20), and the concept permeates discussions of imitation among the Sevillian disciples of Herrera (Vilanova 20–21).

Thus while there appears to be a systematic, although partially veiled, consistency of purpose in the new direction of Part II, this is not the case in the unfolding of the poem through Part I and on into Part II. The contrast between the series of protestations by the poet in the prologues and texts of Parts I and II might seem to support Fernando Alegría's assertion (44) that Ercilla is sailing by dead reckoning, without a preconceived plan, and that the changes of direction and purpose are made ad hoc as the poem wends its way from the mind of its creator to the written page. Another critic, Charles Aubrun, specifically suggests that Ercilla conceived of Part I as a "crónica rimada de los hechos de los españoles en el Arauco," but that by 1578 Part II "ya es otra cosa: un poema épico con episodios galantes" (261–62). Marcos A. Morínigo, in his introduction to the Castalia edition, puts forward the hypothesis that Ercilla wrote all or most of the core narrative that concerns his own presence in Chile—material interwoven into what was published as Parts II and III of the *Araucana*—while still in America. Morínigo refers to this material as a *Diario de la guerra*. According to Morínigo, it only then occurred to Ercilla to provide this *Diario* with an introductory section that would set the stage for the poet's own arrival upon the scene in Arauco. This preliminary material, perhaps begun while Ercilla was in Peru after his falling-out with Don García Hurtado de Mendoza—the leader of the expedition—came to form the bulk of Part I of the *Araucana* when it was published in 1569 (Ercilla, *Araucana*, ed. Morínigo and Lerner, 1:59–60). Morínigo further hypothesizes that, upon Ercilla's return to Madrid and the court in 1563, the poet came to realize the importance of varying the warlike monotony of his original *Diario* with amorous episodes more in accord with courtly conceptions of epic, and above all, of intertwining the colonial subject of his poem into the larger scheme of empire as seen from the metropolitan center (1:47, 51–52). While I find Morínigo's conjectures convincing in regard to the relative periods of composition of the testimonial portions of the poem in contrast with the rest, the Paraguayan philologist's hypotheses still do not explain the fact that in 1569, six years after Ercilla's return to Spain, Part I of the *Araucana* shows no trace of the deliberately showcased imitation and the carefully plotted web of prophecy that distinguish Part II when it is published in 1578.

Nonetheless, while there is clearly an evolution in the poet's approach, especially in regard to the theme of love in Part I, not all critics of the *Araucana* agree that there is any real change between Part I and Part II at all. Maxime Chevalier, for instance, argues that Ercilla's surrender to the theme of love at the end of Part I was intentionally counterpoised by the poet to his opening references to Ariosto, and furthermore, that this tribute to Ariosto and love in Part I precludes consideration of any change in between 1569 and 1578 (Chevalier, *L'Arioste*, 150–51). The French scholar's thesis rests entirely on the issue of the theme of love as opposed to war, and seems to revolve around Chevalier's underlying project of demonstrating the key role of the Ariostesque model in sixteenth-century Iberian letters, especially epic poetry. While I find Ducamin's (117 n. 1) and Alegría's (44) perception of ad hoc improvisation more convincing, Chevalier can certainly demonstrate that Ercilla has already introduced the theme of love in Part I. Nonetheless, Sabat-Rivers (116–17) has pointed out the cogency of the idyll of Guacolda and Lautaro to the martial narrative in Part I, and Pittarello has underlined its distinct focus and function relative to the later amatory passages. Thus it is difficult to sustain the French scholar's thesis that there is no real novelty in the further development of amorous fiction in Part II with the famous episodes of Tegualda and Glaura. Furthermore, what Chevalier's argument fails to address entirely is the introduction of a complex supernatural *machina* and the concomitant sea change in imitative strategy that is evident at the end of the storm in *Araucana* 16 and only becomes more pronounced in the unfolding web of prophecy that binds the metropolitan victories of Saint Quentin and Lepanto, as well as the visionary, imperial mapamundi, into the Araucanian, colonial fabric of the poem.

Perhaps we can gain an insight into the inner, hidden processes of this drastic change in the course of the *Araucana* by recalling one of the most distinctive features of Ercilla's description of the storm at the end of Part I. As I have already indicated above, Ercilla infuses what is really a very literary storm with an air of freshness and authenticity by making liberal use of detailed, up-to-date nautical jargon and by enlivening the traditional topos of the confusion of the sailors with direct speech rather than third-person narration. The poet of the *Araucana* would have found the most highly developed classical model for both the nautical terminology and the direct speech of the despairing pilot, as I have pointed out, in Ovid's best literary storm (*Metamorphoses* 11). Ercilla was not the first sixteenth-century poet to see the possibilities for updating the topos suggested by Ovid's fortunate expansion on this feature of the locus received from Virgil.

Ariosto, like Ercilla after him, writes literary storms that display an eclectic concatenation of elements selected from various versions of the traditional topos. In Ariosto's case, there are both Renaissance and classical models that must be taken into account. The principal Renaissance models are his Italian predecessors, Boccaccio, Pulci, and Boiardo. The most important classical paradigms are Virgil, but above all, Ovid (Ponte 196–98). The Ovidian inspiration is particularly evident in the desperate cries of the helmsman:[11]

> Quel che siede al governo, alto sospira
> pallido e sbigottito ne la faccia;
> e grida invano, e invan con mano accenna
> or di voltare, or di calar l'antenna.
>
> (*Orlando furioso* 41.10e–h)

(The helmsman, his face sickly and pale yellow with terror, sighs loudly and cries out in vain, signaling uselessly with his hand now to trim, now to let go the yard.)

and the frantic activity of the sailors:

> I navegante a dimostrare effetto
> vanno de l'arte in che lodati sono:
> chi discorre fischiando col fraschetto,
> e quanto han gli altri a far, mostra col suono;
> chi l'ancore apparechia da rispetto,
> e chi al mainare e chi alla scotta é buono;
> chi 'l timone, chi l'arbore assicura,
> chi la coperta di sgombrare ha cura.
> (*Orlando furioso* 18.143)

(The sailors go to show off the skills for which they are praised; one of them communicates by whistling on a boatswain's pipe, and tells the others what to do by the sound: who is to make ready the reserve anchor; who is most handy at lowering the sail and who at hauling the main sheet; who is best at lashing the tiller, who at securing the mainmast, who takes charge of clearing the deck.)

In particular, these passages recall Ovid's:

> "Lower the top yards right away!" the pilot
> cries, "reef the sail tightly to the spars!"
> So he orders; but the contrary blasts of the storm
> drown out his orders,
> nor does the uproar of the sea let his voice be heard.
> Nevertheless, some, on their own account, hasten to
> pull in the oars, others to secure the side, some
> to take in the sails;
> here one bails out the waves, another pours the sea
> back into the sea,
> another hastily strikes the spars.
> (*Metamorphoses* 11.482–85)

> ("Ardua iamdudum demittite cornua" rector
> clamat "et antemnis totum subnectite velum"
> hic iubet; inpediunt adversae iussa procellae,
> nec sinit audiri vocem fragor aequoris ullam

> sponte tamen properant alii subducere remos,
> pars munire latus, pars ventis vela negare;
> egerit hic fluctus aequorque refundit in aequor,
> hic rapit antemnas.)

and. "The pilot himself is in terror and admits that he does not know how the vessel stands, nor what either to order or forbid" (ipse pavet, nec se, qui sit status, ipse fatetur / scire ratis rector, nec quid iubeatve vetetve) (*Metamorphoses* 11.492–93).[12]

Such indeed is the authority of the *Orlando furioso* that some critics have ascribed clear imitations of Ovid's storm to the influence of Ariosto. A case in point is Ronsard's *Franciade* of 1572, where the cries and confusion of the sailors (2.197–208) are only one blatant instance among many of imitation of Ovid's storm.[13] Unlike the French poet, however, Ariosto notably increases the density of nautical jargon in his storms, even if this recourse may originally have been suggested by Ovid. In fact, although Ariosto is not known to have spent long months traveling the great oceans of the world like Ercilla, the specific sailor's terminology of the *Orlando furioso* compares favorably with that of the *Araucana*.[14] It would be naive indeed to read the supposedly realistic Iberian seafaring poems of the later sixteenth century without taking into account the exemplary role of Ariosto's poem in the transformation and modernization of the topos of the classical literary storm. Ariosto, however, like Ronsard, regresses toward the standard literary storm description by reporting everything in the third person, omitting the direct speech that sets Ovid's storm apart from the other classical tempests and gives it such immediacy. Expanding upon Ovid's device, it is precisely the direct representation of the sailors' alarm, authenticated by detailed seaman's jargon, that imbues Ercilla's storm with novelty and credibility.

In fact, to find a portrayal of the sailors' confusion with exploitation of direct speech similar to Ercilla's, it is necessary to look to another prestigious poem first published in 1572, and like Ronsard's *Franciade* also charged with a highly nationalistic, imperialistic message: *Os Lusíadas*. Camoens, like Ercilla, had extensive firsthand experience of sixteenth-century sea travel. Thus, at first glance, it is not surprising that Camoens should enliven his otherwise very literary storm that precedes Gama's arrival in India with some authentic shipboard vocabulary, including the following:[15]

> Mas neste passo assi promptos estando,
> Eis o mestre, que olhando os ares anda,
> O apito toca, acordao despertando
> Os marinheiros dhua e doutra banda:
> E porque o vento vinha refrescando,
> Os traquetes das gaueas tomar manda,
> "Alerta," disse, "estay, que o vento crece
> Daquella nuuem negra que aparece."
>
> Não erão os traquetes bem tomados,
> Quando dà a grande e súbita procella
> "Amaina," disse o mestre a grandes brados,
> "Amaina," disse, "amaina a grande vella."
> Não esperão os ventos indinados
> Que amainassem, mas juntos dando nella,
> Em pedaços a fazem, cum ruído
> Que o Mundo pareceo ser destruydo.
>
> (*Lusíadas* 6.70–71)

What immediately stands out, of course, is that like Ovid and Ercilla, Camoens represents the sailing master's exhortations in direct speech rather than through third-person description as do Ariosto or others. The similarities, however, do not end with the use of direct speech; nor did they pass unnoticed.

Manuel Faria e Sousa published his monumental edition of *Os Lusíadas* in Madrid in 1639. In his commentary on *Lusíadas* 6.71, Faria e Sousa prefaces his copious references to and citations of Virgil, Ovid, and Ariosto with a quotation from the *Araucana*:

> "Amayna, amayna," gritan marineros,
> "amayna la mayor, hiça trinquete."
> Esfuerçan esta Voz los passageros
> Y a la triça vn gran número arremete,
> Los otros de tropel corren ligeros
> a la escota, a la braça, al chafaldete,
> Mas del viento la fuerça era tan braua,
> que ningún aparejo gouernaua.
>
> (*Araucana* 15.72)

Indeed, although *Araucana* 15.72 follows the direct speech of the pilot (*Araucana* 15.70) and represents the cries of the sailors, the direct quotation is echoed in *Lusíadas* 6.71, as are the repeated imperative "Amaina" and the references to the mainsail (Sp. "vela mayor"; Port. "grande vela"). The lexical relation between the foresail (Sp. "trinquete"; Port. "traquete") and the topsails (Port. "traquetes de gávea") is also very suggestive.

Faria e Sousa's enthusiasm for Camoens, however, seems to have blinded him to some of the implications of these coincidences between the storm descriptions of the two Iberian poets. Faria e Sousa remarks (2:146): "No ay en toda esta descripcion accion, o palabra que no sea natural de la marineria en aquel tiempo; al fin como de quien lo vio, i tuvo ingenio para saberlo pintar. La repeticion de, *amaina*, especificando que con vozes descompassadas (esso es, *brados*) es propia": Faria e Sousa, in his commentary on the preceding stanza (*Lusíadas* 6.70; 2:144), explicitly acknowledges Camoens's debt to Ariosto (*Orlando furioso* 18.143*cd*) for the detail of the pilot blowing on his bosun's pipe to order the change of sail. The seventeenth-century critic, however, seems to evade the issue of a possible imitation of the *Araucana* by asserting that "every word and action" was appropriate for a person with direct experience of contemporary nautical practices.[16] Regardless of what exactly Faria e Sousa had in mind, the similarities between the two passages suggest that Camoens may have taken a pointer from Ercilla as well as Ariosto in how to modernize and enliven the classical literary storm motif as originally spun out by Ovid. Camoens returned to Portugal from the East in 1569 or 1570 (*Os Lusíadas*, ed. Pierce, ix) and did not publish his poem until 1572. Although the belief that Camoens brought the manuscript of his poem complete back from India has been widely disseminated (Pierce, ed. xi), the license for publication was not granted until September 1571. Thus it is entirely possible, indeed probable, that Camoens was still polishing and correcting the poem after his arrival in Lisbon. Ercilla published Part I of the *Araucana* in the spring of 1569 (Medina, *Vida*, 97), and Camoens would have arrived in Lisbon either shortly after or shortly before the first blast of the Castilian poet's success swept through the literary circles of the Portuguese capital.[17] Engaged as they were in such similar poetic enterprises, it is inconceivable that the two Iberian poets would not have read each other's work as soon as it appeared.

Even if the similar, dense use of nautical terminology to lend verisimilitude and originality to the literary storm was only a serendipitous elaboration on the Ariostesque model, and if the repetition of "Amaina, amaina" (*Araucana* 15.72a; *Lusíadas* 6.71cd) was a strikingly coincidental, creative translation of Ovid's "Ardua iamdudum demittite cornua" (*Metamorphoses* 11.482) on the part of both Ercilla and Camoens, it could only have been read by Ercilla in 1572 as a gauntlet flung into the field of poetic and imperial contention and honor. In fact, there is a great deal more in the *Lusíadas* that would have piqued Ercilla's sense of rivalry and that would have challenged an ardently Castilian poet on crucial imperialist and poetic grounds. It is my thesis that concrete, definite responses by Ercilla in Parts II and III of the *Araucana* to this Lusitanian challenge have long been overlooked or misread. In order to place these in the proper context, however, it will first be necessary to examine Ercilla's approach to imitation and rivalry in a way that heretofore has not been attempted by critics of the *Araucana*.

As the difficulties and uncertainties that have emerged in my discussion of the storm in Parts I and II of the *Araucana* will have made abundantly clear, establishing exact relationships between texts, even where the simple fact of some sort of imitation is quite apparent, can prove to be a delicate and elusive enterprise. Is Ercilla imitating Homer in the opening of his tempest? If so, does he wish to advertise or disguise this fact, or only make it accessible to the erudite few? What does Ercilla's storm owe to Virgil? Ovid? Lucan? Ariosto? And more important, how does Ercilla want his reader to perceive these relationships? As in the case of Ovid, Ercilla, and Camoens, which similarities are inevitable in the treatment of a long-established topos, and which are the deliberate response to a specific model text? Renaissance imitation is too varied and too subtle a practice to yield useful results to the critic on the basis of mere allegations of analogy. For that reason, before passing on to the detailed examination of Ercilla's strategies of imitation and rivalry that occupies Chapters 2 and 3 of this book, and then the direct confrontation with Camoens in Chapters 4 and 5, it is prudent to conclude the present discussion with a brief sketch of the theoretical compass that I employ to chart the *maria incognita* of imitation in the *Araucana*.

1.3. Toward an "Arte de Navegar" of Imitation

The first problem that arises in any discussion of imitation is the often-blurred distinction between two fundamental shadings of the term. Aristotle, among many other ancient Greek authors, used the Greek word *mimesis*, which we translate as "imitation," when referring to the concept of art as a representation or imitation of life. Yet the notion that the most convincing counterfeisance of life and nature is to be achieved by following the models provided by prestigious predecessors is already implicitly present in Aristotle's singling out of Homer as paradigm of the epic poet (*Poetics*, chap. 23). This idea of perfecting *mimesis* through the mediation of superior example acquires increasing momentum in direct ratio to the cultural distance traversed between model and imitator. Thus it is a growing preoccupation among Greek writers during the Hellenistic period, and begins to assume almost obsessive proportions in Rome in the first century B.C. (Greene, *Light*, 56–57). Because this secondary *mimesis*, the imitation of models produced by art rather than nature, is so closely associated with Latin imitation of Greek, later Latin imitation of earlier Latin, and Renaissance imitation of Latin exemplars, it is convenient to distinguish it from unmediated representation by designating it with the Latin *imitatio* and reserving the Greek *mimesis* for the broader concept of "imitation of life." It is with this admittedly artificial and anachronistic distinction that throughout my discussion I will employ the terms "imitation" and "imitatio" as referring specifically to the imitation of literary models. Following the usage of Thomas Greene and other contemporary writers on imitation, where appropriate, the model text will be referred to as the subtext.

The reader of texts written in the tradition of *imitatio* soon becomes aware that the term rather loosely embraces a multiplicity of widely varying literary practices and attitudes toward model texts. George W. Pigman, in his remarkably concise but comprehensive study "Versions of Imitation in the Renaissance," finds that only Bartolomeo Ricci, in his treatise *De imitatione* of 1541, "writes as if there were accepted divisions of the genus *imitatio* into species" (Pigman 3). Ricci, discussing an instance of Virgil's imitation of Catullus, breaks imitative practice down into "following" (*sequi*), "imitating" (*imitari*) and "emulating" (*aemulari*) (Pigman 3). Pigman observes that Ricci's scheme bears close resemblance to ideas expressed on the subject by Erasmus and Bembo, and that an associate of Bembo's, Daniel Barbaro, gives a similar threefold definition—*accostarsi, aguagliarli, superargli*—in a tract published in 1557 (Pigman 26 n. 35). These formulations are particularly cogent for the study of Ercilla's approach to imitation. Ricci's was published some seven years before Ercilla took up his studies with the celebrated humanist Juan Cristóbal Calvete de la Estrella (Medina, *Vida*, 22), and Barbaro's during the early gestation of the *Araucana*. Although there is no particular reason to believe that Ercilla read either, they reflect what were apparently widely held opinions on the subject among humanists at precisely the time Ercilla was experiencing his formation as a poet under the tutelage of the humanist Calvete de la Estrella and in the humanist literary circles of the Spanish court.

While the categories proposed by Ricci and Barbaro may well represent very accurately the state of theoretical thinking on the question of *imitatio* at a crucial period in the development of Ercilla's poetics, their direct and unmediated application to the tangled skeins of imitation in the *Araucana* is problematic at best. As Pigman explains, it is not always clear exactly what Ricci or Barbaro means by each species of imitation, and the only way of arriving at a practical understanding of their terminology is "by studying the imagery, analogies, and metaphors of writings on imitation" (3). Pigman concludes that Ricci's "following" and "imitating" are often indistinguishable, and that "thus the two *major* categories of imitation are imitation (*imitatio*) and emulation (*aemulatio*)" (3). Through his analysis of the "analogies and metaphors" of imitation in a wide selection of classical and Renaissance authors, Pigman devises his own threefold scheme of imitative practice: transformative, dissimulative, and eristic (3).

Pigman's transformative category is extremely broad, and includes frankly nontransformative "following" as well as failed attempts at transformation. Pigman regards the well-known metaphors of the bee collecting pollen and transforming it into honey, the digestion of food, and the resemblance of son to father as all illustrative of what he calls transformative imitation (3–4). Despite Pigman's observation that the apian metaphor can refer to modes of imitation in which no transformation occurs as well as those that involve varying degrees of transformation (4), the theoretical conflation of these is perhaps the least useful aspect of his system. As Ricci and Barbaro indicate, there is a definite sense of a distinct, nontransformative approach to imitation (*sequi, accostarsi*) that must be explicitly distinguished from the various transformative types to yield a useful perception of what a poet is really about in a given context. As both Alicia de Colombí-Monguió, employing Ricci's and Barbaro's typologies (*Petrarquismo peruano*, 182–90), and Thomas Greene (*Light*, 38), with his own taxonomic vocabulary, demonstrate in their respective analyses of Petrarchist poetics, the type of imitation that Ricci dubs "following" plays an active role in the practice as well as the theory of Renaissance poets. This is true even if its only function is to loom as a potential pitfall to be avoided or an inferior type of imitation against which to be measured.[18]

Pigman's transformative category proves to be too inclusive to be useful for other reasons as well. Both *dissimulatio* and *aemulatio* are variations of transformation, but are relegated to separate species. If there is indeed a basic opposition between *imitatio* and *aemulatio* as Pigman admits (3), there is no clear-cut division in his presentation between what he calls transformation and dissimulation. In fact, the two categories seem to slide naturally one into the other (10). For these reasons, as well as others that will become apparent, Pigman's species of transformative imitation will not really help us clarify what Ricci means by *sequi*, *imitari*, and *aemulari*.

Dissimulation (*dissimulatio*), as the term implies, covers all of the strategies of borrowing or stealing and then trying to disguise the debt or theft. Pigman's insistence on the importance of differentiating dissimulative imitation from other types is one of the great strengths of his system. Even in a tradition in which *imitatio* is highly valued, and indeed the only medium for the spontaneous elaboration in definite form for the poet's own *inventio* (Py 17), there is still a stigma of the illicit, of theft, of plagiarism, associated with the use of another's words or ideas. Marco Girolamo Vida, in his *De arte poetica* of 1527 for instance, repeatedly refers to imitation as theft and the subtext as plunder. For example:

> Ergo agite o mecum securi accingite *furtis*
> Una omnes, pueri, passimque avertite *praedam*.
> (3:243–44)

> (Therefore, my pupils, let each of you follow my example; commit your *thefts* fearlessly and draw your *booty* from every quarter.)[19]

Although Vida is using the metaphor of pilferage playfully here, as he makes clear a few lines further on (3:256–63), there are darker undertones. Vida himself had been criticized by unkind contemporaries for his excessively close "following" of Virgil; they vilified him for pilfering (*surripere*) rather than adapting or selecting (*sumere*) from his chosen model (Vida, *De Arte Poetica*, ed. Williams, xvii–xviii, xli–xlii).[20] Thus one of the motors for *dissimulatio* is to be found in the desire to avoid the onus of "following" so closely or in such a servile fashion as to cast doubt on one's own abilities. Vida himself counsels dissimulation from just such motives (3:217–20). That such preoccupations were very operative in Ercilla's ambit can be seen in his contemporary El Brocense's references to, and defense of, Garcilaso's imitative borrowings as "hurtos" (Vilanova 15).

In fact, the seemingly contradictory goals of, on the one hand, milking all of the power and prestige of a consecrated subtext, and on the other, of avoiding the appearance of parasitical vampirism, creates one of the central driving tensions of imitative practice. One of the major carriage springs through which this tension is absorbed in an imitative text is the idea of dissimulation that will only be penetrated by the learned. As Antonio Vilanova observes in his essay on imitation that opens his monumental exploration *Las fuentes y los temas del "Polifemo" de Góngora*, El Brocense and Fernando de Herrera, both learned contemporaries of Ercilla, equate erudition and its resulting difficulty of access with excellence in imitation (17). Vilanova rightly reminds us that the Renaissance cultivations of erudition and imitation are so tightly intertwined as to make their separate study highly unfruitful (34).

Dissimulation through erudite difficulty can be achieved in a number of ways. Clearly, to imitate an obscure model is to miss the point; little advantage accrues from such a source. To imitate a model of great prestige, but known directly by but a few, has certain attractions. A case in point is the imitation of Greek models not accessible to many Renaissance readers. Such extreme inaccessibility, however, presents problems. For instance, Ronsard, perhaps the only important sixteenth-century epic poet to be directly conversant with Greek texts, justifies his focus on imitation of the *Aeneid* in the *Franciade* by noting that the French are more familiar with Virgil than with Homer and the other Greeks, and that therefore they will more readily recognize the subtexts of his imitation. This, of course, corresponds to his intention to set up his poem as a model of imitative practice (Rigolot 70).

Ercilla would perhaps have found exactly the right balance between prestigious remoteness and practical accessibility in the storm descriptions from the *Odyssey*. Homer's storms were notorious as the paradigmatic epic storms of the tradition, but had still been read by very few Spaniards before the publication of Pérez's translation in 1550. The six editions of Pérez's *De la Ulyxea de Homero XIII libros* that had appeared before Part I of the *Araucana*, however, would have assured a sufficiently wide circle of readers "in the know" to make a certain dissimulation advisable in Ercilla's rendering if he wished to preserve the illusion of *verismo* in his storm. This is exactly what we find in the opening scenes of Ercilla's tempest (*Araucana* 15.67). As Ronsard explicitly states, and Ercilla seems to demonstrate, there are practical limits to the uses of extreme erudition in dissimulation.

Indeed, by far the most common context of *dissimulatio* involves the dissembling of well-known subtexts of proven worth and potency. In this type of dissimulation, the subtext must be so successfully scrambled that only the very learned will be able to decode the imitation (Pigman 14), but the model itself must be chosen from among the most authorized and widely read texts. Pigman questions the functional value of disguised imitation, pointing out that sometimes the only role of the allusion is to provide the pleasure of recognition for its own sake. If this pleasure is intended exclusively for, and only accessible to, the author himself, as Pigman suggests it sometimes is (14), there is some justification for denying the imitation a positive function. Regardless of the author's intentions, however, if the allusion is in fact recognized, the reader is bound to derive pleasure from this contact with an old and familiar friend: the dissimulated subtext. I cannot agree with Pigman's assumption that the "pleasure of recognizing a phrase from an ancient poet" is of minimal functionality in a text (14). A great deal of the motive force driving virtually all kinds of *imitatio* proceeds from the anticipation of pleasure shared between poet and reader in renewing acquaintaince with familiar texts. Dissimulation only serves as a screening device, an attempt by the poet to assure that only those worthy of the pleasure will be indulged in its realization. This kind of *dissimulatio* can well play a role in more ambitious types of imitation or emulation, as I demonstrate in Chapter 3.

Pigman's exploration of dissimulation also arrives upon another important but vaguely defined frontier of imitation. Referring back to the metaphors of the bees and of the digestion of food, Pigman questions whether some resemblances between one text and another may not be the result of unconscious recollection. Just as the bee's transformation of pollen into honey, and the body's digestion of nutrients are natural, unconscious processes, some perceived allusions must be the "natural" result of repeated readings (12). Pigman takes his primary example from Petrarch, paraphrasing the poet: "[H]e read and reread Virgil, Cicero, Horace, and Boethius. He digested their works so thoroughly that they entered his bone marrow, not just his memory. They became so much a part of his mind that occasionally their phrases came to his pen without his recognizing the source or even that they came from someone else" (13). Pigman insists on taking Petrarch very much at face value here, and indeed, the issue of "unconscious reminiscence" poses a very real problem for the reading of imitative texts, particularly those where dissimulation is already an issue. As Pigman observes, "Petrarch's explanation of unconscious reminiscence offers particular difficulties because it casts doubts on just those texts to which one would suppose an author would allude. For one usually feels most confident calling a similarity between two texts an allusion when the putative model is a famous work or a work known to be familiar to the author of the 'alluding' text" (13).

In fact, Petrarch's protestation raises two specters to haunt the reader. On the one hand, Petrarch is the arch-prince of self-fashioning poets, and far from just "exaggerating to make a paradoxical, epigrammatic point"—a possibility that Pigman easily brushes aside (13)—it is quite probable that Petrarch's statement is yet another move in the overall strategy of creating an impressive aura of ersatz *sprezzatura* in which to wrap his carefully crafted imitations. On the other hand, it is undeniably difficult to detect the difference between cleverly disguised allusions and genuinely unpremeditated intertextuality. Even more so when the poet is master at the game and intentionally sets out to exploit the reader's doubt.

Nonetheless, this intriguingly ill-defined no-man's-land between *dissimulatio* and late twentieth-century divagations on the unconscious, inchoate, and uncontrollable compenetration of texts referred to as intertextuality has not failed to attract certain interest. Perhaps inevitably, students of the French Pléiade poets have been in the forefront of this movement. Jean-Claude Carron, for instance, quotes Roland

"Con que ilustrar pudiese más su historia"   49

Barthes to support the notion that "every text is an intertext . . . a new interweaving of past quotations" (573–74). The erudite French poets of the late sixteenth century provide plenty of attractive fodder to nurture this trend of interpretation. Responding to much the same type of criticism leveled against Marco Girolamo Vida, Du Bellay, for instance, literally follows in Petrarch's footsteps and asks rhetorically:

> Si, par la lecture des bons livres, je me suis imprimé quelques traitz en la fantaisie, qui après, venant à exposer mes petites conceptions selon les occasions qui m'en sont données, me coulent beaucoup plus facilement en la plume qu'ilz ne me reviennent en la memoire, doibt-on pour ceste raison les appeller pièces rapportées? (Py 12)
>
> (If, through reading good books, I have imprinted a few traces in my imagination, which afterward when expressing some thoughts that come to me, flow more easily to my pen than to my memory, should one then call them imitations?)

Albert Py, perhaps reading Du Bellay less credulously than Pigman reads Petrarch, explains the attractions of this posture very succinctly:

> Conçue de la sorte, l'imitation des anciens serait tout autre chose que la reproduction délibérée d'un modèle. Elle permettrait, grâce à l'acquis de lectures préalables faites dans un esprit à la fois philologique et poétique, qu'afflue dans les vers français un espèce de mémoire involontaire toute bruissante de la parole des poètes grecs ou latins. La poèsie nouvelle pourrait donc s'entendre, non comme un écho servile de la poèsie ancienne, mais comme son prolongement vivant. (Py 12)
>
> (Conceived of in this way, the imitation of the ancients would be a completely different matter from that of the deliberate reproduction of a model. It would allow, due to the acquirement of previous readings undertaken in both a philological and poetic spirit, that a sort of involuntary memory all-a-whisper with the eloquent sayings of the Greek and Latin poets flow on through French verse. The new poetry could consequently be under-

stood, not as a servile echo of ancient poetry, but rather as its living continuation.)

Nonetheless, it is precisely this type of Petrarchist stratagem that allows Jean-Claude Carron to conclude that Barthes's concept of intertextuality puts Renaissance claims of the control of models through imitation into just as much question as it does the Romantic rejection of models (573–77).

Alicia de Colombí-Monguió, again in the context of Petrarchism, addresses thoughtful remarks to this current of criticism that deserve to be quoted in full:

> El poema petrarquista es completamente inteligible sólo a la luz de otros anteriores que abierta o escondidamente continúa, cita, o transforma. El corpus poético del petrarquismo creó un código que determina la significación, la verdadera inteligibilidad de todo texto que se escribe dentro de su espacio cultural. Para Roland Barthes es imposible trazar los intertextos según él siempre anónimos que forman todo texto. Sin embargo, es muy posible identificar muchos, y no meramente como fuentes que sólo determinan la génesis del poema. . . . me inclino mucho a la concepción de Julia Kristeva, quien probablemente fue la primera en formular la noción de intertextualidad. En su estudio de la poesía de Lautréamont insiste en la absoluta necesidad de identificar sus intertextos y, de ser posible, determinar las ediciones que pudo usar el autor, porque «el texto poético se produce en un movimiento complejo de simultánea afirmación y negación de otro texto». Tanto más, he de agregar, cuando se escribe dentro de la poética de la *imitatio*, que presupone la existencia de un pre-texto. Por eso puede ser que toda lectura sea finalmente una equivocación más o menos fecunda, pero de olvidar la realidad imitativa, es decir, la profunda intertextualidad de un poema de estos siglos áureos, mucho me temo que estos *misreadings* sean por cierto errados, y de seguro vacuos. (193–94)[21]

Colombí-Monguió's warning—that to read texts written in a dense tradition of *imitatio* in willful ignorance of that tradition is to court total incomprehension—is timely. Indeed, insistence on the futility of disentangling inchoate, Barthian intertextuality can all too easily serve as the pretext for a particularly seductive species of scholarly sloth. Furthermore, it is important to bear in mind that what Colombí-Monguió has said about lyric poetry written in the tradition of Petrarchism/Garcilasism is equally true for the reading of sixteenth-century learned epic. This is as manifest for Iberian poets such as Ercilla and Camoens who model themselves in the warrior-courtier-poet mold of Garcilaso, in spite of the recent historical nature of their material, as it is for any of their more scholarly European contemporaries whose epics are more patently products of erudition rather than experience.

On the other hand, we must not lose sight of Pigman's caution that the deliberate practice of *dissimulatio*, coupled with the larger problem of unconscious reminiscence, makes the analysis of the function of imitation, in contrast to the mere identification of sources, problematic in many contexts. Pigman points out, however, that there is one species of *imitatio* in which the subtext clearly plays a determining role, and in which the functionality of that role can reasonably be measured by the critical reader (15).

Pigman prefers the term *eristic*, taken from Longinus's metaphor of imitation as strife (16), to *aemulatio* for designating competitive imitation that strives to surpass or supplant the model, or do both. Pigman rejects emulation (*aemulatio*) as a technically useful term because of its morally dubious overtones of envy and because it often seems to be used interchangeably with *imitatio* (23–24). The opposition *imitatio/aemulatio* is so well established in classical, Renaissance, and contemporary usage, however, that Pigman himself, in his own discussion, constantly falls into using the word "emulation" as an economical and practical way to differentiate declaredly competitive imitation from other types. In spite of the vividness of the metaphor of *eris* and the cogency of Pigman's exploration of eristic metaphors, in the interest of keeping the introduction of exotic jargon to a minimum in my analysis of imitation in the *Araucana*, the *Lusíadas*, and other poems, I will use emulation (*aemulatio*) in a general sense to designate the type of imitation that deliberately advertises a specific subtext in a spirit of rivalry. A more precise use for the term will emerge in my discussion below.

As Pigman makes clear through his analysis of metaphors of contention and overtaking, *aemulatio* represents an approach to imitation that is diametrically opposed to *dissimulatio*. Emulation demands that the subtext be made explicit in such a way that the reader is moved to compare directly the emulation with its model; if the emulation is successful, it will clearly outshine the subtext. All potential ambivalence of the role of the model is swept aside, and the subtext unequivocally, and unashamedly, assumes a central, determining function in the unfolding of the imitation (26).

On the one hand, *aemulatio* serves the function of a sacrificial, ritual cleansing of the guilt associated with servile imitation. The emulator assumes a virile posture, and either corrects a perceived imperfection in the model (Pigman 27), or pushes what is already exemplary to new heights, thus covering himself with all the glory of the vanquished text as well as that of his own achievement.

On the other hand, and this aspect of *aemulatio* Pigman does not explore, the emulator may achieve his victory over the model through a parodic deconstruction that leaves the model beyond the pale of further imitation. An excellent example is Quevedo's devastatingly parodic rendering of the Angelica and Medoro theme. Góngora's romance "En un pastoral albergue," itself a superlative emulation resonant with ludic undertones, had left no room for any other approach. Quevedo's vicious parody may seem mean-spirited, but it effectively put a cap on the refashioning of the virtual topos that had emerged from Ariosto's complex, ludic, yet moving, depiction of compassion trespassing into passion (Chevalier, *Los temas*, 317–19; *L'Arioste* 396, 403; Alonso, *Romance*, 17–18).[22] Further examples, which I explore at length in Chapter 3, are Lucan's witheringly parodic emulations of Virgil and Ovid in *Pharsalia* 6; both play a decisive role in Ercilla's most ambitious exercise in emulation.

Pigman's explication of the metaphors of *aemulatio*, however, is extremely revealing for deciphering Ricci's and Barbaro's tripartite schemes of imitation. Pigman shows that one of the most recurrent metaphors is that of the road or path. In this context, one is either a follower, who literally walks in the footsteps of his predecessors, or a leader who blazes the trail (20–22). Barbaro's terminology is particularly transparent if seen in this light. The imitator may draw near (*accostarsi*), pull up equal to (*aguagliarli*), or surpass (*superargli*) the model along the metaphoric path of poetic achievement. It is very probable that Ricci's *sequi*, *imitari*, and *aemulari* can be safely interpreted within the same metaphoric system. The first stage, "following," clearly corresponds to the metaphor of footsteps and the road. Ricci's otherwise enigmatic "imitate" and "emulate," seen in this way, can be coherently explained as "equaling" and "surpassing."[23] This reading is helpful, because it places the whole issue securely into the context of competition and rivalry. *Imitatio* is not a passive process, but one that always invites comparison and value judgment based on a measurement of one's own work against specific models and, ultimately, the entire tradition. Even the first stage of following (*sequi*), if translated through the lens of *accostarsi*, implies forward movement and striving, and cannot be interpeted as passive reduplication. Indeed, it is probable that such lies outside of the system precisely because of the same negative onus that drives *dissimulatio*, the scorn directed toward literary theft. Yet almost everyone admits that borrowing, pilfering, or outright plundering are inextricably involved in the rhetorical vocabulary of imitation. Although it may never represent an explicitly advocated goal or ideal, supinely reduplicative imitation must find a place in any satisfactory theoretical scheme of *imitatio*.

A far graver and more fundamental problem remains unaddressed in the tripartite scheme suggested by Ricci and Barbaro. It must be remembered that the imitative practices, and the metaphors of imitation, so carefully cultivated by Renaissance humanists were sown, sprouted, and grew to maturity in the challenging soils of cultural and linguistic disparities, the *translatio studii* and creeping anachronism. Even as Aristotle was writing on *mimesis*, Homer and the great playwrights and poets of the fifth century B.C. were already beginning to recede into a world that had defined itself culturally, linguistically, and politically in perceptibly different terms. In the centuries between the triumphs of Alexander of Macedon and the Roman conquest of the Hellenistic world, literary activity begins to assume an increasingly antiquarian, philological character concomitantly with an increasing preoccupation with imitation of models in the production of texts. In the Alexandria of the second century B.C., the scholar Aristarchus dealt systematically with the problem of Homer's anachronism. According to Thomas Greene: "The result was to open a space between model and imitator. This Alexandrian consciousness of the historicity of and consequently the remoteness of older texts can be regarded as a permanent acquisition of Graeco-Roman culture" (*Light*, 56).

Indeed, the "space between model and imitator" opens into a formidable crevasse with the transference of the tradition to late republican and early imperial Rome. The problem of linguistic anachronism is no longer posed merely in terms of distinct stages of development of the Greek language, but in options ranging from the literal translation to the total transmutation of the models into the radically disparate, and yet nascent vehicle of literary Latin. The overall cultural dimensions of *imitatio* become equally challenging. This crisis of adapting imitative practice to anachronism produces a definitive response during the reign of Augustus Caesar. The fruit of this creative germination, Virgil's *Aeneid*, sets the agenda for many centuries to come.

The role and stature of Virgil (70–19 B.C.) in this crucial definition of Latin *imitatio* cannot be exaggerated. Virgil achieved a viable and elegant synthesis of the recognizable imitation of the most prestigious Greek models with the new cultural and linguistic circumstances of Augustan Rome. This was almost immediately recognized, and impelled by the powerful influence of Augustus's court, Virgil's work itself had attained the status of a classic model within the overall tradition even before the poet's death (Graves 11). Furthermore, Virgil's exemplary work, particularly his epic celebration of the Julio-Claudian imperial destiny in the *Aeneid*, explicitly intertwines the successful resolution of the problem of imitative anachronism with the ennobling of the Latin language and the legitimation of Rome's position as imperial center of the world.

This lesson was not lost on Renaissance readers of Virgil. The *Aeneid* was understood to be an imitation of Homer, yet was widely considered itself to be a superior model for imitation. Julius Caesar Scaliger in his treatise *Poetices libri septem* of 1561, for instance, singles Virgil out as the only worthy model of imitation (Weinberg 747). Jacques Peletier du Mans, in his *Art poëtique* of 1555, could recommend Virgil as the prime epic model even after a comparison with Homer (Rigolot 68). Peletier astutely raises the issue that Virgil is known to be an imitator, and Homer is reputed to be original, but might well be an imitator himself. If the two were evaluated synchronically, Peletier feels that Virgil would be considered clearly superior (Rigolot 68–69). According to François Rigolot: "One of the consequences of Peletier's meliorative theory is that, under appropriate circumstances, Virgil himself can be improved upon; and that it should be the duty of modern poets to take up that extraordinary challenge. Contrary to common belief among men of letters, Virgil is not an untouchable model, removed from history to be revered endlessly, like Homer, by future generations" (69). Virgil is specifically seen in the context of imitation that had to rise to the challenges of anachronism. The clearly recognizable echoes of Homer's poems in the *Aeneid* lose none of their power, but they have been perfectly brought into play in a radically different time for a purpose that is completely under the imitating poet's control. Furthermore, his exploitation of the possibilities concomitant with the challenge resulted in an exemplary ennobling of his mother tongue harnessed to the chariot of imperial destiny. Virgil's example produces multiple resonances in sixteenth-century poetics, particularly in the epic, but it is as the illustration of an especially productive mode of exploitation of the dilemma of anachronism posed by imitation that I want to insist on it here.

Indeed, if there is a crevasse of anachronism between the world of Homer and that of Virgil, there is a veritable chasm, a Great Rift Valley, dividing the Rome of Augustus from the splintered European world that was emerging from the cultural devastation brought about by the barbarian invasions that we call the Middle Ages. The first great realization of this renewed challenge of anachronism is attributed to the early fourteenth-century Italian poet and scholar Petrarch. Thomas Greene, whose *The Light in Troy* stands as a monument to the study of *imitatio* through the lens of the challenge of anachronism, begins his survey of Renaissance imitation precisely with Petrarch because the Italian poet is the key figure in the realization that rather than an unbroken continuum, there has been a significant rupture with the world of Virgil (Greene, *Light*, 8). Like Virgil, Petrarch makes a virtue of his dilemma, and his innovative exploitation of the unique spaces opened up by the differences between the linguistic and cultural modes of his models and those of his own times itself becomes a model that rivals the ancients in power and prestige. Some two centuries later, Garcilaso was to imitate Petrarch in much the same spirit, with very similar results (Cruz, "Spanish Petrarchism," 86–89). In each case—Virgil, Petrarch, Garcilaso—the element of linguistic and cultural disparity, which can be summed up under the general rubric of anachronism, plays a key role in determining the strategies of imitation and emulation. Ercilla, whose poetics are based on a careful following of Garcilaso's praxis, likewise spins his own most ostentatious imitatio around a conscious exploitation of anachronism.

Curiously, however, neither Ricci, nor Barbaro, nor Pigman for that matter, really engages the question of anachronism in his scheme of imitative practice. Thomas Greene's extensive meditation on the Renaissance theory and practice of imitation takes the problem of anachronism as a central and organizing principle. For this reason, Greene's work proves to be an indispensable magnifying glass for reading the inner workings of Ercilla's most ambitious imitative passages.

Greene, in *The Light in Troy* (37–38), likens the most successful processes of humanist imitation, particularly as practiced by Petrarch, to necromancy—the revival of the dead to make them speak prophetically. Seen in this light, according to Greene, "each imitative literary work contains by definition what might be called a revivalist initiative, a gesture that signals the intent of reanimating an earlier text or texts situated on the far side of a rupture" (37). Expanding on the metaphor of necromancy, and using one of Ronsard's imitations of Horace as an example, Greene indicates that the imitative poet is asking the reader to judge

> whether the necromantic disinterment is brought off, whether the Latin text emerges still mummified from the tomb, or shrunken and thin, or merely ornamented, or whether rather an authentic resurrection has occurred. The reader can ask, *should* ask, not whether anachronism has been suppressed but whether it has been controlled and employed. If it has not and no true renewal is carried out, then the revivalist initiative has to be seen as abortive or failed or in bad faith. But if the revivalist initiative has been made good, if the necromantic metaphor has been validated, then how is this validating process to be described? (37–38)

Greene goes on to suggest an answer to this question by proposing a fourfold framework for the taxonomy of imitative practice (*Light*, 38–47): "reproductive" or "sacramental" imitation that treats its subtext as a hallowed model that must be reduplicated as faithfully as possible; "eclectic" imitation that stirs together a witch's brew of allusions from a variety of sources without privileging any particular subtext; heuristic imitation that, on the one hand, flaunts its kinship with the subtext while, on the other, it deliberately delves and illuminates the chasm of anachronism that cultural and linguistic mutation have interposed between "parent" and "offspring" texts; finally, "dialectical" imitation, an amplification of the heuristic type that not only asserts its independence from the subtext, but also its superiority through what Greene calls "Oedipal aggression" (46). Only the last two types, heuristic and dialectical, are truly necromantic in that they revive a "dead" text and make it sing of new things. Greene's necromantic metaphor is the strongest aspect of his system, and the one that will best help us delve the archaeology of Ercilla's imitative practice.

According to Greene, "Heuristic imitations come to us advertising their derivation from the subtexts they carry with them, but having done that, they proceed to *distance themselves* from the subtexts and force us to recognize the poetic distance traversed" (*Light*, 40). Thus Greene's idea of heuristic or necromantic imitation is very similar to what I have already pointed out as emulation, where the poet takes a deliberately competitive stance to a clearly announced subtext. The essential difference, of course, is Greene's special recognition of the element of anachronism. Poets who are roughly contemporary may well engage in emulative rivalry without ever engaging the issue of anachronism in relation to one another. This is especially true if they are writing in the same language. For that reason I prefer to keep the term "emulation" to use for rivalry between contemporaries, particularly those whose linguistic media of expression are either the same or at least at the same stage of distance from the ancient models, and reserve Greene's terminology for those instances where anachronism and cultural distance are key factors.

Greene suggests Petrarch's sonnet "Erano i capei d'oro a l'aura sparsi" as a basic example of necromantic imitation. This well-known exploration of the topic of the beauty of the beloved illustrates Greene's dictum on what he calls heuristic imitation by unmistakably calling up the reader's reminiscence of Virgil's description of Venus in *Aeneid* 1, but then building on the power of the allusion to create an entirely new and different effect, perfectly under the control of the imitative poet, that depends for its success on the reader's awareness of the "poetic distance traversed" (*Light*, 40–41). This relatively straightforward Petrarchan necromancy suggests another instance of far more ambitiously necromantic imitation that would have been of much more immediate importance for Ercilla: Garcilaso's sonnet "En tanto que de rosa y d'açucena." This often anthologized sonnet presents a convenient case study of the type of sophisticated imitative practice that represented the ideal toward which poets of Ercilla's generation strove in their own exercise of *imitatio*.

Petrarch, in "Erano i capei," engages in a subtle dialogue with several intermediate Ovidian imitations of Virgil's description of Venus in the process of reversing the dynamic of his principal model (Mazzotta 277; Greene, *Light*, 112).[24] Garcilaso's own imitative technique is typically even more eclectic (Cruz, *Imitación*, 71–72), yet frequently "eclectic sources, and their embedded erotic codes, are marshalled to meet the challenge posed by a Petrarchan *incipit*" (Navarrete, *Orphans*, 103). This is certainly the case in "En tanto que," where Garcilaso engages two Petrarchist contemporaries, Pietro Bembo and, especially, Bernardo Tasso, whose respective sonnets ("Crin d'oro crespo e d'ambra tersa e pura"; "Mentre che l'aureo crin v'ondeggia intorno") both recall and, to varying degrees, transform, Petrarch's image of Laura with her hair blowing in the wind. In addition to this emulative rivalry with the "modern" Italians, Garcilaso also performs an act of necromancy on Petrarch's sonnet by specifically alluding to the Virgilian master subtext that underlies the image evoked by all three Italian poets.[25] In this way, Garcilaso not only revives the earlier image to new purpose, but also successfully reduces the daunting "father figure" Petrarch to the status of a predecessor whose own models can be invoked to carry out the act of transformation and rejuvenation.

Ercilla's own essays at necromantic imitation in the unfolding of the web of prophecy in Part II of the *Araucana*, and his rivalry with another extremely talented Petrarchist/Garcilasist imitator—Camoens—can only be appreciated through a precise evaluation and comprehension of the process of necromantic imitation as practiced by Garcilaso, the Iberian master himself. Due to the direct relationship between "Erano i capei d'oro a l'aura sparsi"—Greene's example of necromantic imitation—and "En tanto que de rosa y d'açucena," Garcilaso's famous sonnet presents itself as the ideal laboratory in which to give a practical demonstration of the theoretical concepts discussed earlier in the chapter. Nonetheless, it should be borne in mind that the important point is how the master imitator manipulates the textual material, and not that material in itself. In the same way that Garcilaso imitated, not so much Petrarch's text but his approach, it is the technique that Ercilla imitates, and in order to properly understand his approach to imitation in the *Araucana*, there is no better textbook than the praxis of his model.

1.3.1. An Imperialist Paradigm of Imitation

Thus "En tanto que de rosa y d'açucena" is the mirror of the most ambitious type of imitation that Ercilla would have held before his eyes as he underwent his formation as a poet in the same court that, only a decade before, had occasionally been the theater of Garcilaso's activities as a courtier.[26] By the late 1540s, when Ercilla was receiving his advanced instruction under Calvete de la Estrella in the court of Charles V, and in the succeeding decades as the project of the *Araucana* was taking shape, Garcilaso was being canonized as the ideal poet of the Castilian nobility (Navarrete, "Decentering Garcilaso," 22). Enshrining that *sprezzatura* that Castiglione had established as the sine qua non of the perfect courtier—equal parts man of arms and of letters (Castiglione 1.26; Castellón 73)[27]—Garcilaso was also the literary exemplar of the new, world-scale imperialist enterprise. For the aspiring knight-poets of Ercilla's generation, Garcilaso was "one of their own, a warrior who by fighting against the Turks was a modern crusader and thus a link between national identity (the reconquest of Spain), literary prestige (ascendancy over Italy), and the new international empire" (Navarrete, "Decentering Garcilaso," 22).

This last point is of special significance. Hispanists will recall the circumstances surrounding the genesis of the Italianizing project in sixteenth-century Iberian poetry: the international court of Charles V gathered in Granada, still toasting the great imperial victory over Francis I; Garcilaso's confidant Boscán rapt in conversation with Navagero and Castiglione in the shadow, if not the gardens themselves, of the Alhambra—crown jewel among the spoils of the Reconquest; emblem of the enterprise of the Catholic kings and 1492 (Garcilaso, *Obras*, ed. Rivers, 12). The pecularily Spanish transfomation of Petrarchism, which we may call Garcilasism, could not have been conceived in a context more symbolically charged with the new, universalist imperialism.

Nevertheless, despite Garcilaso's exemplary character as the poetic standard-bearer of the new Spanish-Hapsburg imperialism, there was a major lacuna in the corpus of his work. The learned epic poem written in the tradition overshadowed by the *Aeneid* functions as a cultural practice explicitly centered in a dynamic of legitimization/subversion of authority (Quint, *Epic and Empire*, 8). Sixteenth-century poets certainly conceived of the epic in this light. If Ariosto's enconium to the House of Este seems futile in the face of political realities, the *Orlando furioso* nonetheless follows the Virgilian model of dynastic epic along at least one of its fundamental structural axes (Fichter 71–85). Camoens indisputably writes *Os Lusíadas* as an epic emblem of Portuguese empire. Ronsard considers the epic an essential vehicle of the *translatio imperii* (Carron 571–73). Garcilaso, however, had not lived to write an epic poem, although he flirts with some of the loci proper to epic in his *Egloga II*.

The Spanish imperialist project was the most successful of its time—the only one indeed with genuine hopes of rivaling ancient Rome. Francisco López de Gómara, a Spanish humanist and historian, writing around 1543—the year Garcilaso's poems first saw print—observed that together, the realms of Charles V and Suleiman the Magnificent exceeded those of the ancient Romans, although the possessions of the Catholic monarch in the New World gave him something of an advantage (*Crónica de los Barbarrojas*, 346). Some nine years later, the same writer was to remark that the discovery of the New World was the greatest event since the creation of the universe, with the exception of the birth and death of Christ, and that no other nation, ever, had achieved such dominion over distant lands and oceans by dint of martial effort as the Iberian (*Historia general*, 7). Ever since the beginning of Charles's reign in 1519 many of the emperor's foremost subjects and advisors had been intoxicated by the vision of actually realizing the long-held dream of an ideal, universal Christian monarchy. This sentiment was widely shared by many of Gómara's—and Ercilla's—contemporaries. His courtiers believed that Charles not only equaled his "predecessor" Charlemagne, but was the first to surpass him (Braudel, *Mediterranean*, 674–75). At last, it was believed, the *translatio imperii* could move from the realm of metaphor to that of reality. But if all this was true, if Spaniards had exceeded the Greeks and Trojans in deeds of valor, if the empire of Charles V far outshone that of Augustus, where was their Homer? Who was to be their Virgil? These questions were being asked precisely in the period of Ercilla's poetic genesis (Chevalier, *L'Arioste*, 122).

Thus it should not seem strange if a young aristocrat of poetic inclination should seek to realize the promise of Garcilaso in the crucial field of epic. As studies by Francisco Márquez Villanueva and Isaías Lerner ("Garcilaso en Ercilla"), among others, have made clear, Ercilla unquestionably devises his own poetic persona in the mold struck by Garcilaso. In addition to the imitation of Garcilaso's stance of self-presentation, and formal and lexical elements (Lerner, "Garcilaso," 202), Ercilla also adopts Garcilaso's model of imitation itself, and then transplants it to the New World and imperialist epic contexts of the *Araucana*. Within this Garcilasesque poetic, the highest form of imitation would be that necromantic imitation embodied in "En tanto que de rosa." What the reader must ask, and what Ercilla must have asked himself, is if, in Part II, any passage of the *Araucana* aspires to, or reaches, such heights.

This question cannot be answered, however, solely within the limits of Greene's discussion of necromantic imitation alone. Necromantic imitation, as Greene himself defines it, is only discernible when outlined against the screen of less ambitious practice or result. Furthermore, certain imperatives of the long narrative poem make consideration of Greene's two nonnecromantic categories essential before proceeding to the discovery of Ercilla's web of prophecy, and the answers to the question I have just posed, in the succeeding chapters of this study.

1.3.2. Reproductive and Eclectic Imitation

Greene's first category, what he calls reproductive or sacramental imitation, is less a goal that is explicitly championed by theorists or practitioners of *imitatio*, than an essential epistemological construct. Like Ricci's *sequi*, the taxonomic class of reproductive imitation serves primarily as a low-tide marker against which the ebb of more ambitious, more "successful" strategies of imitation can be measured. Even so, Greene conceives of reproductive imitation within the overall context of the challenge of anachronism: "The model or subtext is perceived as a fixed object on the far side of an abyss, beyond alteration and beyond criticism, a sacred original whose greatness can never be adequately reproduced despite the number of respectful reproductions" (*Light*, 38). Despite functioning in the environment of anachronism, according to Greene, reproductive imitation is a sterile response, "since any reproduction must be made in a vocabulary that is unbecoming the original and whose violations remain out of artistic control. Creative imitation in the Renaissance has to be seen as a challenge to the liturgical repetitions of an age lacking historical consciousness. . . . Sacramental imitation . . . involved a . . . category mistake. Its pursuit of a 'great Original' led it paradoxically away from genuine contact with the Original and also away from artistic discovery" (38–39). Thus Greene tags reproductive imitation as an essentially medieval ("an age lacking historical consciousness") mode of "liturgical repetition" in contrast to the more transformative approach appropriate to the Renaissance dialogue with the past. It is in precisely this context that I will have occasion to refer in Chapter 3 to reproductive imitation in the contrast between Juan de Mena's and Ercilla's imitations of Lucan.

The second type of nonnecromantic *imitatio* in Greene's system is what he calls exploitative or eclectic imitation. Greene identifies this procedure with what the Renaissance rhetoricians called *contaminatio*, and describes it in the following terms:

> Allusions, echoes, phrases, and images from a large number of authors jostle each other indifferently. . . . The art of poetry finds its materials everywhere, materials bearing with them the aura of their original contexts, charged with an evocative power implanted by the poet or the convention from which they are taken. At its slackest, eclectic imitation falls back into mere anachronism and becomes indistinguishable from the ahistorical citations of the Middle Ages. But when it is employed with artistic intelligence, the imitative poet commands a vocabulary of a second and higher power, a second keyboard of richer harmonies, which however are combined with rhetorical skill rather than esemplastic vision. (*Light*, 39)

It is precisely this last caveat, however, that renders eclectic imitation problematic. Like *dissimulatio*, the eclectic, indiscriminate stirring together of disparate elements often muddies the waters to such a degree that the reflection of the discrete imitative element in the new text loses any possiblity of communication on its own. This is especially true, as is often enough the case, if the eclectically selected elements are only there to serve an ornamental function. In this regard, Greene very rightly insists on the necessity of defining allusions as "usages of earlier texts that the reader must recognize in order to read competently" (49). It is only through the identification of true allusions, rather than mere "repetitions," that the reader can recognize what Greene calls a "determinate subtext" (50). As Greene defines it, a determinate subtext "plays a constitutive role in a poem's meaning. The imitative poem need not follow its 'model' throughout, but the earlier poem must count as a major presence if one is to speak of imitation in a valid sense" (50).

While it may be fairly simple to identify a determinate subtext in a relatively brief, lyric poem, the long narrative poem poses special problems for the student of imitation. As Greene indicates, virtually all long Renaissance poems, and most certainly the long narrative poems, are in some sense eclectic imitations "pulling in innumberable subtexts and clusters of topoi, alluding sometimes to conventions and modes by means of a kind of synecdochic shorthand" (*Light*, 50). Yet Greene allows that most Renaissance long narrative poems ultimately "reach out to a single privileged predecessor" (51). However true this may be for the examples Greene offers—Ariosto, Tasso, Spenser, and so on—it is difficult to establish for the *Araucana* as a whole. Ercilla's poem is certainly a melting pot of eclectic imitation, and the question of an overall single "privileged predecessor" that can truly be said to play a determinate role in the whole work has always been extremely problematic.

Nonetheless, in the limited contexts of discrete episodes and passages, many eclectically selected subtexts certainly assume a determinate role. This is especially true in the case of the web of prophecy that Ercilla interweaves with the development of the war in Arauco in Part II of the *Araucana*. The prophetic structure itself has a venerable lineage in the epic tradition and thus imposes a certain succession of model texts on the imitative poet who seeks to invoke its power. This, of course, is also the case with the epic storm, although on a smaller scale. The storm is also a persistent feature of the epic tradition, and usually has a constitutive role to play in the unfolding of the poet's theme. Yet it never assumes the structural central function in the architecture of the whole work that is the province of prophecy. Furthermore, as we have seen, Ercilla chooses not only to whip up his rendition of the storm topos from an eclectic palette of ingredients, but also to veil the literary nature of his creation as far as possible with various strategies of *dissimulatio*. Thus, although Ercilla's storm is a perfect weather vane for reading the shift in the winds of imitation between Parts I and II of the *Araucana*, it is an unpropitious vehicle for studying Ercilla's approaches to imitation at the cutting edge of his practice.

The web of prophecy, on the other hand, although itself eclectic, eschews the dissimulation characteristic of Part I, and unfolds along channels virtually predetermined by the tradition. Within this framework, Ercilla resorts to virtually all of the types of imitation that I have discussed in this chapter. Especially important within the determinate eclecticism of the conventional theme of epic prophecy are a number of specific examples of Ercilla's resort to necromantic imitation of ancient subtexts and intensely emulative rivalry with more immediate predecessors as well as a particularly successful contemporary. Thus I will discuss the essentially determined, but eclectic, imitation of the theme of prophecy in the following chapter, Ercilla's most outstanding necromantic imitation in Chapter 3, and the unfolding of emulation and rivalry in the final sections of this study.

2

Ercilla's Eclectic Web of Epic Prophecy

Ercilla spins his web of prophecy in order to bind the splendor of the metropolitan hub of empire securely into the center of his own celebration of the obscure and inconclusive punitive expedition at its extreme periphery. The result is to create a truly colonial epic, a heroic poem that explicitly integrates the most remote with the most central spheres of imperial enterprise. No account that focuses exclusively on the details of empire-building in the colonial ambit alone can truly achieve this, because as in all manifestations of colonial power, authority flows from a source that lies elsewhere. In order, therefore, to achieve this integration within the *verista* confines of his initial program, Ercilla finds it necessary to resort to a variegated tapestry of eclectic imitation.

Before Ercilla published Part II of the *Araucana* in 1578, the only genuinely successful poem of the Age of Navigations to realize this conjoining of metropolitan and peripheral imperialist enterprise was Camoens's *Os Lusíadas*. However, neither Camoens nor Ercilla, poets deeply steeped in a tradition of *imitatio*, could elude certain fundamental models of epic celebration and legitimization of empire. The theme of prophecy is a central, organizing element in these paradigmatic texts, and although both Ercilla and Camoens bring original and eclectic approaches to their own realizations of imperialist epic and epic prophecy, any discussion of the details of the webs of prophecy in the *Araucana* and the *Lusíadas* must be prefaced by a brief overview of the most urgent and powerful models that presented themselves to cultured Iberian poets around the middle of the sixteenth century.

2.1. Virgil's Prophetic Scheme of Empire

Virgil's *Aeneid* is the principal model of all subsequent learned European epic, particularly that of the Renaissance (Pierce, *La Poesía*, 12–13; "Some Themes," 95–97). As Thomas Greene has observed, the essence of Virgilian epic is that its hero be human rather than divine or superhuman, and yet be called upon to perform prodigious, quasi-divine actions (*Descent*, 12–15). For an epic poem to be successful, the dichotomy between what is asked of the protagonist and his natural limitations as a human being must create a vital tension that in turn produces the necessary effects of fear, awe, and admiration. Virgil masterfully uses the device of prophetic revelation and exhortation to punctuate Aeneas's "epic" struggle with himself, his surroundings, and the inimical consort of Jove, as he reels and stumbles across the Mediterranean world toward the foundation of an empire. A brief examination of the role of prophecy in the first six books of the *Aeneid* reveals exactly how this interplay between the hero's gradually announced destiny and his faltering humanity drives the poem to its central turning point in Book 6. The *katabasis*, or prophetic descent to the underworld, in *Aeneid* 6 goes on to become the underlying model of virtually all prophecy in the occidental tradition of learned epic. This includes, although mediated by subsequent imitations, the mantic scheme of the *Araucana*.[1]

Virgil begins spinning his web of prophecy in Book 2. Just as the Greeks are stealing out of the belly of the wooden horse, the battered shade of Hector comes to Aeneas in a dream, reveals the city's doom, and exhorts his brother (*Aeneid* 2.268–97):[2]

> "Ai! Give up and go, child of the goddess,
> Save yourself out of these flames . . .
> . . . .
> Her holy things, her gods
> Of hearth and household Troy commends to you.
> Accept them as companions of your days;
> Go find for them the great walls that one day
> You'll dedicate, when you have roamed the sea."
> (*Aeneid* 2.293–95)

> ("heu fuge, nate dea, teque his" ait "eripe flammis . . .
> . . . .
> sacra suosque tibi commendat Troia penatis;
> hos cape fatorum comites, his moenia quarere
> magna pererrato statues quae denique ponto.")

In this first prophetic intervention, Aeneas is informed with privileged foreknowledge from the otherworld that further defense of Troy is futile, and that the best he can hope for is to save the *penates* (household gods) of his ill-fated city. His imperial mission is only hinted at by the injunction that he must seek out the place where he will finally erect *moenia magna* (great walls) overseas.

Aeneas follows the advice of his brother's ghost and abandons Troy, but after a false start in Thrace, realizes he does not know where to go. In his quandary, he lands on Delos, the sacred island of the prophetic god Apollo. The Trojans pray for guidance, and are immediately vouchsafed a thunderous reply:

> "Tough sons of Dardanus, the self-same land
> That bore you from your primal parent stock
> Will take you to her fertile breast again.
> Look for your mother of old. Aeneas' house
> In her will rule the world's shores down the years,
> Through generations of his children's children."
> (*Aeneid* 3.94–98)

> ("Dardanidae duri, quae vos a stirpe parentum
> prima tulit tellus, eadem vos ubere laeto
> accipiet reduces. antiquam exquirite matrem.

>   hic domus Aeneae cunctis dominabitur oris
>   et nati natorum et qui nascentur ab illis.")

Apollo makes it clear here that the new homeland awaiting the Trojans carries with it an imperial burden: Aeneas's *domus* and descendants—the dynasty he founds—will rule all the seacoasts (*Aeneid* 3.97–98), which is to say, the Mediterranean world. This, the first, explicit statement of Aeneas's doom, is both a promise and a challenge, and it kicks the ensuing plot complication into motion in a way that can only underline the tension between the Trojan leader's human doubt and confusion on the one hand, and his divinely ordained destiny on the other.

The human limitations that hinder Aeneas are manifest in his father's misinterpretation of the oracle. Anchises recalls that the ancient Teucrians had once settled in Crete before the founding of Troy, and he supposes that Apollo must have been referring to that island when he spoke of their "forefather's land, their ancient mother" (*Aeneid* 3.102–17). The fleet proceeds to Crete, but the Trojans' attempt to settle there does not prosper; Aeneas is racked by doubt and discouragement. Before he can return to Delos to request a second oracular opinion, however, the *penates* visit him in a dream and make it clear to him that it is Hesperia, now called Italy, that he must seek. The household gods also reiterate the glorious future that awaits him if only he will take heart and continue his journey (*Aeneid* 3.147–74). Virgil skillfully embroiders his prophetic web here, having Anchises remember only now that Cassandra, the princess of prophecy, cursed by Apollo to be disbelieved, would often sing of a future Italian home for the Trojans (*Aeneid* 3.182–88). By invoking Cassandra's oracular notoriety, the poet imbues Aeneas's prophesied destiny and human dilemma with reinforced authority.

Yet not all prophecy is positive encouragement, as Aeneas next receives confirmation of his Italian fate from a sinister source. The Harpy Celaeno, first among the Furies, corroborates the previous revelations, adding her own terrible addendum:

> "Italy is the land you look for; well,
> The winds will blow, you'll find your Italy,
> You'll be allowed to enter port;
> But you may never wall your destined city

Till deathly famine, for the bloodshed here,
Has made you grind your tables with your teeth!"
                                   (*Aeneid* 3.253-57)

("Italiam cursu petitis ventisque vocatis:
ibitis Italiam portusque intrare licebit.
sed non ante datam cingetis moenibus urbem
quam vos dira fames nostraeque iniuria caedis
ambesas subigat malis absumere mensas.")

Virgil makes clear here that the hero's prophesied triumph is not a gentle gift to be collected effortlessly in due time. On the contrary, the epic hero is called upon to struggle, to bleed, and to suffer in order to realize his destiny. Virgil's web of prophecy promises a challenge, not a present to be dropped—unearned—into the hero's limp and idle hand.

The Harpy's malediction has disconcerted Aeneas. When next he has the opportunity to consult with a Trojan priest of Apollo—Helenus, son of Priam—Aeneas anxiously pleads for renewed guidance, and reveals the degree to which he has become dependant on prophetic tutelage:

"Prophesy for me! As you know, the powers
Favored me with directions for my sailing:
All the divine speech from the shrines agreed
I must find Italy, must pioneer
In those far lands. The Harpy called Celaeno
Riddled the only strange and evil sign:
Of pallid famine, and the wrath of heaven.
What dangers must I steer away from first?
How set my course to conquer that distress?"
                                   (*Aeneid* 3.362-68)

("fare age, namque omnis cursum mihi prospera dixit
religio, et cuncti suaserunt numine divi
Italiam petere et terras temptare repostas;
sola novum dictuque nefas Harpyia Celaeno
prodigium canit et tristis denuntiat iras
obscenamque famen quae prima pericula vito?
quidve sequens tantos possim superare labores?")

It is clear that Aeneas, almost whining, dares not set sail without first consulting an oracle. If the "powers" have led him every step of the way, encouraged him at every turn, how now can the Fury eclipse the bright vision of the future he had received from the *penates*?

Helenus delivers the looked-for reassurance (*Aeneid* 3.374–462), carefully omitting, by claiming that both the Fates and Juno prevent him from revealing all (*Aeneid* 3.377–80), the various dire and unpleasant vicissitudes awaiting Aeneas along his appointed path. As R. D. Williams points out in his notes to this passage, Helenus's oracular speech is the central nexus of Book 3 and "is by far the longest piece of prophecy about the voyage of Aeneas" (Virgil, *Aeneid*, ed. Williams, 1:299–300). It is of special importance because it is here (*Aeneid* 3.441–60) that Aeneas first learns of his future visit to the Sibyl's cave (Book 6)—the pivotal prophetic experience of the entire poem.

Aeneas's ardor for guidance abates, however, in the arms of Dido. Jupiter, made aware of the hero's torpor, sends Mercury to admonish the dallying Trojan that he has not been the beneficiary of divine intervention for his personal caprice, and that the great empire that he must found and that his descendants will enjoy demands that he forsake his present idyll (*Aeneid* 4.219–37). Mercury duly conveys the Thunderer's impatience, and Aeneas, stung, hurries to abandon his newfound love and once again take to sea in search of his destiny (*Aeneid* 4.265–76). Prophecy, then, serves not only to guide, challenge, and reassure, but also to prod, reprove, and correct the errant hero.[3]

The web of prophetic motivation is spun yet tighter in Book 5. Aeneas, once again at sea, is visited by disaster on the shores of Sicily. In his despair, he pleads for divine aid (*Aeneid* 5.687–92). The shade of his father, whose impending death had been omitted from Helenus's oracle, visits him in answer to his prayer. Anchises not only resolves his son's present quandary (*Aeneid* 5.722–31), but also expands upon the Trojan seer's original admonition to visit the Sibyl at Cumae (*Aeneid* 5.731–37). Helenus had only described the prophetess and her cave, urging Aeneas that he not fail to consult her (*Aeneid* 3.441–60). Anchises' ghost now fills in the oracular picture, making it clear that his son must:

> "First, however, visit the underworld
> The halls of Dis, and through profound Avernus
> Come to meet me, son. Black Tartarus

With its grim realm of shades is not my home,
But radiant gatherings of godly souls
I have about me in Elysium.
To that place the pure Sibyl, after blood
Of many black sheep flows out, will conduct you.
Then you will hear of your race to come
And what walled town is given you: Farewell."
(Aeneid 5.731–37)

(". . . Ditis tamen ante
infernas accede domos et Averna per alta
congressus pete, nate, meos. non me impia namque
Tartara habent, tristes umbrae, se amoena piorum
concilia Elysiumque colo. huc casta Sibylla
nigrarum multo pecudum te sanguine ducet.
tum genus omne tuum et quae dentur moenia disces.")

Just as Aeneas's imperial future in Italy was only gradually revealed to him in cumulative events of prophesy, so now the all-important consultation with the Sibyl and the ensuing journey to the underworld are insinuated in successive ripples of revelation. This piecemeal divulgence of his fate not only creates tension in the plot, but also renders Aeneas a more human, and thus both truly epic and credible, character. If everything had been revealed to him at one stroke, right at the beginning, the narrative structure of the poem would suffer immensely. By the same token, if Aeneas were to have been informed immediately that he must harrow hell and pass on through the Elysian Fields before finding the promised new home for the *penates* and his people, and if he were to have accepted cheerfully, it would reduce our belief in his verisimilitude as a sane, mortal man.

Aeneas does find the Sibyl's cave, and there finally he is told details about the coming war with Turnus (*Aeneid* 6.83–97). Mindful of the parting injunction of his father's wraith in Sicily, the Trojan captain beseeches the prophetess to lead him to the underworld (*Aeneid* 6.103–23). She complies with his request, and Aeneas is able to make his tour of the nether regions. Aeneas at last meets his father's shade in Elysium. Here Anchises leads his son to a hilltop near Lethe's waters, and from this vantage point begins to single out and identify individuals from the swarm of earth-destined souls buzzing about them (*Aeneid*

6.706–9, 752–55). The hero's father, pointing now at one, now at another, passing spirit, delivers an idealized, capsule history of Rome from its remote, legendary origins up to the reinauguration of the *aurea saecula* (golden age) under Augustus (*Aeneid* 6.756–807). Thus, at last, the fullness of Aeneas's destiny is revealed, leaving him no option but to persevere in self-denial and slaughter—even when apprised of the ominous, bloody recapitulation of Roman political history, from Numa the Lawgiver through every grim episode of civil strife up to the death of Marcellus, that follows (*Aeneid* 6.807–86). Virgil's web of prophecy reaches its crux here in Book 6. As Williams puts it, Anchises' revelation of Roman history culminating in Augustus "is the decisive moment of the whole poem" (Virgil, *Aeneid*, ed. Williams, 1:505).

The skeins of prophecy and divine intervention are by no means cut short after Book 6; they extend throughout the remaining six books of the poem. Nonetheless, it is the prophetic trajectory that takes Aeneas first to the Sibyl, and then to the cave entrance to the underworld, that has the most significant impact on subsequent renditions of the theme. This will ultimately include Ercilla's own *katabasis*, although the experience will appear mediated through a number of intermediate imitations and reworkings of Virgil's prophecy. We must leave Aeneas at this juncture, therefore, and leap forward through literary history to a scene inspired by Virgil's account of the hero and his father's ghost examining the encircling swarm of souls from their Elysian hilltop.

2.2. Ariosto's Web of Dynastic Prophecy

When the enchantress Melissa—here playing the role of Anchises to Bradamante's Aeneas—steps into the protection of the pentagram with the warrior maiden of Chiaramonte and begins to single out individual spirits of yet-to-be-born Estensi from the swirling throng in Merlin's cave (*Orlando furioso* 3.20–23), Ariosto already has begun his own essay at spinning a Virgilian web of prophetic motivation for his dynastic lovers. As Andrew Fichter has pointed out, of the two major narrative threads of the *Orlando furioso*, that of Bradamante and Ruggiero most closely imitates the classical foundation epic exemplified by the *Aeneid*, and the prophecy in Merlin's tomb is perhaps the most well-developed exercise in exact Virgilian imitation in the poem (70–71, 84–85).

Unlike Aeneas's prolonged process of gradual initiation into the burdens of destiny, Bradamante plunges directly, although inadvertently, into her confrontation with the prophetic forces of the underworld. Her love for Ruggiero had already been established by Boiardo—Ariosto's immediate poetic predecessor and model (Bigi, ed. 127, 1.70 n. 1)—and Ariosto himself reminds us of their relationship and indicates that she is searching for her lover when she first rides into the action of the *Furioso* (2.31–33). Nonetheless, when shortly afterward the treacherous Pinabello precipitates Bradamante into the enchanted caverns that guard the sorceror's sepulcher (*Orlando furioso* 2.75), she has no inkling of the doom that awaits her. Her arrival has been predicted by prophecy, and, although this foreknowledge has been vouchsafed only to the mage's pupil, Melissa, it has been authorized by the heavens themselves (*Orlando furioso* 3.9). Bradamante reacts with disbelief to the young enchantress's revelations: "Di che merito son io, / ch'antiveggian profeti il venir mio?" ("Of what merit am I, / that prophets would forsee my coming?") (*Orlando furioso* 3.13gh), and Melissa responds by leading the warrior maid into the *sanctum sanctorum* of the subterranean complex, where Merlin's disembodied shade immediately delivers a sibylline peroration (*Orlando furioso* 3.16e19).

The Maid of Chiaramonte is informed that from her womb will come forth the most illustrious line of all Italy and the world (*Orlando furioso* 3.16gh). The Virgilian resonances of this prophecy are reinforced by the reminder that in her offspring will be combined the two best lines of Trojan blood (*Orlando furioso* 3.17ab). Ruggiero himself will explain this genealogy in more detail to his long-lost sister Marfisa (*Orlando furioso* 36.70–75), recalling his Boiardesque prototype's explanation of his Trojan provenience to the Brandiamante of the *Innamorato*— Bradamante's precursor and model (*Orlando innamorato* 3.5.18–37).[4]

Merlin further underlines the analogy to the *Aeneid* by declaring that among the dynastic pair's progeny will be found "marquesses, dukes and emperors" (*Orlando furioso* 3.17h), and that of these some will not only restore Italy's glory in arms, but also, like Numa and Augustus, will usher in a new golden age (*Orlando furioso* 3.18f–g), directly recalling Anchises' prophecy to Aeneas that his descendant Augustus would reinaugurate the *aurea saecula* (*Aeneid* 6.792–93). The old magician's fleshless voice closes its exhortation reminding Bradamante that she has been chosen from the beginning by the heavenly powers for this role, and that she should not quail before the machinations of Atlante (*Orlando furioso* 3.19), recalling the final words of the Sibyl's frenzied prophecy to Aeneas in her cave at Cumae:

> "Never shrink from blows.
> Boldly, more boldly where your luck allows,
> Go forward, face them. A way to safety
> Will open where you reckon on it least,
> From a Greek city."
>
> (*Aeneid* 6.95–97)

> ("tu ne cede malis, sed contra audentior ito
> qua tua te fortuna sinet. via prima salutis,
> quod minime reris, Graia pandetur ab urbe.")

In the same way that Aeneas occasionally faltered or strayed from his predestined path and required a prophetic prodding to take heart and keep moving toward his goal, Bradamante, despite Merlin and Melissa's subterranean revelations, also experiences her moments of doubt and despair. Despondent because Ruggiero, who she knows is in the company of another woman—Marfisa (*Orlando furioso* 30.88–89)—has failed to meet her as agreed, Bradamante abjures the prophecy of the cave (*Orlando furioso* 32.24–25). Only her innate, inalterable, inexplicable love for Ruggiero preserves something of her sanity, but even this is put to a further, more rigorous test. A Gascon knight, met by chance, passes on to Bradamante the rumor that Marfisa and Ruggiero are soon to be wed (*Orlando furioso* 32.28–35). Beside herself, the passionate warrior maiden attempts to run herself through with her own sword, only to be frustrated by the armor she had disdained to remove before throwing herself, disconsolate, upon her virgin's bed to weep (*Orlando furioso* 32.44a–d). Desire for her own death is now complicated by an implacable urge to avenge her pain (*Orlando furioso* 32.45–46).

It is in this state, her dynastic duty forgotten in a welter of despair and vengeful deliria, that Bradamante wins a night's lodging in Tristano's castle (*Orlando furioso* 32.77). She is treated to the ekphrastic examination of the prophesied history of foreign intervention in Italy—a subject of great immediacy to Ariosto and his generation—which, as the castellan explains, had been magically painted on the interior walls of the great hall by Merlin and his demons (*Orlando furioso* 33.3–58). In accord with the Virgilian model, here we would expect a prophetic reminder of the importance of Bradamante's destiny along the lines of Mercury's admonition to Aeneas in Carthage (*Aeneid* 4.265–76) or the dream message of Anchises' ghost on the Sicilian beach (*Aeneid* 5.722–31). For Ariosto, however, such reverential, slavish imitation of the model would undermine his ludic transformation of the materials offered by the literary tradition, and hence, his rivalry with the poets who preceded him and his attempt to supplant them. Merlin's painting depicts nothing at all that can be taken directly as a spur to the warrior maiden. On the contrary, the message of the murals seems to be that all is vain before the capricious winds of Fortune (*Orlando furioso* 33.50*a–d*, 57*e*). There is a bitter *aggiornaménto* of Virgil's dynastic prophecy here. As both Ariosto and his patrons knew very well, given the prostrate political condition of Italy, the only imperial future that awaited them was, like their humiliating present, under foreign flags.

It is only after viewing the enchanted frescoes, as she tosses and turns in her hard-won bed, that Bradamante is visited by Ruggiero in a dream (*Orlando furioso* 3.59*efgh*–61). Yet she is not as credulous an interpreter of dreams as Aeneas, and thus remains unconvinced by her beloved's apparition. Ariosto uses this opportunity to toy with the Virgil-steeped reader's expectations, subverting the topos of the prophetic dream. Bradamante responds to the visitation with a Petrarchist meditation on the differences between appearances and reality, developed as a series of conceits contrasting waking and sleeping, dream and reality, peace and war, and life and death (*Orlando furioso* 33.62–64).[5] Bradamante then continues on her search for revenge, finally encountering Ruggiero and Marfisa during a joust at the Moorish camp in Arles (*Orlando furioso* 35.62), and determined to kill Marfisa and then die herself in front of Ruggiero (*Orlando furioso* 32.45–46, 36.45), the warrior maiden furiously attacks her presumed rival (*Orlando furioso* 36.17–58).

Bradamante's violent negation of Merlin's prophecy can only be set right by the intrusion of another voice from the beyond. Ruggiero interposes himself between the two furious amazons, and completely beside herself, Marfisa aims a deadly blow at his head that chances to strike instead one of the cypress trees that guard the monument over the enchanter Atlante's tomb. The earth shakes, and from the haunted marble crypt issues forth a terrible voice that immediately freezes the violent scene (*Orlando furioso* 36.58). The old magician's disembodied spirit informs the three that Ruggiero and Marfisa are twins, brother and sister (*Orlando furioso* 36.59–66), and thus their relationship can pose no threat to either Bradamante's desire or Merlin's prophecy. Atlante's ghost directly reprimands Bradamante for her jealous lapse (*Orlando furioso* 36.66), and the dynastic lovers are once again reconciled. Characteristically, Ariosto closes this Virgilian episode with a special twist. If fickle Fortune negated prophecy in the ekphrastic depiction of Italian history seen in Tristano's castle, Atlante now informs us that none other than Fortuna herself had preserved Ruggiero's life while still in his mother's womb because he had been singled out for his dynastic mission (*Orlando furioso* 36.61*ab*). Atlante, the antagonistic wizard against whom the Arthurian mage's pupils have had to struggle throughout the poem, finally puts the seal on Merlin's design.

There are at least two additional, explicit, prophetic references to Ruggiero and Bradamante's dynastic destiny in the remaining cantos of the *Furioso*—the saintly hermit's prophetic reassurance to Ruggiero concerning his progeny's future (*Orlando furioso* 41.60–67), and the enchanted pavilion (handiwork of the Trojan prophetess Cassandra herself) that bears the ekphrastic prophecy honoring Ariosto's patron, Ippolito d'Este (*Orlando furioso* 46.76–99). These, moreover, hardly exhaust Ariosto's play with the theme of prophecy. As Andrew Fichter indicates (71–72), both the Orlando/Angelica and the Ruggiero/Bradamante plots of the *Furioso* participate in the exercise in Virgilian imitation. Ariosto divides up the Aeneas role among a number of his characters. Ruggiero, for instance, plays Aeneas to Melissa's Mercury on Alcina's island (Fichter 93), and Ariosto even assigns a certain "anti-Aeneas" or "Aeneas-gone-wrong" function to Orlando. Orlando as well as Ruggiero, then, figures in Ariosto's ludic subversion, transformation, and ultimate Bloomian overcoming of the prophetic system of the *Aeneid*.[6]

Of course it can be argued that Ariosto's imitation of Virgil has been vastly exaggerated by a series of scholars beginning in the sixteenth century and continuing to the present. Daniel Javitch, for instance, demonstrates that in a number of cases, even where Ariosto elaborates an episode that ultimately depends on a Virgilian subtext, Virgil's Homeric models and subsequent, intervening Silver Latin renditions can be of even more importance for the Italian poet's realization of the material than the specific passages in the *Aeneid* ("Imitation of Imitations," 215–39). According to Javitch, the exclusive, and hence distorted, emphasis on the Virgilian model is largely traceable to the influence of Ludovico Dolce's sixteenth-century commentaries on the *Orlando furioso*. Javitch explains that Dolce's aim was to establish Ariosto as the "modern" Virgil, and by setting out the precise equivalence of the *Orlando furioso* to the *Aeneid*, to prove that the vernacular Italian had finally become as "illustrious" as ancient Latin. Thus Dolce not only distorts Ariosto's uses of Virgil, but also suppresses his imitations of medieval and romance models. While placing this initiative of literary canonization in the political and cultural contexts of the mid-sixteenth century, Javitch is particularly impatient with twentieth-century critics who seem to perpetuate Dolce's myopia, and in fact, singles out Fichter as an example ("Shaping," 268–71, 270 n. 3).

It would be futile to deny the complexity and diversity of Ariosto's imitative practice in the *Furioso* as a whole; nevertheless, there are two fundamental reasons why this fact does not undermine the present argument. In the first place, Ariosto's scheme of dynastic prophecy is probably the one aspect of the poem that undeniably is modeled closely on the *Aeneid*, as I have argued above, and as Fichter convincingly demonstrates.[7] The second reason is best supported by Javitch's own research establishing the ubiquity of efforts to construct Ariosto's canonicity from roughly 1540 to 1580, precisely the period of Ercilla's education and the writing of the *Araucana*. In particular, the fact that Dolce's commentary accompanied at least forty editions of the *Orlando furioso* between 1542 and 1566, and no less than sixty-five by the century's end (Javitch, "Shaping," 266–67), indicates that for readers of Ercilla's day, the Virgilian profile of the Italian poem would have been even more authoritatively pronounced than otherwise.[8] This reading is borne out by the fact that all of the early imitations of the *Furioso* in Spain focus almost exclusively on the element of dynastic encomium (see section 2.3 below).

Thus for Ercilla and his contemporaries, it would have been perfectly clear that like Virgil, Ariosto has spun the major encomiastic thread of his poem through a web of epic prophecy that virtually extends from beginning to end. Furthermore, it would have been apparent that, as in the *Aeneid*, this dynamic interplay between prophecy and protagonist plays a constitutive, determining role in the unfolding of the *Furioso*. Where Virgil weaves a subtle web of progressive revelation to finally bring Aeneas to the climactic descent to the underworld at the very center of the *Aeneid*, Ariosto opens at this point with Bradamante's unlooked-for tumble into Merlin's underground sanctum. Nonetheless, Ariosto builds upon this precipitate opening, and like his model, sustains the prophetic tension between his future dynasts and their fate throughout his long poem.

If the grand destiny of the family of the dukes of Ferrara seems somewhat hollow in comparison with the splendor of Augustan Rome, as indeed it must have to Ariosto and his immediate audience, within the world of the poem the theme resonates with authenticity. Orlando recovers his wits and defeats the enemies of the emperor and Christendom, while the "unbeliever" Ruggiero makes a voluntary conversion to the "true faith" before the prophecy is fulfilled and he is united with Bradamante in a Christian world in which harmony has been restored under Charlemagne. Thus the two principal narrative strands of the *Orlando furioso* are tied together at the end in a vision of imperial triumph.

2.3. The Ariostesque Model in Sixteenth-Century Spain

Of course, the real-life Emperor Charles of Ariosto's time was none other than Charles V, and the only empire that could be compared with that of either Augustus or Charlemagne was centered in Spain, not Italy. Ariosto lamented the foreign domination of Italy in the strongest terms, comparing the competing alien armies to filthy harpies gorging themselves while the Italians went hungry in the midst of plenty (*Orlando furioso* 34.1–3). Nor could he entirely restrain himself from turning the full force of his ire and sarcasm on the Spaniards, whom he at his most vitriolic characterizes as "popul la più parte circonciso" (people for the most part who had been circumcised [i.e., Muslims or Jews]) (*Orlando furioso* 42.5*h*). Nonetheless, for the ambitious Castilian poet seeking a model for encomiastic dynastic celebration and epic prophecy, Ariosto's poem enjoyed such success and prestige that it became an inevitable mediator of the Virgilian model into the *mundus significans* of the sixteenth century. It is not surprising, therefore, to find the *Orlando furioso* already serving as fundamental subtext for Iberian poets, notably Garcilaso himself, in the very decade that saw the publication in 1532 of the third, definitive version of Ariosto's poem (*Orlando furioso*, ed. Bigi, 9).

Although Garcilaso did not himself essay the epic proper as a genre, when he sought to incorporate epic-like encomiastic elements into his *Egloga II*, it was to Ariosto that he turned for an *aggiornaménto* of the classic device. Nemoroso's ekphrastic description of the history of the family of the dukes of Alba in Garcilaso's *Egloga II* (vv. 1169–747), probably composed in Naples sometime between 1533 and 1534 (Garcilaso, *Obras*, ed. Rivers, 303), includes three passages from the *Orlando furioso* among the constitutive subtexts (376–77, notes to vv. 1172ff.). The three passages are *Orlando furioso* 33.1–58, 42.13ff., and 46.46ff. Elias Rivers observes that "las alabanzas de los Alba se pueden comparar con las de los Este que se encuentran al final del *Orlando*."[9] Ercilla, obviously a careful reader of both Ariosto and Garcilaso, would not forget the *Egloga II* when he came to crafting his own *machina* for the introduction of a climactic ekphrastic prophecy into Part II of the *Araucana*.

During the remaining years of Garcilaso's life and on into the following decade, detailed acquaintance with the *Orlando furioso* among Iberians was probably limited to the circle of courtiers, soldiers, and diplomats who, like Garcilaso, had served or were serving in Italy (Chevalier, *L'Arioste*, 61–62). The key year in the dissemination of the *Furioso* among Iberian readers and writers, therefore, was 1549, when the first edition of Jerónimo de Urrea's Castilian translation was published in Antwerp by the busy presses of Martín Nucio (Chevalier, *L'Arioste*, 74). Urrea is said to have been the first soldier to scale the walls of the Tower of Muy in Provence on 19 September 1536, reaching the top only a few moments before his comrade-in-arms, Garcilaso, was hit by the falling stone that would bring about the untimely death of the celebrated young poet (71). Author of original works as well as translations, Urrea is yet another example of the Iberian soldier-poet that is exemplified by Garcilaso, and which would soon flourish in the field of epic poetry with Camoens and Ercilla.

Despite a certain lack of critical enthusiasm—Cervantes's village priest condemned Urrea's translation while praising Ariosto's original (*Quijote*, bk. 1, chap. 6), and twentieth-century critics such as Chevalier have complained that it often merits criticism for "indigence artistique" (*L'Arioste*, 70–71, 77)[10]—Captain Urrea's version of the *Furioso* was published at least twelve, and possibly as many as eighteen, times between 1549 and 1583, enjoying an immense popularity (74–75, 74 n. 32).[11] Urrea, like his comrade-in-arms Garcilaso before him, found the prophetic passages of the *Orlando furioso* irresistible. Urrea cut out some forty-seven stanzas describing the "future" of the House of Este in Merlin's prophecy in *Orlando furioso* 3 (Van Horne, "Urrea Translation," 218–19),[12] but more than made up for this by adding one hundred and eleven stanzas of his own invention, most of them praising famous Spaniards ranging from Ferdinand the Catholic to Philip II, as well as a number of illustrious Spanish women (222–24).[13] These patriotic addenda are all introduced into ekphrastic and prophetic passages of Ariosto's original.

Urrea's translation of the *Orlando furioso* may well have played a very special role in Ercilla's development as an epic poet, although not for the reason most frequently adduced by scholars. It is a commonplace of literary history, of course, to recall that the first edition of Urrea's *Orlando furioso* was published in Antwerp by the printer-bookseller Martín Nucio in 1549.[14] What has been largely forgotten, however, is that Urrea and Nucio seem to have coordinated the date of publication to coincide with the most momentous imperial visit of Charles's court to Antwerp of the entire reign. This was none other than the "felicísimo viaje" memorialized in a laudatory tract with the same title written by Juan Cristóbal Calvete de la Estrella, Prince Philip's (and Ercilla's) tutor.[15]

Shortly after the young Ercilla—he was fifteen at the time—joined the court as a page in August 1548, Philip and his entire entourage set out on the highly ceremonial journey to encounter the emperor in Flanders. The royal party arrived in the Low Countries in April of 1549, and spent most of the summer visiting various cities there. In particular, the whole royal party—including the emperor himself—was in Antwerp from 6 to 19 September of that year (Medina, *Vida*, 27–28, 28 n. 36). The first edition of Urrea's translation of the *Orlando furioso* was dated 25 August 1549 (Peeters Fontainas 18). Martín Nucio's bookshop in the Cammerstraat was a magnet for Spanish literati, and Peeters Fontainas assures us that the imperial visit of 1549 brought in an even greater number of Iberian noblemen and scholars both to buy books and arrange for future publications (15–17). José Toribio Medina expresses his confidence that Ercilla's tutor, Calvete de la Estrella, would have been in especially close contact with Nucio on this occasion ("El preceptor," 271). Nucio and Urrea could not have chosen a more propitious moment to launch the Castilian translation of the *Furioso*, and the great success of this work among the courtiers of the imperial retinue could not have failed to impress the young Ercilla. The impact of Urrea's translation on the court can only be judged by the ubiquity and success of Ariosto's poem in the circles through which the imperial party moved. One illustration of this is that on visiting the Council of Trent during the return journey through Italy, the court was feted with mascarades and theatrical pageants based on the *Furioso* (Medina, *Vida*, 28). Thus, whether or not Ercilla could read the original Italian, the launching of Urrea's translation could not have failed to impress the future poet with the prestige and excitement aroused by Ariosto's poem.

Hard on the heels of translators like Urrea came the imitators. First among the latter, in time if not in quality, was the Valencian soldier-poet Nicolás Espinosa, whose *La segunda parte de Orlando* was first published in 1555. Espinosa was perhaps the first to introduce the purely fictional, medieval Spanish hero Bernardo del Carpio into Ariosto and Boiardo's version of the Roland and Roncesvalles material, although his principal preoccupation is the creation of an encomiastic, Carolingian ancestry for the noble Valencian house of Centella. This is represented in Espinosa's poem by the Burgundian Baron Cotaldo, a character loosely based on Catalan chronicles, who at the head of his nine legendary barons leads the reconquest of Spain and marries Marfisa, just as Bradamante and Ruggiero found the line of Este. Espinosa was also one of the first Spanish poets to exalt imperial Spain at the expense of France in the context of Boiardo and Ariosto's reworking of the old, Carolingian epic cycle (Chevalier, *L'Arioste*, 107–15). Significantly, it is precisely the dynastic, encomiastic, and prophetic aspect of the *Furioso* that seems to attract Espinosa, and it is toward these aspects of the model that he directs his imitation.

Another Valencian soldier-poet, Francisco Garrido de Villena, published both a Castilian translation of Boiardo's *Orlando innamorato* and his own *Verdadero suceso de la famosa batalla de Roncesvalles*, also in 1555. This last is, like Espinosa's poem, a continuation of the Roland story as developed by Boiardo and Ariosto. Bernardo del Carpio, elected by Spaniards jealous of their national honor as the predestined slayer of Roland since at least the thirteenth century, also figures in

Garrido's *Roncesvalles*, but as in Espinosa's *Segunda parte del Orlando furioso*, the role of the medieval Spanish anti-Roland is overshadowed by an even more pressing encomiastic project. Garrido has his hero Albert, of both Trojan and Austrian ancestry, marry Marfisa and engender the line of Edward III of England, grandfather of both Philip II of Spain and Mary Tudor (Chevalier, *L'Arioste*, 116).[16]

Nineteenth- and twentieth-century critics have judged harshly the poetic quality, if not the invention, of both Espinosa's and Garrido's poems, and especially these poets' seeming inability to appreciate the essentially ludic, subversive aspects of Ariosto's treatment of chivalric themes (Chevalier, *L'Arioste*, 110, 115, 118–19); and Cervantes's village priest singled out Garrido's *Roncesvalles* for consignment to the housekeeper's bonfire from among other books treating Carolingian material (*Quijote*, bk. 1, chap. 6).[17] Nonetheless, these two Iberian *giunte* of Ariosto and Boiardo must have found a certain public during the third quarter of the sixteenth century. Whatever their artistic faults, Espinosa's *Segunda parte de Orlando* was printed five times in the period 1555–79, and Garrido's *Roncesvalles* at least twice between 1555 and 1583 (Pierce, *La poesía*, 329–30).[18] These numbers may pale before the evident popularity of Ariosto's original and its translations, but nonetheless, they indicate a thirst for further draughts from the marvelous world of enchantment, chivalric prowess, and epic enterprise perfected by the *auctor ferrarense* on the part of the Iberian reading public of the third quarter of the sixteenth century.

More important for the genesis of Ercilla's approach to epic prophecy, this series of translations, adaptations, and imitations indicates that Iberian poets of the period were turning to the Italian *romanzi*, particularily the *Orlando furioso*, for a modern paradigm of dynastic and patriotic epic. Ariosto had become, indeed, the sixteenth-century Virgil: the preferred model for imperialist epic. This becomes patent with the first long poems to celebrate explicitly the reign of Charles V and the sixteenth-century Spanish Empire. Both Jerónimo Sempere, whose *Carolea* was published in 1560, and Luis Zapata, Ercilla's erstwhile fellow courtier whose *Carlo famoso* came off the presses in 1566, look to the *Orlando furioso* as a modernized version of Virgilian epic and the principal model for their poems (Chevalier, *L'Arioste*, 130, 132–38). Although these works were each printed only once in their entirety, and are now little read, Sempere's *Carolea* and Zapata's *Carlo famoso* serve as important indicators; when their authors were moved to sing of recent history and what seemed to be the most transcendent theme possible in their times, they unhesitatingly chose Ariosto as their principal model and source of poetic invention. Thus it comes as no surprise that Ercilla should imitate many of the formal elements of the Italian *romanzi* in the *Araucana*. And indeed, we would expect the most immediate and prestigious model for the prophetic scheme that he introduced into Part II of the *Araucana* to be Ariosto's reworking of the Virgilian web of prophecy.

2.4. Ercilla's Web of Prophecy

Like Virgil and Ariosto before him, Ercilla in Part II of the *Araucana* sets up a web of prophecy in which one revelation leads to another. A radical departure, however, is that the recipient of the otherworldly guidance is none other than the poet himself. Ercilla thus simultaneously casts himself as both Virgil and Aeneas, Ariosto and Bradamante, and interweaves the prophecy of empire with the mantic inspiration of the creative act. Ercilla's insistence on portraying the epic *katabasis* of the *Araucana* as his own becomes one of the most original features of this pioneer colonial epic poem. There is no encomium of his sovereign's dynastic roots in the *Araucana*, but rather of King Philip's two greatest victories, of his empire, and of the process of writing its epic celebration. This subtle shift in the focus of the prophetic projection in the *Araucana* results in an even more complexly eclectic kaleidoscope of imitation.

Part II of the *Araucana* begins with the arrival of the little fleet carrying the Spanish punitive expedition in the Arauco region of southern Chile (*Araucana* 16.1–36). Advised of this renewed threat to their independence, sixteen Araucanian chieftains meet in yet another council of war (*Araucana* 16.39–79). After considerable debate, a messenger is sent to spy out the situation in the Spanish winter quarters—now established on the island where the fleet found shelter from the storm—and if possible, to lure the Spaniards over to the mainland with a false offer of submission to the emperor (*Araucana* 16.79–83, 17.5–16). Two months later, when the fiercest winter weather has abated, an advance guard of one hundred and thirty wary Spaniards, including the poet, establishes a fortified beachhead on the mainland (*Araucana*

17.18–28), and the local Araucanians quickly assemble and move into position to attack at first light (*Araucana* 17.29–33). Up to this point there has been no real deviation from the program announced in Part I, and reiterated in the prologue to Part II. Ercilla has followed the course of the war in Chile, with the sole difference that now he is personally a protagonist as well as a reporter of the action.

It is in this role of recorder, of transformer of experience into poetry, that Ercilla begins to spin his own web of prophecy. While the Araucanian warriors silently gather in the neighboring ravines, the young Spanish soldier-poet relates:

> Aquella noche yo malsosegado,
> reposar vn momento no podía,
> o ya fuesse el peligro, o ya el cuydado,
> que de escriuir entonces yo tenía:
> Assí imaginativo y desuelado,
> reboluiendo la inquieta fantasía,
> quise de algunas cosas desta historia,
> descargar con la pluma la memoria.
>
> En el silencio de la noche escura,
> en medio del reposo de la gente,
> quiriendo proseguir en mi escritura,
> me sobreuino vn súbito acidente,
> Cortóme vn yelo cada coyuntura,
> turbóseme la vista de repente,
> y procurando de esforçarme en vano,
> se me cayó la pluma de la mano.
>
> (*Araucana* 17.34–35)

Now that he himself is a participant in the action of the poem, Ercilla makes patent what he had announced in the prologue to Part I in 1569 where he insists that his poem was written "en la misma guerra y en los mismos pasos y sitios, escribiendo muchas veces en cuero por falta de papel, y en pedazos de cartas, de algunos tan pequeños que apenas cabían seis versos, que no me costó después poco trabajo juntarlos." While this stance has almost always been interpreted in the light of the testimonial quality of so much of the writing about the conquests in America, it must not be forgotten that Ercilla is also constructing his persona as a poet in the mold of Garcilaso. Garcilaso, in his own long poem in *ottava rima*, seeks to create the image of warrior *sprezzatura* by describing his writing process in the following terms:

> entre las armas del sangriento Marte,
> do apenas ay quien su furor contraste,
> hurté de tiempo aquesta breve suma,
> tomando ora la espada, ora la pluma.
>
> (*Egloga III*, vv. 36–40)

Later in Part II, Ercilla, expanding upon the theme, echoes Garcilaso's words, portraying himself as "la pluma ora en la mano, ora la lança" (*Araucana* 20.24h). Here in *Araucana* 17, however, Ercilla is also directly linking the visionary experience that is to follow the "súbito accidente" with the process of writing.

Indeed, this is probably the main reason for Ercilla's choice of model for the opening of his prophetic structure. In place of the sudden descent into the mantic cavern, as in Ariosto, the poet-protagonist of the *Araucana* slips off into "dulce sueño" (*Araucana* 17.37–38) only to be suddenly confronted by "la robusta y áspera Belona" (*Araucana* 17.38–39), his peculiar muse. The identity of his "divine" visitor, and a number of details of the episode, directly allude to the opening of the fifteenth-century Castilian poet Juan de Mena's *Laberinto de Fortuna* (*copla* 13ff.; Lida de Malkiel, *Juan de Mena*, 511–12). Mena, too, is the protagonist of the prophetic experience of his poem. Thus of the constitutive models that underlie Ercilla's mosaic of eclectic imitation in Part II of the *Araucana*, the first determining mediator of the overall Virgilian prophetic scheme is neither Ariosto nor Garcilaso, but rather Juan de Mena.

2.4.1. Imitation of the *Laberinto de Fortuna*

At first glance, Ercilla's elevating of a supposedly outmoded, hopelessly "medieval" poem, one written in the definitively superseded—by 1578—"coplas de arte mayor," to the forefront of his prophetic structure may strike the reader as odd. To put the poet of the *Araucana*'s relationship with Mena in perspective, it is useful to remember that

Ercilla's contemporary Francisco Sánchez de las Brozas ("El Brocense") would say of Mena in 1582:

> Es muy bien que este poeta sea tenido en mucha estima, aunque no fuera tan bueno como es, por ser el primero que sepamos que haya ilustrado tanto la lengua castellana. Aunque en Roma salió Virgilio y Horacio, y otros de aquel siglo, nunca Ennio y Lucrecio, y los muy antiguos dexáron de ser tenidos en gran veneracion. Ansí que no hay razon de desechar á Juan de Mena, porque en nuestra edad hayan salido otros de estilo muy diferente. . . . le pueden leer todas las edades y calidades de personas, por ser casto y limpio y provechoso, donde las costumbres no recibiran mal resabio, lo qual no se puede asegurar de los otros poetas . . . Yo espero que leyéndose agora este poeta con mas claridad . . . será mi trabajo bien recibido, principalmente de aquellos que estan hartos ó apartados de leer cosas lascivas y amorosas. (*Obras del famoso poeta Juan de Mena*, "Al lector," n.p.)

Thus, according to El Brocense, himself also the author in 1574 of the first important commentary on Garcilaso, Mena was the first to have truly "ennobled the Castilian language." The use of the verb *ilustrar* in this context reinforces the idea of elevating the vulgar tongue to the level of the classical languages, not only through careful polishing of the lexicon and the refined use of poetic tropes, but also through the dense accumulation of learned allusion: in effect, through imitation.[19] El Brocense goes on to set up a simile that has Mena in the role of Ennius or Lucretius compared with Garcilaso and the other Italianizers as Virgil or Horace.[20] This is especially important for Ercilla because Mena is prized as a native poet, working in the Castilian tradition, and this accords well with Ercilla's own evident literary Spanish chauvinism in respect to the French, the Italians, and even the Portuguese. Furthermore, Mena is seen as "casto," a martial alternative or antidote to the Italianate poets who concern themselves exclusively with "cosas lascivas y amorosas." This, of course, concords well with Ercilla's own initial outright rejection, and later temporizing, of the theme of love in the *Araucana*. Although most of Ercilla's amorous episodes may be based on models in the *Orlando furioso* (Schwartz Lerner 624), in the same way that Ercilla's version of Carthaginian Dido is the antithesis of Virgil's libidinous queen (Lida de Malkiel, *Dido*, 127-34), the indigenous heroines of the *Araucana* are all considerably more chaste than their Italian models. Mena would have recommended himself to Ercilla from the beginning as a singer of great deeds unsullied by overly enthusiastic attention to the salacious details of his characters' amours.[21]

It is also clear that El Brocense was not alone in his estimation of Mena.[22] Including the edition first prepared by Fernán Núñez in 1505 and that readied by El Brocense himself in 1582, in all of their various reprintings, the complete text of the *Laberinto de Fortuna* is known to have appeared at least sixteen times between 1505 and 1586, seven of these after 1540 (Kerkhof and Le Pair, "El *Laberinto*," 322-24).[23] The only conclusion that can be drawn is that, despite the revolution in taste introduced by the publication of *Las obras de Boscán y algunas de Garcilaso de la Vega* in 1543, as well as Jerónimo de Urrea's widely disseminated 1549 translation of the *Orlando furioso* in octava rima, Mena's *Laberinto de Fortuna* continued to be read widely and to enjoy considerable literary prestige. For a work written in a style that conventional literary history assumes to have been hopelessly out of fashion, the sixteen printings of the *Laberinto de Fortuna* do not compare unfavorably with the twelve to eighteen printings registered by Urrea's translation of *Orlando furioso* up to about 1583-88 (Chevalier, *L'Arioste*, 74-75).

As Daniel Javitch has shown for Ariosto ("The Shaping," 265-66), and Ignacio Navarrete for Garcilaso ("Decentering Garcilaso," 24), the production and publication of commentaries stressing the prestigious sources of authors writing in the modern, spoken languages is a fundamental medium in the process of their canonization. Fernán Núñez's monumental commentary on Mena's *Laberinto de Fortuna*, first published in 1499, substantially revised in 1505, and reprinted at least fourteen times before serving as the basis of El Brocense's edition and commentary of 1582, is the first such humanist canonization of a Castilian poet.[24] Furthermore, between 1499 and 1582 only one edition—Toledo 1501—was to appear without Núñez's commentary (Kerkhof, "El *Laberinto*," 322). Thus it is virtually certain that Ercilla could have read Mena only in the context of Núñez's pioneering exercise in literary canonization. I examine some of the implications of Ercilla's reception of Mena through the medium of Núñez's commentary in detail in Chapter 3, but here it is sufficient to underscore the impact on Ercilla of Mena's prestige as the first truly canonized Castilian poet.

Mena's poem would have suggested itself to Ercilla as a privileged subtext for the opening of the prophetic scheme of the *Araucana* for thematic reasons as well. The *Laberinto de Fortuna*, it must be remembered, played a key role in the unfolding of Spanish imperialism. Mena addressed his poem to John II of Castile as a goad to the king's ambition, promising his sovereign that he could be a "new Augustus" if only he would unite his fractious nobles and complete the reconquest (Deyermond 159, 163–64; *Laberinto de Fortuna* 230).[25] As Dorothy Clotelle Clarke has pointed out, although the *Laberinto de Fortuna* may have fallen on deaf ears in the case of Mena's monarch, its prophetic power reached on to inspire the imperialist enterprise of Isabel the Catholic (9).[26] Two precise echoes of the connection between the *Laberinto de Fortuna* and the ideology of Castilian imperial expansion will be examined in detail in Chapters 3 and 5, respectively. Here it will suffice to indicate how the opening framework of Ercilla's prophetic machinery is inspired by that of the *Laberinto de Fortuna*.

Mena turns the prophetic scheme of the *Aeneid* inside out, as does his principal model in this regard, Dante. While the debate over the exact role of the *Divina commedia* as a subtext for the *Laberinto de Fortuna* has been a critical quagmire into which it is perhaps imprudent to tread, it is nonetheless apparent that the overall structure of Mena's visionary journey through the Spheres owes a great deal to the Florentine master (Lida de Malkiel, *Juan de Mena*, 16–20; Street, "Allegory," 8; Foster 345).[27] Thus Mena, like Dante, foregoes the complex web of prophecy, one revelation leading to the next, interwoven with other plot elements that characterize the *Aeneid* and the *Orlando furioso*. In an inversion of this model, Mena enters directly into a cosmic allegory that can easily accommodate the diverse historical personages and examples that he presents didactically to his reader.[28] It is with this same initial machinery that Ercilla, in turn, sweeps himself toward the prophetic illumination of his own poem.

The *Laberinto de Fortuna* opens with the poet inveighing against the caprices of Fortune. As he challenges the fickle goddess to lay bare the inner workings of "la casa . . . do anda tu rueda" (*Laberinto de Fortuna* 12f), he is furiously swept up by another allegorical goddess, "la madre Belona," in her dragon-drawn chariot (*Laberinto de Fortuna* 13). As I indicated above, after falling asleep with his pen in his hand in the

Spanish camp on the eve of the Araucanian attack, Ercilla is confronted by the same personage, this time without her chariot, but "de las horribles Furias rodeada" (*Araucana* 17.39f). Unlike Mena's sudden but silent visitor, however, Ercilla's Bellona pauses to address her mortal poet:

> ". . . O moço venturoso,
> el ánimo leuanta y confiança,
> reconociendo el tiempo presuroso,
> de la diestra fortuna, y buena andança:
> Huye del ocio torpe pereçoso,
> ensancha el coraçón y la esperança,
> y aspira a más de aquello que pretendes,
> que el Cielo te es propicio, si lo entiendes.
>
> Que viéndote a escriuir yo aficionado,
> y de tu inclinación el claro indicio,
> pues nunca te han la pluma destemplado,
> las fieras armas y aspero exercicio:
> Tu trabajo fiel considerado,
> sólo mouida de mi mismo officio,
> te quiero yo lleuar en vna parte,
> donde podrás sin límite ensancharte.
>
> Es campo fértil lleno de mil flores,
> en el qual hallarás materia llena,
> de guerras más famosas y mayores,
> donde podrá correr largo la vena:
> Y si quereys de damas y de amores,
> en verso celebrar la dulce pena,
> tendrás mayor sugeto y hermosura,
> que en la passada edad y en la futura."
>
> (*Araucana* 17.40–42)

Just as Ercilla's preoccupation before this sudden visitation has been with the writing of his poem, so now the warlike muse offers to reward with richer possibilities the poet's faithful constancy to the harsh theme of colonial war. Specifically, she urges him to aspire to "más de aquello que pretendes" (*Araucana* 17.40g). This is a clear reference to the shift in focus and approach that Ercilla has announced in the prologue to

Part II.²⁹ "Aquello que pretendes" must surely be interpreted as the narrow delimitation of Ercilla's subject as the *verista* account of the war in Chile that the poet has saddled himself with from the outset of the poem in Part I, only to chafe and temporize at the self-imposed bounds in the final cantos.

In fact, here Ercilla makes a specific allusion to his protestations about the monotony and harshness of his chosen theme in Part I when he has Bellona describe the place she will take him as "campo fértil lleno de mil flores." The reader will recall that in Part I Ercilla explains, and complains, that

> Que si a mi discreción dado me fuera
> Salir al campo, y escoger las flores,
> Quiçá el cansado gusto remouiera
> La vsada variedad de los sabores:
> pues como otros han hecho, yo pudiera
> entretejer mil fábulas y amores:
> mas ya que tan adentro estoy metido,
> hauré de proseguir lo prometido.
>
> (*Araucana* 15.5)

Bellona is, in effect, freeing him from his obligation to "proseguir lo prometido." But his new opportunities now explicitly include more than "amores"; the belligerent goddess also promises him "guerras más famosas y mayores" (*Araucana* 17.42c). This is implicit acknowledgment that the campaigns of the colonial periphery must be exalted by direct connection with the more prestigious enterprise of the imperial center.

Ercilla's pursuit of the metaphor of the "field of flowers" first essayed in canto 15 also serves to underline the eclectic nature of his imitation, leading into the first of two *loci amoeni* (*Araucana* 17.44–49, 18.66–69) in the style of Garcilaso that will adorn this phase of his visionary trajectory.³⁰ He abruptly returns the reader to the prophetic context of the *Laberinto de Fortuna*, however, as Bellona sweeps him up to a great height from which the whole world can be observed (*Araucana* 17.49–51). This recalls the immediate prelude to Mena's vision of the cosmos, where Divine Providence leads the fifteenth-century poet to the highest place in Fortune's mansions "donde podía ser bien devisada / toda la parte terrestre e marina" (*Laberinto de Fortuna* 32). In Ercilla's version, this is at the summit of a pyramid-shaped hill, "redondo en ygual círculo y esento" that itself rises from the center of the upland *locus amoenus* (*Araucana* 17.49*bc*).

Ercilla's description of his vantage point offers some interesting variations on its model:

> Era de altura tal que no podría,
> vn liuiano Neblí subir a buelo,
> y ansí no sin temor me parecía,
> mirando abajo estar cerca del Cielo:
> De donde con la vista descubría,
> la grande redondez del ancho suelo,
> con los términos Bárbaros ygnotos,
> hasta los más ocultos y remotos.
>
> (*Araucana* 17.51)

The great pyramidal mountain from which all the world can be seen, and which cannot be reached by the high-flying bird of prey, prefigures Sor Juana's description of a more profound visionary journey in her *Sueño* (1:342–43, vv. 292–339). The sensation of being nearer the heavens than the earth recalls the entire tradition of such visionary dreams and journeys, not the least the *Somnium scipionis*, itself a model for both Dante and Mena (Curtius 359–60; Macrobius 45–46; Scarpa 54–55; Lida de Malkiel, *Juan de Mena*, 31). Ercilla veers back toward the immediate subtext of the *Laberinto de Fortuna* with the mention of "la grande redondez del ancho suelo," recalling Mena's spherical imagery at the corresponding juncture (*Laberinto de Fortuna* 32*gh*, 34*a*). In a manner typical of Ercilla's eclectic approach, he retains Bellona for this segment of his journey, and postpones the introduction of the mysterious woman in white—who corresponds to Mena's allegorical figure of Divine Providence (Lida de Malkiel, *Juan de Mena*, 512)—until a later stage of the unfolding of his web of prophecy. Bellona provides a description of the initial layout of the battle of Saint Quentin in northern France (*Araucana* 17.52–58), and she takes leave of her mortal pupil at this point, to perform her allegorical function by diving down into the lines before Saint Quentin to goad the opposing armies into a murderous frenzy (*Araucana* 17.59–61).[31]

Before leaving Bellona to her grisly work, however, there is one point that should be clarified because it strikes to the heart of Ercilla's imitative stance in regard to both classical epic and his contemporary rival, Camoens. Maxime Chevalier asserts that "la seule trace de la machinerie mythologique dans *L'Araucana* est la presence de Bellone" (The only trace of mythological machinery in the *Araucana* is the presence of Bellona) (145 n. 154), an observation that has been frequently repeated (for instance, Morínigo y Lerner, eds. 2:43 n. 22).[32] It is significant that Chevalier makes this remark in the context of his discussion of the overall importance of Lucan's *Pharsalia* as a determining subtext of the *Araucana* (144–48). Chevalier notes that Ercilla, like Lucan, rejects the mythological machinery that is so typical of Homeric and Virgilian epic (145). The French scholar does not develop this interpretation any further, as his purpose is actually to minimize as much as possible the importance of Lucan over that of Ariosto in Ercilla's poem (148–49).

Perhaps for this reason, the point is so easily misread. Bellona, as we have seen, enters the *Araucana* through the *Laberinto de Fortuna*. As Lida de Malkiel points out (*Juan de Mena* 16), Mena probably found this image in Lucan, who uses Bellona brandishing her flail as a simile for Caesar's battle rage during the decisive confrontation with Pompey (*Pharsalia* 7.568–70).[33] Lucan himself may be echoing Virgil's description of Bellona, seen in company with Mars and the Furies on Aeneas's shield (*Aeneid* 8.700–703).[34] The key factor, however, lies in Lucan's rejection of Virgil's mythological apparatus. Whether this is due to a conscious effort to contrast his poem to Virgil's, as many critics suppose (Graves 11–12), or because by Lucan's time the Olympians "have ceased to exist" as W. R. Johnson would have it (4), is a question perhaps best left to the specialist.

For the Christian poet of the late Middle Ages or Renaissance, however, Lucan's suppresion of the conventional, Olympian machinery offered a very attractive model: prestigious as a famous ancient author, yet free of the contamination of outright paganism. Although the learned poets of the twelfth-century Renaissance found doctrinally acceptable ways to incorporate the pagan apparatus of Virgilian epic into an essentially Christian *mundus significans* (Bernardus, *Cosmographia*, 2), the general tendency, especially in vernacular works, was to transform the overtly pagan supernatural into less questionable guise, either wizardry or allegory. This is perhaps especially true in Iberia, where, for instance, the anonymous adaptor of the twelfth-century Latin *Alexandreis* systematically excises the mythological from his rendition of the model into the vernacular *Libro de Alexandre* (Willis, *The Relationship*, 12–13, 75–76).

Mena, although he employs them in similes and examples, likewise avoids involving the Olympians in the vital machinery of the *Laberinto de Fortuna*, except as the names of the spheres, a usage that corresponds to Neoplatonic cosmology and not pagan religion. As does Ercilla, Mena clearly sees Bellona for what she is, one of the allegorical personifications who begin to proliferate in Silver Latin poetry at the expense of the true Olympians, and who supersede the old gods almost completely in medieval literature. These personified abstractions were particularily apt for the depiction of the inner conflicts of conscience that so preoccupied the intellectual transistion from paganism to Christianity (Lewis 73). Although Bellona, like Fortuna, had her temples in pre-Christian Rome,[35] her essential character as an allegorical personification rather than one of the vital deities of the Olympian pantheon permits her to intervene in both the *Laberinto de Fortuna* and the *Araucana* in the company of Divine Providence without any hint of irreverence or heresy.[36]

This stance in regard to pagan mythology seems to have been the most comfortable for Ercilla from the outset, and it is significant that he is careful not to stray from it even under the pressure of intensified *imitatio* in Part II. Camoens, of course, does introduce a complete Virgilian, pagan apparatus as a mediator between Divine Providence and his mortal protagonists in *Os Lusíadas*. This aspect of Camoens's poem proved to be one of the most controversial, even resulting in the publication of the ludicrously sanitized so-called "Piscos" edition of 1584 in which the rich mythological fabric of the original is systematically suppressed (Camões, *Obras*, ed. Cidade, 4:xviii–xxii).[37] Ercilla might well be implicitly counterpoising his own, sober Ibero-Christian supernatural machinery in Part II of the *Araucana* to the suspect, pagan indulgence of his Portuguese rival.

Bellona, then, is clearly not a genuinely mythological figure. That she plays a relatively more prominent role in Ercilla's visionary journey than in the *Laberinto de Fortuna* is because Ercilla's subject, even more than Mena's, is war. It is therefore most fitting that the allegorical personification of organized slaughter should preside over the poet's linking of the grand conflicts of the metropolitan empire to the sordid suppression of rebellion at its periphery. Ercilla, however, does not want the reader to lose sight of his subtext completely here, and so returns to Mena's scheme with the advent of the mysterious woman in white. Left to observe and report the battle of Saint Quentin on his own once Bellona has disappeared into the fray (*Araucana* 17.61–18.28), it is only after Ercilla has praised the clemency of his sovereign in victory that the poet tells us:

> El Sol ya poco a poco declinaua
> al Emispherio Antártico encendido,
> cuando yo que alegríssimo miraua
> todo lo que en mi canto aueys oído,
> Vi cerca vna muger que me hablaua
> más blanco que la nieue su vestido,
> graue muy venerable en el aspecto
> persona al parecer de gran respecto.
>
> Diziendo: "Si las cosas que dixere
> por cierta y verdadera profecía,
> dificultosa alguna pareciere
> créeme que no es fición ni fantasía,
> Más lo q*ue* el padre eterno ordena y quiere,
> allá en su excelso throno y hierarchía,
> al qual está sujeto lo más fuerte
> el hado, la fortuna, el tiempo y muerte".
> (*Araucana* 18.29–30)

We are reminded here that Ercilla's mantic mountain vantage point, a fixture in the medieval allegorical tradition (Patch, *The Goddess Fortuna*, 132–36), is securely located in the Andes—he observes the sun setting in the "hemísferio Antártico" (*Araucana* 18.29*ab*)—and not in some ambiguous literary limbo. The nameless woman in white who addresses the poet here, however, has walked straight out of a long series of allegorical landscapes, beginning with Boethius's *Consolatione* and Alan of Lille's *Anticlaudianus* (Lida de Malkiel, *Juan de Mena*, 25; Patch, "Chaucer's Desert," 324), although Ercilla makes his own contribution to the tradition by referring to her as Reason when he recalls her prophecy some cantos further on (*Araucana* 23.28*b*).

Ercilla also innovates by restoring the gift of prophesying the future to his white-clad Sibyl. Mena's guide, who identifies herself with the remark "Divina me puedes llamar Providencia" (*Laberinto de Fortuna*

23h), proclaims that the future is unknowable to mortals (*Laberinto de Fortuna* 59), and advises her poet pupil to scorn those who presume to know what God has in store for them (*Laberinto de Fortuna* 60). Mena is consistent in this as well: he reserves a particularly inauspicious place at the bottom of the Sphere of Venus for fortune-tellers and other prestidigitators (*Laberinto de Fortuna* 129-30); the major necromantic prediction of the poem—examined in detail in Chapter 3—is explicitly revealed to be false (*Laberinto de Fortuna* 263-65). Ercilla would seem to be responding directly to Mena's cautious orthodoxy when he has the woman in white reassure the poet that, in spite of how difficult it may be to believe, what she foretells is neither "ficción ni fantasía" but rather what God himself has ordained (*Araucana* 18.30).

The transformative initiative of Ercilla's imitation is also apparent in the transposition of the sudden blindness that overcomes the poet as a prelude to his visionary experience. Mena is affected by this after being swept up by Bellona as a prelude to his encounter with Providencia (*Laberinto de Fortuna* 18-19), and it is a constitutive element in his meditation on the unreliability of appearances—a theme closely related to the inconstancy of Fortune. Ercilla transposes this experience to just before his initial encounter with Bellona at the very beginning of his visionary journey (*Araucana* 17.35-37). He also adapts it, as the bees are said to transform the pollen into honey, to his own purpose. Here the blindness and confusion serve to underline the extraordinary, abnormal state of the poet and the visionary nature of the experiences to come.

Ercilla's transformative use of Mena's guide is further evident in the way he has the woman in white foretell how the poet will encounter his next supernatural mentor and then take her leave from the poem. After laying out the political and military fortunes of the Hapsburg imperial enterprise in Europe (*Araucana* 18.31-59) from the denouement of the battle of Saint Quentin up to the eve of Lepanto, and particularly the labyrinthine forging of the Holy League against the Ottoman Turks, all of which is "future" relative to the narrative time of the *Araucana*, the woman in white declares:

> "Mas si quieres saber desta jornada,
> el futuro suceso enteramente
> y la cosa más grande y señalada,
> que jamás se aya visto entre la gente,

> Quando passares solo la Cañada,
> que ciñe del río Rauco la corriente,
> verás al pie de vn líuano a la orilla
> vna mansa y doméstica Corzilla.
>
> Conuiénete sequirla con cuydado,
> hasta salir en vna gran llanura,
> al cabo de la qual verás a vn lado
> vna fragosa entrada y Selua escura:
> Y tras la Corza tímida emboscado,
> hallarás en mitad de la espesura,
> debaxo de vna tosca y hueca peña,
> vna oculta morada muy pequeña.
>
> Allí por ser lugar inabitable,
> sin rastro de persona ni sendero,
> viue vn anciano viejo venerable,
> que famoso soldado fue primero,
> De quien sabrás do auita el intratable
> Phitón mágico grande y hechicero,
> el qual te informará de muchas cosas,
> que están aún por venir marauillosas,
>
> No quiero dezir más en lo tocante,
> a las cosas futuras pues parece,
> que abrá materia y campo asaz bastante,
> en lo que de presente se te offrece:
> Para lleuar tus obras adelante,
> pues la grande ocasión te fauorece,
> que a mí sólo, hasta aquí me es concedido,
> el poderte dezir lo que as oydo."
>
> (*Araucana* 18.60–63)

Once again, the thrust of prophecy is aimed toward writing. The imitation of Mena is useful to Ercilla here, for in addition to bearing in mind Mena's prestige as the pioneer Castilian poet of empire, it must be remembered that Mena deliberately provoked his encounter with the supernatural forces represented by Bellona and Divine Providence in order to further his writing of Fortune's vagaries (*Laberinto de Fortuna* 2). Ercilla intensifies this relationship in his revision of *Araucana*

18.60*d*, when he changes the woman in white's advertisement of her visionary wares from "la cosa más grande y señalada, / que jamás se aya visto entre la gente" (1578) to "la cosa más grande y señalada / que jamás en historia se ha leído" (1589–90).³⁸ Although this modification also corresponds to the development of one of the balanced oppositions so beloved by Garcilasist poetics—the final, rhyming "enteramente" of 18.60*b* is also changed to "oído"—the overall effect is to anchor the prophecy to come more securely in the realm of writing. The woman in white reiterates the literary destiny of her revelations with the remark that "abrá materia y campo asaz bastante, / . . . / Para lleuar tus obras adelante" (*Araucana* 18.63*c, e*). By unmistakably alluding to Mena here, Ercilla is able to figuratively wrap himself in the flag of Castilian imperialism as he sets up the machinery that will allow him to contravene the limitations of his original program and speak directly to the "guerras mayores" of the metropolitan ambit.

Ercilla's interweaving of the subtext of the *Laberinto de Fortuna* into his web of prophecy does not end with the departure of the woman in white from the poem. On the contrary, Ercilla returns to Mena for key material in his presentation of the prophetic nexus of the *Araucana* that he spins in Fitón's cave in cantos 23 and 27. Several instances of this merit far more detailed discussion than can be given them in the context of the overall structure of prophecy and and its underlying, and previously uncharted, terrain of eclectic imitation. The emulation of Mena's culminating scene of necromancy that Ercilla essays in *Araucana* 23, therefore, is the principal subject of Chapter 3, and Ercilla's use and expansion of Mena's mapamundi in *Araucana* 27 falls naturally into the province of Chapter 5. For the present, the woman in white's prophecy must lead us back into the forest of eclectic imitation that is ultimately based on Virgil as transformed by Ariosto.

2.4.2. The Ariostesque Approach to the Cave of Prophecy

As the pattern laid down by the *Aeneid* dictates, one prophecy must lead to the next, and the complete revelation is reserved for the central nexus of the poem. Ercilla follows this scheme in an extremely eclectic fashion, having his woman in white—taken as we have seen from the

Laberinto de Fortuna—announce that the poet will be wise to follow the roe deer when he sees her by Rauco's water, and that he will be led in turn, first to one human guide, and finally to the fearsome sorceror Fitón, who will put the seal on his prophetic experience (*Araucana* 18.60–63). Ercilla has read Ariosto too well, however, to compress all of this into one seamless narrative.

The woman in white, later referred to as "La Razón" by the poet, does not take immediate leave of her pupil, but lingers long enough to point out the second of the *loci amoeni* of Part II (*Araucana* 18.67–69). Ercilla seems to be anxious to relieve the grime of battle with this type of poetic exercise, and takes particular pleasure here in indicating a garden blooming with the flower of Spanish womanhood. This recalls, if only faintly, Ariosto's ekphrastic monument to eight illustrious Italian women (*Orlando furioso* 42.79–93), and the sixteen stanzas praising eight Spanish women added by Urrea in his translation of 1549 (Van Horne, "Urrea Translation," 224). Yet Ercilla puts his own stamp on the motif, literally launching himself from his visionary mountaintop aerie down into the flowery scene below with the observation that:

> Y desseoso luego de ocuparme,
> en obras y canciones amorosas,
> y mudar el estilo y no curarme,
> de las ásperas guerras sanguinosas,
> Con gran gana y codicia de informarme,
> de aquel assiento y damas tan hermosas,
> en especial y sobre todas, de vna,
> que vi a sus pies rendida mi fortuna.
>
> (*Araucana* 18.72)

Once again, it is anxiety over his subject matter, and his desire to essay his powers in praise of Venus as well as Mars, that preoccupies him. The woman who catches his eye proves to be none other than his future bride, the young Doña María de Bazán (*Araucana* 18.73). Significantly, although no hint of sculpture, tapestry, or painting has been insinuated, she is identified in the manner of ekphrasis by an inscription at her feet.[39]

The poet's reverie among the amorous blossoms is brief, however, as Ercilla is abruptly awakened by the Araucanian assault that comes sweeping over the ramparts with the dawn (*Araucana* 18.74–76). The fifty-two stanzas of *Araucana* 19 are devoted to the ensuing combat, the first real battle in Chile in which the young poet personally takes part, and the first colonial combat described at length in Part II. Following his tried and true Ariostesque narrative strategy, Ercilla breaks off the canto with the outnumbered Tucapel—one of the poet's favorites, a character most surely modeled on Ariosto's irrepressible Moor Rodomonte (Chevalier, *L'Arioste*, 149)—furiously exchanging blows with a group of Spaniards (*Araucana* 19.51–52).

Ercilla again airs his angst over the conflict between his original program and the theme of love in the Ariostesque exordium to the following canto:

> ¿Quién me metió entre abrojos y cuestas,
> tras las roncas trompetas y atambores
> pudiendo yr por járdines y florestas
> cogiendo varias y olorosas flores
> Mezclando en las empresas y requestas
> cuentos ficiones fábulas y amores
> donde correr sin límite pudiera
> y dando gusto, yo le recibiera?
>
> ¿Todo ha de ser batalla, y asperezas,
> discordia, fuego, sangre, enemistades,
> odios, rencores, sañas, y brauezas,
> desatino, furor, temeridades,
> Rabias, iras, venganças, y fierezas,
> muertes, destroços, riças, crueldades,
> que al mismo Marte ya pondrán hastío,
> agotando vn caudal, mayor quel mío?
>
> (*Araucana* 20.4–5)

The poet sustains the metaphor of flowers, fields, and gardens for amorous themes, variety, and imitation initiated at the end of Part I in *Araucana* 15.5, and renewed in Bellona's speech at 17.42a–d. Here, however, he is more explicit. Not only love, or "guerras mayores" for that matter, will be found in these flowery glades and gardens, but also "cuentos, ficciones, fábulas": in effect, the entire Ariostesque ensemble so bravely, and prominently, defied in the opening stanzas of the poem (*Araucana* 1.1–3).

The complaint of the exordium leads back into the interrupted narration of Tucapel's prowess (*Araucana* 20.6–17). The authentic answer to Ercilla's rhetorical question, posed in *Araucana* 20.4–5, follows quickly on the intrepid Tucapel's retreat from the Spanish lines under a hail of missiles, which occasions a general Araucanian withdrawal (*Araucana* 20.17). Once again, just as the night before, when on the eve of the battle he was visited by Bellona (*Araucana* 17.34–35), the poet finds himself dozing off when he is confronted with a fittingly Ariostesque "fábula" with which to adorn his poem (*Araucana* 20.21–27). The ensuing tale of Tegualda and her ill-fated swain Crepino occupies no less than forty-eight stanzas, almost as many as the preceding battle (*Araucana* 20.28–75).

As has often been pointed out, the main inspiration for this intercalated amorous episode is Ariosto's tale of Isabella and Zerbino (*Orlando furioso* 13ff.; Ducamin 149 n. 1; Chevalier, *L'Arioste*, 152). Although Lía Schwartz Lerner has underlined the typically eclectic nature of Ercilla's imitation in his rendering of his encounter with Tegualda (620–21), it is nonetheless apparent, as Chevalier insists (152), that the overall invention of form and narrative strategy as well as of episodic content, draws its inspiration from Ariosto; Schwartz Lerner herself comes to much the same conclusion (624). It is important to bear this in mind in the analysis of Ercilla's web of prophecy in Part II, as the supernatural introduction of metropolitan, imperial themes itself forms a part of the larger framework of novel variety that the poet constructs. If Ercilla does not have the *Orlando furioso* "open on his lectern" as he writes Part II, it is certainly very present in his mind, just as it was the principal foil for his stance of dour, stout, Spanish *verismo* in Part I. The carefully balanced narrative structure of Part II, throughout which episodes of war in Chile are systematically and symmetrically balanced with either unearthly encomia of metropolitan empire or Ariostesque amorous adventures,[40] is patently and solidly grounded in a careful reading of the *Orlando furioso*.[41]

Thus when Ercilla finds himself, as the woman in white predicted (*Araucana* 18.60), "por donde corre Rauco más estrecho" and comes across a "mansa corcilla junto al río / gustando de las hierbas y rocío" half hidden beneath a "selva de árboles copados" (*Araucana* 23.27), it is not surprising that the whole episode should exude a certain Ariostesque flavor, although the precise allusions prove elusive. In the most general terms, of course, Ercilla has certainly brought his prophetic machinery back into line with the underlying Virgilian model by having one prophecy lead incrementally to the next. It is here, in fact, that we learn the name of the mysterious woman in white:[42]

> Ocurrió luego a la memoria mía
> que la razón en sueños me dixera
> cómo auía de topar acaso vn día
> vna simple Corçilla en la ribera,
>
> (*Araucana* 23.28a–d)

Furthermore, by explicitly alluding back to the woman in white's prophecy, the poet reminds the reader that the visionary experiences recalling the *Laberinto de Fortuna* are not isolated, self-contained elements of eclectic imitation, but rather the preliminary pieces in a more complex, Virgilian or Ariostesque mosaic of gradual revelation.

The ambience is also extremely reminiscent of the *Orlando furioso*. Ercilla tries to follow the roe deer, just as Reason had urged him to do, but becomes lost in a dense, dark wood (*Araucana* 23.30–32). As the woman in white had intimated, this is the "selva escura" that surrounds the enchanter's cave (*Araucana* 18.61). As Curtius indicates (201–2), the trackless, wild forest is one of the mainstays of medieval epic landscape, and reaches its full flower as a characteristic motif of the *Orlando furioso*. Dante, of course, recalls the locus with his "selva selvaggia e aspra e forte" in which the poet wanders lost at the opening of the visionary journey of the *Divina commedia* (*Inferno* 1.5; Curtius 201). Although Dante is using the forest here as a metaphor for worldliness (*Divina commedia*, ed. Grandgent and Singleton, 9), it is also doubtlessly a reminiscence of the impenetrably thick, shady forest that surrounds Virgil's entrance to the underworld (*Aeneid* 6.238). This Virgilian contribution to the exterior landscape of hell is reinforced by Lucan, whose anti-Sibyl, the necromantic witch Erictho, has her cave in "a dim wood with forward-bending trees . . . yew trees that the sun cannot penetrate" (*Pharsalia* 6.644–45).[43]

It is, then, through a combination of the trackless forest of medieval romance with the darker, more ominous wood that guards the classical cave entrance to the underworld that Bradamante and Pinabello ride as they lose their way in a "selva oscura" (*Orlando furioso* 2.68cd). From the midst of this "dark forest" rises the crag that conceals the cavern entrance to Merlin's tomb, the medieval-romance equivalent of Virgil's "jaws of Hell" and Lucan's "caverns of Dis," predestined site of *katabasis* and prophecy. Ariosto is deliberately, and characteristically ludically, alluding to Dante's "mi ritrovai per una selva oscura" (I came to myself in a dark forest) (*Inferno* 1.2) here by saying of Pinabello that "ritrovossi in una selva oscura" (he came to himself in a dark forest) (*Orlando furioso* 2.68d) as he veers off the beaten path, lost in thought over how to bring his erstwhile companion Bradamante to a bad end, but, unbeknownst to either, in fact leading her to prophetic revelation of her destiny (*Orlando furioso*, ed. Bigi, 161–62). Ercilla clearly has this in mind when he has the woman in white describe the environs of the enchanter's lair as a "selva escura" (*Araucana* 18.61d), although he typically dissimulates a little with the less Latinate form "escura" in place of "oscura."[44]

Indeed, once Ercilla has found his guide, the aging Araucanian warrior Guaticolo, he is led

> por vna estrecha y intricada senda,
> La qual seguida vn trecho nos hallamos,
> en vna Selua de árboles horrenda
> que los rayos del Sol y claro Cielo,
> nunca allí vieron el vmbroso suelo.
>
> Debaxo de vna peña socauada
> de espessas ramas y árboles cubierta
> vimos vn callejón y angosta entrada,
> y más adentro vna pequeña puerta,
>
> (*Araucana* 23.46d–47d)

This is truly the heart of the "selva selvaggia." Again, Ercilla's rendition of this locus calls up the whole tradition, rather than any one specific model. The cave under a rocky outcrop perhaps most recalls Lucan's description of Erictho's necromantic den "beneath a high rock of the hollow mountain" (montisque cavi . . . / . . . alta sub rupe) (*Pharsalia* 6.640–41), itself, as we have seen, surrounded by funereal yew trees that admit no light (*Pharsalia* 6.644–45).[45] Nonetheless, this is not inconsistent with Ariosto's "pietra dura" (stony crag) that rises out of the "selva oscura" (*Orlando furioso* 2.68f) with its:

> . . . nel sasso . . . una caverna,
> che si profonda più di trenta braccia.
> Tagliato a picchi et a scarpelli il sasso
> scende giù al dritto, et ha una porta al basso.
> *(Orlando furioso* 2.70*e–h)*

> (. . . within the stony crag . . . a cavern,
> more than thirty yards deep.
> The stone hewn by picks and chisels,
> it descends straight downwards, and there was a door at the bottom.)

In fact, Ercilla seems to engage deliberately in *dissimulatio* when he describes the entryway as narrow and the door as small. This is clearly designed to distinguish his prophetic cave from Ariosto's, with its "porta ampla e capace" (wide and capacious door) *(Orlando furioso* 2.71*a)*. This interpretation is supported by a number of other details of Ercilla's *katabasis*.

Ariosto describes the antechamber of Merlin's tomb as emitting a light, as if of torches *(Orlando furioso* 2.71*cd)*. As Bradamante enters, she discovers that

> Surgea nel mezzo un ben locato altare,
> ch'avea dinanzi una lampada accesa;
> e quella di splendente e chiaro foco
> rendea gran lume all'uno e all'altro loco.
> *(Orlando furioso* 3.7*e–h)*

> (There stood in the middle a well-placed altar,
> in front of which there was a burning lamp;
> and this, with bright and clear flame
> gave out bright light to both chambers.)

In a very similar fashion, Ercilla and his guide Guaticolo enter the first chamber of the enchanter Fitón's cave to discover themselves "do vna lámpara eterna en medio ardía" *(Araucana* 23.48*d)*. This would seem to be a clear reminiscence of Ariosto's "lampada accesa." In his revision of 1589, however, Ercilla changes this to "do una perpetua luz en medio ardía."[46] The essential idea, of the large cavern illumined by a central light source, is left intact. The exact verbal correspondence, the telltale allusion of "lámpara" to "lampada" is dissimulated with the substitution of "luz." This can be read as a refinement of what has been Ercilla's approach to imitation of Ariosto throughout Part II of the *Araucana*.

This deliberate dissimulation of the model provided by the *Orlando furioso* perhaps explains why critics, although they have long intuited an Ariostesque subtext for the episode of Fitón's cave, have had so little success in establishing the concrete allusions that would substantiate such an imitation. Chevalier, for instance, affirms that "quand *L'Araucana* cesse d'être un poème uniquement guerrier, c'est pour se rapprocher du grand modèle offert par le *Roland furieux*" (when the *Araucana* leaves off being a poem exclusively about war, it is in order to approximate more closely the great model presented by the *Orlando furioso*) (*L'Arioste*, 152), but feels it necessary to qualify this judgment by admitting:

> On a voulu rapprocher les épisodes de Bellone et de Fiton de fragments du *Roland furieux*. . . . Ces parallèles nous semblent peu probants. Il est vrai que le merveilleux d'Ercilla est comparable à celui de l'Arioste. On ne peut rien affirmer de plus. (*L'Arioste*, 152 n. 186)
>
> (Some have wanted to compare the episodes of Bellona and Fitón with fragments of the *Orlando furioso*. . . . These parallels seem unconvincing to us. It is true that the marvelous in Ercilla is comparable to that of Ariosto. One can say no more with certainty.)

Chevalier mentions two authors who had proposed Ariosto as a model for the Fitón episode. The first, José Toribio Medina (Ercilla, *Araucana*, ed. Medina, 5:450), without giving exact references, suggests a relationship between "algunas pinturas de las guerras de Francia en Italia" which occur in *Orlando furioso* 32 (of Urrea's translation) and are presumably to be taken as a model for either Ercilla's description of the battle of Saint Quentin or the Battle of Lepanto seen in Fitón's magic globe.[47] The other critic indicated by Chevalier, Joseph G. Fucilla, briefly asserts in a footnote that Ariosto provided the model for "la bajada del Mago Fitón" (37 n. 6). A good argument can be developed to support this view, in spite of Chevalier's lack of enthusiasm for the thesis. In order to do so, however, it is necessary to understand Ercilla's approach to the Ariostesque subtext here as essentially dissimulative.

Ercilla's descent into the magician's cave, and the revelation there of his sovereign's future glories, are clearly reminiscent of Bradamante's precipitate *katabasis* in Merlin's tomb. The essentially ekphrastic vision of the Battle of Lepanto that Ercilla witnesses in Fitón's globe likewise corresponds both to the "future" history of House of Este represented by the swirling throng of Merlin's demonic familiars (*Orlando furioso* 3.22–59), the patently ekphrastic "future" history of Italy painted on the walls of Tristano's castle (*Orlando furioso* 33.3–58), and the similarily ekphrastic prophecy honoring Ippolito d'Este adorning the enchanted pavilion (*Orlando furioso* 46.76–99). But just as the intercalated stories of Tegualda and Glaura recall but do not neatly correspond to their Ariostesque models, Ercilla has also deliberately distanced his *katabasis* and ekphrastic vision of the future from the models in the *Orlando furioso*. Thus, presented with the opportunity of revising the poem in 1589, Ercilla further disguises the too-close correspondence of "lámpara" = "lampada" with "luz." Seen in this light, it becomes clear why Ercilla's essentially Virgilian, Ariostesque web of prophecy is so devoid of easily identifiable allusion, even when other models are being brought into the foreground and ostentatiously paraded before the reader.

A motivation for this emerges if we consider the extent to which Ercilla has tried to set himself up as a poetic antidote to Ariosto in Part I. This is especially cogent if we take into account the predominance of the Ariostesque model in the series of long poems in *octava rima* that precede the *Araucana* in Spain. As set out in section 3 of this chapter, with the notable exceptions of Garcilaso's *Egloga II* and Jerónimo de Urrea's translation of the *Orlando furioso*, Spanish imitations of Ariosto such as Espinosa's *La segunda parte de Orlando*, Garrido de Villena's *Roncesvalles*, Sempere's *Carolea*, and Zapata's *Carlo famoso* are all essentially both critical and artistic failures.[48] Ercilla, although he adapts much from the model presented by the *Orlando furioso*, deliberately distances his work from its less successful predecessors by setting himself in opposition to Ariosto from the outset. Thus it is precisely because he must rely on Ariosto's verse form, his narrative structure, and many of his descriptive devices, that he is so careful to dissimulate his imitation of specific episodes. This becomes especially true in Part II, where Ercilla feels obliged to vary the monotony of colonial war with diverse poetic "flowers," and the model of the *Orlando furioso* becomes even more imperative. Because he has set his dour Spanish *verismo* so sternly against the "laxity" of the Italian in Part I, he is constrained to dissimulate his "hurtos" from Ariosto as cleverly as he can.

On the other hand, the great success of *Os Lusíadas* may also partially explain why Ercilla avoids direct imitation of Virgil in Part II of the *Araucana*. Precisely because Camoens casts his modern, colonial-imperial poem so smoothly into a nearly perfect Virgilian mold, Ercilla may have wished to distance his response by avoiding direct imitation of Virgil, even when spinning out an essentially Virgilian web of prophecy. There is, in fact, an easily discernible logic that underlays Ercilla's choice of advertised, as opposed to dissimulated, models. This will become even more apparent when we take into account another major contributor to the mosaic of eclectic imitation that constitutes the prophetic scheme of Part II of the *Araucana*: Garcilaso.

2.4.3. Garcilaso and the Powers of the Natural Mage

If, as postulated in the preceding chapter, Ercilla crafts his self-fashioned image as a poet on the model of Garcilaso, it is certainly Garcilaso's example of highly transformative imitation that suggests itself as the most valid, and valued, imitative praxis for Ercilla.[49] Thus it is not surprising that Ercilla should find occasions to introduce examples of his own imitation of Garcilaso into the prophetic machinery of Part II of the *Araucana*.

In addition to generally following Garcilasist practices and approaches to *imitatio*, Ercilla also engages in direct allusion to subtexts taken from the master, considered by Ercilla to be the premier Iberian poet.[50] As studies by Eugenio Florit and Isaías Lerner have established, there are clear allusions to Garcilaso in the two *loci amoeni* that Ercilla interweaves into the early phases of his prophetic trajectory (Florit 48–49, 52; Lerner, "Garcilaso," 204). There is an even more cogent allusion to Garcilaso, however, in the very heart of the prophetic nexus of Part II, which has gone unnoticed by critics. In order to appreciate how this deliberately foregrounded imitation of Garcilaso meshes into the vatic system of Part II of the *Araucana*, it is necessary to return to Ercilla as he makes his way toward his *katabasis* in Fitón's cave.

The poet-protagonist Ercilla stumbles out of the "selva escura" to find himself, as the woman in white predicted (*Araucana* 18.62), face-to-face with an old man, his guide-to-be Guaticolo (*Araucana* 23.32). The young Spaniard explains that he seeks the enchanter Fitón (*Araucana* 23.34), and Guaticolo relates that he is the dread magician's nephew (*Araucana* 23.39). Before leading Ercilla to the sorceror's subterranean abode, Guaticolo delivers a peroration detailing the powers of the fearsome Araucanian wizard (*Araucana* 23.41–44). This speech along with Guaticolo's ingratiating, laudatory preamble to his request that Fitón aid Ercilla (*Araucana* 23.58–59) constitute Ercilla's rendering of a well-established literary topos: the description of the powers of the practitioner of the forbidden arts.

With roots in Greek letters, the locus flourished in the Augustan Age (Morford 67–68; Martindale 370), and Virgil gives an extremely abbreviated version when he has Dido describe an African priestess to her sister Anna as she secretly prepares her suicide (*Aeneid* 4.83–91). Ovid makes a far more detailed contribution to the topos, having Medea, along with Circe, the most notorious sorceress of Greek literature (Morford 67), boast of her own previous exploits as she invokes Hecate (*Metamorphoses* 7.199–209). Lucan's uncle Seneca the Philosopher has the Colchian witch reprise this performance in his *Medea* (752–70). But it is Lucan himself who brings the locus to its apogee (Morford 67), glorying first in the exploits of the witches of Thessaly (*Pharsalia* 6.434–506), then outdoing himself with the bizarrely hyperbolic excesses of the arch-necromanceress Erictho (*Pharsalia* 6.507–68). The locus is subsequently retailed on down through the Middle Ages and into the Renaissance.

As we have seen with the topos of the storm in Chapter 1, the long repetition, rearrangement, and reworking of the same or similar elements in the development of an essentially set-piece topic of this kind can render the analysis of imitation in a specific example very problematic unless the poet deliberately calls attention to a particular subtext. Ercilla, following in the footsteps of Garcilaso in this regard, always brings a certain eclecticism, originality, and enthusiasm for transformation to his imitative passages. Yet, unlike the systematic dissimulation of sources in the rendering of the storm at the end of Part I of the *Araucana*, Ercilla's essay of the locus of the mage's powers advertises its direct parentage.

Guaticolo begins his accolade of Fitón's thaumaturgical prowess with

> "Mas su saber y poder es tanto
> sobre las piedras, plantas y animales
> que alcança por su ciencia y arte quanto
> pueden todas las causas naturales,"
>
> (*Araucana* 23.41a–d)

None of the Latin authors mentioned above commence their versions of the topos in an even remotely similar manner. Garcilaso, however, opens his description of the sage Severo by having the shepherd Nemoroso declare:

> "A aquéste Phebo no le 'scondió nada,
> antes de piedras, yervas y animales
> diz que le fue noticia entera dada."
>
> (*Egloga II* 1074–76)

The sequence "piedras, plantas/yerbas y animales," occurring precisely at the beginning, is the telltale allusion that unequivocally signals Garcilaso's rendition of the locus as a privileged subtext. As Isaías Lerner has observed, it is typical of Ercilla to vary a single word, engaging in a sort of dialogue with Garcilaso, when he borrows a phrase from the master ("Garcilaso," 205–6). Thus Ercilla substitutes "plantas" for "yerbas" without altering the sense. Clearly, in keeping with his avoidance of Olympian mythological machinery, Ercilla must suppress Garcilaso's very first line. The constitutive character of the allusion, however, is unequivocal and is reinforced by further correspondences throughout the passage.

Although most of the remaining reminiscences are common to the tradition of the topos, there are still direct lexical points of contact between Ercilla's version and his Garcilasian subtext. For instance:

> "El raudo *curso* de los *Ríos enfrena*,
> y las aues en medio de su buelo
> vienen de golpe abaxo, amodorridas
> por sus *fuertes palabras* compelidas."
>
> (*Araucana* 23.42e–h; my italics)

"Este, quando le plaze, a los caudales
ríos el *curso* pressuroso *enfrena*
con *fuerça* de *palabras* y señales;"
                    (*Egloga II*, vv. 1077–79; my italics)

There are further correspondences, although perhaps less compelling. Clearly, too, Garcilaso's rendition of the topos is relatively brief, and he is trying to portray an Orphic enchanter capable of remedying "mal de amores," although Severo is also the medium of the ekphrastic prophecy of the urn, not a mantic mage like Fitón. For Ercilla, therefore, it is doubly necessary to expand and transform the model, adding material from the other major subtext employed in this passage, for reasons that I will explain below. The most important point here, however, is the initial linkage established with Garcilaso's prestigious rendering of the topos. This is significant, not merely for an ornamental, or even patriotic, identification with the great predecessor Garcilaso, but for the vital, constitutive sense of Ercilla's refashioning of the locus.

The development of the topos of the "powers of sorcery," in the Latin authors referred to above, centers around the figure of a witch: a female practitioner of illicit magic as opposed to established pagan religion.[51] She typically invokes the "unclean" deities of the infernal regions, not the "healthy" Olympians of the upper air. These female figures range from the highly idealized and attractive, like Virgil's African priestess and Ovid's Medea, through progressively more sinister representations such as Seneca's Medea, Horace's Canidia, and Ovid's Dipsas, to arrive at their most grotesque, and deliberately "anti-idealized," literary incarnation in Lucan's Erictho.[52] Nonetheless, all of these literary "daughters of Hecate" represent the dark, female side of the supernatural. They are typically associated with poison, and one trait commonly attributed to them, and a major constituent of the locus describing them, is their power to "pull down the Moon," and make it deposit poison on the earth. As emerges in Chapter 3, this is traditionally associated with menstruation and menstrual discharge.

Garcilaso includes this salient feature of the traditional rendition of the topos, but mitigates the subversive, female element by transmuting it into a hypothetical, contrary-to-fact statement:

"la luna d'allá 'riba baxaría
si al son de las palabras no impidiesse

el son del carro que la mueve y guía."

(*Egloga II*, vv. 1083–85)

Significantly, although this power is prominently featured in both of his principal subtexts, Ercilla suppresses it entirely. The explanation lies in the type of wizard that Ercilla wants to construct in Fitón.

El Brocense was the only early commentator on Garcilaso to link the figure of Severo to the wise Enareto of Sannazaro's *Arcadia* (Sánchez 205 n. 166; Azar 160 n. 17). Modern critics have, on the whole, concurred in this view (Azar 124).[53] It would appear that many have extrapolated the correspondences between the verses describing Severo's powers in the *Egloga II* and the citations from Sannazaro's "Prosa 9" indicated by El Brocense into an oft-repeated, if not entirely accurate, commonplace of the critical literature. Rafael Lapesa, for example, would have it that "los prodigios de Severo reproducen los de Enareto" (113). In fact, the sentences from "Prosa 9" of the *Arcadia* quoted by El Brocense in his commentary on *Egloga II* 1074–85 (Sánchez 204 n. 162; Garcilaso, *Obras*, ed. Rivers, 369) do not refer to the masculine, Apollonian mage Enareto at all, but rather to the female witch with whom he is contrasted.

Sannazaro has one of his lovesick shepherds, in desperation, ready to seek the aid of a certain "famosa vecchia, sagacissima maestra di magichi artifici. A la quale . . . Diana in sogno dimostrò tutte le erbe de la magica Circe e di Medea" (a famous old woman, a most shrewd mistress of magical arts. Diana, in dreams, taught her all the herblore of the enchantress Circe and of Medea) (*Arcadia* 137). This old woman, then, possesses precisely the arts of the two most famous literary witches of the tradition. Furthermore, she received her knowledge from Diana, who like Hecate is associated with the Moon; just as her brother Apollo often stands allegorically for the Sun, so the name Diana can represent the reflecting orb of illicit magic.[54] Sannazaro combines typically "low-genre" elements in her description with the standard "high-genre" features of the topos (see my note 52 above; Martindale 370–71). Thus, she is a shapeshifter, sprouting feathers to fly though the night "in forma di notturna strega" (in the shape of a nocturnal witch) (Sannazaro, *Arcadia*, 137). These qualities of the rustic witch of folklore are exalted and amplified by the powers over weather, the ability to reverse the course of rivers and turn night into day associated with the Medea figure of the "high" literary tradition.

Most significant, she can "imporre con sue parole legge al corso de la incantata luna" (control with her words the course of the enchanted Moon) (Sannazaro, *Arcadia*, 137). This, of course, is the key power of "pulling down the Moon," so central to the classical rendering of the locus and which Garcilaso mitigates and Ercilla completely eliminates from his imitation.

Sannazaro has deliberately created his female witch with this combination of folkloric elements and the lunar qualities of the literary witch in order to propose a superior alternative. The lovesick shepherd's companions are aghast at his desperate resolve, and one of them suggests another, healthier course, less dangerous to his future salvation. There is a wise old shepherd, Enareto, whom Sannazaro at one point calls a "santo pastore" (holy shepherd) (*Arcadia*, 140). The contrast with the witch figure could not be more clear. Clonico, the lovesick rustic, is urged to take advantage of the wisdom of Enareto, who in fact can counteract the nefarious effects of illicit magic (*Arcadia*, 140), rather than succumb to the temptation of the lunar, female sorceress. Enareto is represented as an Apollonian, Neoplatonic, masculine wiseman who, commanding saner, more licit forces, can bring genuine peace to the disturbed herdsman.[55]

In this sense, Garcilaso's Severo is indeed modeled on Enareto, although the textual imitation in the passage describing his powers is actually based on the description of the witch. As El Brocense indicates by the positioning of his glosses, only a brief part of the second description of Severo (*Egloga II* 1167) alludes directly to the powers of Enareto himself (Sánchez 205 n. 166).[56] Nonetheless, Severo receives his inspiration from Phoebus, not Phoebe (*Egloga II* 1074).[57] Much like Enareto, Severo is a Neoplatonic, Renaissance mage who represents the diametric opposite of the lunar witch. As Inés Azar explains:

> La sabiduría de Severo posee, en suma, los atributos básicos de la *magia natural*, que en la especulación de Ficino y de Pico era manifestación directa de los poderes del alma y resultado de su ascenso cognoscitivo hacia Dios. Por eso mismo, Severo es capaz de producir en los elementos naturales la *coincidentia oppositorum* postulada por Pico como principio operativo de su filosofía natural. Esa coincidencia de opuestos es, para el pensamiento neoplatónico renacentista, la cifra misma del Universo (múltiple, infinito y uno). Y es el conocimiento de esa realidad

última el que permite al neoplatónico Severo reconciliar contrarias calidades en el ámbito de la naturaleza física y en el de la humana. *Coincidentia oppositorum, discordia concors* son la cifra del universo, la fórmula íntima de la armonía y de la belleza, el principio operativo de la magia y del arte de Severo. (125)

The literary witch, in both her "high" and "low" avatars, draws her powers, if not directly from what W. R. Johnson calls the *discors machina* (16–18), at best from the least stable, most negative energies of the cosmic engine. The Renaissance mage who, like Enareto, Merlin, and Severo, stands on the threshold between pagan religion and doctrinally acceptable Neoplatonist theory, on the other hand, is the agent of *discordia concors*.

Thus it is no idle search for ornamentation that draws Ercilla unerringly to Garcilaso's Severo when he seeks a model for the enchanter Fitón. Like Severo, Fitón is a practitioner of what Azar calls "magia natural" (125) as opposed to the illicit witchcraft derived from the Moon. When Ercilla opens his description of Fitón's powers with the unequivocal allusion to Garcilaso's sketch of Severo, the reader is to understand that Fitón is cut from the same mold. Like Severo, Fitón will also be the medium of transmission for an ekphrastic, prophetic vision that enshrines an encomium to the poet's patron—in Garcilaso's case the duke of Alba, in Ercilla's Philip II.

Nonetheless, as Azar observes, this Orphic, Neoplatonic mage is also a master of *coincidentia oppositorum* (125). Severo can integrate most, if not all, of the powers of the witches into his Neoplatonic harmonizing of cosmic forces, as Garcilaso's rendering of the topos makes clear. In the same way, Fitón can reconcile the powers traditionally associated with Virgil's African priestess and Medea, as filtered and sanitized through Severo, with others that directly recall the most hyperbolic sorceresses of all Latin literature: the Thessalian witches of the *Pharsalia*.

As María Rosa Lida de Malkiel indicates, there is a strong odor of Lucan wafting about Ercilla's portrait of Fitón's powers (*Juan de Mena*, 503). Thus, although control over meteorological phenomena is a standard element of the locus, when Ercilla says of Fitón that "el mar rebuelue, el viento le obedece / contra la fuerça y orden de la Luna" (*Araucana* 23.43cd), we are perhaps meant to be reminded especially of

Lucan's "when the tide is driven on by the moon, the spells of Thessalian witches drive it back and defend the shore" (Impulsam sidere Tethyn / Reppulit Haemonium defenso litore carmen) (*Pharsalia* 6.479–80).[58] Even more reminiscent of Lucan are these lines of Ercilla's:

> "Tiembla la firme tierra, y se estremece
> a su voz eficaz sin causa alguna
> que le altere y remueua por de dentro
> apretándose rezio con su centro."
>
> (*Araucana* 23.43e–h)

Although the ability to shake the earth is a fairly common feature of the locus, only Lucan proclaims that as a result of the spells of the Thessalian witches:[59] "Tambien la tierra comouer el exe y asiento de su firmeza y titubear estribando y apretando se hazia el centro: y vn cuerpo de tanta espessura y quantidad como es, henderse por medio de manera que se pareciese el cielo de la otra parte" (Terra quoque inmoti concussit ponderis axem, / Et medium vergens nisu titubavit in orbem. / Tantae molis onus concussum voce recessit / Prospectumque dedit circumlabentis Olympi) (*Pharsalia* 6.481–84). Significantly, these two allusions to Lucan follow one upon the other both in the subtext and in Ercilla's imitation.

In a manner typical of his eclectic approach, Ercilla weaves in reminiscences of Erictho—the very incarnation of the *discors machina* (Johnson 19–20)—in his portrayal of Fitón's powers. Thus Ercilla concludes the second section of his rendition of the locus—recalling that Garcilaso's portrait of Severo falls into two parts—with an anticipation of Erictho's conjuring of the infernal powers:

> "Y por Mágica ciencia y saber puro,
> rompiendo el cabernoso y duro suelo,
> puedes en el profundo reyno escuro,
> meter la claridad y luz del Cielo:
> Y atormentar con áspero conjuro,
> la caterua infernal que con recelo,
> tiembla de tu eficaz fuerça que es tanta,
> que sus eternas leyes le quebranta,"
>
> (*Araucana* 23.59)

Unlike the other allusions to Lucan's description of the powers of the witches of Thessaly, this is less a textual imitation than an abbreviated paraphrase of Erictho's tongue-lashing invocation of the gods of the underworld, itself a well-worn topos (*Pharsalia* 6.695–718, 730–49). Specifically, Ercilla alludes to the second phase of Erictho's conjuration where, the infernal powers slow to comply, she threatens them with the light of the upper world (*Pharsalia* 6.733). Ercilla here anticipates his own textual imitation of this passage that he puts into Fitón's mouth in the conjuration of the mantic globe (*Araucana* 23.83).

This Lucanesque side of Fitón's character, however, must always been seen in Neoplatonic equilibrium with the Renaissance mage that Ercilla has found in Ariosto's Merlin and Atlante, and especially, Garcilaso's Severo. This is the sage enchanter of whom Ercilla has Guaticolo say:

> "Los otros poderosos Elementos
> a las palabras deste están sujetos,
> y a las causas de arriba y mouimientos
> haze perder la fuerça y los effectos,
> Al fin por su saber y encantamentos
> escudriña y entiende los secretos,
> y alcança por los Astros influentes
> los destinos y hados de las gentes."
>
> (*Araucana* 23.44)

We have here precisely the master of *magia natural* that Garcilaso has sketched in Severo. In this way, Ercilla has transformed what could otherwise be seen as merely one more piece in an eclectic imitation of Garcilaso into a determining, constitutive element of his own prophetic scheme.

This imitation of Garcilaso is significant for more than just the development of the character of Fitón. Unlike the imitations of Ariosto, and ultimately of Virgil, which we have seen Ercilla systematically dissimulate, this reminiscence of Garcilaso is pushed forward so that the competent reader cannot fail to notice the subtext. The importance of Garcilaso in general, and his *Egloga II* in particular, cannot be overemphasized in a reading of the *Araucana* that takes into account the dynamics of imitation.

2.4.4. The Logic of Ercilla's Dynamics of Dissimulation/Imitation of Subtexts

Contrasting the subtexts that are highlighted by unmistakable allusion with those that are dissimulated, we provide ourselves with a key for reading Ercilla's eclectic patchwork quilt of imitative practice in Part II of the *Araucana*. As we have seen, Ercilla goes out of his way to call our attention to his imitations of a number of passages from Juan de Mena's *Laberinto de Fortuna*. As demonstrated in detail in Chapter 3, Ercilla's most elaborate and unequivocally allusive imitation of the entire poem places Lucan's *Pharsalia* squarely in the spotlight. Garcilaso, particularly the *Egloga II*, is also foregrounded rather than dissimulated as a poetic model.

On the other hand, Ercilla borrows from Virgil, Ariosto, and other authors, but systematically disguises his debts as much as possible, despite the great prestige that these writers enjoy. In fact, Ercilla seems to be deliberately constructing his own poetic genealogy for the reader. Perhaps we can best elucidate Ercilla's practice in this regard by means of an analogy to an astute reading of learned commentaries that were current in Ercilla's time.

As mentioned above (section 2.2), Daniel Javitch has shown that sixteenth-century commentators on vernacular poets often deliberately distort the imitative provenience of the texts under discussion in order to further their canonization. Thus, for instance, Ludovico Dolce, in his oft-published commentary on the *Orlando furioso*, systematically foregrounds Ariosto's imitations of Virgil at the expense of medieval and vernacular Italian authors. According to Javitch's reading, Dolce evinces a programmatic effort to support Ariosto's candidacy as the modern Virgil ("Shaping," 265–69). Javitch notes that El Brocense engages in a similar exercise in his commentary on Garcilaso. Javitch suggests that El Brocense's purpose is to emphasize the prestigious classical genealogy of Garcilaso's imitations, and to demonstrate that the Spanish poet operates at parity with the newly canonized Italian poets. Thus, although El Brocense acknowledges the analogies between Garcilaso's texts and works of Italian poets such as Petrarch, Sannazaro, and Ariosto, the commentator always emphasizes the classical, and particularly the Virgilian, provenience of Garcilaso's imitations, even where the mediating, Italian subtext is patently more cogent (Javitch, "Shaping," 271–76).

This activity of deliberately staking a claim to a prestigious genealogy through the careful selection and foregrounding of certain authors in delineating the poetic ancestry of the text, however, is not always confined to the sphere of the commentator. Indeed, the first initiative in this type of project is always in the hands of the author, especially when the poet is working in a tradition deeply steeped in the practice of *imitatio*. Ercilla had before him the example of Garcilaso, a highly eclectic, selective, and transformative imitator, who, as even Javitch acknowledges, manipulates his subtexts in such a way that his filiation with the most prestigious classical models is recognizably insinuated, as is his parity with a select group of vernacular poets who have themselves achieved status almost comparable to that of the most exalted of the ancients (Javitch, "Shaping," 275–76). It should not be forgotten, furthermore, that Ercilla had before him not only the examples of the Italian commentaries on Ariosto, but also those of Fernán Núñez's editions of Juan de Mena and El Brocense's commentary on Garcilaso. It is thus far from surprising that Ercilla should attempt to create his own genealogy by clearly signaling his imitations of certain authors and systematically dissimulating his debts to others.

As I have indicated, the three poets who are most unequivocally invoked by Ercilla in Part II of the *Araucana* are Lucan, Juan de Mena, and Garcilaso.[60] Lucan, as explained at length in Chapter 3, was considered a particularly Spanish poet by Ercilla's contemporaries. Juan de Mena, as El Brocense's comments above illustrate, occupied a privileged position as the first to "make illustrious" the Castilian language. Garcilaso, clearly, was the optimum poet to have written in Spanish up to that time. Ercilla had begun the *Araucana* by contrasting his poetic enterprise with the morally lax Italian tradition of the *romanzi*. He had subsequently been obliged to temporize his initial outright rejection of the contamination of the historical epic with amorous fictions in his search for variety. In the all-important prophetic structure that, more than merely providing relief from monotony, serves the crucial function of tying the colonial action of his Castilian epic into the metropolitan sphere of empire, he is careful to preserve the "purity of blood" of the genealogy of his imitations. The reader is meant to recognize the allusions to Lucan, Mena, and Garcilaso, and either to ignore, to minimize, or in the case of the most perceptive reader, to admire as highly eclectic Garcilasist transformations, those to Ariosto and others, precisely because Ercilla is constructing an encomium to the Spanish empire of his sovereign Philip II.

Ercilla is not content to rely entirely on an eclectic mosaic of allusions that merely recall the prestigious, Castilian ancestry of his poem, however. As I demonstrate in the following chapter, Ercilla puts the seal on his cycle of prophecy by engaging in the most challenging type of imitation and emulation of a clearly identified model text, significantly invoking precisely Lucan and Juan de Mena. This in turn illustrates the degree to which Ercilla's imitative praxis is driven by the spur of poetic and dynastic rivalry.

3

Ercilla's Literary Necromancy

Shades of Lucan and Juan de Mena
in Fitón's Cave

Overshadowing the entire episode of the poet-protagonist Ercilla's descent into the cave of the enchanter Fitón in *Araucana* 23 looms the specter of *Aeneid* 6. Although Aeneas's penetration of Pluto's realm is, in part, an imitation of *Odyssey* 11, the immediate model for the *nekuia* or prophetic visit with the dead for most Renaissance poets, including Ercilla, is Virgil's poem rather than Homer's (Pierce, "Some Themes," 99–101).[1] It is the Roman poet who places the entrance to the underworld in a cave, and it is in a cave that Ariosto's dynastic heroine Bradamante has her prophetic encounter with Merlin's entombed spirit (*Orlando furioso* 2.70–3.23).[2] This last episode, itself recalling *Aeneid* 6 in important ways (Bigi, ed. 171; Fichter 84–85), is probably the immediate overall model for Ercilla's tour of the Chilean wizard's subterranean manse.[3] Nonetheless, as I have demonstrated in the preceding chapters, within this Ariostesque, and ultimately Virgilian, framework Ercilla weaves a complex fabric of essentially eclectic imitation that systematically dissimulates these models. In contrast, Ercilla deliberately foregrounds his "Spanish" predecessors Lucan, Juan de Mena, and Garcilaso in this intricately woven tapestry of imitation.

By far the most garish skeins that he draws upon are two episodes from the Latin poet Lucan's *Pharsalia*,[4] especially Lucan's own response to *Aeneid* 6, and Juan de Mena's imitation of that response. These are particularily significant for our exploration of Ercilla's web of prophecy because they reveal the poet's approach to another kind of imitation. As Thomas Greene points out (*Light*, 50), only where a "determinate subtext plays a constitutive role in a poem's meaning" can we really gauge the limits of a poet's imitative praxis. Because Ercilla does engage in a clearly identifiable, extended imitation of prestigious primary and secondary subtexts in the passages in question, and because they do play a key role in the spinning out of "constitutive meaning" in the web of prophecy, they present themselves for close examination as prime examples of how the author of the *Araucana* approaches what Greene calls necromantic imitation and Oedipal rivalry. This in turn will be fundamental for our reading of the climactic, decisive encounter with Camoens in the Araucan enchanter's shining globe to be explored in Chapters 4 and 5.

3.1. Lucan's Agonistic Invocation of the Shade of Virgil

If ever an epic poet struggled in a truly Bloomian, agonistic relationship with an awesomely successful and immediate predecessor, it was Marcus Annaeus Lucanus. The author of the *Pharsalia* suffered the peculiar doom of writing during the reign of Nero (A.D. 54–68), last and not the most loved of the Julio-Claudian emperors. Lucan, nephew of the poet, statesman, and imperial tutor Seneca the Philosopher, was born into the Roman aristocracy, and because of this, inherited both a close relationship with the megalomaniac young emperor and the prejudice of his class against the usurpation of republican liberties under the Caesars (Ahl 36–37, 40). The young poet also inherited a literary education, standard preparation for public life for a young aristocrat, that, along with the Greek classics, placed a highly canonical value on the exemplary work of a member of his grandfather's generation—Virgil (Graves 11).

Virgil had begun to write the *Aeneid* in 30 B.C., a year after Octavian's victory at Actium finally put an end to the horrendous cycle of civil wars that had wracked Roman society in the last years of the Republic. By the time he finished the poem in 19 B.C., his former acquaintance Octavian, now the emperor Augustus Caesar, had already gone a long way toward establishing the peace, order, and world empire that the shade of Anchises had proclaimed to Aeneas as the coming of a new golden age in *Aeneid* 6.791–94 (Virgil, *Aeneid*, ed. Williams, 1:xi–xiv). Although some modern critics may find Virgil's celebration of "Rome, Aeneas and Augustus . . . highly ambivalent" (Ahl 65), there is no doubt that the *Aeneid* immediately became the literary standard, the poetic *aquila legionis* of the empire of the Julio-Claudians, and that early on its author came to be touted as the Roman Homer (Graves 11). Roman poets who attempted the epic after Virgil, such as Lucan, Statius, or Silius Italicus, found it impossible not to become enmeshed in a struggle of imitation and rivalry with the Mantuan master that was much more immediate and intimidating than any Latin poet's relationship to the ancient Greek bard.

For Lucan the political element was easily as pressing as any purely poetic competition. The imperial golden age so lauded by Virgil was perceived by aristocrats of Lucan's generation as an insufferable despotism (Ahl 23). The brilliant young poet Lucan took up his pen not only to outdo but also to undo the literary emblem of Caesarism, just as Lucan the young senator would engage—fatally for himself and his family—in a doomed revolutionary conspiracy.[5] Although the Julio-Claudians had come to power as a result of a series of bloody civil wars, Virgil either glossed over or cautiously disguised the theme of civil war in the *Aeneid*; Lucan made indictment of the war between Julius Caesar and Pompey the leitmotiv of his *Pharsalia* (Ahl 65–67).

The *nekuia* of *Aeneid* 6 contains the "the decisive moment of the whole poem" (Virgil, *Aeneid*, ed. Williams, 1:505), where Anchises' ghost points out to Aeneas his future descendent, the emperor Augustus, and asks his son if he still fears to conquer Italy and found Rome (6.790–807). Lucan cannot hope to surpass his predecessor and deconstruct the Virgilian vision of Roman history without creating a devastating retort to *Aeneid* 6 (Tupet 419–20). This he attempts to do in *Pharsalia* 6. M. P. O. Morford summarizes the result very succinctly (66–67):

Wisely Lucan deliberately contrasts his *nekuia* with those of Homer and Virgil: he describes superstition, not religion; his inquirer is not an Odysseus or an Aeneas, but Sextus Pompeius, the unworthy son of a great father (6.420); the guide and interpreter is not a Teiresias, a Sibyl or an Anchises, but a witch capable of every sort of foul crime and unfit to live with other human beings (6.507–13). No rational account of the Underworld, compatible with Stoic doctrine is attempted; finally, the utterance of the dead man (6.777–820), far from presenting a pageant of Rome's future greatness (*Aen.* 6.756–853), brings onto the stage the demagogues who had destroyed the Roman constitution and foretells the immediate end of Roman law and liberty.

The episode is very long; it is morbid, sensational, hyperbolical. It is usually dismissed as mere rhetoric: yet it is still a careful account of the practice of necromancy, the fullest in Latin literature.

Much like Ercilla's tour of Fitón's cave, Sextus Pompey's consultation with the Thessalian witch Erictho often has been dismissed as digressive, yet a perceptive reader of the *Pharsalia* remarks that "la scène de magie, avec son horreur atroce, est le symbole et le pivot de l'oeuvre entière et qu'elle signifie beaucoup plus que les misérables pratiques qui y sont décrites" (the witch scene, with its atrocious horror, is the symbol and the central hub of the entire work and its significance goes far beyond the despicable practices that are described in it) (Tupet 425). Yet for Ercilla it is just these "misérables pratiques" that seem to offer the principal attraction. In order to understand both Ercilla's and Juan de Mena's disinterments of Lucan's hyperbolic "horreur atroce" it will be necessary to describe briefly the *nekuia* of *Pharsalia* 6.

3.1.1. Lucan's Model Necromancy: The Shades of Virgil and Ovid in *Pharsalia* 6

Pharsalia 6 opens with a siege and a series of military engagements on the Adriatic coast that end with Caesar withdrawing eastward toward

Thessaly and Pompey marching in pursuit (1–332).[6] This is followed by a description of Thessaly that includes both the physical and the mythological landscape and becomes increasingly sinister as it develops (vv. 333–412).[7] Toward the end of this sequence Lucan mentions that it was from Thessaly that the great oracular serpent Python slithered down to Delphi (vv. 407–9). It is quite probable that Ercilla, who seems to have been a careful reader of this section of the *Pharsalia*, was inspired to name his Chilean wizard by this passage.[8]

Lucan begins the episode of the *nekuia* by explaining that both armies are now encamped in Thessaly and that the imminence of the decisive battle weighs especially heavily on the minds of the morally degenerate in the opposing camps. One of these, Great Pompey's son Sextus, is driven by his fear to try to divine the future course of events. In keeping with his "unworthy" nature, Sextus rejects all respectable forms of divination in favor of the most repugnant and illicit means of foretelling his destiny, necromantic witchcraft (6.413–34). As Morford (66–67) has pointed out, the contrasts with *Aeneid* 6 could not be more clearcut or deliberate: Sextus, the depraved seeker, is the exact opposite of "pius Aeneas," and whereas Aeneas is motivated by self-abnegating patriotism, Sextus is impelled by craven fear and self-interest. Lucan underlines the reprehensible nature of Sextus's preferred oracle by creating a careful parallelism between the *nekuia* in Book 6 and Appius Claudius's unfruitful attempt in *Pharsalia* 5 to consult the licit, but defunct and inefficacious, oracle at Delphi out of a similar desire to save his own skin (Ahl 130–33).

Lucan now remarks that Sextus was influenced in his choice of oracle by the proximity of Thessaly and its witches (6.434–37). It is here that he reveals the immediate subtext for his necromancy by mentioning that it was in Thessaly that the "Colchian foreigner" once gathered magic herbs (6.441–42). The direct reference is to Ovid's description of how Medea, the "foreigner from Colchis," gathered potent ingredients for a necromantic potion from the vales and mountain slopes of Thessaly (*Metamorphoses* 7.222–31). Although *Aeneid* 6 is the target of his deconstructive imitation, Lucan clearly models many of the details of his necromancy on Medea's successful rejuvenation of her lover's moribund father and subsequent deceit of the daughters of Pelias in *Metamorphoses* 7.159–349 (Morford 67–68).[9]

The reference to Medea, along with Circe, the most famous witch of Greek literature (Morford 67), opens the door to a long description of

Thessalian witches and their exceptional magical prowess (*Pharsalia* 6.434–506). This passage develops with progressively hyperbolic intensification and culminates with reflections on the witches' power to overawe the gods themselves and control the movements of the celestial bodies (6.491–506). This, however, is only the preamble; Lucan goes on to tell us that there is one even more execrable witch, Erictho, who considers the abominations of the rest to be far too pious. She specializes in utilizing the illicitly gained body parts of the dead or dying in her ghoulish rites and is in regular communication with the Stygian regions (6.507–68).[10] In keeping with the rhetorical development of the whole episode, Lucan closes the description of Erictho by describing how she often rips open the mouth of a freshly buried corpse with her teeth and bites into its lifeless tongue in order to send an arcane message down into the shadows of the infernal realm (6.563–67). This is a clear prefiguration of the necromancy she will perform for Sextus in the passages that follow.

Sextus hears of Erictho and, seeking her out, explains that he must know how the coming battle will go (6.569–603). Erictho readily agrees to use her powers to aid him and explains how she will proceed (6.604–23). Thus the degenerate Sextus finds his sordid sibyl; again, the contrast with *Aeneid* 6 could not be more starkly drawn. The *nekuia* proper begins as Erictho sets out across the fields to select the body of a freshly killed, unburied soldier. Choosing a suitable corpse, the witch drags it by the neck to a cave mouth in a mountain gorge that falls away all the way down to the caverns of Dis (6.624–53). Because the basic subtexts for the actual necromantic revival of the dead man that follows are found in Ovid and Seneca, Lucan here draws special attention to details from *Aeneid* 6 so that the reader will not lose sight of the real target of his deconstructive imitation. The dark cave mouth surrounded by a thick wood that allows no light to enter directly recalls Virgil's description of the entrance to the underworld in *Aeneid* 6.237–41.[11]

After preparing herself and reassuring the frightened Sextus (*Pharsalia* 6.654–66), Erictho cuts open the corpse and pours in her necromantic brew (*Pharsalia* 6.667–84). According to Morford (71) this is principally an imitation of Medea's decoction described by Ovid in *Metamorphoses* 7.262–78, but Lucan expands and improves considerably on his source. In fact, not only does Erictho's potion contain substances more grotesque and more magical than Medea's, its ingredients are, for the most part, quite distinct from those used by Ovid's witch.[12] The exact contents of Erictho's decoction will be dealt with at some length when we examine Mena's and Ercilla's imitations of this passage.

Erictho's necromantic elixir still lacks an essential element before it can revive the corpse: her voice. Ovid merely tells us that Medea placated the gods of the underworld with "prayers and long murmur" (*Metamorphoses* 7.251). Seneca follows the nurse's description of how Medea prepared her poison with the Colchian witch's incantation (*Medea* 740-839).[13] Lucan improves upon his uncle's formula, and Erictho's invocation of the infernal powers becomes the classic model for subsequent renditions of this locus. The structure of the scene displays Lucan at his rhetorical best. The poet first describes the horrific qualities of Erictho's voice, and then has the witch call upon the familiar inhabitants of Pluto's realm with a hair-raising litany of her own criminal devotion (*Pharsalia* 6.685-718). This, however, is not sufficient, and the spirit of the dead soldier is still reluctant to reenter the corpse (6.719-25). Erictho, enraged, now threatens the denizens and powers of hell that she will reveal their true names, allow the light of the sun to illumine the depths, and, most terrible of all, call upon the nameless deity who dwells even below the halls of Tartarus and holds an oath sworn by Styx as nothing (6.725-49). The corpse instantly warms up as the blood begins to flow again, and Erictho is able to interview the spirit about what it has learned in the underworld (6.750-820). The vision is one of civil war among the shades of the great Romans of the past and looming disaster for the Roman future. It is a vicious satire of the patriotic, encomiastic presentation of Roman history in *Aeneid* 6.[14]

3.2. Ercilla's Motives for Resuscitating the *Nekuia* of *Pharsalia* 6

Why then, if Lucan's imitation of *Aeneid* 6 is a deliberate cheapening, a grotesque distortion, does Ercilla choose to privilege it in the telling of his own *katabasis*? There are probably three complementary answers. The first lies in the raw, horrific impact of Lucan's imagery. It must be remembered that the account of Erictho's necromancy, especially the list of magical substances and the witch's invocation of the powers of hell, is the most complete account of necromantic practice in Latin literature, probably based on a detailed knowledge of actual practices as well as literary sources (Morford 67, 71). Ercilla needs to imbue both the wizard Fitón and his abode with the maximum of awe and terror as economically as possible, precisely because the dread Araucanian sorcerer will prove, in the event, to be quite tame in his dealings with his poet-pupil. Fitón sets Ercilla no test of wit, strength, or skill, no golden bough is required, and the poet is not conducted past the fearsome guardians of the underworld as was Aeneas by the Sibyl. Even the craven Sextus Pompey had to steel himself to endure the sight of Erictho's gruesome rites, something his followers could not stomach (*Pharsalia* 6.657–58). In contrast, the wizened old Araucanian mage accepts a very meager ration of flattery and explanation (*Araucana* 23.63–64) in exchange for revealing the workings of the magic crystal that has cost him forty hard years of thaumaturgical application in solitude to fabricate (*Araucana* 23.71cd),[15] and Ercilla is not obliged to stain his hands by participating in any act of bloody witchcraft. Just like Bradamante in Merlin's tomb, Ercilla is the foreordained and somewhat passive recipient of forbidden knowledge. Of course, all this has come about as the result of prophecy, and like Aeneas, who also arrives at his katabasis as the result of a succession of prophecies, Ercilla must first pass through the terrors of the entrance to the underworld in some way, albeit considerably ameliorated in comparison with his classical predecessors, before being shown the glories of the future. If both Aeneas's consultation with his father's shade and Sextus Pompey's grisly interview with the revived corpse are types of the overtly pagan *nekuia*, Bradamante's instruction by the powers of Merlin's entombed spirit represents a transitional modification of this necromancy that is acceptable in late medieval romance and pre-Tridentine Italian epic. For Ercilla, however, writing in the second half of the sixteenth century and, moreover, a Spaniard, the only possible necromancy is purely literary—the revival, appropriation, and transformation of powerful ancient poetic images. No unquiet soul can literally be called back from the first porches of the pit here, no ancestral ghost can be consulted on the further banks of the Styx. As Ercilla and his guide, Guaticolo, walk entranced through the "bóveda de sustancias mágicas" (*Araucana* 23.48–55) the awe and terror inspired by the catalog of poisonous, grotesque, and magically potent substances and the reminiscence they invoke of the ghastly scenes in Thessaly and Libya must serve the same purpose as the dreadful specters passed by Aeneas and the Sibyl in their descent into the "jaws of hell" (*Aeneid* 6.273-425).

The second probable motive for Ercilla's recourse to the *Pharsalia* is closely linked to the third. For Ercilla, as for most literate Iberians of his time, Lucan was not only a revered but hopelessly remote figure from a distant, culturally superior Latin past; but born in Roman Corduba, he was also perceived as a direct ancestor, a fellow Spaniard (Curtius 387).[16] Ercilla must deal with the *Pharsalia* because it was seen as part of the national literature, the first great epic poem written by a "Spaniard." This point has not always been adequately elucidated. Dieter Janik, for instance, in his excellent overview of Lucan's influence on the *Araucana*, explains that Ercilla chose the *Pharsalia* from among the possible classical models because it was the only well-known prototype of a historical rather than a mythological poem (103).[17] This is undisputably true, but it is not the whole story; literary tradition should not be ignored in this matter. Sulpitius, in his oft-consulted commentary on the *Pharsalia*, indicates that the study of Lucan is of special relevance to the Spaniards (*M. Annei Lucani Cordubensis*, fol. AAv v).[18] The introduction to Lasso de Oropesa's early sixteenth-century (c. 1535) translation of the poem also emphasizes Lucan's Spanish nationality (fol. Aii v).[19] This tradition continued in the seventeenth century. Francisco Cascales referred to "nuestro Lucano" (50), and Sebastián de Armendáriz, in the introduction to his 1684 edition of Juan de Jáuregui's translation of the *Pharsalia*, insisted on the point at length (2:307-14). According to León Pinelo, a representation of Lucan was included among those of nine "Spanish" poets that adorned a "Monte Parnaso" erected for a festival in Madrid in 1649 (Mena, *Laberinto de Fortuna*, ed. Blecua, c).[20] The most compelling testimony, however, comes from a close contemporary of Ercilla. Fernando de Herrera, in his commentary on Garcilaso's *Elegía II*, mentions that Lucan, too, contributed to the tradition behind verse 175 in the following terms: "Lucano, si permiten los que aborrecen el nombre español que se cuente entre los poetas que tienen estimación, trató también este lugar" (Gallego Morell H-401).[21] It is the weight of this tradition, at least in part, that drew Ercilla into a necromantic relationship with his Cordovan forerunner.

The third reason for resuscitating Lucan's frightful imagery arises from Ercilla's perception of his own relationship with another powerful, much more immediate, predecessor, Juan de Mena. As has been demonstrated in Chapter 2, Ercilla launches the prophetic structure that brings him to Fitón's cave on the model provided by Mena's *Laberinto de Fortuna*.[22] Nowhere, however, is the complexity of Ercilla's relationship with Mena more apparent than in his imitation of *Pharsalia* 6. If in the episodes of Bellona and the "Lady in White" Ercilla follows Mena as a dutiful son follows a beloved father, in the passages that describe the "chamber of magical substances" and the "conjuration of the infernal powers" Ercilla exerts himself both to invoke the power of Mena's verses and, at the same time, to distance himself from Mena's imitation of Lucan in order to demonstrate the superiority of his own necromantic revival of the common subtext. This shift in Ercilla's approach to his predecessor's work is due to two factors: (1) because both Mena and Ercilla are engaged in the imitation of the same prestigious and powerful model, it is Ercilla's best opportunity to measure himself against the tradition and Oedipally replace Mena's revivification of Lucan with his own; and (2) because Mena's imitation of Lucan's *nekuia* introduces the culminating episode of the *Laberinto de Fortuna*, Ercilla is able to draw attention to the importance of his visit to Fitón's cave by positioning his imitation of both Lucan and Mena as the introduction to his "prophetic" vision of the Battle of Lepanto. This last point requires some explanation before we proceed to examine Mena's imitation of Lucan.

3.3. The Witch Episode in the Structure of the *Laberinto de Fortuna* and Its Significance for Ercilla

Mena's mid-fifteenth-century *Laberinto de Fortuna* is no abstract medieval meditation on the vagaries of fortune, as the title might suggest. On the contrary, it is an intensely political, propagandistic attempt on the part of the poet to influence his monarch in favor of the person and policies of Alvaro de Luna, the powerful but controversial constable of Castile (Deyermond 163–64). As King John II's chief minister, Luna was struggling to assert the central authority of the crown over the unruly and fractious great nobles so that the stalled enterprise of the Reconquest could be sparked back into motion. The high nobility, however, resisted this program tenaciously and sought to undo the constable by every means possible—perhaps even resorting to witchcraft (Deyermond 159; Lida de Malkiel 79). On the other hand, the emerging class of royal bureaucrats supported Luna. Juan de Mena, the king's Latin secretary, dedicated his poem to his literarily inclined royal master, with the clear intention of convincing John II that his best and only chance of achieving greatness and lasting fame lay in continued support of his constable (Deyermond 159, 163–64).[23]

The basic architecture of the *Laberinto de Fortuna* has been amply delineated.[24] On one hand, Mena sets up the system of the three wheels of Fortune (*Laberinto de Fortuna* 56–61)—past, present, and future—and on the other, the Ptolemaic scheme of a geocentric universe composed of concentric spheres ascending through the medieval solar system of seven planets (*Laberinto de Fortuna* 62). Of the three great wheels, only two can be clearly descried. Mena's guide, Divine Providence, admonishes that knowledge of the future belongs to God alone, and that it is vain for mortals to presume to penetrate the veils that enshroud the third wheel (*Laberinto de Fortuna* 59–60). Nonetheless, time and space intersect in a grand allegory as the poet perceives that each of the other two of Fortune's wheels is woven of seven orbs.[25] Each of the seven rings is crowded with human figures, all worthy of note (*Laberinto de Fortuna* 62e–h).

Philip Gericke, in his groundbreaking 1968 article "The Narrative Structure of the *Laberinto de Fortuna*" (514), has pointed out that Mena's "wheels of Fortune turn out not to be wheels of Fortune at all. They are 'wheels of Providence' in that they allegorize the reward of virtue and the punishment of vice; they symbolize, not instability, but its opposite." Gericke goes on to demonstrate that Mena has ordered his allegorical universe in a very deliberate manner. Spheres I–IV, which is to say those of the Moon, Mercury, Venus, and the Sun, contain primarily examples from the past that illustrate the power of Providence. According to Gericke, this section prepares the ground for what is really the central core of the poem (515–16). Spheres V–VII, those of Mars, Jupiter, and Saturn, stand in an antithetical relationship to I–IV (515). Where I–IV are characterized by order, V–VII are dominated by Fortune and chaos, and the focus shifts to the present and, more important, to Spain. In sphere V Mena presents a series of eight contemporary noblemen who achieve transitory greatness through their own moral rectitude, but who are inevitably brought down by the hand of fickle Fortune (*Laberinto de Fortuna* 138–213; Gericke 517–18). Mena opens sphere VI with Augustus Caesar (*Laberinto de Fortuna* 215) as the first of a group of exemplary figures from the past, and then passes on to the present with none other than his own master, King John II of Castile (*Laberinto de Fortuna* 220–22). Mena clearly indicates that John II, too, may be another Augustus, if only he will seize the occasion (*Laberinto de Fortuna* 230). The direct appeal here is that the king exercise "justiçia" against those who serve him falsely. The practical application of this advice becomes immediately apparent as Mena passes on to the seventh sphere, that of Saturn, and beholds the figure of none other than the constable, Alvaro de Luna (*Laberinto de Fortuna* 233–35).

As Gericke has indicated, Luna is directly contrasted with the noblemen of sphere V who were undone by Fortune (519). Divine Providence, still Mena's guide, declares that: "Este cavalga sobre la Fortuna / y doma su cuello con ásperas riendas" (*Laberinto de Fortuna* 235*ab*). It is clear that Mena has reached the most crucial moment of his poem; here he must demonstrate to his sovereign the decisive superiority of Alvaro de Luna over the treacherous grandees who oppose the constable and his policies. Simply put, at this juncture Mena has need of his most brilliant literary fireworks. It is no mere coincidence, then, that the poet calls upon the shade of Lucan and places his imitation of the Erictho episode from *Pharsalia* 6 at this point in the text.

Furthermore, it must be remembered that the *Laberinto de Fortuna* is no eclectic string of imitative episodes of more or less equal density. Mena, of course, engages in highly selective imitation of a multiplicity of models in individual verses and passages, as María Rosa Lida de Malkiel has so amply demonstrated (*Juan de Mena*, 15–83). Nevertheless, apart from the mapamundi (*Laberinto de Fortuna* 34–53), the scene of the sorceress of Valladolid stands alone as a long, highly developed narrative passage that is so closely hewn to the exact measure of a single, clearly identifiable subtext.[26]

Ercilla shows himself throughout the *Araucana* to have been a very careful reader of the *Laberinto de Fortuna*, just as he was a careful reader of the *Pharsalia*. It is thus very improbable that he was unaware of the importance of the Erictho episode in Lucan's poem and its imitation in Mena's. All of this supports Jaime Concha's argument that, far from being a digression, Ercilla's depiction of Spain's great naval triumph is a key element in the imperialistic unity of the poem ("El otro nuevo mundo," 41–45). Ercilla, cognizant of Mena's use of the common subtext, signals the importance of his own central prophetic episode by placing his own imitation of *Pharsalia* 6 at this particular point in the *Araucana*.

Before proceeding with the examination of Mena's use of the Erictho episode, however, it is first prudent to establish that Mena did, indeed, find his essential subtext in Lucan. This is necessary because no less a scholar than María Rosa Lida de Malkiel has called into question the importance of *Pharsalia* 6 for the "maga de Valladolid" passage.

3.3.1. Mena's Witch Episode: Confluence of *Imitatio* and Historical Event?

María Rosa Lida de Malkiel, in her intimidatingly erudite *Juan de Mena: poeta del prerrenacimiento español*, begins her section on "La maga y el Condestable" by calling it the best opportunity to appreciate Mena in the demanding role of historical poet (79). This, of course, comes as something of a surprise for the reader who is accustomed to thinking of the episode as an exercise in imitation. The Argentine scholar bases her affirmation of the historicity of the event on some remarks included by Fernán Núñez ("El Comendador Griego") in his commentary on *Laberinto de Fortuna* 238. In one of his extensive glosses, Núñez includes an account of the matter that makes a claim to tie the poetic necromancy to a historical séance, and which forms the basis of Lida de Malkiel's position:

> Estando en la villa de Llerena oy a un hombre anciano y digno de creer que los de la valia del Condestable se aconsejaua*n* con vna maga que estaua en Valladolid, y los que seguian el partido de los Infantes se aconsejauan con vn religioso frayle de la Mejorada que es Monesterio cabe la villa de Olmedo, el qual era gran nigromantico, y assi mismo co*mo* Do*n* Enrrique de Villena, y que la sobredicha maga dixo que el Condestable auia de ser

> hecho pieças, lo qual salio despues verdad quando lo degollaron aunq*ue* Iuan de Mena por fauorecer al Co*n*destable, dize q*ue* ya fue complido en el bulto del dicho Condestable, segun dicho es. (1552 [Nucio], fol. 202r)

That we are dealing here with at least a semihistorical, rather than a purely poetic, version of events is apparent from the denouement. Luna was ultimately executed by John II in 1453, some nine years after Mena completed his poem (Deyermond 165). Obviously, when Lida de Malkiel says, "Quedó entre las gentes, todavía en la época de Hernán Núñez, el recuerdo de las consultas hechas ya por los partidarios, ya por adversarios de don Alvaro de Luna a una hechicera de Valladolid o a un fraile nigromante de Olmedo" (79), she is referring directly to what Núñez claimed to have heard from "un hombre anciano y digno de creer."

Of course, that an old man of Núñez's aquaintaince might have conserved the memory of a rumor about the recourse to forbidden arts by the followers of, on the one hand, the constable, and on the other, the grandees, is not in itself conclusive evidence that such consultations in fact took place. Mena finished the *Laberinto de Fortuna* in February of 1444 (Deyermond 164), so the necromantic séance in Valladolid, if something like it did indeed occur at all, must have taken place before that date. In fact, another comment by Fernán Núñez, in the gloss on *Laberinto de Fortuna* 263, permits us to place the episode with some precision. Núñez states that

> estando el rey Don Iuan en la villa de Medina del campo le cercaron el rey de Navarra y el Infante don Enrrique su primo y el principe Don Enrrique su hijo, y otros muchos caualleros. Y como se entro en la villa por fuerça, y el Condestable don Aluaro de Luna se saluo a vña de cauallo y se vino huyendo a Castilla a su villa de Escalona. Por lo qual ento*n*ces muchos de los que antes eran de su valia pensando que yua ya su estado en diminucion y que no tornaria mas al ma*n*do que solia tener le desampararon, avnque el Poeta fingia auer sido otra la causa. (1552 [Nucio], fols. 218v–219r)

The situation that Núñez describes here, when Luna was forced to flee precipitately from Medina del Campo, occurred on the night of 28–29

June 1441 (Suárez Fernández 170–71). Because Núñez specifically links this incident to the abandonment of Luna by his fainthearted followers that the "Poet represented as being due to another cause" in the context of the denouement of the "maga" episode, we can say with considerable certainty that the fictive time of Mena's necromancy was late June of 1441.

Fernán Núñez's commentary on the *Laberinto de Fortuna* was first published in 1499 (Street, "Hernán Núñez," 58–59), but Núñez did not add the reference to the "old man of Llerena" until his revision of 1505.[27] Thus there is a gap of sixty-four years between the putative séance conducted by the "maga de Valladolid" and the first report of it independent of Mena's own verses. It is still not totally improbable that Núñez—born about 1470–75 (Street, "Hernán Núñez," 53)—could have heard the tale from an elderly informant contemporary with the supposed event. Nevertheless, it should not be forgotten that the *Laberinto de Fortuna* circulated widely in manuscript between 1444 and 1505—at least twenty-one manuscripts containing the poem are known to have survived from the period[28]—and there were at least three printings between about 1481 and 1496 before Núñez's first edition appeared in 1499 (Street, "Hernán Núñez," 55). The poem itself could easily have planted the seed of a popular belief that such an episode in fact occurred. Furthermore, even if the story circulated independently of the *Laberinto de Fortuna*, it would more likely represent malicious political propaganda than a truly "historical" event, however people, Mena included, may have taken it.[29] Finally, it is not particularily compelling that the unique source of the supposed anecdote should himself explicitly state, as we have seen above, that Mena, engaging in poetic licence, feigned (*fingía*) that Luna's partisans sought to disassociate themselves from their former benefactor because of the witch's prophecy when the "historical" cause was the reverse suffered by the constable in Medina del Campo (Núñez 1552 [Nucio], fol. 219r). Unlike the "old man in Llerena" story, this version of events is found in both the 1499 and 1505 versions of Núñez's commentary (1499, fol. 177r).

Curiously enough, some classical scholars have made an argument very similar to Lida de Malkiel's in regard to the Erictho episode itself, proposing that Lucan, in addition to the apparent literary models, was reflecting some historical circumstance. Pierre Grenade, for instance, dredges up a number of ancient references to the practice of necromantic sorcery on the part of Pompey's descendants, positing that such activities may have inspired Lucan to portray a prominent Pompean engaged in forbidden arts (28–36). Both Grenade and Frederick M. Ahl are impressed by the similarities between Lucan's rendition of the dead soldier's prophecy for Sextus Pompey and a story told by Pliny about a Caesarian soldier executed by Sextus in Sicily who prophesied before he expired (Grenade 37–40; Ahl 133–37). In fact, the case for Lucan drawing on some historical or "real life" elements is perhaps, in a very general sense, somewhat more convincing than that proposed for Mena. Even so, the preponderance of available evidence—the obvious references to literary subtexts—points to the most plausible and least tortuous hypothesis. C. A. Martindale makes a convincing argument that the *nekuia* of the *Pharsalia* is based on Lucan's reading of both literary texts and manuals of magic, and not any historical event (367–73). I think that much the same case can be made for Mena's necromancy as well. Lida de Malkiel, in fact, may well have suspected as much herself, because she quickly goes on to temper her initial remark about how the episode reveals Mena as a "historical" poet by saying that "es la recreación de una anécdota actual, apenas fijada en sus rasgos más generales, a través del episodio de la hechicera Ericto en la *Farsalia* y de los datos prestigiosos de la poesía antigua" (Lida de Malkiel, *Juan de Mena*, 79). As the reader rapidly discovers, her principal concern here is not so much the aspect of historicity, but demonstrating Mena's originality and independence from his models, especially Lucan. Where she has drawn on Fernán Núñez's meticulous commentary for the possibly historical anecdote, she sets up Menéndez y Pelayo and Francisco Sánchez de las Brozas (El Brocense), as the straw men whose assertion that "esto todo es de Lucano" she will demolish (79). She is particularly harsh with El Brocense, who "emprendió como trabajo de vacaciones la edición y anotación del *Laberinto*, y más de una nota arrastra la huella de tal precipitación" (83). What she "left in her inkwell," however, is how closely Fernán Núñez collates the *coplas* of Mena's "maga de Valladolid" passage with the Erictho episode of the *Pharsalia*.

Núñez begins his gloss on the "maga" section with *Laberinto de Fortuna* 238, where he commences "Lucano en el sexto libro de la *Pharsalia* escriue que estando Pompeyo y Cesar en Macedonia," reprising Lucan's entire account of the matter in some detail, and concluding "esta fabula y fiction de Lucano imita aqui Iuan de Mena, siguiendo en todo las pisadas de Lucano" (1552 [Nucio], fol. 202r).[30] Indeed, Núñez's verse-by-verse comparison of Mena's imitation—Núñez himself uses the term—is far more extensive and detailed than that of El Brocense (Sánchez 292–96).

Lida de Malkiel pursues two other lines of attack. She notes, quite aptly, that Mena abbreviates his subtext considerably (Lida de Malkiel, *Juan de Mena*, 79–80), and she makes every effort to demonstrate that Mena has introduced elements from a variety of poetic models as well as his own experience (81–83). Throughout, she insists on not only Mena's relative independence from Lucan, but also his aesthetic superiority (80–81). Yet the surest method of demonstrating that Mena indeed was engaged in an exercise in imitation, and what type of imitation it is, will be a close analysis of the "maga de Valladolid" episode, bearing in mind what has already been discussed about *Pharsalia* 6. There will be several occasions to refer back to Lida de Malkiel's "defense" of Mena as this examination unfolds. Before we enter into the magic circle of Mena's *nekuia*, however, yet one more essential parameter must be established.

3.3.2. The Importance of the Fernán Núñez Editions of the *Laberinto de Fortuna* for the Composition of the *Araucana*

Editors of post-1968 editions of the *Laberinto de Fortuna* for the most part have based their texts on MS. 229 of the Bibliothèque Nationale in Paris, which they considered closer to Mena's original than any of the early printed editions and which was thought perhaps to reproduce Mena's own glosses on difficult passages. A partial exception to this trend is Maxim P. A. M. Kerkhof's 1995 critical edition, which is based on a careful comparison of all of the extant manuscripts as well as the early printed texts (Mena, *Laberinto de Fortuna*, ed. Kerkhof, 81–83). Kerkhof's edition seems destined to serve as the basis for serious study of the *Laberinto de Fortuna* for some time to come. Nonetheless, just as A. E. Housman's highly regarded 1926 revision of the text of the *Pharsalia*—upon which the Loeb edition is based (Lucan, *The Civil War*, ed. Duff, vii)—is not as useful for the investigation of Ercilla's possible knowledge of Lucan as the various "less accurate" sixteenth-century editions, so too Fernán Núñez's highly emended text of the *Laberinto de Fortuna*, in spite of its possible deviations from Mena's "original," is to be preferred for the study of Ercilla's reception and transformation of elements of Mena's poem.[31]

Curiously, José Toribio Medina omits the *Laberinto de Fortuna* from the books with which he thought Ercilla would have been familiar (*Vida*, 23–25). Nonetheless, it is obvious to any observant reader of the *Araucana* that Ercilla must have studied Mena's poem very carefully. Although it is conceivable that Ercilla could have come across one of the many manuscript copies or one of the pre-1499 printings of the *Laberinto de Fortuna*, the most probable case is that he would have consulted one of the numerous reprintings of Fernán Núñez's 1505 edition. This is especially likely if it was the royal tutor, Juan Cristóbal Calvete de la Estrella, who introduced the young Ercilla to Mena's most important poem. It is inconceivable that a scholar such as Calvete de la Estrella would not have known or insisted on using Núñez's highly glossed and corrected text. Although a well-connected humanist such as Calvete de la Estrella might indeed have possessed a copy of the relatively rare 1499 version of Núñez's edition, it is far more likely that Ercilla's preceptor would have had his pupils read one of the many, more available reprintings of the revised 1505 edition.[32] No less than eleven printings of this text appeared between 1505 and 1548 (including one in Toledo precisely in 1548), the year when Ercilla came under Calvete de la Estrella's tutelage (Kerkhof, "El *Laberinto*," 322–23; Medina, *Vida*, 22).[33] Three further reprintings appeared (the last in 1566) before Ercilla published Part I of the *Araucana* in 1569, and, in fact, no competing edition of the *Laberinto de Fortuna* was to appear in print at all between 1505 and 1582 (Kerkhof, "El *Laberinto*," 322–24).[34]

That Ercilla almost certainly knew the *Laberinto de Fortuna* through Núñez's edition is important for more than just details of the text of Mena's verses. It means that in his approach to both Lucan and Mena, Ercilla would have had the benefit of Núñez's considerable scholarship in addition to his own, perhaps very limited, reading in classical texts. Thus in the examination of Mena's rendering of the *nekuia*, Fernán Núñez's commentaries on the *Laberinto de Fortuna* will illuminate not only Mena's imitation of Lucan, but also Ercilla's necromantic strategies relative to both of his principal subtexts.

3.4. The Principal Subtexts Underlying Ercilla's Most Ambitious Literary Necromancy: Mena, Lucan, and Ovid

The resuscitation of two key passages from the scenes of necromantic witchcraft portrayed by Lucan, and then imitated by Mena, represents Ercilla's most clearly advertised and poetically ambitious exercise in what Thomas Greene has characterized as heuristic imitation. As has been delineated in detail in Chapter 1, section 1.3, Greene uses the metaphor of necromancy to describe the revival of "dead" verses inscribed with the cultural and linguistic codes of a former age (*Light*, 37–38). The poet engaged in this highly competitive type of imitation must select a subtext that is well known, and through the transformative magic of his imitation, bring that text back to life and make it sing of new things without dissipating the aura of power conferred by the subtext's original authority. For the Iberian poets of Ercilla's generation, the most compelling model of this type of imitation was Garcilaso. In chapter 1.3, Garcilaso's sonnet "En tanto que de rosa y d'açucena" has been referred to as a particularly cogent example of this type of literary necromancy. The reader will recall that one of the most distinctively "necromantic" features of Garcilaso's imitation in that sonnet is the calculated invocation of a layered series of related subtexts. Garcilaso not only engages contemporaries like Bernardo Tasso and Pietro Bembo, but also alludes to their model, Petrarch. Nor is it sufficient for Garcilaso to highlight the Petrarchan subtext; he must also engage in a subtle dialogue with Petrarch by inserting a sly reminiscence of the Italian master's own key subtext, Virgil's description of Venus. This dynamic excavation of the complex archaeology of the subtext is a key feature of Garcilasist imitative practice. Because Ercilla brings exactly this type of necromantic approach to his revivification of crucial passages from the famous *nekuia* episode of the *Pharsalia*, it is therefore necessary to explore the underlying strata of imitations evoked by the poet of the *Araucana* in some detail. Juan de Mena's rendition of Lucan's model necromancy plays a pivotal role in Ercilla's imitation, and therefore this exploration of the locus in question begins from the perspective of Mena's approach to Lucan. This, in turn, requires that we investigate Lucan's own emulation of his major subtext, Ovid's description of Medea's rejuvenation of Aeson. The comparison of Mena's essentially reproductive approach to imitation in this passage with the competitive transformation that characterizes Lucan's emulation of Ovid will then provide the essential context for deciphering Ercilla's most ambitious exercise in necromantic Garcilasist *imitatio*.

3.4.1. Mena's Imitation of Lucan's Nekuia

Mena is characteristically economical in his approach to exhuming the ghoulish potency of Lucan's *nekuia*. Lucan takes advantage of the greater space afforded by the more porous and extensive framework of his poem and dedicates approximately 415 hexameters—half of *Pharsalia* 6—to the development of Erictho's necromancy. He takes care to orchestrate the rhetoric of horror and revulsion in an incremental series of crescendos, because he is literally working against all of the density and majesty of *Aeneid* 6. Mena, on the other hand, is writing within a much more circumscribed structure. In order to highlight Alvaro de Luna's dominion over Fortune, Mena needs to select only the most memorable, and the most appropriate, passages from his model. Lucan has to establish the hyperbolically depraved nature of his anti-Sibyl at great length, in part because her immediate prototype, Medea, is far too appealing a figure for his purpose (Martindale 371). In contrast, Mena has the luxury of being able to rely on a reasonably well-read reader's recollection of Erictho and her Thessalian sisterhood's outrageous crimes and degeneracy to imbue his own "persona muy encantadera" with more than enough of an aura of evil and the forbidden to suit the requirements of the episode without going into great detail in the description of her powers. In the same way, the timorous, fair-weather friends of the constable stand revealed in the spectral aura of cowardice projected across the centuries by Lucan's rendering of the craven Sextus Pompey. Lucan's forty-five hexameters describing how Erictho selects the unburied body of a legionnaire, drags it with a hook to a gloomy cave and prepares to begin her grisly rites, likewise permit Mena to condense the whole process into one eight-line *copla* without losing either the hair-raising revulsion of the subtext or the rapid pace of his own narration (*Pharsalia* 6.624–66; *Laberinto de Fortuna* 245).

Because he has chosen to reproduce the device of the necromantic revival of a corpse that will become the vessel of prophecy, Mena selects for detailed imitative resurrection precisely the segments from his model that deal most directly with the sorceress's violent and transitory resuscitation of the unfortunate soldier's cadaver. The two most thoroughly developed of these are the list of horrendous ingredients that make up the witch's necromantic decoction and the hair-raising invocation of the infernal powers that finally results in the prophetic revival of the dead soldier. Not coincidentally, these are also the two Lucanesque loci that Ercilla conjures up in his descent into Fitón's subterranean manse. Consequently, a close examination of the successive recreation or transformation of either of these two passages will provide one of the best opportunities to evaluate Ercilla's approach to imitation in a context where he is most eager to display his powers at their fullest. Because the "horrísono conjuro" is more of a set piece and is recreated by so many authors, in so many contexts, over the centuries, it is the less apt of the two for a study of necromantic imitation. Therefore, the following analysis will concentrate on the list of frightful ingredients.

According to C. A. Martindale, Lucan's list of magically charged ingredients is based entirely on literary models. The principal subtext is Ovid's description of the potion prepared by Medea for the rejuvenation of Aeson in *Metamorphoses* 7.262–78. Martindale characterizes Lucan's approach as *aemulatio* (372). As George Pigman has pointed out, *aemulatio*, or emulation, is an inherently competitive mode of imitation that demands that the subtext be made explicit in such a way that the reader is moved to compare the emulation directly with its model; if the emulation is successful, it will clearly outshine the subtext (26).[35] Reading Mena's and Ercilla's common subtext as itself a notoriously triumphant instance of *aemulatio* provides the "magic formula" that unlocks and reveals the inner processes of their respective imitations.

3.4.1.1. Erictho's Necromantic Brew as an Emulation of Medea's Recipe for Rejuvenation

Ovid's Medea may well seem charming and benign in comparison with Erictho, but she is no garden-variety gatherer of herbs and brewer of philters. The entire world serves as her apothecary chest: into her bronze cauldron Medea pours roots, seeds, blossoms, and juices collected in the high vales of Thessaly (*Metamorphoses* 7.264–65), and she has fetched stones from the remotest reaches of the Orient and sands washed by the waters of world-girdling Ocean's stream to season her potion (*Metamorphoses* 7.266–67). To these she adds frosty dews garnered beneath the full moon, the wings and flesh of a horned owl, and the entrails of a shape-shifting werewolf (*Metamorphoses* 7.268–71). Up to this point Ovid has used verbs (*adjicio, addo*) that express a positive act of enhancement to indicate how Medea introduces ingredients into her concoction. Now, perhaps for the sake of variety, he switches to impersonal litotes, saying that there lacked neither (*nec defuit*) the scaly skin of a Libyan water snake nor the liver of an aged stag (*Metamorphoses* 7.271–73). Shifting back to positive enumeration (*addo*), Ovid relates that Medea throws in the eggs and head of a crow that has endured for nine generations (*Metamorphoses* 7.273–74).[36] Ovid wraps things up by saying that the witch prepared for her design with all of the aforementioned substances, as well as a thousand other, nameless things (*Metamorphoses* 7.275–76).

Ovid's rendition of the list of Medea's magic ingredients is one of the longest and most developed descriptions of the mixing of a magic elixir that Lucan could have found in Latin literature.[37] Quite aside from its obvious cogency for the *nekuia* of the *Pharsalia*, the passage would have presented a tempting target for emulation on its merits alone, as the best of its type. For this reason, Lucan invokes all of his considerable powers of hyperbole and skill at evoking horror in his attempt to surpass it.

For his opening, Lucan eschews anything as mundane as herbs stewing in a cauldron. On the contrary, Erictho slices open the corpse, washes out the rancid gore with fresh, hot blood, and decocts her potion directly in the unfortunate legionnaire's chest cavity (*Pharsalia* 6.667–69). As the first ingredient, the witch pours in a generous measure of "lunar poison" (virus lunare) (*Pharsalia* 6.669). This is the first point of direct contact with the subtext, and it sets the tone for how Lucan will approach this exercise in *aemulatio*. Ovid's Medea adds "frosty dews garnered beneath the full moon" (exceptas luna pernocte pruinas) to her brew (*Metamorphoses* 7.268), for poets had long expressed the belief that witches could, by power of incantation, "draw down the Moon" and make it secrete "poisonous dew" or "foam" upon the plants of the earth.[38] Lucan himself explicitly describes this process in the grand finale of his general introduction to Thessalian witches that immediately precedes the first appearance of Erictho (*Pharsalia* 6.499–506). Lucan, then, refers back to this when he begins his list of substances, but where Ovid is characteristically "poetic," delicately suggesting both "dew" and whitish "foam" with *pruina* (hoarfrost) and leaving it to the reader to make the connection "moon plus dew/foam equals poison," Lucan is brutally direct and typically "antipoetic" with his "lunar poison."

Lucan also begins to set up a rhetorical structure for his emulation that will surpass the relatively simple development of the model, just as his substances will be more exotic and horrific than Ovid's. The blood and lunar poison will serve as the liquid medium in which "whatever Nature has perversely produced is mixed together" (*Pharsalia* 6.670–71).[39] Up to this point Lucan has avoided using simple, generic verbs of addition like those employed by Ovid (*adjicio, addo*), preferring more complex, specific ones such as *suppleo, ministro* and *misceo*. Where Ovid throughout utilizes the active voice, even when switching to impersonal litotes, Lucan creates a sense of flow, of transition, by first using the active voice (*supplet, abluit, ministra*) and then shifting to the passive with *miscetur*. This in turn leads into a series of discrete items that "Nature has produced," each introduced by a *non* (*Pharsalia* 6.671–80), that orbits around the single, impersonal verb *desum* (*Pharsalia* 6.673). This is far more than just another allusion to the subtext, however. Ovid's use of the construction is casual, merely a way to vary the presentation of the substances, and only leads to the introduction of two of them, lacking as well the anaphora in "non." Lucan, on the other hand, seizes upon this fortuitous expedient in the subtext and amplifies it into one of the main motors of the rhetorical machinery of the whole passage. By adopting this recourse, Lucan is able to give a finite list of things "perversely produced by Nature" that "were not absent" from the mixture, all the while implying that Erictho was able to include an overwhelming "everything" (quidquid fetu genuit natura sinistro) (*Pharsalia* 6.670).

Ovid, of course, had been attempting to give his list a similar amplitude by winding it up with "the barbarian woman, after having with *these and a thousand other nameless things* prepared to carry out her more than mortal design" (his et mille aliis postquam sine nomine rebus / propositum instruxit mortali barbara maius) and relating that Medea then stirred it all together with an olive branch (*Metamorphoses* 7.275–76).[40] Lucan has been alert to this all along and is now ready to deliver his master stroke. He closes his list of "things not absent" from among all of "whatever Nature had perversely produced" with "After she has brought together hither (in the chest cavity full of blood and lunar poison) these *common, name-having banes*, she added . . ." (quo postquam viles et habentes nomina pestes / contulit . . . / . . . / addidit . . .), going on to enumerate things produced by Erictho herself in contrast to Nature (*Pharsalia* 6.681–84).[41] Lucan archly links these last substances to Ovid's *sine nomine rebus* by having the first of them be "leaves infused with unutterable incantations" (infando saturatas carmine frondes) (*Pharsalia* 6.682). What, indeed, could be more "nameless" than a spell so potent as to be unspeakable?

The allusion to the subtext is unmistakable, as is the success of the emulation. Both sum up the contents of a list, both imply that something new is going to be related with *postquam*, and, above all, there is the common reference to things either named or nameless. Lucan is openly thumbing his nose at the whole tradition of this locus, as exemplified by Ovid, by referring to his own magnificently more exotic and bloodcurdling emulation of Medea's ingredients as "common banes having names" (Martindale 372). Housman makes it clear that the *viles et habentes nomina pestes* of *Pharsalia* 6.681 are the substances listed in *Pharsalia* 6.671–80 that "were not absent" from the brew (178), which in turn correspond to, and clearly excel, those of *Metamorphoses* 7.264–74.[42]

The genuine triumph of Lucan's emulation, however, resides in the distinction that is established between the things provided by Nature and those by Erictho herself. The ravishing sorceress Medea, faithful priestess of "three-headed Hecate" (*Metamorphoses* 7.194), is the consummate manipulator of natural forces (*Metamorphoses* 7.192–219). Erictho, on the other hand, is a literally "supernatural" force in her own right. Lucan begins developing this idea in the description of the witches of Thessaly by asserting their power to turn nature on its head and then asking, perhaps rhetorically, why it is that the Olympians themselves seem to be subject to the will of the sisterhood—could it be that the Thessalian hags have dominion over a deity that can overawe even the conventional powers of heaven and hell? (*Pharsalia* 6.461–99). This conception, embodied in Erictho as a truly "supranatural" entity, will reach its culmination in her browbeating of the infernal potentates that follows the mixing of the necromantic elixir and that finally results in the revivification of the corpse (*Pharsalia* 6.730–51). It is in the list of substances, however, that Lucan first specifically insinuates that Erictho must be seen in contradiction to, rather than as part of, Nature. Whereas the "commonplace banes produced by Nature" that she employs merely outshine Medea's arcane exotica by an order of magnitude, those generated by Erictho herself, beginning with the poison she spits out of her mouth and culminating in her terrible voice (*Pharsalia* 6.681–93), totally eclipse the Colchian sorceress's philters as common indeed. Ovid's Medea bends the orderly processes of Nature to her will with the aid of her patron, Hecate, and the other powers of the underworld. Lucan's Erictho is herself a manifestation of the dire, but unfocused, fury of Chaos that capriciously wells up now and then to reveal all of Nature's apparent order, heaven, hell, and Middle Earth included, to be a cruel illusion. She is, in fact, emblematic of the *discors machina* that W. R. Johnson has identified as the central theme of Lucan's epic cosmology (15–33).

3.4.1.2. The Sorceress of Valladolid's Potion: Sacramental Reflections of Erictho and Medea

It can be appreciated, then, that Juan de Mena set himself a daunting task when he chose to empower the key episode of his own poem with an imitation of this scene from the *Pharsalia*. Nor should it be taken as any aspersion on Mena's talents as a poet and a scholar to find that he was, in fact, daunted by his subtext. At least he makes no attempt to dissimulate the identity of the model. As we have seen, one of the most distinctive features of Lucan's emulation of Ovid is the organization of the list of explicitly named substances around the impersonal litotes of "non . . . defuit" (was not lacking) (*Pharsalia* 6.671–80). Mena commences his list with a virtual quotation from this passage that, furthermore, functions in exactly the same way: "Pulmón de Linçeo allí non fallesçe, / de yena non menos el nodo más tuerto" (*Laberinto de Fortuna* 241*ab*), and he reinforces the allusion by returning to the litotes in the following stanza with "non menos falta" (*Laberinto de Fortuna* 242*e*).

This highlighting of the subtext might be seen in terms of attempted *aemulatio*, as much the same as Lucan's care to remind his reader of Medea's potion with references to the "hoarfrost/lunar poison," the things "not lacking" and the "nameless" substances. But there is a fundamental difference. Lucan clearly makes the subtext explicit in order to demonstrate unequivocally that he can surpass it; Mena, on the other hand, appears to be adhering closely to his model so as not to risk losing any of its power. In fact, Mena's imitation of *Pharsalia* 6 fits very closely Thomas Greene's category of reproductive or sacramental imitation that "celebrates an enshrined primary text by rehearsing it liturgically, as though no other form of celebration could be worthy of its dignity" (Greene, *Light*, 38). This becomes increasingly evident as one reads through the list of ingredients employed by the sorceress of Valladolid.

Ovid names fifteen discrete substances that Medea mixed in her cauldron, while Lucan has Erictho blend sixteen in the chest cavity of the dead legionnaire.[43] It is not surprising, then, that Mena limits himself to just fifteen. Of these, ten are taken directly from *Pharsalia* 6, and several are almost exact translations. A good example of these last is "Espuma de canes que el agua reçelan" (*Laberinto de Fortuna* 243a), which virtually translates "spuma canum quibus unda timori est" (*Pharsalia* 6.671), and which, with its latinate "espuma" and "canes," approximates its original at least as closely as Martín Lasso de Oropesa's very literal prose translation of Lucan (c. 1535), which reads: "espumajo de aquellos perros q[ue] temen del agua" (123). The following verse, "membranas de líbica sierpe çerrasta" (*Laberinto de Fortuna* 243b), is also hewn very closely to its model, "viventis adhuc Libyci membrana cerastae" (*Pharsalia* 6.679), which Lasso de Oropesa renders, more completely than Mena, as "el hollejo dela serpiente cerastres del libya antes que muera" (123). This verse was, of course, Lucan's own most direct allusion to his Ovidian subtext (Morford 71), and as such plays a key role in his strategy of emulation. No other line from this passage in the *Laberinto* more instructively illustrates the difference between "reproductive" imitation and transformative emulation.

Medea stirs into her cauldron the "squamea Cinyphii tenuis membrana chelydri" (*Metamorphoses* 7.272), which Fernán Núñez translates somewhat clumsily as "la sotil membrana de la serpiente que se cria en Africa, la qual se llama chelidro" ([1499], fol. 168v).[44] She has chosen the delicate, scaly skin shed by the water snake (chelydrus) because the purpose of her potion is rejuvenation (Broccia 226 n. 124). The Alexandrian poet Nicander, in Greek, and Virgil, in Latin, had already established the image of the water snake shedding its skin as an indelible metaphor of renewed youth and vigor, and hence, longevity.[45] Virgil's amphibious serpent frequented the mountain streams and pastures of Calabria (*Georgics* 3.425). Ovid is not content with anything so prosaic, and has Medea fetch her snake skin from the river Cinyps, now the Wadi Khahan, near Leptis Magna (Broccia 225 n. 122), because Libya had long been famous for the number and extraordinary venom of its reptiles.

Lucan himself uses "Cinyphian" as a synonym for "Libyan" in another herpetological context (*Pharsalia* 9.787),[46] and so in his emulation of *Metamorphoses* 7.272 he reinforces the allusion to the subtext not only with "membrana" but also by reversing the synecdoche with "Libyci" for "Cinyphii" (*Pharsalia* 6.679). For *aemulatio* to succeed, of course, it is not sufficient to merely highlight the model; there must be meaningful transformation as well. Lucan transforms Ovid's water snake (chelydrus) into a horned viper (cerastes). A subtle link already existed between the two serpents: according to Celsus (*De Medicina* 5.27.8), the venom of either one could be counteracted by the same remedy. The horned viper, furthermore, serves Lucan's purpose better because it is visually the most "infernal" of the poisonous snakes—not for nothing do poets describe the writhing reptilian locks of the Furies as *cerastae*.[47] No other serpent in the classical canon is more directly associated with death, and hence more appropriately juxtaposed to an image of renewed life and vigor. Additionally, the horned viper is associated with dry desert and rough sand, while both Ovid's and Virgil's emblematic snakes of rejuvenation are amphibious and gleam with moisture.

But this is not all; just as in the case of the "nameless" ingredients, Lucan must have his fun at the expense of the tradition. Here he is playing with Ovid's emblems of longevity. As Broccia (226 n. 124) points out, these are the water snake, the stag, and the crow. *Cerastes* is derived from the same Greek word meaning "horn" as *cervus* (stag).[48] Both are linked to the Moon and magic by the shape of their horns. Lucan then gilds the lily by qualifying the horned viper as "vivens adhuc," which can mean either "still" or "up to now," "living" or "alive." The model has been both magnificently surpassed and deconstructed at the same time.

Keeping in mind that this is the closest that Lucan comes to an exact reproduction of his subtext, it is apparent that Mena's "membranas de líbica sierpe çerrasta" (*Laberinto de Fortuna* 243b) is seeking to identify with its own model for some purpose other than transformation or emulation. The same can be said without further argument of "Pulmón de Linçeo" (*Laberinto de Fortuna* 241a) which corresponds closely enough to "viscera . . . lyncis" (*Pharsalia* 6.672) and "de yena non menos el nodo más tuerto" (*Laberinto de Fortuna* 241*b*) which mirrors "non dirae nodus hyaenae" (*Pharsalia* 6.672) in everything but the adjective. Not all of Mena's more obvious allusions to *Pharsalia* 6 are such exact translations, however, and before labeling the whole as reproductive or sacramental, it is only fair to examine what kinds of modifications or transformations Mena works on the remaining ingredients.

Lucan had, in fact, set up the ludic interplay between the "horned" and reptilian emblems of longevity a few lines previous to the mention of the horned viper by metamorphosing Ovid's "liver of a long-lived stag" (vivacisque iecur cervi) (*Metamorphoses* 7.273) into the "marrow of a stag nourished on snake" (cervi pastae serpente medullae) (*Pharsalia* 6.673). As Fernán Núñez notes at some length, a number of ancient authors claim not only that stags feed on snakes, but that they do so in order to rejuvenate themselves when they get old and infirm ([1499], fol. 166r).[49] That such goods can be found retailed in Pliny, Solinus, or especially, the church fathers, is no sure guarantee that they circulated independently of the *Pharsalia* when Lucan was composing the poem; nonetheless, it is clear that Lucan must be referring to some belief of this kind. There is certainly no doubt that Mena read it in this way, because the fifteenth-century poet feels obliged to amplify the model as "medula de çiervo que tanto envegesçe / que traga culuebra por rejuvenir" (*Laberinto de Fortuna* 241*ef*).

While still operating far below the dimension of ludic transformation seen in Lucan's emulation of Ovid, Mena is doing more with the "stag's marrow" than simply translating the subtext: he is translating it hermeneutically. It is one of the few glimmers in this passage of acknowledgment on Mena's part of a potential difficulty with anachronism. Clearly, Lucan was confident that his readers would understand that "stags that ate snakes" did so in order to recover their youthful vigor. Mena's "intended reader" is, in the first instance, King John II, and by extension, the court of Castile (Deyermond 163). Fernán Pérez de Guzmán, in his less than flattering portrait, informs us that John II was much given to literary pursuits, that he could read well, and that he could even speak and understand Latin (118). Yet whatever the extent of the king's direct acquaintance with Latin texts may have been, it is certain that many if not most of his courtiers were limited to the vernacular, if they could read at all. Even such a distinguished man of letters as the poet-courtier Iñigo López de Mendoza, marqués de Santillana, was sufficiently unsure of his Latin as to prefer his classics in translation (Santillana, *Comedieta*, ed. Kerkhof, 11–12). Although a certain "difficulty" of style may well have been "part of Mena's strategy of persuasion" as Deyermond has suggested (164), Mena could not afford to lose his audience completely. By expanding his translation of the model to include, in effect, the gloss, Mena is not only making a concession to his audience's lack of erudition, he is skating very close to explicit recognition of the abyss of anachronism. This is, of course, not a problem that concerned Lucan, who was writing within the confines of the same *mundus significans* as Ovid, and who could strive to outshine or undermine his model, or do both, confident in the relative stability of the shared system of signifiers and things signified.

Mena seems to engage in a similar attempt at hermeneutic translation in the immediately following, final verses of *Laberinto de Fortuna* 241. Medea had merely added "stones fetched from the remotest reaches of the Orient" (extremo lapides Oriente petitos) (*Metamorphoses* 7.266) to her potion. Lucan makes this more specific as "stones that rattle when warmed beneath the great breeding bird" (quaeque sonant feta tepefacta sub alite saxa) (*Pharsalia* 6.676). While Ovid probably meant to imply only "exotic stones" or possibly "pearls,"[50] Lucan again does his model one better by giving Erictho the fabulous "eagle-stones" (aëtitae), which, according to Pliny, do indeed come from the East (10.4; 36.34, 39). In the case of the lunar frost/lunar poison, Lucan's strategy was to be more explicit than his model; here, on the other hand, he prefers to allude rather than name. Mena, however, again seems to be unsure how far he can challenge his reader's knowledge of either the subtext or the *mundus significans* that lies behind it, and so renders Lucan's delicate periphrasis into "e de aquella piedra que sabe adquerir / el águila cuando su nido fornesçe" (*Laberinto de Fortuna* 241*gh*).[51] Mena finds himself in a difficult position here. He has said more, but also considerably less, than Lucan. While it is now clear that the "great winged creature" (ales) is an eagle, the dimension of the stones' musicality has been sacrificed, as has the brooding warmth of *tepefacta*, and the uninformed reader is still none the wiser about what role the stones might play in the bird's nesting. In fact, Mena's near contemporaries seem to have realized that many of these *coplas* required further explanation, and one fifteenth-century commentator glosses 241*gh* in an early manuscript as follows (*Laberinto*, ed. Cummins, 165):[52] "El aguila quando faze los huevos por criar los fijos halla y pone en el nido ciertas piedras marmoreas por temperar su calor el qual es tanto que sin aquellas piedras cozería los huevos y mactaria los fijos estas piedras dize lucano caber en el encantamiento." The assiduous reader of Pliny and other ancient authors will, of course, learn a great deal more about the therapeutical and magical properties of the "eagle-stones"; Fernán Núñez would give generations of sixteenth-century readers a partial summary of this literature ([1499], fol. 166v). As Mena has left it, even with the additional gloss, the salient feature in Lucan's rendition—the sound made by the stones—is still left "buried in the inkwell."[53] Nor has he gained much in the exchange. Like the verses that reveal the stag's peculiar motivation for eating snake, those that seek to spell out the nature of the eagle-stones betray a nascent recognition of the difficulty of communicating the essence of the model across the ever-widening cultural and linguistic fracture running back from the Spain of John II to Nero's Rome. In the case of the *aëtitae*, however, the expedient of hermeneutic translation does not totally succeed in transmitting a satisfactorily "sacramental" version of the subtext. Nor is there any indication that anything except an intelligibly "liturgical" reproduction of the model was intended.

Such a reproduction is achieved with certain success in the case of the remora. Lucan is at his most expansive when he gives Erictho the "sucking-fish that holds the ship still in the water although the wind is filling out its cordage" (puppim retinens Euro tendente rudentes / In mediis echenais aquis) (*Pharsalia* 6.674-75). Mena's paraphrase "Allí es mesclada grand parte de echino, / el qual, aunque sea muy pequeño pes, / muchas vegadas e non una vez / retiene las fustas que van de camino" (*Laberinto de Fortuna* 242*abcd*) conveys the substance of the model with charm but without ambition. The detail of this fantastic fish's very small size is probably taken from Pliny (9.41), and again, is more of an attempt to transmit effectively than to transform the model.

"Çeniza de fénix, aquella que basta" (*Laberinto de Fortuna* 243*c*) is an adequate, although somewhat lackluster, rendition of "ash of the phoenix which lays itself on the eastern altar" (cinis Eoa positi phoenicis in ara) (*Pharsalia* 6.680). Considering that the "phoenix" is Lucan's answer to Ovid's "nine-lived crow" (*Metamorphoses* 7.274)—the avian third of the triad of rejuvenation[54]—Mena's imitation barely passes muster as "reproductive." Mena's "de otras vipéreas sierpes que velan, / dando custodia a las piedras preçiosas" (*Laberinto de Fortuna*

243*ef*) for the "viper born by the Red Sea, guardian of the precious shell" (innataque rubris / Aequoribus custos pretiosae vipera conchae) (*Pharsalia* 6.677-78) is only slightly more satisfactory, and certainly never presumes to exceed the bounds of a "sacramental" recreation of the model.

Although Mena's essential attitude toward his subtext is clearly respectful to the point of diffidence in regard to the majority of the ingredients, his natural exuberance and creativity as a poet cannot be entirely bridled. Just as he has made some tentative efforts to deal with the problem of anachronism, he also attempts some transformations worthy of his model. Among his more original contributions are "lo que chimerino / se engendra por yerro de naturaleza" (*Laberinto de Fortuna* 242*ef*),[55] although this may well represent, as Fernán Núñez ([1499], fol. 167v) and El Brocense (293) suppose, a misreading of Lucan's "whatever Nature has perversely produced" (quidquid fetu genuit natura sinistro) (*Pharsalia* 6.670), and "ojos de loba después que encanesçe" (*Laberinto de Fortuna* 241*d*), which probably represents the combination of elements suggested by Lucan's "eyes of dragons" (oculi draconum) (*Pharsalia* 6.675), Ovid's "werewolf's entrails" (*Metamorphoses* 7.270-71), and Pliny's remark that the gaze of wolves was "noxious," and would strike men dumb if the wolf were the first to see the other (8.34), all perhaps conflated with some aspect of contemporary occult practice (Lida de Malkiel, *Juan de Mena*, 82).[56] A similar fusion of matter insinuated by the subtext—Lucan's "eastern altars" (*Pharsalia* 6.680)—with fifteenth-century ideas about witchcraft can be seen in "e pieças de aras que por grand alteza / son dedicadas al culto divino" (*Laberinto de Fortuna* 242*gh*). According to Lida de Malkiel, that Mena may have blended his own presumed knowledge of "real" sorcery with literary models of necromancy in the cases of the "pieças de aras" and the "ojas de loba" is not only an important demonstration of his independence and originality, it also indicates that Mena can function on the same level as Lucan and Ovid—that he is in some way their peer (*Juan de Mena*, 82-83). The "pieças de aras" and the "ojos de loba" are certainly signs of a more transformative approach than that evidenced in the case of the majority of the ingredients.

Mena, in fact, does effect one imitative transformation that recalls, albeit palely, some of the technique of Lucan's most directly allusive imitation of Ovid. At least, as in Lucan's reworking of the "skin of the Cinyphian water snake" into the "skin of the Libyan horned viper," there is an effort to recombine elements from the two most prestigious subtexts into something that can take its own place in the tradition. Lucan, of course, brings both Virgil and Ovid to mind with *Pharsalia* 6.679. Mena, likewise, looks back to both Lucan and Lucan's own model, Ovid, with "huesos de alas de dragos que buelan" (*Laberinto de Fortuna* 243d). Medea had put "the wings, along with the flesh itself, of the ill-famed horned owl" (strigis infamis ipsis cum carnibus alas) (*Metamorphoses* 7.269) into her pot.[57] Lucan, with his clear preference for ultra-exotic reptiles, had Erictho introduce the "Arabian winged serpent" (Arabum volucer serpens) (*Pharsalia* 6.677) as well as the "eyes of dragons" (oculi draconum) (*Pharsalia* 6.675) into her brew. Mena, of course, would have understood *draco* as virtually a synonym for *serpens*, and makes his original contribution with the suitably macabre "huesos." Mena's originality, however, is far less interesting than his focusing on the one element Lucan's "flying serpent" had in common with Ovid's "screech owl"—the wings. Although the ludic, deconstructive dimensions witnessed in Lucan's emulation of Ovid's snake skin, for instance, seem still to be quite lacking here—substituting the "wingbones" for the whole creature itself makes no particularly cogent commentary or improvement on the model—if Mena is deliberately drawing attention to the immediate subtext of his own principal subtext, he is pushing his imitation to the extreme limits of the sacramental or reproductive.

If the "huesos de alas" were the only evidence for a conscious harkening back to Lucan's subtext on Mena's part, it would form a very tenuous basis indeed for any revision in the evaluation of his imitative practice as being fundamentally "sacramental." María Rosa Lida de Malkiel, however, has pointed out at least two apparently far more direct allusions to the *Metamorphoses* in this section of the "maga de Valladolid" passage. Because of the potential importance of these presumed references to Ovid for our understanding of Mena's approach to imitation, and because of certain difficulties they present, it is worthwhile to examine them in some detail.

Lida de Malkiel is primarily concerned with demonstrating that Mena's imitation of Lucan is not only not "servile," but also far from "exclusive" (*Juan de Mena*, 81). Although she, of course, does not use Greene's terminology, she is essentially arguing that Mena's imitation is "eclectic" rather than "reproductive." For this reason it does not matter where in the *Metamorphoses* Mena may have found his additional inspiration; the important point is that it was somewhere other than *Pharsalia* 6. The first of her two proposed Ovidian allusions in the list of ingredients, is, in fact, an alleged correspondence between *Laberinto de Fortuna* 241c and *Metamorphoses* 15.389–90, a passage with no direct bearing whatsoever on Medea's rejuvenation of Aeson. This, however, is not the principal difficulty.

Lida de Malkiel is referring, in the first instance, to one of the most problematic verses in Mena's poem. As noted above, the list of the sorceress's ingredients begins with "Pulmón de Linçeo allí non fallesçe / de yena non menos el nodo más tuerto" (*Laberinto de Fortuna* 241ab). When Fernán Núñez was preparing his 1499 edition, he found the next verse given as "después que formada de espina de muerto" (*Laberinto de Fortuna* 241c). Florence Street has demonstrated convincingly that Núñez based his 1499 text almost exclusively on the Seville 1496 edition, itself based on Zaragoza 1489, which in turn was based on the princeps of Salamanca (c. 1481), this last itself replete with unresolved difficulties ("Hernán Núnez," 55–57; Bataillon, "L'édition," 328; Kerkhof, "Hacia una nueva edición," 180–81, "El *Laberinto*," 328–30). Errors in the text had multiplied with each printing, and Núñez was justified in approaching murky readings in Seville 1496 with a healthy skepticism (Street, "Hernán Núñez," 56). "Después que formada de espina de muerto" initially perplexed Núñez as thoroughly as it has twentieth-century editors and elicited a memorable response:

> En estas palabras esta vn grand flagicio y error de los impressores que me touo asaz dias suspenso los quales por escreuir de sierpe formada de espina de muerto escriuieron corruptissima y viciosamente despues que formada de espina de muerto. Y este es vno de los logares muy difficiles que en esta obra sacamos nosotros primero a luz, lo qual sea dicho syn arrogancia. Nascer culebra o sierpe del tuetano que esta en el espinazo del hombre muy notorio es entre los letrados y traelo Plinio en el libro .xii. de la historia natural asy. ([1499], fol. 165r)

Based upon this reasoning and several other authorities in addition to Pliny, Núñez has no compunction about emending *Laberinto de Fortuna* 241c to conform to his own hypothesis: "de sierpe formada de espina de muerto."

Núñez's happy solution to the difficulties posed by the reading he found in Seville 1496 has had great success. A number of subsequent editors of the *Laberinto de Fortuna* have embraced it, and Lida de Malkiel bases her assertion that Mena was imitating Ovid's "there are those who believe that when the backbone has decomposed in the closed grave, the human marrow is changed into a snake" (sunt qui, cum clauso putrefacta est spina sepulcro, / mutari credant humanas angue medullas) (*Metamorphoses* 15.389–90) on Núñez's "de sierpe" without making any reference to the problematic provenience of this reading (81). Such confidence, however, is not entirely merited. Núñez assumed that the reading he found difficult, and hence corrupt, was due to the carelessness of the printers, for whose professionalism, in any case, he had scant respect (Street, "Hernán Núñez," 57). All seventeen of the manuscripts examined by Kerkhof, as well as the three earliest printed editions, however, read "después que" rather than "de sierpe" (Mena, *Laberinto de Fortuna*, ed. Kerkhof, 225).

Among recent editors Vasvari Fainberg (195) and Gómez Moreno and Jiménez Calvente (137) accept Núñez's emendation, while Cummins (165), Pérez (155), and Kerkhof (225) deem it more prudent to retain the reading of the manuscript tradition. As Pérez Priego points out (155), the only authority for "de sierpe" is the erudite guesswork of Núñez, reinforced somewhat by Lida de Malkiel, and the emendation is not entirely necessary to make some sense of the verse in question.[58] The preponderance of the evidence tends to support Cummins, Pérez, and Kerkhof, and it remains highly questionable that Mena ever meant to evoke the image of a corpse's spine metamorphosing into a serpent. Consequently, this particular example adduced by Lida de Malkiel to demonstrate the "eclectic" nature of Mena's imitation in the "maga" episode emerges from close analysis as tenuous at best. Furthermore, although it is true that a reader of Ercilla's time would more than likely read this verse in Núñez's version, the commentator makes no reference to Ovid himself, and it would have been left to the reader's own erudition to make the connection.

Lida de Malkiel is on much firmer, as well as more fruitful, ground with her second example of an allusion by Mena to the *Metamorphoses* in the sorceress of Valladolid passage. When Mena wraps up his list of the witch's ingredients with "e otros diversos millares de cosas / qu'el nombre non saben aun los que las zelan" (*Laberinto de Fortuna* 243gh), there can be no doubt about the allusion to Ovid's "these and a thousand other nameless things" (His et mille aliis . . . sine nomine rebus) (*Metamorphoses* 7.275). Again, all Lida de Malkiel would make of this is yet one more example of the independent, "eclectic" nature of Mena's imitation (81). There are, however, without denying their ultimate parentage in *Metamorphoses* 7, at least two different ways to read these lines. Furthermore, whichever way the reader chooses to interpret them, far from pointing away from *Pharsalia* 6, these verses prove to be the final, decorative knot in the ribbon of Mena's imitation of Lucan's list of ingredients.

As discussed above, Medea rounds off her recipe with "these and a thousand other nameless things" (His et mille aliis . . . sine nomine rebus) (*Metamorphoses* 7.275) in order to imbue her magic potion with hyperbolic grandeur. Lucan, in turn, makes his own "common banes having names" (viles et habentes nomina pestes) (*Pharsalia* 6.681), which both excels and deconstructs Ovid's device, the central axis of his emulation of Medea's widely gathered exotica. Like Ovid's "nameless things," Lucan's "named things" wraps up an enumeration of discrete items: the individual things "Nature has perversely produced" that are given in *Pharsalia* 6.671–80. Mena, then, quite deliberately places his "e otros diversos millares de cosas / qu'el nombre non saben aun los que las zelan" (*Laberinto de Fortuna* 243*gh*) precisely at the conclusion of his catalog of the ingredients the sorceress of Valladolid stirs into her decoction. Position alone demonstrates that this cannot be the result of any casual eclecticism. Whatever else we may infer, there can be no doubt that Mena is letting us know that he, too, is aware that Erictho's necromantic brew is modeled on Medea's philter of rejuvenation.

As we have seen, up to this point Mena has followed Lucan very closely. Ten of the fifteen ingredients have ranged from nearly word-for-word translations to "hermeneutic" paraphrases of their models in *Pharsalia* 6, only one of which—243*d*—may betray some cross-pollination from *Metamorphoses* 7. Even the three additional items that showcase Mena's own powers of invention all have some link to elements of the Erictho passage. Of the remaining two that Lida de Malkiel ascribes to immediate imitation of Ovid, one—241*c*—is highly problematic, and the other—the only direct and unchallengeable allusion to the *Metamorphoses*—is the case in point: 243*gh*. Moreover, this unmistakable, virtual quotation from Lucan's principal subtext occupies a key position and plays a pivotal role in both the model and the emulation. How, then, are we to read Mena's abrupt conjuration of

Lucan's model at the close of what has been so thoroughly a "sacramental" imitation of Lucan's rendition of this locus?

Can we interpret Mena's invocation of Ovid here as a necromantic, heuristic, or even dialectical (in Greene's terms) distancing device, perhaps even of the same order as Garcilaso's nod to Virgil while winking at Petrarch in the cuartets of "En tanto que de rosa y d'açucena"?[59] Does Mena transform an otherwise dutifully reproductive imitation into something much more subtle and ambitious with one master stroke in the final two verses? Perhaps. The answer depends on how Mena himself read *Pharsalia* 6.681.

Unfortunately, the critic's task is complicated here by a long-running problem in the editing and interpretation of *Pharsalia* 6.681. As Housman points out (178), many editors of Lucan down the centuries have held that because the model for Erictho's necromantic concoction was clearly Medea's recipe for rejuvenation, and that because Ovid had written "these and a thousand other *nameless* things" (His et mille aliis . . . sine nomine rebus) (*Metamorphoses* 7.275), that therefore Lucan could only have corresponded with "common banes *not* having names" (viles nec habentes nomina pestes) (*Pharsalia* 6.681). Such editors have not hesitated to emend *et* to *nec*. Essentially, this school of thought misreads Lucan's emulation of the passage from *Metamorphoses* 7, and consequently denies this master of parodic *aemulatio* the possibility of anything other than a purely "reproductive" imitation.

Curiously enough, Fernán Núñez vehemently subscribes to this interpretation of *Pharsalia* 6.681. In his commentary on *Laberinto de Fortuna* 243*gh* in his 1499 edition he explains indignantly: "Lucano (quo postquam viles et habentes nomina pestes contulit.) Que quiere dezir: 'Donde como echaste estas ponçoñas y otras muchas que no tienen nombre,' avnque en el lucano mendosamente se lee (Quo postquam viles et habentes nomina pestes.) por dezir (Quo postquam viles nec habentes etc.) Esta es la verdadera escritura de lucano para que concuerde con ouidio que al mismo proposito dize en el libro ya muchas vezes alegado" (fol. 169v). As already demonstrated in the case of *Laberinto de Fortuna* 241c, Núñez had little faith in the accuracy of the printed or copied texts he had to deal with, and had as little compunction about "correcting" them according to his own lights. As far as Núñez is concerned, Lucan must be engaged in "following" imitation (Ricci's *sequi*, Pigman 3); Núñez does not seem to understand or admit the possibility of transformative emulation. For Núñez, then, there is no question of Mena doing anything other than "following" as well. Mena, in fact, is merely preserving the "correct" sense of the passage by imitating Ovid rather than Lucan.[60]

Nor is Núñez alone among Spanish scholars of his generation in insisting on "rectifying" the text of *Pharsalia* 6.681 to make it read as a "faithful, following" imitation of *Metamorphoses* 7.275. Martin Lasso de Oropesa, whose Castilian translation of the *Pharsalia* appeared sometime in the 1530s, renders *Pharsalia* 6.681 as "Quando tuuo alli allegadas todas estas pestilençias, y otras que no sabria yo dezir" (124). The principal virtue of Oropesa's prose is that it generally follows the sense of Lucan's difficult hexameters very literally (Herrero Llorente 764–65). Here "otras que no sabría yo decir" clearly comes down on the side of "things without names." Oropesa, like Núñez before him, obviously must have felt the Latin text was defective if it did not reflect a "sacramental" reproduction of the Ovidian subtext.

What we cannot really know, of course, is if Mena shared this view of his subtext. Juan de Mena was one of the most erudite Iberians of his day, and there can be little doubt that he was at least aware of the controversy. Fernán Núñez, however, for all of his scholarship, was no poet, and in his commentary he is often blinded to poetic nuance by the splendor of his own learning. Mena, on the other hand, was not only a fine poet, he also had the closest to a "humanist" understanding of classical letters of any Iberian poet of his age (Lida de Malkiel, *Juan de Mena*, 549). It seems unlikely, then, that Mena would have so misconstrued Lucan's brilliant emulation of Ovid's Medea passage. But if he was also capable of misreading "whatever Nature has perversely produced" (quidquid fetu genuit natura sinistro) (*Pharsalia* 6.670), a fundamental part of the same astute emulative strategy, into "lo que chimerino / se engendra por yerro de naturaleza," (*Laberinto de Fortuna* 242*ef*), as Fernán Núñez ([1499], fol. 167v) and El Brocense (293) suppose, might he not also misread the other binding cord of Lucan's deconstruction of Ovid? For all his poetry, and all his reading, Mena was still often medieval in his approach to his classical sources (Lida de Malkiel, *Juan de Mena*, 529–35). Lacking any extratextual commentary directly attributable to Mena, we are left with only his verses, and it is upon our reading of those that we must ultimately base our judgment.

Close analysis of Mena's sorceress's brew has demonstrated that Mena pursued an extremely sacramental or reproductive imitation of his model in all but a very few particulars. The only really possible challenge to the authority of Lucan is the one Ovidian allusion at the conclusion. This, I think, we should give to Mena. Although he may indeed have believed that Lucan meant to say the same thing, it is Ovid's words that he most closely imitates. That Mena's imitation of Lucan is largely "sacramental" should not be taken as a denigration of his achievement. On the contrary, Mena did not set out to outshine or deconstruct Lucan, but rather to borrow his poetic power and authority and lend it to the needs of his own poem. Lucan is deliberately much more macabre than Ovid, and it is the hyperbolic horror of the witch's brew that Mena uses to grip the reader's attention and paint the constable's enemies in a suitably negative light. That Mena's imitation was very successful within its limited scope can be seen in Ercilla's reworking of the locus. A more ambitious, necromantic imitation would have been exceedingly difficult for Mena to carry off, given the linguistic and cultural circumstances of his time. As it was, he pushed the limits of the possible. Only after the introduction of the printing press had more widely disseminated classical learning, and the "invasion" of Italian letters had prepared the ground, could a truly necromantic imitation of this most paradigmatic of necromancies be undertaken in Iberian letters. But these alone were not enough: it would also require Mena's own Promethean effort, ahead of his time, and the broad dissemination of his work in Fernán Núñez's meticulously glossed editions to create the cultural space that allowed Ercilla to attempt a genuinely literary necromancy.

3.5. A Renaissance Necromancy: Ercilla's Revivification of Lucan and Oedipal Supplanting of Mena

Ercilla begins his necromantic revival of the locus of the magical substances by leaving no doubt that he is alluding to the sorceress of Valladolid's recipe as well as Erictho's. This he accomplishes by opening, just as Mena did, with a reference to Lucan's lynx. Ercilla, however, with his "del Lince preparados / los penetrantes ojos virtuosos / en cierto tiempo y conjunción sacados / y los del Basilisco ponçoñosos" (*Araucana* 23.49a–d),[61] is also announcing that his approach to imitation in this passage is going to be much more ambitious than that of his fifteenth-century predecessor. Mena's "pulmón de Linçeo" (*Laberinto de Fortuna* 241a) reflects Lucan's "viscera . . . lyncis" (*Pharsalia* 6.672) fairly faithfully. After all, butchers and other dissectors of carcasses, including, presumably, witches, normally include the "lungs" among the "entrails" (viscera). As demonstrated above, the element of transformation is as minimal as the differences in language, metrical convention, and overall cultural outlook will permit. Ercilla's technique, on the other hand, recalls the emulative alchemy that Lucan worked on his own Ovidian subtext. In that case, the element anchoring the allusion was the "entrails" (Lucan's "viscera," Ovid's "prosecta," *Metamorphoses* 7.271), while Lucan transmuted Medea's "werewolf" into the lynx and the hyena—both considered extremely exotic creatures if ancient authors are to be believed.[62] Ercilla, in much the same way, leads off with the lynx for its double value as a flag that signals a reference to both Lucan and Mena. In the *Araucana*, however, the focus immediately shifts back to a specific body part: in this case, the eyes.

By Ercilla's time the most well-known quality of the lynx was indeed its vision (Ducamin 172 n. 4). The author of the *Araucana*, or his potential reader, would have had to look no further for this information than Fernán Núñez's ever popular edition of the *Laberinto de Fortuna*, where the tireless commentator begins his gloss on *copla* 241a with the remark, "Escriue Plinio en la historia natural que el Lynce es animal de muy acutissima vista" ([1552 Nucio], fol. 203r).[63] Like so much of Núñez's commentary, the reference is not particularily germane to either the text of the *Laberinto de Fortuna* or its subtext in the *Pharsalia*, but becomes significant in terms of subsequent reception and interpretation. Nonetheless, Morínigo and Lerner (*La Araucana* 2:147 n. 25) are correct in singling out Boethius's remark:[64]

> But if, as Aristotle says, men possessed lynxes' eyes so that their sight could penetrate obstacles, would not that outwardly very beautiful body of Alcibiades, once the entrails were examined, seem most foul? (*De consol. philos.* 3.8)

> (Quod si, ut Aristoteles ait, Lynceis oculis homines uterentur, ut eorum uisus obstantia penetraret, nonne introspectis uisceribus illud Alcibiadis superficie pulcherrimum corpus turpissimum uideretur?)

The similarity in lexical choice is particularily convincing, with Ercilla's adjective "penetrantes" recalling Boethius's use of the verb *penetro*. Curiously, Boethius also makes a reference here to entrails in close conjunction with a mention of lynxes, although the context is totally different from that in *Pharsalia* 6.[65]

If bringing the reference to the lynx into accord with the prevalent erudition of his own day was the only transformation that Ercilla worked on his subtext here, we would still read it necromantically. There is a fundamental difference between Mena's amplificatory "hermeneutic translation," designed to clarify and fix the "original" reference for a reader whose mastery of the poetic *mundus significans* the poet must assume a priori to be inadequate, and Ercilla's metamorphosing the subtextual citation into rejuvenated referentiality. The poet's alchemical transmutation of his models here does not end with the lynx's eyes, however. Ercilla leaves no doubt about how he is going to deal with both the primary subtext, *Pharsalia* 6, and the secondary, *Laberinto de Fortuna* 241–243, by bringing the "basilisk" into play as well at this juncture. The eyes of the lynx, aside from their greater recognition value for the sixteenth-century reader, also make a much more compelling image as the macabre contents of a labeled glass jar gracing a necromancer's workbench than the far less specific "entrails," or even, "lungs." Having opted to exploit the possibilities presented by exotic eyeballs preserved in vitro, Ercilla did not have to look far in his primary subtext for an opportunity to magnify the power of the image, and in so doing, truly "imitate" the transformative, emulative, and ludic qualities of his model.

Erictho had added the "eyes of dragons" (oculi . . . draconum) (*Pharsalia* 6.675) to the seething, blood-based brew in the legionnaire's chest cavity. Mena, as discussed above, seems to have converted this to "ojos de loba," perhaps reflecting some contemporary belief or practice of witchcraft (Lida de Malkiel, *Juan de Mena*, 82), perhaps recalling Pliny's observation that the wolf's glance is harmful to men (8.34), but in either case without achieving much of anything recognizable in the way of revivification or dialogue with the subtext. Mena may or may not have known why Lucan chose to use the eyes of the *draco* rather than some other reptile. Ercilla, at least, seems to have been aware that the "dragon," like the lynx, was renowned for the acuity of its vision (Covarrubias 485–86),[66] and that its eyes were the essential ingredient in a thaumaturgical ointment that would render even the most timorous person proof against nocturnal apparitions (Pliny 29.20).

Perhaps not, it now appears, entirely coincidentally, the paragraph in Pliny immediately preceding that explaining the virtue of the dragon's eyes concerns the prowess of the basilisk (29.19). It is tempting to imagine Ercilla hunting for the key to unlocking the significance of Lucan's *oculi draconum* in the pages of the *Naturalis historia* and coming across, on the same page, the perfect means of transforming his subtext in a way that would genuinely "bring it back to life."[67] Sound critical practice does not permit such flights of fancy, but nonetheless, the mutual proximity of Pliny's references to the pertinent qualities of these two reptiles is extremely suggestive, and can, at least, open a door for our reception of Ercilla's imitative praxis.

Because both the *draco* and the *basiliscus* are serpents, Ercilla was able to work a transmutation similar to Lucan's recasting of Ovid's "water snake" (chelydrus) as a "horned viper" (cerastes). According to Pliny, the basilisk can kill a man by merely looking at him (8.32–33, 29.19).[68] This well-known quality, as proverbial among sixteenth-century readers as the lynx's acuity of vision, permits Ercilla to place the eyes of the basilisk beside those of the lynx in the labeled flasks in the Araucanian wizard's workroom, and at the same time incorporate yet another immediately recognizable allusion to the subtext—"eyes of serpents" (oculi draconum)—into one of the antithesis so favored by the Italianate poetics of his age. The eyes of the lynx, like those of the "dragon," are "virtuosos" because they see with great clarity, even, as in Boethius, allowing one to see the corrupt inner nature of outwardly "virtuous" and seductively attractive men such as Alcibiades. Those of the serpent basilisk are "ponzoñosos" because they set to flight or destroy all living creatures that they behold, even the most poisonous and fearsome of the other reptiles (Pliny 8.33, 29.19; Lucan *Pharsalia* 9.724–26; Covarrubias 198).

The juxtaposition of the two opposing qualities of this antithesis is emblematic of the image of Fitón that Ercilla is trying to convey. The putatively indigenous mage must, on the one hand, be imbued with much, if not all, of the macabre and awesome aura of necromantic power proper to Erictho—a figure who excites hair-raising horror and revulsion. On the other hand, Fitón is to be the protagonist Ercilla's mentor in prophecy and his guide to the revelations first intimated by white-clad Reason—the future triumph of the poem's "intended reader" over the seaborne forces of the Antichrist, and the vast expanse of King Philip II's universal, Christian, world-spanning empire. Clearly, then, Ercilla's imitation of Erictho's hyperbolically depraved assault on all order, even that of hell, must find an avenue of mitigation. The poet must conjure up a means of suggesting the balanced, potentially beneficent manipulation of essentially illicit forces that is characteristic of the ideal Renaissance magus without sacrificing the awe-inspiring "otherness" of the original. If Erictho embodies the unbridled *discors machina* (Johnson 20), Fitón must represent the "sage enchanter" who, while operating outside the strict confines of Christian order, will be capable of using his extraordinary powers over Nature for the furtherance of the designs of Providence. As I have demonstrated in Chapter 2, the Araucanian sorceror is cast in the mold first struck by the Merlin of medieval romance. Like Ariosto's Merlino or Atlante, Fitón may be the master of the forbidden arts, may rule the unclean spirits with his wand, may himself be hopelessly trapped beyond redemption, but where the fate of the mortal protagonist is concerned, it is still the wizard who commands, and not the infernal powers. With one foot in the dark and the other in the light, this mage, whether by his own volition or in spite of it, presides over the spinning of the *concors machina*, not its unraveling.

The eyes of antithetical potency in their respective flasks, which Ercilla first descries as he enters into direct imitation of Lucan's necromancy, impart exactly the desired message about the wizened Araucan thaumaturge. While recalling with spine-tingling horror the handiwork of the witches of both Thessaly and Valladolid, the reader cannot fail to recognize that he has stepped, not into Erictho's cave or the "maga's" illicit "circle," but into the workroom of a Renaissance mage who balances the dark forces of Nature with the light. The turning of the subtext's potency to Ercilla's own purpose without losing any of its impact is certainly as thorough as Lucan's transformation of Ovid. But the processes are not exactly equivalent. For Lucan's emulation to succeed, it need only transform the model in such a way that the subtext is clearly refocused and surpassed. Ercilla faces two additional problems. On the one hand, he must also deal with Mena's intermediary imitation, and on the other, he must span the chasm of anachronism that separates the *mundus significans* of the sixteenth century from that of the first.

The first four verses of *Araucana* 23.49 unequivocally announce

Ercilla's strategies for engaging both of these issues. Ercilla alludes directly and unmistakably to Mena's "sacramental" imitation, just as Lucan referred to Ovid, in order to provoke a comparison. As I shall demonstrate, not only with the lynx and the eyes, but throughout, the poet of the *Araucana* spares no effort both to recall and, at the same time, to distance his own imitation from that of Mena. Although it may go against the grain of the conventional distinction defining Castilian poetics of the fifteenth century as medieval and those of the sixteenth as Renaissance, Ercilla clearly conceives of the *Laberinto de Fortuna* as operating within the same *mundus significans* as his own poem, to the extent that it presents itself as a legitimate object of emulation. The enduring popularity of Mena's poem, as evidenced by its frequent republication throughout the 1500s, tells us that Ercilla was not entirely out of step with his countrymen in this regard.[69] As El Brocense was to say in 1582, Mena was the first to have truly "ennobled the Castilian language" (Mena, *Las obras*, ed. Sánchez, n.p.).[70] The *Laberinto de Fortuna* was clearly still a fair and compelling target for the most "Oedipal" type of *aemulatio* in 1578. Outshining and supplanting Mena's imitation of Lucan with devastating totality, in fact, becomes one of the organizing principles of Ercilla's own imitation of the common subtext.

As for *Pharsalia* 6 itself, Ercilla adopts a strategy that can only be called necromantic. Ercilla's goal does not seem so much to outdo or supplant his primary model as to revive it, adapt it to his own time and needs, and make it sing again in a new reincarnation without dissipating any of its power or authority. As I shall demonstrate, Ercilla's approach here cannot be described adequately in terms of Ricci's or Barbaro's tripartite *schemata*, nor does it fit neatly into Pigman's category of "eristic" imitation. I think that close analysis will reveal that the best tool for measuring Ercilla's practice in relation to Lucan will prove to be Greene's concepts of heuristic and dialectical imitation, with emphasis placed more on Greene's metaphor of poetic necromancy than on the element of "Oedipal aggression."[71]

The first thing to strike the reader about Ercilla's imitation of the catalog of magical ingredients is that it is about double the length of its models. Ovid recites Medea's recipe in a mere fifteen hexameters (*Metamorphoses* 7.262–76); Lucan dedicates eighteen to his emulation (*Pharsalia* 6.667–84), which Mena reprises in three *coplas* of eight lines each (*Laberinto de Fortuna* 241–43). Ercilla devotes no less than six *octavas*—a total of forty-eight verses—to his resuscitation of the topic. Where Ovid, Lucan, and Mena all cut their rendition of this locus to the measure of fifteen or sixteen distinct substances, Ercilla expands his to include at least twenty-nine discrete elements or groupings of elements. Of these, seventeen allude, some less directly, some more, to the ingredients of Erictho's potion. Many of the remainder recall the herpetological nightmare of *Pharsalia* 9, and a few appear to be entirely of Ercilla's own invention. The whole passage, however, revolves around the central axis of the imitation of *Pharsalia* 6, and any analysis of Ercilla's imitative practice must begin with the seventeen substances that directly reflect the principal model.

Of these seventeen, five simply reproduce, without significant modification or transformation, elements of the subtext. When Mena follows this type of procedure with virtually all of the ingredients, it can only be called "sacramental" or "reproductive" imitation. In the case of Ercilla, however, the five "reproductively" transmitted loci form the nucleus of direct allusion that serves to assure unequivocal identification of the subtext and thus anchor the much more ambitious, heuristic imitation that orbits around it. Not surprisingly, the same five ingredients appear in the "maga de Valladolid's" recipe, but Ercilla carefully avoids direct translation and, even in his closest rendition of the subtext, is able to distance his imitation from that of his fifteenth-century predecessor.

This is abundantly clear in the case of Lucan's "the foam of dogs that fear water" (spuma canum quibus unda timori est) (*Pharsalia* 6.671), which Mena had translated almost verbatim as "Espuma de canes que el agua reçelan" (*Laberinto de Fortuna* 243a), leaving the reference as enigmatic as in the original. Late fifteenth-century commentators on Lucan such as Sulpitius and Beroaldus saw the need for exegesis, and concur in clarifying *Pharsalia* 6.671 by explaining that the Latin poet is referring to foam produced, not by aconite poisoning, but by rabies (*M. Annei Lucani*, fol. 159r, 159v). Lasso de Oropesa, in his early sixteenth-century (c. 1535) translation, renders the verse as literally as Mena—"espumajo de aquellos perros que temen del agua" (123)—but adds a note to the effect that: "Rauiosos entiende, que se espantan del agua" (n. 20). Fernán Núñez, in his commentary on *Laberinto de Fortuna* 243a, characteristically buries the pertinent reference in a mass of irrelevant recapitulation of Pliny and other ancient authorities, but nonetheless does not fail to observe that Pliny mentions that rabid dogs flee from water (1552 [Nucio], fol. 208v). Ercilla, then, has plenty of authority for making the subtext more explicit with "espumajos de Perros, que rauiosos / van huyendo del agua" (*Araucana* 23.49*fg*). This is very much like what I have called "hermeneutic" translation in Mena, but the significant point is that Ercilla engages in the practice precisely where Mena has failed to do so. Even when Ercilla is establishing the parentage of his imitation most explicitly, he does not pass up the opportunity to point out a weakness in the rival, secondary subtext and, by rectifying it, surpass and supplant it.

The same sort of strategy prevails in Ercilla's reprise of Lucan's "dirae nodus hyaenae" (*Pharsalia* 6.672). Probably because Mena sacrificed the adjective "dira" with his "de yena non menos el nodo más tuerto" (*Laberinto de Fortuna* 241*b*) in order to preserve the litotes with "non menos," Ercilla counters with "la coyuntura de la dura Hiena" (*Araucana* 23.50*b*). Not only does he restore the adjective,[72] he also modernizes Mena's Latinate "nodo" to "coyuntura."[73] As I have demonstrated, Mena foregrounds the litotes in his imitation of Lucan, making it one of the first and most important points of allusive contact. Ercilla, perhaps deliberately to distance his imitation from Mena's, relies on other means of implicating the subtext and reserves his single echo of Lucan's litotes for the final stanza of the passage (*Araucana* 23.54).

Ercilla pursues the same course of implacable emulation with respect to Mena in the remaining three substances taken virtually unmodified from Lucan. Ercilla's "y ceniza del phénis que en Oriente / se quema él mismo de viuir cansado" (*Araucana* 23.53*cd*) is not only more faithful to Lucan's "ash of the phoenix that lays itself on the eastern altar" (Aut cinis Eoa positi phoenicis in ara) (*Pharsalia* 6.680) than Mena's "çeniza de fénix, aquella que basta" (*Laberinto de Fortuna* 243*c*), it is also much more alive. The same can be said for "y el pescado Echineys, que en mar ayrado / al curso de las naues contrauiene / y a pesar de los vientos las detiene" (*Araucana* 23.53*fgh*) when compared to "Allí es mesclada grand parte de echino, / el qual, aunque sea muy pequeño pes, / muchas vegadas e non una vez / retiene las fustas que van de camino" (*Laberinto de Fortuna* 242*abcd*) in the light of Lucan's "the sucking-fish that holds the ship still in the water although the wind is filling out its cordage" (puppim retinens Euro tendente rudentes / In mediis echenais aquis) (*Pharsalia* 6.674–75). Although here it can be said in Mena's defense that his rendering has a certain innocent charm, it is essentially static in spite of its length. Ercilla clearly excels his fifteenth-century predecessor in restoring the movement of "the wind filling out its cordage" (*Euro tendente rudentes*) and the resulting palpable tension with "holding the ship still in the midst of the waters" (*puppim retinens . . . in mediis . . . aquis*) with his insistence on the "mar airado" and "a pesar de los vientos las detiene."[74] The final and fifth of the five ingredients in question is, perhaps, the least successful. Ercilla's "y las piedras del Aguila preñadas" (*Araucana* 23.54*d*) recalls Lasso de Oropesa's "las piedras aguila que suenan como preñadas, las quales auian sido tomadas de nido calientes" (123) for Lucan's "stones that rattle when warmed beneath the great breeding bird" (*quaeque sonant feta tepefacta sub alite saxa*) (*Pharsalia* 6.676). Nonetheless, in both economy and accuracy, Ercilla still surpasses Mena's "e de aquella piedra que sabe adquerir / el águila cuando su nido fornesçe" (*Laberinto de Fortuna* 241*gh*) here. It must be remembered, of course, that with these five substances, Ercilla's principal goal is to establish an unmistakable identification with the main subtext, and that outshining the secondary subtext is entirely an ancillary consideration.

The direct overshadowing and surpassing of Mena's "sacramental" imitation moves into the foreground, however, in Ercilla's transformative confrontation with at least seven of the remaining twelve substances that have roots in *Pharsalia* 6.667–84. The first two of this group—"eyes of the lynx and the basilisk"—as I have already demonstrated, introduce and set the tone for the whole passage. It is the closing locus of the same, first stanza which opens the imitation of Erictho's potion with the "eyes of lynx and basilisk," however, that best reveals the true depth of Ercilla's daring and ambition.

Following immediately on the heels of the highly "reproductive" and unabashedly allusive "espumajos de perros," the words "y el pellejo / del pecoso Chersidros, cuando es viejo" (*Araucana* 23.49*gh*) confront the reader. The juxtaposition of the clear-cut allusion to both Erictho's and the "maga's" recipes—the "foam of dogs"—with the "cast-off skin of the spotted amphibious viper" is obviously intended to prevent the reader from losing track of the context, and thus missing the point of the poet's truly necromantic, emulative audacity. As it is, even so perceptive and knowledgeable a modern reader as Ducamin (172 n. 9) has been led off the scent by the fact that the serpent called the *chersydrus* also makes an appearance in the herpetological freak show of *Pharsalia* 9 (710–11), whence Ercilla does borrow some of his other, most bloodcurdling snake lore.

The key to the presence of the *chersydrus* here, however, is not to be looked for in *Pharsalia* 9, but rather back in Lucan's emulation of Ovid in *Pharsalia* 6. We have already seen how Lucan ludically appropriates Ovid's "slender scaly skin of the Cinyphian water snake" (squamea Cinyphii tenuis membrana chelydri) (*Metamorphoses* 7.272) and maliciously transmutes it into the "skin of the yet-living Libyan horned viper" (viventis adhuc Libyci membrana cerastae) (*Pharsalia* 6.679). The alienated poet of the *Pharsalia* has taken one of his model's chief emblems of longevity—proper to a potion destined for a relatively "wholesome" rejuvenation—and transformed it into something much more suitably infernal and apropos of his own thoroughly "unwholesome" necromancy. The success of the emulation hinges upon changing the type of snake in a way indicative of the shift in meaning while maintaining the readily identifiable common metaphor of renewal embodied in the shed skin.

As I have previously pointed out, Ovid owes much of the impact of this image of rejuvenation to a "set portrait" established in Latin poetry by his most prestigious predecessor, Virgil. As the culmination of the same passage of *Georgics* 3 that opens with an admonition to the husbandman to clear his stock pens of venomous water snakes (chelydri) (3.414–15), Virgil gives a compelling description of the amphibious viper of Calabria that approaches its climax with "renewed and shining with youth when it has shed its old skin, it slithers along" (cum positis novus exuuiis nitidusque iuuenta / uoluitur) (3.437–38). This image of deadly vigor and renewal, which Virgil found so successful that he recycles it with appropriate modifications as a terrifying epic simile of youthful strength and menace in *Aeneid* 2.471–75 (Virgil, *Georgics*, ed. Thomas, 2:123), undulates just below the surface of Ovid's "skin of the water snake" and Lucan's "skin of the horned viper." Virgil does not explicitly name this amphibious serpent, but glosses its Greek name in his description of its habits (Virgil, *Georgics*, ed. Thomas, 2:121). Furthermore, in the Alexandrian poet Nicander's *Theriaca* 366–71, Virgil's principal subtext, this amphibious viper is explicitly called the *chersydrus* (Virgil, *Georgics*, ed. Mynors, 245). Servius, in his widely disseminated commentary on Virgil's work, insured that this reference would not become obscure down the centuries (309).

Ercilla, moreover, not only recalls that the *chersydrus* inhabits the same passage in *Georgics* 3 as the *chelydrus*, but that the section that deals with the amphibious viper (chersydrus) itself begins:

> There is, also, in the mountain pastures of Calabria that evil serpent, coiling its scaly back, with breast erect, and its long belly speckled with large spots. (*Georgics* 3.425–27)
>
> (est etiam ille malus Calabris in saltibus anguis
> squamea conuoluens sublato pectore terga
> atque notis longam maculosus grandibus aluum)

Ercilla's "chersidros" is "pecoso," not because he is mixing up his snakes from *Pharsalia* 9 as Ducamin suggests,[75] but because he is engaging in audacious dialogue with Lucan. The adjective "pecoso," corresponding to Virgil's "speckled" (maculosus) removes any possible doubt. Ercilla is not only indicating that he appreciates the process of *aemulatio* exemplified by his principal subtext, he is doing so by demonstrating that he, too, is capable of creative, "dialectical" imitation of his model emulation; in fact, that he can beat the master at his own game.

The parentage of Lucan's *membrana cerastae* out of Ovid's *membrana chelydri* was notorious. Ercilla, indeed, would have had to look no further than his copy of Fernán Núñez's edition of the *Laberinto de Fortuna* to find the two passages quoted one after the other in the commentary on 243*b* (fol. 208v). If he had done no more than turn the "horned viper" back into the "water snake" he would have equaled the most daring single stroke of Mena's imitation: the quotation of Ovid at the close of the passage (*Laberinto de Fortuna* 243*gh*). By going back to Virgil's "amphibious viper," however, Ercilla is doing far more than just pointing out the timidity of Mena's "liturgical" rendition of the Lucanian subtext as "membranas de líbica sierpe çerrasta" (*Laberinto de Fortuna* 243*b*). He is challenging, on the one hand, the foundations of meaning in his principal subtext by conjuring up the underlying metaphor, and on the other, the erudition of his reader. As Landino—in the fifteenth century—and Sturm and Parthenio—in the sixteenth—all indicate, for many, the best type of imitative practice reserves recognition of the allusion to the "learned" (Pigman 11, 14). Pigman, rightly, is very cautious about the pitfalls inherent in trying to disentangle such potentially "dissimulative" imitation (15). Nonetheless, in the case of

Ercilla's "pecoso Chersidros," the solidity of allusion that surrounds this covert reference to Lucan's model's model is so persuasive and unequivocal as to rule out the hermeneutic problems concomitant with *disimulatio*. None of the subtexts is the least bit obscure; on the contrary, all three were extremely prestigious and well known and their interrelationship widely understood. Clearly, Ercilla himself probably derives pleasure from the cleverness of his allusion, and he intends that his reader also derive pleasure from divining how he has unraveled Lucan's web of *aemulatio* and struck right back to the core substratum of significance that lurks below the surface of Lucan's emulative transformation of Ovid. This pleasure, however, is not based on the sort of idle fiddling with meaning described by Marco Girolamo Vida in his *De arte poetica* of 1527 and used by Pigman to underscore the difficulty of assessing the "function" of this type of imitative play (Pigman 14). On the contrary, far from "using the same words to express another meaning" as Vida boasts of doing (102–3),[76] Ercilla is intentionally shifting the words back toward the ursubtext of his own principal subtext in order to set up a dialogue with his model that can only be resolved in his own favor.

Ercilla gilds the lily here with "cuando es viejo." The fundamental metaphor is one of youth and rejuvenation, which Lucan playfully alludes to with his *vivens adhuc*. The poet of the *Araucana* turns this back upon itself and cleverly exposes the other side of the coin by focusing on the state of the snake before the skin is shed, rather than after. This insistence on the "aged" quality of the substance is far more fitting for the context of the enchanter's workroom. Once again, he has succeeded in appropriating the potentially anachronic image and necromanitically incorporating it into the *mundus significans* of his own poem.

None of the four remaining substances of this group is as audaciously transformative as the "pellejo del pecoso Chersidros," but all are specifically targeted at rounding out the direct confrontation with and triumph over Mena's "sacramental" imitation of *Pharsalia* 6. Ercilla's "y la espina también descoyuntada / de la Sierpe Cerastas" (*Araucana* 23.51*ef*) brings the "horned viper," passed over in his emulative rendering of *Pharsalia* 6.679, back into play. Here, however, Ercilla does have recourse to *Pharsalia* 9, where Lucan lists the "spinaque vagi torquente cerastae" (*Pharsalia* 9.716), translated by Lasso de Oropesa as "las Cerastas con la espina del lomo tan descoyuntada, que facilmente se rebueluen à todas partes" (198), in his catalog of the terrifying serpents of Libya. Fernán Núñez (1552 [Nucio], fol. 209r), in his gloss on *Laberinto de Fortuna* 243*b*, directs the reader to *Pharsalia* 9, and this was perhaps the initial stimulus for Ercilla to seek ammunition for his competitive overwhelming of Mena's imitation among the hyperbolic reptiles that harass Cato and his troops as they march through the sands of Libya.

The "meollo del Cencris, que se cría / dentro de Lybia en la caliente arena" (*Araucana* 23.50*cd*), represents the same type of strategy. The substance that links it to *Pharsalia* 6 is the "marrow," recalling Lucan's "marrow of the stag that feeds on snakes" (*cervi pastae serpente medullae*) (*Pharsalia* 6.673). Ercilla, throughout this passage, has clearly decided to take even further Lucan's tendency to transform various substances from Ovid into snakes or reptilian references. Thus if Lucan was successful in giving Ovid's "long-lived stag's liver" a herpetological spin, Ercilla will be even more successful by, on the one hand, assuring identification of the allusion with "marrow," and on the other, transforming the "stag that feeds on snakes" itself into a snake. Again, the chief point seems to be showing up the "reverential" nature of Mena's highly reproductive "medula de çiervo que tanto envegesçe / que traga culebra por rejuvenir" (*Laberinto de Fortuna* 241*ef*).

Mena is even more clearly the target in the case of Ercilla's "las dos alas del Iáculo temido" (*Araucana* 23.52*d*). As I have already shown, one of Mena's few attempts to implicate Lucan's Ovidian subtext and create some dialogue with his model in his otherwise "sacramental" imitation is his "huesos de alas de dragos que buelan" (*Laberinto de Fortuna* 243*d*). As such, the verse attracts special attention from a competitive emulator. Although the explicit mention of the "wings" is probably Mena's gesture toward Ovid, it is the Lucanian subtext that calls the most attention to itself here. Ercilla, even if he had not recognized it otherwise, would have had to look no further than Fernán Núñez's commentary (1552 [Nucio], fol. 209r) to discover that the principal model is Lucan's "winged Arabian serpent" (*Arabum volucer serpens*) (*Pharsalia* 6.677), that this fantastic reptile is called the *iaculus*, and that it can also be found in *Pharsalia* 9.

As it is, the exploit of the *iaculus* in the reptilian assault on Cato's troops seems to have occupied a special place in Ercilla's poetic imagination. Already in Part I of the poem, Ercilla had used the vivid image of the flying snake (Iáculo), speeding faster than slingshot or ballista bolt, piercing one temple of the unfortunate soldier, Paulus, and then speeding on without slowing out the other (*Pharsalia* 9.822–27) in a delightful simile to describe how Doña Mencía de Nidos's words went in one ear and out the other of the inhabitants of La Concepción, terrified by rumor of the approaching Araucanians (*Araucana* 7.30).[77] Ercilla deliberately invokes the "flying serpent's" proper name to conjure the power of the image from *Pharsalia* 9, just as he brings in other references to the same "place" for the same purpose. Additionally, however, he is able to surpass Mena's vague "dragos que buelan" by making explicit the "scientific" name of the snake that Lucan has veiled with an epithet in the common subtext of *Pharsalia* 6.

The final direct reference to both the primary and secondary subtexts in this passage is found, fittingly, in the closing verses of the final stanza devoted to the contents of the flasks in Fitón's antechamber. By winding up the list of substances with "landres, pestes, venenos, quantas cosas, / produze la natura ponçoñosas" (*Araucana* 23.54*gh*), Ercilla neatly skirts around the potentially problematic reading of *Pharsalia* 6.681 that plays such a central role in my discussion of Mena's imitation of Lucan and Ovid. Perhaps to circumvent just such a difficulty, but more probably to distance his own imitation from that of Mena, Ercilla avoids referring to either "named" or "nameless" things, and instead insists on making explicit the link back to the "everything perversely produced by Nature" (quidquid fetu genuit natura sinistro) of *Pharsalia* 6.670. As my discussion in the previous pages of this chapter indicates, the dynamic between *Pharsalia* 6.670 and 6.681 becomes the central axis of Lucan's devastating emulation of *Metamorphoses* 7.262–78. Mena overlooks the opening move in this emulative strategy—*Pharsalia* 6.670—in his own imitation, as indeed he must if he is to restore Ovid's "these and a thousand other nameless things" at the close of the whole passage. Ercilla, significantly, introduces a direct echo of *Pharsalia* 6.670 with "Vello de cuantos monstruos prodigiosos / la superflua natura ha producido" (*Araucana* 23.52*ab*) at about the middle of his imitation of the passage from Lucan, a position that recalls, if imperfectly, the place and function of the model. By explicitly recalling Lucan's *pestes* of *Pharsalia* 6.681 with his "landres, pestes, venenos," as well as the "quidquid fetu genuit natura sinistro" (*Pharsalia* 6.670) with "cuantas cosas / produce la natura ponzoñosas," Ercilla brings his imitation of Erictho's recipe to a close by demonstrating that he, in contrast to Mena, does understand the underlying dynamics of the most devastatingly overwhelming aspect of Lucan's emulation of Ovid.

Pharsalia 6.670 is not the only element from the brewing of Erictho's potion that Mena fails to include in his imitation. Lucan opens the passage by telling us that the witch washes out and fills the legionnaire's chest cavity with "hot blood" (*Pharsalia* 6.667). According to Lida de Malkiel (*Juan de Mena*, 505), when Ercilla finds "sangre de hombres bermejos enojados" (*Araucana* 23.49e) among the first flasks he descries in the Araucan enchanter's antechamber, he is making an original contribution to the locus, and perhaps referring to contemporary ideas about witchcraft. I think it more likely, however, that Ercilla has found a way to necromantically revive yet another element from his primary subtext in a way that fits the context of his own time. From ancient times red-haired or so-complected persons were believed to be "quick-tempered," and hence, "hot-blooded." Again, Ercilla is also able to outshine Mena, simply by divining the means of including something that his rival left out.

The same is probably true of two other substances that Lida de Malkiel also ascribes to Ercilla's originality combined with "hechicerías contemporáneas" (*Juan de Mena*, 505). "Moho de Calauera destroncada / del cuerpo que no alcanza sepultura" (*Araucana* 23.51ab) perhaps reflects some sixteenth-century necromantic custom, but more likely is derived from Lucan's description of Erictho's grave-robbing habits in the section immediately preceding the mixing of her potion (*Pharsalia* 6.529–68). There can be no doubt that "Carne de Niña por nacer, sacada / no por donde la llama la natura" (*Araucana* 23.51cd) is directly inspired by some hexameters from the same passage that read "she pierces the pregnant womb, and delivers the child by an unnatural birth, and places it on the fiery altar" (volnere sic ventris, non qua natura vocabat, / Extrahitur partus calidus ponendus in aris) (*Pharsalia* 6.558–59),[78] as Ducamin so astutely observes (173 n. 7). Both of these excursions beyond the confines of the mixing of the concoction proper are similar to Ercilla's raid on Book 9. They reinforce the macabre atmosphere from the same general source, helping to insure that Ercilla's version of this locus will permanently supplant Mena's in the tradition.

The necromantic quality of Ercilla's effort, in terms of a revival of lost meaning, can be seen most clearly in the case of another ingredient that Mena omitted entirely. The reader will recall that Lucan, at the very beginning of his catalog of Erictho's potion, mentions that the witch generously pours in "lunar poison" (virus . . . lunare) (*Pharsalia* 6.669), an emulatively blunt rendition of Ovid's more elliptical "hoarfrost gathered under the full Moon." Mena does not reproduce all of Lucan's substances, and may well have left this one in his "inkwell" either because he did not understand it or because he found it too "explicit." Ducamin, still the best commentator on Ercilla as far as the Erictho passage as a whole is concerned, suppressed the verse in question in keeping with prevalent Victorian mores and replaced it with a string of dots, without further explanation (175). The author of *La Araucana*, however, seems to have suffered no such compunction in evoking a sly reminiscence of his model. On the contrary, he boldly amplifies this allusion by including a further reference to Pliny (*Naturalis historia* 7.15–16) when he adds "menstruo y leche de hembras azotadas" (*Araucana* 23.54*f*) to the flasks in the wizard's workroom. The key here, that Mena himself may or may not have understood, is supplied by Sulpitius and Beroaldus in their commentary on the 1514 edition of the *Pharsalia*: the "lunar poison" is understood to be nothing less than the menstrual discharge of mortal women (fol. 159r–v). That Ducamin, not to mention Mena, may have been a little skittish about mentioning such a thing is not really surprising—even as recently as 1923, Thorndike, a thoroughly "scientific" writer, would refer directly to menstrual fluid in only Latin (1:82). Again, Ercilla brings an obscure reference in his subtext "up-to-date" across the chasm of anachronism, while at the same time exposing a weakness in the rival, secondary version.

What, then, can Ercilla's imitation of the *nekuia* from *Pharsalia* 6 and its subsequent imitation by Mena tell us about the imitative strategies of Part II of the *Araucana*? The first, and perhaps the most important, lesson we can take from this is that Ercilla is driven to go beyond the "eclectic" and dissimulative practices that have characterized his approach up to this point. He is willing to take the risks involved in measuring himself with a more than "reproductive" stance against a subtext of tremendous power and prestige. Furthermore, he does this necromantically, playing with the shifts in meaning that have intervened over the centuries and turning them to his own pupose as in the case of the "eyes" of lynx and basilisk.

As Stephen Greenblatt has pointed out, the "old world" marvels retailed by ancient authors such as Lucan and Pliny had become somewhat shopworn over the centuries. The encounter with the New World and its "genuine" marvels might have been the final blow, depriving the oft-recited, bookish fantasies of their last glow of wonder by cruel comparison with truly unheard-of, undescribable things that were being "discovered" every day. Curiously, however, this does not seem to be the case. On the contrary, the undeniable discovery of the unquestionably marvelous tended to revive people's credulity; if some marvels were true, why not others? (Greenblatt 22). Ercilla exploits this renewed belief in the wondrous in his litany of the fantastic, hyperbolic contents of the flasks in the Chilean wizard's cave. Unable, in large measure, to communicate the truly "marvelous" of the Araucanian landscape and customs due to the briefness of his acquaintance and the total lack of adequate metaphors, the poet of the *Araucana* falls back upon a necromantic revivification of the ancient tradition of the marvelous to imbue the cave of prophecy and its necromancer with the requisite aura of awe and wonder.

He is also confident enough of his powers to engage his principal subtext in the kind of dialogue that Garcilaso addressed to Petrarch in "En tanto que de rosa y d'açucena," as exemplified by his substitution of the "skin of the spotted amphibious viper" for that of the "horned snake of Libya." This is one of the fundamental requirements of what Greene calls a heuristic imitation (*Light*, 40–41). Ercilla challenges the authority of his principal subtext even as he conjures up its power. Yet I do not think that Ercilla wishes to "Oedipally" supplant Lucan. His ambition does not reach that far; rather, he wants to revive temporarily the corpse of the "dead Latin verses" and make them sing again in a new context, for a new master. In this he succeeds admirably. If critics such as Dieter Janik (100) can complain that Ercilla's imitation is "static" when compared to the "fluidity" of the model in the *Pharsalia*, it is only because they have limited themselves to the establishing and comparing of analogues that characterize traditional "source criticism" and have failed to delve the dynamics of imitative practice in a way that reveals the audacious and transformative, even emulative, movement that swirls through these verses. It is the "action," not of a witch literally stirring ingredients into her decoction, but rather of a poet resuscitating long-dead colleagues so that they can engage in a heuristic dialogue across the years.

It is toward the more contemporary poet, Mena, that Ercilla bares his Oedipal fangs. No recapitulation is necessary here to underline how thoroughly, how consistently, Ercilla strives to outdo and supplant his "father" Mena in this passage. Close reading of the complex, competitive imitation of the "witch" passage reveals just how hotly the blood of rivalry could rise in Ercilla. It is especially significant that this should occur on the doorstep, in the very antechamber, of the mantic grotto where Ercilla unveils the ultimate, underlying relationship of rivalry that drives the engine of prophecy throughout Parts II and III of the *Araucana*. Now that we have seen Ercilla's most ambitious stance before prestigious ancient models, and the intensity of his competitive spirit when matched against a near contemporary, we are ready to explore his encounter with Camoens in the Araucan enchanters' all-seeing globe in the two remaining chapters of this exploration of the intertwining of prophecy and imitation in the service of world-girdling empire.

4

The Light of *Lusíadas* in Fitón's Cave

Inscribing Imperial Rivalry in Magic Crystals

At the very heart of the inner sanctum of Fitón's subterranean manse, Ercilla encounters the enchanter's all-seeing globe. The chamber that contains the great crystal reminds us of Merlin's cave in the *Orlando furioso* and, perhaps, of one of its models in Boiardo's *Orlando innamorato* (2.8.18–20) or other medieval romances (Ariosto, *Orlando furioso*, ed. Bigi, 170–71). Yet the crystalline, thaumaturgical sphere in which the Araucanian wizard conjures up first the "future" Battle of Lepanto and then, during a second visit, a triumphant mapamundi, however, alludes directly neither to the classical epic tradition nor to that of the *romanzi*. As I indicated at the outset, Ercilla finds the model for the Araucanian wizard's prophetic orb in the culminating prophetic passages of Camoens's *Lusíadas*, and unraveling the nuances of the competition expressed in this imitation leads, in turn, to the revelation of the underlying poetic and imperialist rivalry that Ercilla expresses in the two visions displayed in Fitón's globe. In order to establish, however, that the mantic crystal of the *Araucana* is indeed modeled upon the prophetic *globos* of the *Lusíadas*, it is first necessary to survey the literary tradition of crystallomancy, and then to examine certain key representations of the Neoplatonic Intelligible All. This is a journey that may seem to lead down strange paths, yet we will find our way with greater certainty with the aid of a guiding image provided by the twentieth-century Argentine writer Jorge Luis Borges, whose concept of the aleph will prove to be the lodestone that brings us to a vantage point from which we can fully comprehend the light cast by the *Lusíadas* in Fitón's cave.

4.1. Optical Instruments of Prophecy as Revealed by the *Aleph*

As I have demonstrated in the preceding chapters, the Latin epics, medieval romances, and Castilian narrative poems that Ercilla appears to have relied on as models deliver their prophecies by a variety of means. Dreams are not uncommon, either as a component of the topos of "celestial descent" that Thomas Greene examines so exhaustively in his *The Descent from Heaven*, or simply conveying the thought of a loved one, as in Bradamante's dream (*Orlando furioso* 33.59). Two of Ercilla's favorite Spanish forerunners, Lucan and Juan de Mena, for instance, both employ literal necromancies in the key prophetic moments of their poems. On the other hand, in a number of Ercilla's principal models, detailed historical prophecies are seen etched into works of art, or viewed as painted on walls or tent folds. Virgil, Ariosto, and Garcilaso make especially productive use of this ekphrastic recourse for prophecy (*Aeneid* 8.608–731; *Orlando furioso* 33.3–58, 46.76–99; *Egloga II*, vv. 1169–747). Nonetheless, the two most pivotal prophecies, in terms of the narrative structure of the works in which they are found, and most influential in the tradition by Ercilla's time, rely neither on dreams, necromancy, nor ekphrasis per se. Anchises points out the Romans of the future from among the stream of souls swarming about the banks of Lethe like bees around summer blossoms (*Aeneid* 6.706–9). Ariosto deliberately invokes this Virgilian prophetic paradigm when he has the enchantress Melissa pick out the ancestors of the Estense from the throng of *longaevi* swirling about Merlin's subterranean tomb (*Orlando furioso* 3.20–23). Although this last device vaguely suggests a glowing, globular shape in which a prophecy is revealed, nowhere in any of these poems can we find a great, translucent crystal sphere that can represent, depending on the will of its master, the entire cosmos or any part or time contained within the universal whole.

Nonetheless, other avenues beg to be explored. At least two critics have sought to interpret Ercilla's *globo* in the light of the idea of the aleph elaborated by the Argentine writer Jorge Luis Borges in the short story "El aleph" (Hayes 349; Monterroso 231). According to Borges, the aleph is one small space (Borges describes it as two or three centimeters across ["El aleph," 169]) where "están, sin confundirse, todos los lugares del orbe, vistos desde todos los ángulos" (166). One of Borges's characters, Carlos Argentino Daneri, elaborates with enthusiasm: "¡El microcosmo de alquimistas y cabalistas, nuestro concreto amigo proverbial, el *multum in parvo!*" (167). Indeed, Fitón's orb is something of an aleph, although, as Monterroso points out, the precise correspondences between Borges's and Ercilla's descriptions of their respective mantic spheres are loose enough that they could be attributed to mere coincidence (Monterroso 231). Nonetheless, both Hayes (349) and Monterroso (231) affect surprise that Borges fails to mention the *Araucana* among the texts that inspired him in the invention of his aleph. Given Borges's enthusiasm for the recondite and the exotic, this is hardly as surprising as these critics would have it. As Monterroso himself inadvertently makes clear (230), many a Spanish American student makes his or her first, and often only, contact with the *Araucana* as a tedious schoolroom chore. Nothing so tainted with what Robert Graves has aptly called the "classroom curse" would do for the self-created parentage of Borges's little masterpiece.[1] Borges's self-generated, carefully selected literary genealogy of the aleph does, however, lead down intriguing, and ultimately rewarding, paths for the reader of the *Araucana*.

Borges makes references to literary creations analogous to his aleph in two places: in the central episode of "El aleph" where he affects to search for a way to describe the indescribable (169), and in the "Posdata" which forms the conclusion of the tale (173–74). The first passage includes a reference to Alanus de Insulis (otherwise known as Alan of Lille) and his image of "una esfera cuyo centro está en todas partes y la circunferencia en ninguna" (Borges, "El aleph," 169). This is an essentially Neoplatonic notion, and its presence in Alan is ultimately traceable back to Plotinus, as is the occidental concept of the aleph in general (Stefanini 53). As I shall make clear below, Plotinus's formulation of the mental construct of an all-embracing sphere lies at the very heart of Fitón's orb.

In the postscript/conclusion of "El aleph," Borges weaves a deliberately abstruse mantle of orientalia and erudition in which to swathe the parturition of his aleph. The majority of these references, which Borges attributes to the English adventurer, scholar, and arch-orientalist Richard Burton ("El aleph," 173-74), pertain to the topos of the magic mirror—to a certain extent, an analogue of Fitón's globe. Last in the series of allusions is a brief quotation from the work of a near-contemporary of Ercilla. Like the *Araucana*, Edmund Spenser's *Fairie Queene* is an epic poem written at least partly in imitation of the *Orlando furioso* (Fichter 156; Greene, *Descent*, 298; Lewis 298, 304-5). First published in 1590, some twelve years after the first appearance of Part II of the *Araucana*, the *Fairie Queene* enfolds an encomiastic prophecy intended to celebrate and legitimize the monarchy of Elizabeth I (Dobin 140; Fichter 168). Spenser's dynastic heroine, Britomart, catches a glimpse of her destined mate in a "glassie globe" that

> The great Magitian *Merlin* had deuiz'd,
> By his deepe science, and hell-dreaded might,
> A looking glasse, right wondrously aquiz'd,
> Whose vertues through the wyde world soone were
>   solemniz'd.
>
> It vertue had, to shew in perfect sight,
> What euer thing was in the world contaynd,
> Betwixt the lowest earth and heauens hight,
> So that it to the looker appertaynd;
> What euer foe had wrought, or frend had faynd,
> Therein discoured was, ne ought mote pas,
> Ne ought in secret from the same remaynd;
> For thy it round and hollow shaped was,
> Like to the world it selfe, and seem'd a world of glas.
>
> (*Faerie Queene* 3.2.18f–19)

To the extent that this is a "glassie globe"—as Spenser describes it further on (*Faerie Queene* 3.2.21a)—that is, "round and hollow shaped . . . / Like to the world itself . . . a world of glas," Merlin's "looking glasse" is a close analogue of Fitón's thaumaturgic orb. At least one English critic, Warton, noted that Camoens had created a similar mantic sphere in the *Lusíadas*, although he attributes the coincidence to use of similar sources rather than direct imitation (quoted in Spenser 3:216). As far as I know, no modern critic of Spenser seems to have recalled the all-seeing globe of the *Araucana*. Both Iberian *globos* anticipate Spenser's "glassie globe," and as the English poet is himself a highly eclectic imitator, it is not impossible that he may have seen in the Iberian imperialist epics a clever way to update Virgil and Ariosto. But another of the explicitly specified qualities of Spenser's magic mirror, the ability to reveal "What euer foe had wrought, or frend had faynd," as well as the fact that Spenser can call it a "mirrhour plaine" (*Faerie Queene* 3.2.17d), anchor Merlin's glass deeply in the many-layered sediments of a discrete literary tradition.

Spenser had before him, as well as the *romanzi*, a rich heritage of Middle English and medieval French poetry. Chaucer, to name only one, introduces just such a mirror into his "Squire's Tale." The Grand Khan of Tartary is holding court, when in comes riding "a knyght upon a steede of bras, / And in his hand a brood mirour of glas" (vv. 81–82). The intruder describes his gift:

> "This mirour eek, that I have in myn hond,
> Hath swich a myght that men may in it see
> Whan ther shal fallen any adversitee
> Unto youre regne or to yourself also,
> And openly who is youre freend or foo.
>
> And over al this, if any lady bright
> Hath set hire herte on any maner wight,
> If he be fals, she shal his tresoun see,
> His newe love, and al his subtiltee,
> So openly that ther shal no thyng hyde."
>
> (vv. 132–41)

As is plain to see, this mirror, often called Canacee's Mirror after the recipient of the marvelous gift, is a very use-specific brand of aleph.

Indeed, this thaumaturgical instrument is dedicated exclusively to spying out "friend or foe" in both love and war. As the reader of Spenser will recall, Merlin first wrought his "looking glasse" for King Ryence for use in statecraft and war (*Faerie Queene* 3.2.18-19), and Britomart puts it to work—although most chastely—in the service of Venus (*Faerie Queene* 3.1.8*hi*).

Such mirrors are legion, and it would not particularly further the elucidation of Fitón's globe to detail the specific, and usually quite repetitive, marvels of each and every one. Suffice it to say that Virgil's Mirror as described by John Gower in his fourteenth-century allegorical poem *Confessio amantis* (5.2031-44), pertains to the type.[2] The fifteenth-century Scottish poet Gavin Douglas explicitly compares his Mirror of Venus with both Canacee's Mirror from Chaucer and with Virgil's Mirror (*Palice of Honour* 3.24*ghi*). Even Jean de Meun, in his reprise of the optics of Al-Haçen, cannot resist the temptation to play with the topos, claiming that if Mars and Venus had had such a mirror, Vulcan would never have trapped them in his net (*Roman de la Rose* 18060-89). There are many more examples in a variety of European literatures,[3] and the reason for the wide extension of the locus is quite plain.

Chaucer, Gower, and Douglas all make specific reference in their renditions of the topos to a similar mirror that was supposedly once in Rome ("Squire's Tale" v. 231; *Confessio amantis* 5.2031-36; *Palice of Honour* 3.24*g*). As Gower makes quite explicit, this is the mirror reputed to have been crafted by Virgil the Mage—a peculiarly medieval transmutation of our poet Virgil—and given to the emperor of Rome so that he might be apprised of the approach of his enemies. By far the most perdurable medium for the diffusion of this locus is the collection of tales known in Spanish-speaking lands as the *Siete sabios de Roma*.

What is known as the occidental branch of the *Seven Sages of Rome* is thought to have first appeared sometime before 1150, probably in Latin or Old French (Campbell xv, xxi). It became one of the most widely read texts of the Middle Ages and the early modern period. Killis Campbell, writing before 1907, mentions forty distinct versions transmitted in no less than two hundred manuscripts and almost two hundred and fifty editions (xvii). The collection normally contains fifteen stories, and in the majority of versions, one of these is the tale called "Vergilius" (Campbell xxi, xxxv). In most of the versions of "Vergilius," the mage is credited with supplying Rome with a magic mirror that will warn of the approach of any enemy (Campbell xciv). This is the "Mirror that was in Rome" mentioned by so many late-medieval poets.

It is probably futile to inquire after the original of this locus of the magic mirror, and even if we could identify a certain text as the "source," it would not tell us a great deal about Fitón's globe. The important point is the wide diffusion of this particular brand of magic looking glass in European literature. In Spain, the version of *Siete sabios de Roma* containing the tale of Virgil's Mirror was first published in Castilian translation toward the beginning of the sixteenth century, and was frequently reprinted, often in the form of inexpensive *libros de cordel*, up until the end of the nineteenth (Farrell 92, 101).[4]

It is entirely conceivable that Ercilla could have been acquainted with some chapbook version of the *Siete sabios de Roma*. Like the *Historia de Carlo Magno y los doce pares de Francia*, the *Siete sabios de Roma* was just the type of book that found its way into the conquistadors' kit in large numbers during the sixteenth century. Nonetheless, even if Ercilla was well aware of the entire tradition of literary magic looking glasses of the type of Virgil's Mirror, both high and low, it was clearly not the model he chose for Fitón's mantic orb. Gower's mirror, the most closely modeled on that of the *Siete sabios de Roma*, has a range of only thirty miles (*Confessio amantis* 5.2035). Even in the case of the most advanced of the type—and posterior to Part II of the *Araucana*—Merlin's mirror wrought for King Ryence, the principal function is to distinguish friend from foe, whether in love or in war, not to serve as a universal aleph.

Perhaps the closest analogue to Fitón's *globo* in this tradition is the mirror described by the Scottish bishop Gavin Douglas, who also translated the *Aeneid*.[5] Douglas's narrator steals a glance into Venus's radiant mirror, only to be confronted with a vision of "All thingis gone like as thay war present" (*Palice of Honour* 3.26) that begins with the fall of Lucifer, follows on up through Old Testament and Roman history, concluding with the kings of Scotland and famous necromancers such as Roger Bacon (*Palice of Honour* 3.26–49). Although Douglas claims, "All plesand pastance and gammis that micht be, / In that mirrour war present to my sicht" (*Palice of Honour* 3.50*bc*), his vision is declaredly historical, focused on the past, and makes no pretense of prophetic scope. Douglas's Mirror of Venus is similar to Fitón's globe in that it conveys a vision of a sequence of historical events—a précis of world history, in fact—rather than the approach of an enemy or the visage of the beloved, but it still lacks a great deal of the scope and universality of Fitón's globe.

While the orb that Ercilla describes in the Araucanian enchanter's cave is a Neoplatonic representation of the cosmos in which the "claras ideas," which is to say the perfect, Platonic forms that exist beyond the phenomenal universe, are represented in microcosm (*Araucana* 23.71), the magic mirrors are, as Borges has Captain Burton say, "meros instrumentos de óptica" ("El aleph," 174). Although Fitón's orb retains traces of being an optical instrument—it required Fitón forty years of dedication to construct it (*Araucana* 23.71c)—it is a truer aleph than any of the innumerable magic mirrors of the tradition that orbits the *Siete sabios de Roma*.

Borges's Captain Burton also complains that the various literary analogues he enumerates have the additional defect "de no existir" (174). Although Borges takes this observation in a very different direction, for the reader of the *Araucana*, it might suggest that inspiration for Fitón's globe could be found beyond the realm of purely literary models. Certainly, there was no lack of real-life interest in "shewe stones" and crystal gazing in Ercilla's time.

Perhaps the most notorious contemporary crystal gazer was Dr. John Dee. Among the many celebrated séances of his long and checkered career, in at least one Dee entertained no less a seeker than Elizabeth I herself in March 1575 (Dobin 1). Howard Dobin suggests that this encounter inspired Spenser's episode discussed above where Britomart, the dynastic maiden, espies her future mate in Merlin's Mirror (Dobin 5). Although I find a literary genealogy more convincing, there is no reason to deny Dobin's conjecture that Spenser might have found the coincidence of art and life attractive for his allegory (Dobin 5-7). Nor was Dee the only celebrated practitioner of crystallomancy to make his mark in the sixteenth century. The German Cornelius Agrippa, whose infamous career crisscrossed the court of Charles V, was widely reputed to possess a magic mirror that could reveal the circumstances of absent persons (Warton, quoted in Spenser 3:216; Thorndike 5:132). But Agrippa was hardly unique; to judge from the fulminations of such debunkers as Libavius,[6] there was no lack of those who pretended to "construct from the motion of the stars and from the constellations magic mirrors, gems, globes, and many similar devices for exploring the future" (quoted in Thorndike 6:243).

Indeed, such activities often exposed their exponents to considerable risk. Dee's house at Mortlake was burned by a superstitious mob in 1583 (Dobin 4), while Cornelius Agrippa was hounded from venue to venue (Thorndike 5:128–29), and his writings earned an early place on the Index of the Inquisition (Thorndike 6:146). The seriousness with which such illicit forms of divination were viewed increased dramatically in the second half of the century (Thorndike 6:146), and, at least in terms of prohibited books, the climate was less favorable in Spain than elsewhere in Europe (Thorndike 6:148). It does not surprise us, therefore, that Manuel de Faria e Sousa, in his commentary on the first mantic globe described by Camoens, should remark:

> En un globo de materia diafana, como cristalina, vio Proteo esas Ideas, o modelos: aludiendo a estilos de la devinacion, que seria por cierto agora infinito rebolver, y que aun oy usan mugerzillas endemoniadas, i embelecedoras, que encandilando la vista de ignorantes, les asseguran que estan viendo en vidrios, o vacias de agua las personas ausentes que se desean ver: i finge el P. la forma del globo esferica, porque los circulos son mucho de semejantes artes: al fin materia larga; i los que saben no han menester que nos dilatemos; i para los ignorantes mejor es callar: porque no soy yo de los que estan mostrando el camino de las maldades, a quien las ignora, i luego dizen, que es para que se huya del. Escusa dañosissima, con que oy se permite la lecion de muchos libros, que devieran formar una hoguera, porque mas dignamente se ocuparan sus Autores. (col. 4:309–10)

Faria e Sousa's ambivalence is revealing. The poet's invention is to be admired, as it is based on Neoplatonic principles—the "ideas" or "modelos"—but it skirts dangerously near the shoal waters of heresy. The underlying assumption is that the instructed—"los que saben"—are capable of sorting out the licit from the illicit, but the statement that the ignorant are best left in the dark betrays how closely to the rocks Faria e Sousa feels his poet is sailing. The formulaic recommendation that books that delve too explicitly into these matters be burned does not entirely conceal the anxiety that hovers around even the "informed" reference to such topics.

What truly authorizes the poet's use of such potentially risky ideas, however, is the respectable genealogy of imitation that the commentator constructs for the passage. As I explain in some detail below, Faria e Sousa is able to thoroughly legitimize Camoens's prophetic strategies by demonstrating the links binding this potentially heretical "globo" to the most Christian prophecy of all, that of the baptism of Christ in Sannazaro's *De partu Virginis*. The point that I want to insist on here, however, is the centrality of imitation in the poet's development of this prophetic device. Ercilla, like Camoens and Spenser, was probably well aware of the practice of crystallomancy, but the sordid charlatan in the mold of Dee or Cornelius Agrippa is hardly the image that the poet is working so hard to evoke. Where for Borges's Captain Burton "not existing," or rather existing primarily as a literary topos, is a fatal defect, for the sixteenth-century epic poets under discussion it is a saving grace.

This is especially true in the case of the *Araucana*. As I have demonstrated in the preceding chapters, Ercilla deliberately embeds the séances of Fitón's cave in a carefully crafted setting of intensified *imitatio*. More than any other part of the poem, the web of prophecy of Part II of the *Araucana* revolves around advertised, recognizable imitation of literary models. In fact, Ercilla's two most outstanding examples of set-piece imitations—imitations that betray no dissimulative initiative at all—are the litany of magical substances (*Araucana* 23.49–54) and the conjuration of the infernal powers (*Araucana* 23.80–82), and they embrace the introduction of Fitón's globe (*Araucana* 23.68–71) like two finely polished diamonds set immediately to either side of a central cabochon of mantic chrysoberyl. It being far more likely than an allusion to questionable contemporary practices, we must look for a carefully focused imitation of a particular literary subtext when we seek to understand Fitón's orb.

Just such a prophetic globe—a sequence of two, in fact, precisely as in the *Araucana*—can be found in the final, most important prophetic passages of *Os Lusíadas*. As I have pointed out in Chapter 1, Camoens's poem was published in 1572, six years before the appearance of Part II of the *Araucana* in 1578. As I have indicated, there were a number of points of contact, and potential rivalry, between the two works from the outset. That precisely such a rivalry drives the prophetic machinery of Part II of the *Araucana* becomes clear as we compare Ercilla's mantic crystal with its models in the *Lusíadas*.

In order to appreciate the dimensions and motives of this poetic and imperialistic rivalry, it is first necessary to examine Camoens's presentation of the two prophetic spheres of *Lusíadas* 10 and their literary and philosophical pedigree. Then it becomes clear how Ercilla's rendition of Fitón's globe alludes directly to that of his Portuguese rival. This in turn suggests, as I believe Ercilla meant it to, a comparison of the prophetic visions encapsulated in the respective crystals. In this regard, I discuss the first vision displayed in the aleph of both poems as the final section of the present chapter. The following chapter focuses on the rival mapaemundi portrayed in the second appearance of the all-seeing globe in both poems, and its particular significance for colonial epic. In conclusion, I elucidate the circumstances of both the political and poetic rivalry revealed by the conjunction of the prophetic conclusion of the *Lusíadas* with the nexus of Ercilla's web of prophecy in Part II of the *Araucana*.

4.2. The Prophetic Spheres of the *Lusíadas*

In its structural unity and in its well-articulated integration of the recent history of overseas colonial expansion beyond the familiar confines of Europe with classical models of imperialist epic, principally the *Aeneid*, the *Lusíadas* is in many ways everything the *Araucana*, seen as a whole, is not. Ercilla opens the *Araucana* with a challenge to—and thus a backhanded invocation of—Ariosto, implying a return to the gravity of *Arma virumque cano*; Camoens commences the *Lusíadas* by at once invoking the *Aeneid* while at the same time throwing down his poetic gauntlet before the entire tradition of European epic (*Lusíadas* 1.1–3).[7] Unlike the initial program of the *Araucana*, however, Camoens claims for his poem a worldwide scope from the outset, and the struggle for empire is clearly focused through the lens of the crusade for the Faith (*Lusíadas* 1.2). Furthermore, in contrast to the *Araucana*, there is no major change of program in the *Lusíadas*; the project announced in the first stanzas is systematically fulfilled throughout the ten cantos of the poem. Finally, Camoens incorporates the full Olympian mythological apparatus of Homeric and Virgilian epic into the Christian providentialist scheme of the *Lusíadas*, while Ercilla, and most of his other contemporaries, elect to exclude the pagan gods from decisive interference in the *machina* of their poetic universes.[8]

As could be expected in a work that stakes out its own genealogy in the ground of the *Aeneid*, the narrative development of the *Lusíadas* features a deliberately deployed web of prophecy. This series of prophecies, however, lacks some of the dynamic interplay of gradual revelation that characterizes the prophetic pattern of the *Aeneid* that I explored in Chapter 2. Camoens wastes no time in bringing the prophetic machinery into play in a council of the gods at the very outset of the poem (*Lusíadas* 1.24–29), by having Jupiter foretell the future Portuguese dominion over the seas. This loosely corresponds to the same deity's initial reassurance of Venus and prophecy of Aeneas's ultimate triumph, with which Virgil had opened the prophetic scheme of the *Aeneid* (1.257–97). Jupiter's revelations provoke the ire of Bacchus, fearful that his own legendary achievements in the East might be eclipsed (*Lusíadas* 1.30–32). Thus the basic supernatural apparatus of the poem is established, with Bacchus taking the role of Juno, opposing the progress of the Portuguese, and Venus, as in the *Aeneid*, assuming the mantle of protectress of the seafaring imperialists.

Jupiter reiterates his support of the Lusitanians, prophesying further details of the future dominions in the East to reassure an anxious Venus (*Lusíadas* 2.44–55), again recalling Venus's entreaties of Jupiter at the opening of the *Aeneid* (1.229–53). Up to this point, the human protagonists have remained outside of the magic circle of prophetic knowledge. Venus's remonstrances, however, prod Jupiter into dispatching Mercury down to earth (*Lusíadas* 2.56), where the messenger appears to Gama in a dream, warning the Portuguese captain of his present danger and spurring him on toward India (*Lusíadas* 2.61–65). This episode clearly recalls the dispatch of Mercury to pry Aeneas loose from the arms of Dido and set him back on course toward the future Rome (*Aeneid* 4.219–76). While lacking the dynamism of Virgil's rendition—Gama has no Dido holding him back—the episode serves to anchor Camoens's creation in the prestigious subtext of the *Aeneid*.

Camoens next takes a prophetic step backward in time, having Gama describe the visionary dream of King Manuel (*Lusíadas* 4.67–75). This opens as a celestial ascent reminiscent of the *Somnium Scipionis*, and culminates in the prophecy of a river god (*Lusíadas* 4.73–74). As a result of this revelation, King Manuel, upon awakening, convokes a royal council to plan nautical explorations of new climes, thus setting in motion the chain of events leading up to Gama's expedition (*Lusíadas* 4.75–76).

The next prophecy occurs at the very heart of the poem. Gama, still relating his story to the king of Melinde, recounts that as his fleet prepared to navigate the southernmost cape of Africa, a gigantic, menacing figure condensed out of a black cloud (*Lusíadas* 5.37–40). This proved to be the Titan Adamastor who inveighed against the Portuguese for their temerity in breaking through the "vedados términos" that he guards (*Lusíadas* 5.41). Adamastor, as the personification of the Cape, acknowledged the Portuguese's future success, but warned them of the price he will extract from them in storms, shipwrecks, and lost lives (*Lusíadas* 5.42–48). In a very general way, this sobering prophecy corresponds to the imprecations of the Harpy Celaeno, when she warns the Trojan wanderers of the high price they must pay for their eventual success (*Aeneid* 3.253–57). Celaeno's admonition occurs at roughly the halfway point of the first, *Odyssey*-like half of the *Aeneid*, tempering the incrementally positive flow of prophecy with a reminder of the dark side of empire-building. The *Lusíadas*, focusing on Gama's voyage, is all *Odyssey*; the struggle for supremacy that occupies the second half of the *Aeneid*, reminiscent of the *Iliad*, is only hinted at in the prophecies of the final canto of the *Lusíadas*. Thus Adamastor's prophecy occupies the same structural position, and performs the same function, as Aeneas's encounter with the Harpy.

After Gama concludes telling the king of Melinde the tale of his voyages, the Portuguese set out on the final leg of their journey to India, and Bacchus exhorts an undersea council of the marine deities to do their worst against the European interlopers. Proteus, the "shepherd of Neptune's flocks," attempts to prophesy the success of the Lusitanians (*Lusíadas* 6.36), but his voice is drowned out in the clamor roused by Bacchus and his partisans. The storm, which I discussed in Chapter 1, follows as a result of Bacchus's machinations. The party inimical to Portuguese success continues to dominate the prophetic wavelengths of this section of the poem. Thus, the diviners predict to the Indian ruler the coming disaster at the hands of the Portuguese (*Lusíadas* 8.45–46); Bacchus appears to a Muslim cleric in a dream (*Lusíadas* 8.47–50), reprising a standard epic topos, and incites the locals against the westerners. The Portuguese are able to overcome all obstacles, however, and set sail for home with their mission accomplished.

Gama and his men are rewarded for their perserverance with a romp on the Isle of Love, prepared for them by Venus and administered by Tethys and her sea nymphs (*Lusíadas* 9). The Portuguese and their Nereid companions having made their sport, the leading nymph

(Tethys) takes Gama by the hand and guides him to a palace built of gold and crystal at the summit of an island peak:

> Pera lhe descobrir da vnida esphera,
> Da terra immensa, & mar não nauegado
> Os segredos, por alta profecia,
> O que esta sua naçam só merecia.
>
> (*Lusíadas* 9.86e–h)

First, however, the Portuguese heroes and their semidivine hostesses settle down to a sumptuous banquet (*Lusíadas* 10.2–5).[9] To complete their entertainment, one of the nymphs begins to sing to musical accompaniment (*Lusíadas* 10.5e–f). Camoens describes the nymph's song:

> Cantaua a bella Ninfa, & cos acentos
> Que pellos altos paços vão soando,
> Em consonancia ygoal, os instromentos
> Suaues vem a hum tempo conformando:
> Hum subito silencio enfrea os ventos,
> E faz hir docemente murmurando
> As agoas, & nas casas naturais
> Adormecer os brutos animais.
>
> (*Lusíadas* 10.6)

This of course is Orphic song, much like that attributed to Severo by Garcilaso in *Egloga II*.[10] Camoens, however, is far more explicit about the other, Neoplatonic nature of the nymph's singing:

> Com doce voz está subindo ao ceo
> Altos varões, que estão por vir ao mundo,
> Cujas claras Ideas vio Protheo,
> Num globo vão, diafano, rotundo,
> Que Iupiter em dom lho concedeo
> Em sonhos, & despois no reino fundo,
> Vaticinando o disse, & na memoria
> Recolheo logo a Ninfa a clara historia.
>
> (*Lusíadas* 10.7)

Here, at last, we have a visionary globe similar to that of Fitón. We also have found the key to deciphering a complex puzzle of imitation and intertextuality that will ultimately reveal the inner secrets of the Araucanian enchanter's mantic crystal.

Where Garcilaso found many of the attributes of Severo's verbal powers in Sannazaro's *Arcadia*,[11] Camoens has gone to the same Italian author's other most famous work, a Christian epic in Latin hexameters, the *De partu Virginis*.[12] As Faria e Sousa points out in his commentary on the *Lusíadas* (4:col. 311), Camoens is alluding here to the final, culminating prophecy of Sannazaro's epic treatment of the birth of Christ (*De partu* 3.281–504). Specifically, Sannazaro has the tutelary god of the River Jordan recall that he had heard the prophecy of future glory from "sea blue Proteus" (caeruleus Proteus) (*De partu* 3.336).[13] Camoens anchors this allusion by quoting from Sannazaro's rendition of the prophecy, echoing Sannazaro's rendering of the river Jordan's summation of Proteus's revelations:[14]

> Prophesying these things with a happy heart, old Proteus, one time, when by chance he had passed through my cave, foretold that . . . (*De partu* 3.486–87)

> (Haec senior quondam felici pectore Proteus
> *vaticinans*, ut forte meo diverterat antro,
> praemonuit . . .)

Camoens reinforces the connection with Sannazaro's Proteus by insisting that, the marine deity having seen the Neoplatonic prototypes of these future things in Jupiter's globe, "despois no reino fundo, / Vaticinando o disse" (*Lusíadas* 10.7fg).[15] The "reino fundo" corresponds to the river god's deep cave, described earlier as "resounding with waves" (undisonum) (*De partu* 3.281), as does "vaticinando," the Portuguese "-ndo" form functioning here as a present active participle, with "vaticinans." But this is not the limit of the reminiscences evoked by this reference to the *De partu Virginis*.

By alluding so unmistakably to this prophetic passage of Sannazaro's epic poem, Camoens is also implicitly positioning his own prophecy in a competitive poetic relationship with Garcilaso's epic prophecy in the *Egloga II*. It will be recalled that Garcilaso's Neoplatonic mage,

Severo, receives his prophetic, encomiastic vision of the House of Alba from the tutelary deity of the river Tormes. Garcilaso says of Severo:

> A aquéste el viejo Tormes, como a hijo,
> le metió al escondrijo de su fuente,
> de do va su corriente començada;
> mostróle una labrada y cristalina
> urna donde'l reclina el diestro lado,
> y en ella vio entallado y esculpido
> lo que, antes d'aver sido, el sacro viejo
> por devino consejo puso en arte,
> labrando a cada parte las estrañas
> virtudes y hazañas de los hombres
> que con sus claros nombres illustraron
> quanto señorearon de aquel río.
>
> (*Egloga II*, vv. 1169–80).

Thus, just as in the *De partu Virginis*, a river god plays a crucial role in the transmission of the prophecy. Of far more significance, however, is the plastic medium of the prophecy: the ekphrastic urn. As E. Mele has noted (Garcilaso, *Obras*, ed. Rivers, 375–76), the river Tormes's urn described by Garcilaso directly recalls the similar vessel possessed by Sannazaro's personification of the river Jordan:

> Ipse antro medius pronaque acclinis in urna
> fundit aquas: nitet urna novis variata figuris
> crystallo ex alba et puro perlucida vitro,
> egregium decus et superum mirabile donum
>
> (*De partu* 3.298–301)

> (In the middle of the cave, leaning on a tilted urn, he [King Jordan] pours the waters: the urn glows, decorated with novel figures made out of white crystal, and is translucent with pure glass; an uncommon honor and marvelous gift of the gods.)

Sannazaro goes on to describe the prophetic, emblematic scene portrayed on the urn (*De partu* 3.302–17), and the leaning river god establishes the correspondence beyond doubt. The urn itself, in both cases, is made of crystal, is worked with figures, and above all, bears the images of things to come. Like Camoens's *globo* with its depiction of "Altos varões, que estão por vir ao mundo," Garcilaso's bears witness to the future "virtudes y hazañas de los hombres," while Sannazaro's heralds the baptism of Christ and the consequent descent of the Holy Spirit in the form of a dove (*De partu* 3.313–15). This is not an unfitting parentage for Camoens's prophecy that proclaims the triumph of Christian arms over the might of the infidel. Nevertheless, both Sannazaro's and Garcilaso's urns presage Camoens's *globo* in an even more fundamental sense.

In the same way that Camoens's translucent spheres, both this one referred to by the nymph in her song and its double shown to Gama by Tethys in the second phase of the final prophecy of the *Lusíadas* (10.77–79), are Neoplatonic representations of the cosmos, so too are Sannazaro's, and ultimately Garcilaso's, urns. To appreciate this point, it is necessary to return to Sannazaro's presentation of the river Jordan in his cave. At the beginning of the passage, just before mentioning the urn, Sannazaro paints the following scene:

> Herboso tum forte toro undisonisque sub antris
> venturas tacito volvebat pectore *sortes*
> caeruleus rex, humentum generator aquarum
> Iordanes.
>
> (*De partu* 3.281–84)

> (Then by chance in his grassy bed below the caves resounding with waves, the azure king, begetter of the dewy waters, Jordan, was silently reflecting on the future *lots of destiny*.)

Thus, while reclining on his prophetic urn, the river god is mulling over the fates of events yet to occur. This, doubtlessly, is meant to remind the well-read reader of the established image of a deity drawing or pouring the *lots* (sortes) of future lives or deaths from an urn. Perhaps the most well-known example is from Virgil. As Aeneas and the Sibyl gain entrance to the lower reaches of the underworld, Virgil describes the placing in the geography of hell of some of the souls of the dead:[16]

> nec vero hae sine *sorte* datae, sine iudice, sedes:
> quaesitor Minos *urnam* movet . . .
>
> (*Aeneid* 6.431–32)
>
> (Yet not without *lot*, not without a judge, are these places given: Minos, presiding, shakes the *urn*.)

Indeed, the shaking of lots in an urn to determine the chances of either death or reincarnation is something of a poetic commonplace (Shanzer 142–43).[17]

There is one rendition of the topos, however, that is of special interest. Martianus Capella, in his *De nuptiis Philologiae et Mercurii*, describes a conclave of the gods. As the various deities assemble:[18]

> quaedam femina, quae Adrastia dicebatur, urnam caelitam superamque sortem inrevocabilis raptus celeritate torquebat excipiebatque ex volubili orbe decidentes sphaeras peplo inflexi pectoris Imarmene. (Shanzer 214; Martianus Capella, *Martianus*, ed. Willis, 19 [*De nuptiis* 1.64])
>
> (a certain woman who was called Adrastia twirled the divine urn and the fate of the immortals with a speed of irrevocable momentum; and Imarmene of the unbending heart caught in her peplos the spheres that fell from the turning globe.)

Danuta Shanzer's comments on this passage are very suggestive: "The metaphor of the *urna* full of lots is a standard one, but the presence of this adjective *caelitem* coupled with the *ex volubili orbe* below suggests a further refinement: that the urn is the world itself, contained within the *aplanes* or outermost sphere" (142).

Shanzer goes on to propose that Martianus's development of this image of the cosmic urn is grounded in Plato's presentation of the spindle of the Fates in the "Vision of Er the Armenian" that occurs at the end of the *Republic* (Shanzer 143).[19] According to Shanzer, Martianus may have found this conflation of Plato's spindle of the universe with the urn containing the lots of life in a now-lost commentary on Plato's *Republic*, perhaps that of Porphyry (201). However Martianus may have come by the idea, it is rich in implications for later developments of the locus of the urn as a medium for portrayal of future events. The urn, just like the diaphanous globe, is an aleph, a representation of the Neoplatonic Intelligible All.[20]

It would seem that Camoens, aware of the prestige of Garcilaso's example, and of the fact that Garcilaso modeled his urn on that portrayed by Sannazaro, has deliberately alluded to the same passage in the *De partu Virginis* in order to surpass Garcilaso in the prophetic climax of his poem. This he accomplishes, in part, by a certain indirection or dissimulation. Thus Camoens, by mentioning Proteus and alluding directly to the finale of Proteus's prophecy in the *De partu Virginis*, reminds the reader that both Garcilaso and his model have used the crystalline urn as the aleph, or representation of the totality of the universe in which future events may be seen because the Neoplatonic Intelligible All contains the "forms" or "exemplars" of all perceptible phenomena, past, present, and future. This indirect reference to the ekphrastic prophecy of the *Egloga II* being established, Camoens proceeds, in place of the cosmic urn, to substitute an image of the universe that is even truer to the Neoplatonic source of the idea of this type of representation. To appreciate the brilliance of Camoens's stroke here, it is necessary to visit the fountainhead of Neoplatonism: the *Enneads* of Plotinus.[21]

Along with the works of Plato himself (many of them only recently made available in Latin translations thanks to the labor of the humanists), Plotinus's reflections on Platonic philosophy continued to form the backbone of sixteenth-century Neoplatonic thought. Like Plato's works, Plotinus's were newly edited and translated into Latin at the end of the fifteenth century by Marsilio Ficino (Wallis 171). If Camoens knew Plotinus at first hand, it would almost certainly have been in Ficino's Latin translation. In a very suggestive passage on beauty as a means of understanding the visible world as a reflection of the world of Intellect, Plotinus remarks:[22]

> Accipiamus igitur nostrum hunc mundum cogitatione sic se habentem, ut pars unaquaeq[ue?]: maneat quidem quod est: sed singulae sibi invicem insint. Fingamus inquam in unum cuncta simul pro viribus congregata: adeo ut quod cunque singulorum prius sese oculis offert: velut si sphaera sit exterior, continuo sequatur solis quoque spectaculum simulque reliquarum stellorum imago. Intusque videantur terra, mare, animalia omnia: velut in sphaera quadam ubique perspicua. Et denique re ipsa

contingat cuncta in uno quoque conspicere. Esto igitur in animo lucida quaedam imaginatio sperae, in se habens omnia, sive agitata, sive manentia, aut partim quidem mobilia, partim vero stabilia. (*Enneades* 5.8.9)

(Let us then apprehend in our thought this visible universe, with each of its parts remaining what it is without confusion, gathering all of them together into one as far as we can, so that when any one part appears first, for instance the outside heavenly sphere, the imagination of the sun, and, with it, the other heavenly bodies follows immediately, and the earth and sea and all the living creatures are seen, as they could in fact all be seen inside a transparent sphere. Let there be, then, in the soul a shining imagination of a sphere, having everything within it, either moving or standing still, or some things moving and others standing still.) (*Plotinus*, ed. Armstrong, 5:243)

This is the Neoplatonic vision of the sensible universe in its seminal form, conceived of as a transparent, shining sphere. All things are visible within it, yet as Plotinus goes on to make clear in the same passage, they are but phantasms of the true forms that exist in the Intelligible world beyond the bounds of our limited bodily perceptions (*Enneads* 5.8.9).[23] Camoens hints at this Neoplatonic maxim when he stipulates that Proteus saw the "claras Ideas" in the glowing, diaphanous sphere (*Lusíadas* 10.7c).[24]

In order to better understand the import of these "claras Ideas" it is necessary to return to the image of the mirror, but here a much more sophisticated version of an all-seeing mirror than that circulated in the tradition of the "Vergilius." The twelfth-century poet Bernardus Silvestris describes the Mirror of Providence:[25]

Erat igitur speculum Providentiae, cuius magna admodum circumferentia, intermina latitudo, extensa semper facies, perspicuus introspectus ut, quas olim contineret imagines, non rubigo detereret, non deleret antiquitas, non turbaret incursus. Vivebant ideae, vivebant exemplaria nullo nata in tempore nulloque in tempore desitura. Speculum igitur Providentiae mens aeterna, in qua sensus ille profundissimus, in qua rerum genitor extortorque omnium intellectus. Erat in exemplaribus invenire simulacrum, cuius velis generis, quale, quantum, quando et quomodo proventurum. Illic silva prioris adhuc nubilo vestustatis obducta. Exinde sub aedificatore Deo vultus novitios induebat. Illic elementorum amicitia mediator et conplectibilis ex se, in se coincidens et mutuus internexus. Illic orbiculata caelique volubilis magnitudo. Illic fomes ille vivificus, endelechia molem illam intrinsecus atque extrinsecus circumplexa. Illic ignes siderei, illic propietate partili ministra mundo lumina, sol vitalis et generans, luna coadiuvans incrementis. Illic planetae, illic signa planetarum hospitiis et potentiis deputata. Illic pedestrium, natatilium, pennatorum genera, sicut suas conplectitur species familiaritas elementi. . . . Ea speculi tabulaeque differentia, quod in speculo specialiter status naturarum caelestium indeflexus, in tabula quidem quam maxime temporales qui permutantur eventus. (*De Mundi Universitate* 2.11.16–51; pp. 57–58)

(The Mirror of Providence was of vast circumference and boundless breadth, its surface extending forever, its shining glass such that whatever reflections it had once received no rubbing might erase, nor age make faint, nor destruction mar. There lived ideas and exemplars, not born in time and destined not to pass away in time. This Mirror of Providence is the eternal mind, in which resides that unfathomable understanding, that intellect which is the creator and the destroyer of all things. Among the exemplars might be discovered the model of anything, of whatever sort, and its quality and quantity, and when and how it had come to be. Here was Silva, still hidden by the darkness of her ancient condition; now she assumed the shapes of new creations, through the refining work of God; now came the balancing and self-containing harmony of the elements, containing and interweaving them with each other. Now appeared the rounded and revolving vastness of the firmament, now emerged the vital fire, Endelechia embracing the whole, within and without. Now the fiery bodies of the sky, now those orbs jointly empowered to provide for the world, the vivifying and generative sun, and the moon, assisting all birth. Now the planets and their signs. Now the races of land-going, swimming, and feathered creatures, as the friendly quality of this or that element received their several species. . . . The difference between the Mirror and the Table was that the Mirror was particularly concerned with the unchanged state of heavenly natures, while the Table for the most part exhibited such products of the temporal order as were subject to change.) (114–15)

Bernardus distinguishes between "ideas and exemplars, not born in time" and their perceived reflections. The Mirror is the "mens aeterna," wherein reside the discernible images of the true forms of the various phenomena perceived in the visible world.[26]

Another twelfth-century poet, Alan of Lille, expands on this image, also insisting on the difference between the eternal, immutable forms or ideas, and their temporal manifestations.[27] In Book 6 of Alan's *Anticlaudianus*, the allegorical personification Prudence (Phronesis) has penetrated the fiery heavens in search of a soul for the Perfect Man. She swoons. Upon recovering, she cannot bear the brightness of the Intelligible world. Faith, who accompanies her, comes up with a solution:[28]

> Sed quamvis oculus mentis resplendeat intra,
> Languescit tamen exterior nec ferre nitorem
> Sustinet empireum nec tantum fulgur Olimpi.
> Ergo suam solers matrona recurrit ad artem
> Et presigne, decens, rutilans, immitabile, tersum,
> Grandi diffusum spacio scriptumque figuris
> Presentat Fronesi speculum, quo cuncta resultant
> Que locus empireus in se capit, omnia lucent,
> Que mundus celestis habet, sed dissona rerum
> Paret in hiis facies. Hic res, hic umbra uidetur,
> Hic ens, hic species, hic lux, ibi lucis imago.
> Detinet hoc speculum mentem uisumque Sophye
> Sistit, ne maior oculis lux obuiet, illos
> Offendens, uisumque simul cum mente fatiget.
> Hoc speculum mediator adest, ne copia lucis
> Empiree, radians uisum, depauperet usum.
> Visus in hoc speculo respirat, lumen amicum
> Inuenit et gaudet fulgens cum lumine lumen.
> Cernit in hoc speculo uisu speculante Sophia,
> Quicquid diuinus in se complectitur orbis.

. . . .
. . . sed cuncta stupet que nuncius offert
In speculo uisus, ubi nil mortale, caducum,
Defficiens, terrestre micat, solumque refulget
Eternum, celeste, manens, immobile, certum.
Hic uidet ingenitas species, speculatur ydeas
Celestes, hominum formas, primordia rerum,
Causarum causas, racionum semina, leges
Parcarum, fati seriem mentemque Tonantis,
    (*Anticlaudianus* 6.113–29, 210–17)

(But however clear the mind's eye within becomes, the bodily eye nevertheless is still weak and cannot bear the fiery brightness or the great flash of Olympus. The resourceful maiden, then has recourse to a device of her own. She presents Phronesis with a mirror that is outstanding, symmetrical, of a reddish hue, reflective, polished, very broad of surface, equipped with images. In this mirror is reflected everything which the fiery region encompasses: in it shines clear everything which the heavenly universe holds, but the appearance of these things differs from the real objects. Here one sees reality, here a shadow; here being, here appearance; here light, there an image of light. This mirror holds Phronesis' attention and steadies her eyes lest a light too strong for them strike them, injure them and tire both mind and eyes. The mirror acts as an intermediary to prevent a flood of fiery light from beaming on her eyes and robbing them of sight. By use of the mirror her eyes recover, find a kindly brightness and enjoy the clear, gleaming light. As her eyes explore the mirror, Sophia sees there all that the divine world embraces. . . . Nothing that flashes there is mortal, transitory, waning, earthly: there is reflected only the eternal, the heavenly, the permanent, the immovable, the fixed. Here she sees ungenerated species, views celestial ideas, the form of man, the first beginnings of things, the causes of causes, the seeds of reason, the laws of the Fates, the procession of Destiny, the mind of the Thunderer.) (160–63)

Alan has taken Bernardus's Mirror, and the Neoplatonic conceptions that it represents, and rendered them in a more recognizably Christian form (Alan of Lille, *Anticlaudianus*, ed. Sheridan, 32). According to the formulations of Plotinus, the Intelligible world, what Prudence can only bear to see reflected in the mirror, is timeless, containing all times; itself nonspatial, but containing the possibility of all spaces. Plotinus uses the Greek term *Nous* to designate this Intelligence (Wallis 49–53). Bernardus personifies Noys, and it is she that bestows the mirror on Urania (*De Mundi Universitate* 2.9.89, 2.11.16). Alan has Faith give Prudence her mirror and identifies the realm of Noys as that of God (*Anticlaudianus* 6.1, 6.116). Additionally, Alan has taken Plato's metaphor of the cave dweller who, blinded upon emerging into the light, must at first rely on shadows for his perceptions of reality (*Republic* 7.514–17), and conflated it with the mythical account of how Perseus was able to slay Medusa (Alan of Lille, *Anticlaudianus*, ed. Sheridan, 28–29, 141 n. 14).[29] The essential concept, in Plotinus, Bernardus Silvestris, and Alanus de Insulis, however, is the same. The visible universe may be conceived of as a shining sphere of light that contains all possible phenomena—a perfect aleph, in fact—but this aleph that is perceived with the human mind is but an imperfect reflection of the glowing sphere that contains the "claras Ideas," the "forms and exemplars," the "causes of causes."[30]

This, then, is Camoens's first mantic "globo." According to Camoens, Jupiter revealed it to Proteus in a dream (*Lusíadas* 10.7c–f). In the Plotinian tradition, especially in *Enneads* 5.8, Jupiter—the Thunderer—is often identified with Intelligence (Wallis 135). Proteus, on the other hand, in the tradition of *Georgics* 4 represents the "totality of natural creation" (Quint, *Origin*, 75–78). The globe Proteus describes in his song, as overheard and retold by the nymph, is a true aleph, and no mere optical instrument. This becomes even more explicit with the second "globo" of the *Lusíadas*.

When the nymph has concluded singing the prophecy seen by Proteus in the first diaphanous globe, Tethys addresses Gama:

> "Faz te mercê barão a Sapiência
> Suprema, de cos olhos corporais
> Veres o que não pode a vã ciência
> Dos errados & míseros mortais:
> Sigueme firme, & forte, com prudencia

Por este monte espesso, tu cos mais."
Assi lhe diz, & o guia por hum mato
Arduo, difficil, duro a humano trato.

(*Lusíadas* 10.76)

Again, we are going to be shown what the "corporeal eyes" are normally not able to see. This unique vision will be perceived only by grace of Supreme Wisdom. "Sapiência Suprema" is easily enough glossed as "Deus," but betrays the Neoplatonic substratum of Camoens's prophetic vision. Can we not sense the presence of Plotinus's Intelligence, or Bernardus's Noys, or Alan's Sophia underlying this turn of phrase?

The thick wood is, again, the "selva selvaggia" of prophecy that I discussed in Chapter 2. Camoens continues:

Não andão muito que no erguido cume
Se acharão, onde hum campo se esmaltaua,
De Esmeraldas, Rubis, tais que presume
A vista, que diuino chão pisava:
Aqui hum globo vem no ar, que o lume
Claríssimo por ele penetraua,
De modo que o seu centro está euidente,
Como a sua superficia, claramente.

(*Lusíadas* 10.77)

The high peak, surrounded by the forbidding wood, and the enchanted garden blooming with precious stones, will of course remind the reader of the *Araucana* of the upland *locus amoenus* from which rises the pyramidal peak where Bellona leads Ercilla (*Araucana* 17.43–51), or of the garden where the woman in white presents him with the vision of his future bride (*Araucana* 18.67).[31] Ercilla, of course, describes those *loci amoeni* as blossoming with true flowers, and saves the precious stones for the great chamber in Fitón's cave that contains the mantic globe:

El Cielo alto Diaphano estrellado,
de innumerables piedras reluzientes,
que toda la gran cámara alegraua,
la varia luz que dellas rebocaua.

(*Araucana* 23.66d–h)

Although Ercilla places his orb in a subterranean vault, and Camoens uses the alternate visionary platform of a high peak, both the "divino chão" studded with relucent gems and the "cielo alto diáfano estrellado" suggest the dome of the starry heavens. If these were the only similarities, of course, it would be risky to posit any connection beyond the purest coincidence, almost implicit when dealing with essentially the same theme.[32] The luminous globes suspended in the air, however, are unmistakably related. Compare Ercilla's description of Fitón's mantic orb:

> En medio desta cámara espaciosa,
> que media milla en quadro contenía,
> estaua vn Globo o Bola poderosa,
> que vna luziente Esphera ceñía:
> Que por arte y labor marauillosa,
> en el ayre por sí, se sostenía,
> que el gran círculo y máchina de dentro,
> parece que estribauan en su Centro.
>
> *(Araucana* 23.68)

In both cases, the globe is radiant, translucent, and suspended in the air; in both, the center is as visible as the surface. The exact correspondence did not escape the eye of Faria e Sousa, who remarked on how both Tethys's globe and Fitón's are "supernaturally" suspended in the air (4:col. 448). Faria e Sousa, writing in the early seventeenth century, is also the only critic, as far as I know, to have suggested that Ercilla's globe is a direct imitation of Camoens's (4:col. 447–48).[33] Before developing this point, however, which I believe is crucial to the understanding of Part II of the *Araucana*, it is prudent to insist on the essential identity shared by this globe shown to Gama by Tethys and the first globe, revealed to Proteus in dreams by Jupiter, and then celebrated by the nymph in her song. This is especially important, because, as I will demonstrate, Fitón's orb is cast in the same mold.

In the discussion above of the "globo" experienced by Proteus, it has been established that the diaphanous sphere described by Camoens is the poetic representation of the Neoplatonic Intelligible All, or aleph. We have seen how Plotinus describes the visualization of just such an orb in which the great sphere of the Heavens—the Empyrean of the Ptolemaic system—contains the stars, the planets, the earth, the seas, and all the kinds of living creatures (*Enneads* 5.8.9). Bernardus Silvestris and Alan of Lille, while enumerating similar range of contents, both insist, perhaps less subtly than Plotinus, on the fundamental difference between the true form of this sphere—the Intelligible All—and its reflected representation—the sensible universe (*De Mundi Universitate* 2.11.16–51; *Anticlaudianus* 6.113–29, 210–17). Camoens's first globe, that reported by the nymph as seen by Proteus, as I have demonstrated, corresponds to the authentic model of the aleph. It contains the "claras ideas," the immutable exemplars that produce, by their reflection in the crude material of the phenomenal universe, the stars, planets, earth, and living creatures that we experience. The second globe is, then, a sensible visualization *in parvo* of the archetypal model vouchsafed to Proteus. This becomes even more apparent as Camoens continues his description:

> Qual a materia seja não se enxerga,
> Mas enxergasse bem que está composto
> De varios orbes, que a diuina verga
> Compos, & hum centro a todos só tem posto:
> Voluendo, ora se abaxe, agora se erga,
> Nunca se ergue, ou se abaxa, & hum mesmo rosto
> Por toda a parte tem, & em toda a parte
> Começa & acaba, em fim por diuina arte.
>
> Vniforme, perfeito, em si sostido,
> Qual em fim o Archetipo, que o criou:
> Vendo o Gama este globo, comouido
> De espanto & de desejo ali ficou,
> Dizlhe a Deosa: "O trasunto reduzido
> Em pequeno volume aqui te dou,
> Do mundo aos olhos teus, pera que vejas
> Por onde vas, & yrás, & o que desejas."
>
> "Ves aqui a grande máchina do mundo,
> Etérea, & elemental, que fabricada
> Assi foy do saber alto, & profundo,
> Que hé sem principio, & meta limitada,
> Quem cerca em derredor este rotundo
> Globo, & sua superficia tão limada,

> Hé Deos, mas o que hé Deos ninguém o entende,
> Que a tanto o engenho humano não se estende."
>
> "Este orbe que primeiro vay cercando
> Os outros mais pequenos, que em si tem,
> Que està com luz tão clara radiando,
> Que a vista cega, & a mente vil tambem,
> Empireo se nomea, onde logrando
> Puras almas estão de aquelle bem,
> Tamanho, que elle só se entende & alcança,
> De quem não ha no mundo semelhança."
>
> (*Lusíadas* 10.78–81)

The conventional gloss on these and the following stanzas is that they are "the cosmography of Ptolemy, then current in Europe, and made up of eleven spheres, with the earth at the centre" (Camões, *Lusíadas*, ed. Pierce, 240 n. 5). This is certainly true; but more important, as Luciano Pereira da Silva points out in a now-classic monograph, they are not only a very complete and subtle rendering of the most widely accepted sixteenth-century cosmographic theories, they also represent a very sophisticated presentation of the Neoplatonic doctrine of the Intelligible All.

In spite of the publication of Copernicus's *De revolutionibus orbium coelestium* in 1543, Ptolemy's geocentric cosmography remained the dominant system taught in the universities up through the end of the sixteenth century (Pereira da Silva 3). Ptolemy's works were known in the West through ninth-century Arabic versions as reworked in the thirteenth century by John of Holywood, generally known as Sacrobosco. Sacrobosco's treatise *De Sphaera* remained the principal text on astronomy for more than three hundred years and was the most widely read work on the subject in sixteenth-century Europe (Pereira da Silva 16–19). In addition to numerous Latin editions, Sacrobosco's *De Sphaera* was known in a variety of vernacular translations that often updated the original with extensive commentaries and annotations. One of the most influential of these was that of the Portuguese royal cosmographer (*cosmógrafo-mor*) Pedro Nunes, who taught mathematics at the university in Coimbra from 1544 up through 1562 (Pereira da Silva 15). It is not entirely improbable that Camoens may have studied with Nunes himself.[34] As Pereira da Silva demonstrates, Camoens certainly incorporates many of the nuances of Nunes's presentation of Sacrobosco into the cosmographical passages of the *Lusíadas* (3). It is another vernacular version of Sacrobosco's *De Sphaera*, however, that most concerns us here. Pereira da Silva reports finding an Italian translation of Sacrobosco with commentary in the Astronomical Observatory of the University, titled *Annotationi sopra la lettione della Spera del Sacrobosco, authore M. Mauro Fiorentino*, Florence 1550. In addition to a faithful translation of Sacrobosco, this includes *Vna Spera Theologica Diuina, & Christiana e Vna Spera Platonica, con Alcune eccitatione mathematiche, Theologiche & diuine* (64). Pereira quotes from this section:

> Presupponendo la spera materiale, colli suoi dieci circuli (come *figura perfetta*, alla quale non si puo aggiungnere, o minure cosa alcuna, & doue *il principio è vnito col fine*) significare quella diuina & ideale spera intelligibile, qual' è la nuda, pura, & inuisible essentia di Dio glorioso & benedetto. . . . Et cosi il circulo & spera, significare quella intelligibile, & Platonica, intelletuale spera, della quale il centro è per tutto, & la circunferencia in nessun' luogo. (p. 161; quoted by Pereira da Silva 64)

> (Presupposing the sphere to be material, with its ten circles [as a *perfect shape*, to which nothing can be added or taken away, and where *the beginning is joined with the end*] it signifies that divine and ideal intelligible sphere, which is the unadorned, pure, and invisible essence of glorious and blessed God. . . . And thus the circle and sphere represent that intelligible, Platonic, intellectual sphere, whose center is in all places, and its circumference in none.)

This passage, in conjunction with the accompanying illustrations taken from Mauro Fiorentino showing a "Spera Platonica" alongside a "Spera Theologica Christiana & diuina" (Pereira da Silva 66–67), makes it clear beyond a doubt that in the sixteenth-century reception of Sacrobosco, the complete representation of the eleven-sphered Ptolemaic universe was read as the visual encoding of Plotinus's *Nous*. Camoens's second "globo" is indeed the detailed, sensible visualization of the Neoplatonic Intelligible All "reduzido / Em pequeno volume." This is truly the *multum in parvo* so prized by Borges's Carlos Argentino

Daneri: the living Neoplatonic aleph as it can be visualized, as proposed by Plotinus, in the meditation of the human mind.

What I have proposed in the preceding discussion of the Neoplatonic nature of the two "globos" of the *Lusíadas* is not that Camoens necessarily read, or imitated, Plotinus, Bernardus, or Alanus. On the contrary, it is not necessary that he have had direct contact with any of these particular texts—the ideas they contained permeated Camoens's intellectual world so thoroughly that the exact source is of little moment. What is significant is that Camoens has raised the prophetic machinery of his poem to the highest conceptual level attainable within the confines of the Neoplatonic system. These cosmographical ideas represent the culmination of at least two thousand years of an intellectual tradition nurtured in a constant dialogue between literary images and metaphors, on the one hand, and philosophical, mathematical, and astronomical formulations on the other. In both totalizing scope and philosophical profundity, Camoens's prophetic globes are worthy rivals of Virgil's combined *nekuia* and *katabasis* of *Aeneid* 6.[35] No epic poet between Virgil and Camoens approaches the conceptual grandeur and polished execution of this integration of cosmology with human history, and the Portuguese poet undisputably performs an unprecedented *aggiornaménto* on the traditional prophetic machinery of epic, bringing it into line with the development of post-Plotinian Neoplatonism that was unavailable to Virgil.

For an ambitious poet attempting the historical epic on a grand scale who was aware of the prophecy of *Lusíadas* 10, there would be no question that it would loom large as an object of *emulatio*. As we have seen, Spenser may well have drawn upon Camoens's "globos" to ennoble the long tradition of the magic looking glass in his rendition of Merlin's Mirror.[36] For an Iberian poet such as Ercilla, who like Camoens was engaged in rendering the worldwide Iberian imperialist enterprise into historical epic verse, Camoens's prophetic tour de force would have posed, on the one hand, a daunting, and on the other, an irresistible, challenge.

4.3. The Mantic Globes of the *Araucana*

To understand how Ercilla responded to the challenge of Camoens's Neoplatonic globes, it is first necessary to examine the Castilian poet's presentation of Fitón's orb in some detail. Once the exact nature of the Araucanian wizard's mantic "bola" has been established, the contents of the prophecies themselves will reveal the dimensions of Ercilla's poetic and imperialist rivalry with Camoens. The first vision in the respective globes occupies the final section of this chapter. The second vision, proffering in both cases a mapamundi crucial to the competition between the two rival empires, forms the principal matter of Chapter 5. In conclusion, I explore how the dynamics of *emulatio* determine the sea change in the course of the *Araucana* that I delineated at the outset in Chapter 1.

Camoens takes two looks at the Neoplatonic *sphaera* in *Lusíadas* 10, each encapsulating a prophetic vision of Portuguese imperial domination in the East. In the same way, Ercilla makes two visits to Fitón's cave, and in each the prophetic revelation concerns a salient aspect of Philip II's empire and is portrayed in the Araucanian mage's globe. As I have explained above, there is a subtle difference between the globe shown by Jupiter to Proteus and the *sphaera* revealed to Gama by Tethys. Proteus, as a god, can perhaps apprehend more directly the realm of *nous* than Alan's Prudence, while Tethys's sphere is clearly a "sensible" representation of the Intelligible world. In contrast, Ercilla perceives Fitón's globe as essentially the same in both of his descriptions. In both of these, Fitón's orb closely corresponds to Tethys's sphere, for the most part, although it also displays an important reminiscence of Proteus's "globo."

Thus when Fitón himself describes his mantic creation to the poet-protagonist Ercilla, he insists that

> Mas no haurá en larga edad cosa futura,
> ni oculto disponer de inmóbil hado:
> que muy claro y patente no me sea,
> y tenga aquí su muestra y viua ydea.
>
> (*Araucana* 23.71e–h)

We are reminded that Camoens explicitly states that Proteus saw the "claras ideas" of the future Portuguese conquerors of the East in the globe shown him by Jupiter (*Lusíadas* 10.7bc). Ercilla here is making sure that his reader recognizes the full range of Neoplatonic implications inherent in his wizard's crystal, while at the same time establishing the parity of his prophetic medium with that of Camoens. If the Portuguese poet's prophecy originates in the timeless space-beyond-space of the Neoplatonic *nous* where exist the archetypal exemplars, the "causes of causes," Ercilla can certainly do no less. Thus Fitón must be able to call up at will the "viva idea" of future people and events.

As I have already pointed out, Faria e Sousa recognized the most direct similarities between Ercilla's and Camoens's "globos" in the context of Tethys's *sphaera* and suggested that Ercilla's is an imitation of Camoens (4:col. 447–48). Faria e Sousa makes this assertion in the context of Camoens's initial description of Tethys's globe and Ercilla's first depiction of Fitón's orb:

> Aqui hum globo vem no ar, que o lume
> Claríssimo por ele penetraua,
> De modo que o seu centro está euidente,
> Como a sua superficia, claramente.
>
> (*Lusíadas* 10.77e–h)

> estaua vn Globo o Bola poderosa,
> que vna luziente Esphera ceñía:
> Que por arte y labor marauillosa,
> en el ayre por sí, se sostenía,
> que el gran círculo y máchina de dentro,
> parece que estribauan en su Centro.
>
> (*Araucana* 23.68c–h)

The principal points of correspondence are the spherical shape—both are referred to as "globos"—the translucence, and the fact that the center and the surface are simultaneously, and equally, visible. The further detail that it sustains itself in the air with no visible means of support recalls Camoens's observation that Tethys's globe exists "em si sostido" (*Lusíadas* 10.79a), but also directly repeats Camoens's "no ar" (*Lusíadas* 10.77e) with "en el ayre" (*Araucana* 23.68f). As we have seen in Ercilla's imitations of Garcilaso (Chapter 2) and Lucan and Mena (Chapter 3), when Ercilla wants to signal a specific subtext, he will do so at the very outset of his imitation. This is clearly the case here. The allusion to Camoens's globe is unmistakable.

Ercilla, however, does not try to match Camoens's masterful cosmic icon point for point. Once the allusion has been established, the Castilian poet incorporates Camoens's peerless aleph into his own carefully constructed conception of Fitón as a Renaissance mage. Thus

Fitón himself describes the globe and how he himself has managed to conjure it into visibility:

> "Y esta bola que ves, y compostura,
> es del mundo el gran término abreuiado,
> que su difficilíssima hechura,
> quarenta años de estudio me ha costado,"
> *(Araucana* 23.71a–d)

In the same way that Tethys says of her globe: "O trasunto reduzido / Em pequeno volume aqui te dou, / Do mundo" (*Lusíadas* 10.79e–g), Fitón can say of his that it is "del mundo el gran término abreuiado" (*Araucana* 23.71b). In other words, both are examples of the *multum in parvo*, authentic alephs. But there is also an essential difference. Proteus was shown his globe by Jupiter, identified by Camoens in his palinodal stanzas as Divine Providence (*Lusíadas* 10.83ab). Tethys attributes the grace that provides Gama's opportunity of viewing her globe to the same source—"a Sapiência Suprema" (*Lusíadas* 10.76ab) and asserts that it is itself the archetype of its creator (*Lusíadas* 10.79b), which is to say the Intelligible All, glossed by Camoens himself as "Deus" (*Lusíadas* 10.80g). Tethys serves as a guide figure, as does Fitón, but her nature is very different in every other important respect. There is no way that Tethys could be considered the fabricator of the globe that she displays to Gama. Fitón, on the other hand, has devoted forty years of thaumaturgical study to the crafting of the globe that occupies the inner sanctum of his cave.

In a sense, then, this cannot help but diminish the scope of Ercilla's imitation. Where Camoens's "globos" are highly accurate and sophisticated representations of the Intelligible All and its sensible visualization—the highest type of the aleph—Ercilla's aleph is poised on the brink of sliding back into the category of "mere optical instrument." In fact, Ercilla's description of Fitón's globe calls to mind that toward the end of the self-reflecting gallery of magic mirrors cited—according to Borges—by Captain Burton, we find a deliberately skewed reference, as if itself seen in a funhouse mirror, to a gentle parody of the Neoplatonic aleph, and a close analogue of the Araucanian enchanter's orb. Borges affects to quote Burton as mentioning, just before the culminating reference to Spenser, "la lanza especular que el primer libro del *Satyricon* de Capella atribuye a Júpiter" ("El aleph," 174).

The one known work of the fifth-century-A.D. writer Martianus Capella is generally considered a Menippean satire, but the title is customarily given as *De nuptiis Philologiae et Mercurii* (Shanzer 29–43).[37] And indeed, there is a kind of combination aleph/optical instrument in Book 1, although it is hardly a "lanza especular." Martianus, in his description of the same council of the gods in which he describes the cosmic urn we have examined in our discussion above, has both Jupiter and Juno seated on elaborate thrones in full regalia. Martianus portrays the scene:

> his igitur uterque regum indumentis decenter ornati ante concessum in suggestu sidereo positam quandam sphaeram caelatam varietate multiplici conspicantur, quae ita ex omnibus compacta fuerat elementis, ut nihil abesset, quicquid ab omni creditur contineri natura. illic caelum omne, aer, freta diversitasque telluris claustraque fuere Tartarea; urbes etiam, compita cunctarumque series animantum tam in specie quam in genere numerandae. quae quidem sphaera imago quaedam videbatur ideaque mundi. in hac quid cuncti, quid singuli nationum omnium populi cotidianis motibus agitarent. Pythei reformantis speculo relucebat. ibi quem augeri, quem deprimi, quem nasci, quem occidere Iuppiter vellet, manu propria ipse formabat; quam terrarum partem disperdere, quam beare, quam vastam quamque celebrem cuperet, fictor arbitrarius variabat. (*Martianus Capella*, ed. Willis, 21; *De nuptiis* 1.68)

(Thus beautifully decked out in these garments they [Jupiter and Juno] looked at a certain sphere carved with multifarious complexity which was placed before their seat on a starry platform. This was formed of all the elements in such a fashion that nothing was absent of all that which is thought to be included in nature as a whole. All of the aether was there, the lower air, the seas, the diverse areas of the earth, and the gulfs of Tartarus, as well as cities, crossroads, and the whole line-up of living things to be counted as much in species as in genera. The sphere appeared to be the very image and Platonic Form of the universe. And in this orb shone forth, in the mirror of the metamorphosizing Apollo, what each and every people of all nations got up to in its daily activities. There Jupiter directed with his own hand who he wished to rise, who to sink, who to be born, who to die. The arbitrary Maker showed no consistency about which part of the earth he desired to destroy, which to bless, and which to lay waste, and which to make populous. (Shanzer 215; *De nuptiis* 1.68)

The sphere is clearly a representation of the *multum in parvo*. It is not the Intelligible All itself, since it is represented as being mounted "on a starry platform," which is to say upon the Eighth Heaven or Firmament, and set before the thrones of the gods.[38] This sphere then, like Plotinus's sphere (cf. Shanzer 151), is a visualization or model of the sensible universe, although it displays the "ideas."[39] Furthermore, this model suggests the object of art as medium of ekphrasis in the sense that it is "carved with multifarious complexity" (caelatam varietate multiplici). Most important of all, it is explicitly an "optical instrument" as well as an aleph. Not only does Jupiter view the world through this sphere, but he also points out "with his hand" what he decides will occur within it. This reminds the reader of the *Araucana* of Fitón, who causes his orb to come to life by striking it with his wand, accompanying this action with terrible spells (*Araucana* 23.79–82), and obliges the image of the wreck-strewn sea off Lepanto to cloud over in the same way (*Araucana* 24.96).

Ercilla insists on the "optical instrument" nature of Fitón's globe, as does Martianus. Thus the poet-protagonist of the *Araucana* recounts that as he looks into the globe:

> Yo con mayor cudicia por vn lado,
> llegué el rostro a la Bola trasparante
> donde vi dentro vn Mundo fabricado,
> tan grande como el nuestro y tan patente:
> Como en redondo espejo releuado,
> llegando junto el rostro claramente,
> vemos dentro vn anchíssimo palacio,
> y en muy pequeña forma grande espacio.
>
> (*Araucana* 23.76)

Again, there is the reiteration of the *multum in parvo*, but there is also the metaphor of the mirror. Thus Ercilla utilizes the simile "como en redondo espejo revelado," while Martianus refers to his aleph as a "metamorphosising mirror."[40] Both authors also insist on the same type of details, including even the most ignoble species of animal life. Thus Ercilla describes the globe on his second visit:

> Era en grandeza tal que no podrían,
> veynte abraçar el cerco enteramente,
> donde todas las cosas parecían,
> en su forma distincta y claramente:
> Los campos y Ciudades se veían,
> el tráfago y bullicio de la gente,
> las aues, animales, lagartijas,
> hasta las más menudas sauandijas.
>
> (*Araucana* 27.4)

Martianus is engaged in satire, or at least wishes to disguise his compendium of pagan knowledge as such (Shanzer 43), and the all-seeing sphere follows a series of other metaphoric world models that Shanzer believes Martianus found in some Neoplatonic commentary (201). In the case of the "carved sphere," Martianus has taken the Plotinian image of the aleph that I have discussed at length above, in the section on Camoens, and transformed it into another comical element in his satire. Thus the noble philosophical concepts of the Intelligible All and its sensible visualization are diminished into an optical instrument. The satirical twist is made patent by the final sentence, where Martianus asserts that Jupiter wreaks his will with capricious abandon in the world represented in the sphere. Is Ercilla engaged in a similar enterprise in his imitation of Camoens?

As has been pointed out in Chapter 1, section 1.3, parody can be the last resort of the emulator when the model itself has exhausted the possibilities of "serious" treatments of the locus in question. The example of Ercilla's devastating emulation of Mena's imitation of Lucan in Chapter 3 has clearly established the intensity of Ercilla's emulative initiative. Camoens's rendering of the aleph as medium of prophecy, as indicated in section 4.1 above, is a conceptually sophisticated and poetically polished elevation—more than a mere emulation—of the highly canonic ekphrastic prophecies of Sannazaro and Garcilaso. In fact, it is a clear case of the modern surpassing the ancient, outdoing even Virgil. To engage Camoens's cosmic icon feature by feature, as Ercilla has done with Lucan's list of magical substances, for instance, and surpass the Portuguese poet's performance in the same way would be a challenging enterprise indeed. It is not surprising that Ercilla does not attempt to do so. Is his rendition, then, parodic, like that of Martianus Capella?

Certainly, the passages describing the chamber of alchemical ingredients and the conjuration of the infernal powers are both heavily laden with hyperbole, and it is not difficult for the modern reader to interpret their macabre exuberance as comic. One of the charges frequently leveled against Ercilla is that he lacks the ludic dimension of his Italian models, especially Ariosto (Alegría 35). Ercilla certainly displays a sense of humor in the *Araucana*, but it tends to the same kind of dry gallows irony so beloved by Lucan, and is often exhibited in the Castilian poet's imitations of the *Pharsalia*.[41] But these are never parodies, and I find it difficult to read Ercilla's rendering of Fitón's globe as parodic. Certainly, it would be odd for Ercilla to frame the encomiastic prophecies of Lepanto and the Spanish Empire in a destructive parody of the type seen in Quevedo's parody of Góngora's "En un pastoral albergue" or Lucan's of *Aeneid* 6.

As Shanzer points out (43), Martianus Capella may have clothed his pagan images in parodic guise in order to avoid problems with the ecclesiastical authorities. Camoens's cosmic icon does tread on treacherous ground, dealing directly as it does with the nature of God and the cosmos. But would it have been any safer for Ercilla to have reduced Camoens's Neoplatonic aleph to a necromancer's crystal ball, albeit a very large one? Although Camoens certainly threads his way admirably through what could easily be a theological minefield, and Ercilla may have doubted his own powers to surpass the performance, the Ptolemaic cosmological description contained in *Lusíadas* 10 was hardly controversial in the mid-sixteenth century.[42]

Ercilla himself begs off from direct competition with Camoens's description of the eleven cosmic spheres on the grounds of brevity. At the end of his description of the mapamundi in the second vision of the globe, Fitón informs Ercilla:

> "Y como ves en forma verdadera
> de la tierra la gran circunferencia
> pudieras entender si tiempo vuiera
> de los celestes cuerpos la excelencia,
> la Máchina y concierto de la Esphera

> la virtud, de los Astros y influencia,
> varias reboluciones, mouimientos,
> los cursos naturales y violentos."
>
> *(Araucana* 27.53 [1578 27.52])[43]

Characteristically, Ercilla turns the plan of the model around. Where Camoens works from the highest heavens down to the earth, using the extended cosmological description as a preface to his mapamundi, Ercilla does exactly the reverse. In this position, after the terrestrial content of the vision has been detailed, of course, the careful delineation of the celestial spheres would indeed seem digressive. In this way Ercilla excuses himself from what would probably have been a doomed project in terms of emulation.

If Ercilla avoids direct competition with the celestial machinery of Camoens's aleph, then, what has he to gain from alluding so precisely to it in the description of his own prophetic medium? We can find a clue in the denouement to this episode. After Fitón has excused himself from describing the celestial spheres on grounds of lack of time (*Araucana* 27.53 [1578 27.52]), he amplifies the point, saying that the sun is setting. The Araucanian enchanter then conducts the poet back to where he can encounter his friends (*Araucana* 27.54 [1578 27.53]). These verses recall Severo's farewell from the personified River Tormes after viewing the ekphrastic prophecy of the urn (*Egloga II* 1802–6). Ercilla has invested a great deal in the creation of Fitón as a Renaissance mage, modeled on Garcilaso's Severo as well as Merlin, as delineated in Chapters 2 and 3. By rendering the Neoplatonic aleph as an optical instrument fashioned by Fitón, Ercilla may diminish his cosmic icon, but at the same time he increases the stature of his guide figure and necromancer. This leaves, however, the problem of how Ercilla will deploy his emulative forces in the context of poetic rivalry with Camoens.

We have seen enough of Ercilla's imitative and emulative practice to assume that he does not allude to Camoens's masterful *globos* out of a poverty of invention. Ercilla clearly wishes the reader to recognize the Camoenian subtext. Given the ferocity of Ercilla's emulative impulse that I have explicated in Chapter 3, it is unlikely that the Castilian poet invokes the *Lusíadas* in a passive, sacramental, or reproductive spirit. As demonstrated, the flame of competition with contemporaries and near contemporaries burns hotly in Ercilla's imitative praxis. In this confrontation with an Iberian imperial and dynastic competitor, however, the rivalry, unlike that in the case of the witch passages from the *Pharsalia* and the *Laberinto de Fortuna*, is to be played out not in the machinery of prophecy but in the content. It is important that Fitón's globe be an aleph because it must have a certain vatic parity with Camoens's prophetic globes, but Ercilla seems to have been aware that an attempt at close emulation of the model was unlikely to be successful. Where he can be confident of challenging and besting his subtext is in the arena of the respective glories of the two rival empires as portrayed in the aleph. In order to fully appreciate this point, it is necessary to examine Ercilla's two visions in the Araucanian enchanter's *globo* in turn, comparing them with their Camoenian counterparts.

4.3.1. The Naval Battle

In what seems to be an unmistakable allusion to the *Lusíadas*, Ercilla, like Camoens, describes two prophetic visions in his aleph. The first of these is the Battle of Lepanto. If Saint Quentin was the military episode most closely associated with the accession to power of Philip II—celebrated in stone and painting in the Escorial (Cabello Lapiedra 85), Philip's principal monument and favorite lair—Lepanto was considered by many to be the crowning achievement of his reign, and of all Christendom in the sixteenth century (López del Toro 30–31; Mas 1:189–92; Braudel, *Mediterranean*, 1088, 1104). There were two problems involved with its inclusion in the *Araucana*, however. The first is that the naval battle occurred almost twenty years after the action Ercilla is narrating about the war in Chile. The second is that the Mediterranean sea fight has no obvious connection with the central action of the *Araucana*.[44] The device of prophecy solves the first problem, although Fitón's rationalization for transgressing the prohibition on prophesying "los casos no llegados" on the grounds that Ercilla's initial guide, Guaticolo, is his nephew, is perhaps a little weak (*Araucana* 23.64). Ercilla explicitly addresses the second difficulty by having Fitón declare:

> "Que pues en nuestro Arauco ya se halla,
> materia a tu propósito quadrada,
> donde la espada y defensiva malla,

>   es más que en otra parte frequentada:
>   Sólo te falta vna Nabal batalla,
>   con que será tu historia autorizada,
>   y escriuirás las cosas de la guerra,
>   así de mar también como de tierra."
>
>   (*Araucana* 23.73)

This echoes Ercilla's statement in the prologue to Part II that he would try to relieve the monotony of colonial warfare and elevate the subject of his poem, not by deviating from his martial muse, but rather by including more illustrious battles, including one at sea.[45]

That a sea battle crucial to empire should occupy the central portion of an ekphrastic prophecy rendered in a cosmic icon has highly canonical antecedents. Even if Ercilla and his contemporaries had not read the *Iliad*, they probably knew that the Shield of Achilles (18.483–607) was interpreted in Augustan Rome as a cosmic icon, or representation of the universe (Hardie 340–46). Ovid refers to it as such: "the shield engraved with a representation of the vast universe" (clipeus vasti caelatus imagine mundi, *Metamorphoses* 13.110). Sixteenth-century readers likewise understood very well that the concept, if not the specific contents, of the Shield of Aeneas (*Aeneid* 8.625–731) was modeled on that of Achilles. Virgil inscribes his hero's shield with the culmination of the prophetic history of Roman imperialism begun with Jupiter's prophecy at the opening of the poem (*Aeneid* 1.257–96) and amplified in the central prophecy of Book 6 (Hardie 339, 364).[46] At the very center of the Shield of Aeneas, Virgil portrays the naval battle of Actium, where the future Augustus Caesar defeated the combined fleets of Anthony and Cleopatra (*Aeneid* 675–731). Virgil describes the central boss of the shield as having three panels (Virgil, *Aeneid*, ed. Williams, 2:271). The first two depict the battle itself, and the third the subsequent triumph in Rome where all the nations of the East are brought under Augustus's imperial yoke. In terms of the structure of the ekphrastic passage describing the shield, the naval battle and its outcome occupy the entire second half, and represent "the divinely favoured achievement of Roman world empire" (Hardie 350–51).[47] Virgil, the most canonical of epic poets, then, provides a model of an ekphrastic cosmic icon that enshrines a naval battle emblematic of worldwide, ultramarine imperial domination.

It did not escape the attention of Ercilla and his contemporaries that the Battle of Lepanto was fought near the scene of Actium. Ercilla underlines the coincidence at the outset of his description of the vision in Fitón's globe:

> Y por aquel lugar se descubría,
> el turbado y rebuelto mar Ausonio,
> donde se difinió la gran porfía,
> entre César Augusto, y Marco Antonio:
> Assí en la misma forma parecía,
> por la vanda de Lepanto y Fabonio,
> junto a las Curchularas hazia el puerto,
> de Galeras el ancho mar cubierto.
>
> (*Araucana* 23.77)

Although Ercilla does not insist on the parallels in his depiction of the battle itself, this reminder at the outset serves to alert the reader to the full range of correspondences between the two sea fights.

As mentioned in Chapter 1, at midcentury the Spanish historian López de Gómara described the relative situations of the Ottoman and Hapsburg empires in the following terms: "Estos dos emperadores, Carlos y Soliman, poseen tanto como poseyeron los romanos, y si digo mas no erraré, por lo que españoles han descubierto y ganado en las Indias; y entre estos dos está partida la monarchia: cada qual dellos trabaja por quedar monarcha y señor del mundo" (*Crónica de los Barbarrojas*, 346).

It is particularly significant that Gómara sets out the paradigm of universal empire in terms of "tanto como poseyeron los romanos." The Roman Empire was still the metaphorical model of world dominion. Many things had changed between the 1540s, when Gómara was writing, and the 1570s, but the basic sense of being locked in rivalry for mastery of the world with the Ottomans had not diminished. In fact, for much of the century the Spaniards had felt themselves to be at a distinct, if inexplicable, disadvantage in their implacable struggle with the upstart, infidel Turks (Mas 1:2–29). Although the successful defense of Malta in 1565 did something to bolster injured Spanish pride, Lepanto was the victory that truly "washed" the Spaniards' honor and gave them the assurance that they would prevail in this struggle to the death with the representatives of the Antichrist on earth (Mas 1:189–90). Although many historians tend to denigrate the actual long-term results of Lepanto, it did mark the beginning of the decline of Turkish sea power (Braudel, *Mediterranean*, 1088). Furthermore, in the immediate aftermath of the battle, no one had that kind of perspective on events, and it was widely felt that Christendom, led by Spain, was on the brink of recovering the Holy Land and Constantinople, as well as the lucrative trade routes to the East that had been so long under Muslim control (Braudel 1104). Thus if Actium, as celebrated in ekphrastic prophecy by Virgil, represented the triumph of order over chaos and the concomitant extension of the power of the metropolitan center out to the periphery of the physical world (Hardie 351), Lepanto promised as much to the Spaniards of the 1570s. It is in this light that Ercilla casts the battle by his explicit reference to Actium at the outset, and it is in this light that we can appreciate Ercilla's strategy for surpassing his Portuguese rival.

Virgil's Shield of Aeneas becomes something of a paradigm for ekphrastic prophecy in all subsequent poetry. We can see its mark, if faintly, in Garcilaso's ekphrastic vision in the urn. Although the river god's urn—a higher type of aleph—has replaced the shield, Garcilaso portrays Charles V's relief of Vienna—the culminating victory with its attendant triumph of the *Egloga II*—as much as possible as a naval action (*Egloga II* 1575–691). The emperor's success at Vienna in 1532, like his similar feat in 1529, was widely credited with saving Europe from total domination by the Grand Turk. Suleiman had brought the largest military force ever assembled by an Ottoman sultan, the most awesome army imagined by sixteenth-century Europe, to the very threshold of the heartland of the Christian West.[48] The threat was such that, unlike during the previous Turkish advance on Vienna in 1529, Charles was able to rally the full support of his Spanish subjects to the distant shores of the Danube (Mas 1:18–19). The Christian force assembled in response by the Hapsburg monarch was also deemed the largest of modern times.[49] Although Suleiman opted to withdraw before Charles and the main body of the Christian army arrived, the Turks suffered heavy losses and western Europe was spared the fate of Hungary and the Balkans.[50] Despite the fact that both armies fought primarily on land, the Danube squadrons played a key role (cf. *Egloga II* 1635–38); the Christian fleet alone numbered over one hundred ships (Braudel 848–49). If not exactly an Actium, the relief of Vienna was a precursor of Lepanto, fought against the same enemy, and the enterprise was conceived of in terms of a crusade and a defense of Christendom in both cases.

As indicated above, Camoens alludes to Garcilaso's prophecy of the urn in his rendition of the prophecy seen in Proteus's globe. Camoens elevates the ekphrastic vision inscribed in a work of art to a revelation of the Neoplatonic ideas in an aleph, but once again, the manically delivered message centers on the war between Christians and Infidels, European expansion to the East, and naval warfare. The prophecy sung by the nymph covers the history of the Portuguese viceroys and their struggles to expand and maintain domination of the Indian Ocean and the spice trade from the time of Gama up to c. 1550 (*Lusíadas* 10.10–73). This series of contests, of course, centered on the deployment of sea power. Thus, throughout the prophecy seen in Proteus's globe, Camoens narrates, not one naval battle, but a whole series of naval operations. The enemies vary; sometimes they are characterized as alliances of "Gentios e de Mouros" (*Lusíadas* 10.43d); at others Camoens specifies the Turks who came to reinforce their Muslim brethren in the struggle against the Christian imperialists (*Lusíadas* 10.62b, 68a).[51]

One of the most outstanding episodes, which dominates the final stanzas of the prophecy and which itself was expanded by Ercilla's rival Jerónimo Corte Real into the subject of an entire epic, is the second siege of Diu in 1546–47 (*Lusíadas* 10.67–71).[52] Camoens makes special mention of the fearsome Turkish heavy artillery that played such a prominent role in the siege (*Lusíadas* 10.69ab). Although the actions described in this prophecy, like the siege of Diu, were not strictly speaking sea battles, they were often amphibious operations, and always involved the deployment of forces by sea for both the Portuguese and their Turkish rivals.

Near the outset of the vision, Camoens explicitly states that the deeds of the Portuguese in these wars eclipse those of the most famous Greeks and Romans (*Lusíadas* 10.20–21). Thus, although Actium is not specifically invoked, it is implicitly surpassed. The nymphs have foretold that the Portuguese are destined to rule the seas, and that the prophecy will provide the details of this dominion (*Lusíadas* 9.86h). If Virgil's ekphrastic prophecy of Aeneas's shield implies the extension of empire to the periphery, Camoens's prophetic vision in the globe explicitly delineates this expansion of European imperialism to rich, long-coveted lands beyond even the most ambitious dreams of Augustan Rome.

I do not mean to suggest that Garcilaso, Camoens, or Ercilla is imitating Virgil's Shield of Aeneas in the precise sense of specific textual allusion discussed in Chapter 1. Nonetheless, there is an inescapable, generic affinity running as a deep undercurrent through all three of the Iberian poets' imperialist prophecies that ultimately flows from Virgil's own imitation of Homer's cosmic icon, the Shield of Achilles. This can be briefly summarized as a series of historical events, centered on naval triumph or sea power, of crucial importance to European imperialist ambitions in the face of the age-old challenge of the East, depicted in the prophetic medium of a cosmic icon or aleph. In the case of the three sixteenth-century poets, the East is personified in Muslim civilization and its most aggressive imperialist standard-bearer, the Turkish Empire. Clearly, in the same way that Camoens's sophisticated Neoplatonic prophetic machinery transcends Garcilaso's carved urn, the Portuguese domination of the East overwhelmingly surpasses Charles V's lifting of the siege of Vienna. As seen in the light emanating from Aeneas's shield, Charles's barring the gateway to western Europe in the face of the Ottoman advance stands out in very low relief indeed.

Lepanto, on the other hand, reflects back the full splendor of Actium, at least for Spaniards of the 1570s. If Camoens can be sure that he has bested Garcilaso's ekphrastic imperial prophecy, Ercilla no doubt rests secure in the belief that his "naval batalla" outshines both his Castilian predecessor and his Portuguese rival. By focusing his mantic "optical instrument" on the single action of what was considered the most crucial sea fight of modern times, Ercilla's ekphrasis surpasses Camoens's in artistic unity as well as imperial transcendence. Where Camoens can vaunt the turning of the Turk's flank on the colonial periphery, Ercilla is able to display the decisive breaking of his fearsome naval power in the central theater of worldwide imperial rivalry. Moreover, the Castilian is able to draw directly on all the most potent resonances of the poetic tradition. As Ercilla is very careful to point out, the gulf of Lepanto was filled with galleys in 1571 "in what appeared to be the same manner" as in 31 B.C. (*Araucana* 23.77e–h). Thus the glow emitted across the centuries by the boss on Aeneas's shield directly infuses the Castilian imperial prophecy with overwhelming vatic power.

Nonetheless, if we had only the correspondence between the prophecy of sea power described in Camoens's first *globo* and Ercilla's portrayal of Lepanto in his first séance with Fitón and his orb, it would be risky indeed to define the whole web of prophecy and sea change in Part II of the *Araucana* in terms of rivalry with the Portuguese bard. The second prophecy vouchsafed in the aleph in both poems, however, removes any possible doubt, as will be demonstrated in the following chapter.

5

Plotting Imperial Rivalry

The *Mapaemundi* of the *Lusíadas*
and the *Araucana*

Both Ercilla and Camoens present their readers with a second opportunity to gaze into the glowing sphere of the aleph. Once the prophecy seen in the first *globo* is concluded, Camoens, as I have indicated in the preceding chapter, has the nymph Tethys lead Gama to a mountaintop where she shows him a visualization of the Neoplatonic Sphere (*Lusíadas* 10.76–77). Tethys describes the eleven heavens of Ptolemaic cosmology from the Empyrean on down, culminating in the center, the earth (*Lusíadas* 10.81–90). She then embarks on a geographical description of the planet, with emphasis on the newly explored areas of the globe brought into the Portuguese ambit by the voyages of Gama and his successors (*Lusíadas* 10.91–141). Ercilla, likewise, returns to Fitón's cave and, anxious to see more of the magician's mantic orb, is vouchsafed a second séance with the "gran poma lucida" (*Araucana* 26.46–27.4). Fitón announces that

> "sin que vn mínimo punto oculto reste,
> verás del vniuerso la gran traça:
> lo que ay del Norte, al Sur, del Leste, al Oeste,
> y quan ciñe el mar, y el ayre abraça,
> ríos, montes, lagunas, mares, tierras,
> famosas por natura y por las guerras,"
>
> (*Araucana* 27.5c–h)

The mage then proceeds to point out the various geographical features of the earth to his poet-pupil (*Araucana* 27.5–53 [1578 27.5–52]). As previously mentioned, although Fitón promises "del universo la gran traza," he in fact limits himself to terrestrial geography. Thus both Tethys and Fitón present minute geographical descriptions, or mapaemundi, in the second appearance of their respective alephs.

The mapamundi per se is not a feature of the prestigious classical epics that loomed so large as models for Renaissance poets.[1] María Rosa Lida de Malkiel has suggested that the Homeric topos of the catalog of ships or hosts, imitated by all of the canonical Latin epic poets, contributed in some way to the development of the literary mapamundi in the Middle Ages (*Juan de Mena*, 31). If this is true, in a certain sense the locus does have roots in the epic poetry of antiquity. However that may be, the mapamundi as a discrete, set-piece literary exercise seems to flourish in the Middle Ages (Lida de Malkiel, *Juan de Mena*, 30ff.). One of its earliest manifestations is found in Book 14 of Isidore of Seville's (d. 636) *Etymologiae*, a prototypical medieval compendium of universal knowledge in twenty books. Other compilers expanded and varied Isidore's condensation of ancient geographical lore, and works such as the *Speculum naturale* of Vincent of Beauvais (d. 1264) seem to have proliferated during the twelfth and thirteenth centuries. Of particular interest in this regard is the treatise *De imagine mundi* once attributed to Saint Anselm, then later to Honorius of Autun (c. 1120), and now considered to be of anonymous authorship (Mena, *Laberinto de Fortuna*, ed. Kerkhof, 113 n. 265),[2] which rather than being a collection of universal information, only pretends to a monographic study of what was then known of world geography. The *De imagine mundi*, believed by both Mena's and Ercilla's contemporaries to be the work of Saint Anselm,[3] became the principal source for late medieval authors who wanted to incorporate classical geographical knowledge into easily accessible vernacular works (Wright 103–5). It is this Isidorean itinerary, and especially the version disseminated by the *De imagine mundi*, that dominates the medieval epic elaboration of the topos up to well into the Age of Navigations.

5.1. The Mapamundi Enters the Epic: The Medieval Alexander Poems

The first incorporation of the locus of the mapamundi, ultimately based on Saint Isidore, into epic poetry is found in a number of twelfth-century poems pertaining to the medieval Alexander cycle. The most extensive rendering, and the most cogent insertion in terms of overall narrative structure, of the topos is found in the *Alexandreis* of the twelfth-century French poet Walter of Châtillon. Walter belongs to that same great revival of Latin learning in northern France that produced Bernardus Silvestris and Alan of Lille. Walter had a solid firsthand acquaintance with classical Latin poetry (Walter of Châtillon, *Alexandreis*, trans. Pritchard, 3), and incorporated respectable imitations of Virgil, Ovid, Lucan, and Statius into his own Latin epic (Walter of Châtillon, *Alexandreis*, trans. Pritchard, 15).[4] Reading between the lines of the obligatory topos of modesty in his prologue makes it clear that Walter not only wants to revive the ancient epic, but also to join the ranks of the canonical poets such as Virgil. Walter tells us that he chose the story of Alexander the Great for the subject of his poem because of its "sublime" nature, and perhaps more important, because no ancient poet "dared to tackle it" (*Alexandreis*, Prologue, vv. 34–35).[5] Writing at the apogee of the first blush of crusading spirit in the West, it is probable that Walter found the tale of Alexander's conquests in the East particularly sublime precisely because the Macedonian king was the first European to exert wide dominion over the lands of Asia.[6]

Joseph J. Duggan has suggested that the experiences of Norman mercenaries returned from service in Anatolia and the developing tradition of the vernacular *chanson de geste* combined to play a significant role in the preaching of the First Crusade (70). It is clear that the reality of the crusades helped to bolster the burgeoning popularity of the romance epics that dealt with the legendary wars of Charlemagne and his peers against the Saracens. That an ambitious poet desiring to work in the field of learned epic should pick the deeds of Alexander of Macedon as his theme accords well with the crusading spirit and interplay between art and life that is found in the vernacular epics of the same period. Within the context of an epic poem celebrating the first great European imperialist enterprise beyond the familiar confines of the Mediterranean, the mapamundi so dear to the didactic inclination of learned medieval literary taste also finds a natural place.

Near the outset of the *Alexandreis*, once Alexander's army has landed in Asia, Walter finds it appropriate to give the reader a brief geography lesson (*Alexandreis* 1.396–426). Isidore of Seville begins his survey of the planet with the remark that Asia, taking its name from the woman who once ruled it, represents a third of the earth (Isidorus, *Etymologiae* 14.3.1). Walter of Châtillon, in the opening lines of his own mapamundi, comes as close to quoting Isidore as his hexameters permit (*Alexandreis* 1.396–401). Walter continues to follow Isidore throughout the remainder of the description (*Alexandreis*, trans. Pritchard, 13), although he varies the order of presentation of specific elements of the subtext. Walter, apparently anticipating the criticism that would be directed at later interpolators of mapaemundi into epic poems, also condenses his model considerably. He breaks off with the remark:[7]

> Totque Asiae partes, quas si meus exaret omnes
> Aut seriem scindet stilus aut fastidia gignet.
> (*Alexandreis* 1.425–26)

> (There are so many parts of Asia. If my pen were to note them all, it would disrupt the flow of my tale or be very tedious.)

Probably for the same reasons, Walter refrains from retailing Isidore's passages on Europe and Africa beyond the brief comments at the outset placing Asia in relation to the other two continents (*Etymologiae* 14.2; *Alexandreis* 1.402–6). At an appropriate point, as Alexander enters India, Walter does have occasion to make a brief reference to the geography of the subcontinent (*Alexandreis* 9.9–34). As this selectivity suggests, Walter is deliberate in his use of geographical lore and is hardly succumbing to some hypothetical, indiscriminate medieval didacticism.

In the initial mapamundi of Book 1, Walter focuses on those aspects of Asia that are calculated to impress the reader with the wealth and grandeur of Alexander's conquests. Thus he mentions the "gems and elephants" of India (*Alexandreis* 1.409), the scents and spices of Arabia (*Alexandreis* 1.415–17), and, of course, Jerusalem and the Holy Land with all its—here totally anachronistic—significance for Christians (*Alexandreis* 1.420–24). All of these features represent precisely the combination of lust for wealth with religious enthusiasm that motivated the Crusades, exactly the same impulses that were to fuel the colonial enterprises of the sixteenth century. Thus it is of particular significance for our reading of Camoens and Ercilla that the first epic mapamundi is found in a poem that celebrates the deeds of Alexander, the prototype of the European imperialist and colonizer, in the context of the original crusading fervor of the twelfth century. Seen in this light, the mapaemundi of the *Lusíadas* and the *Araucana*, far from seeming digressive, come into sharp focus as essential elements of colonialist epic.

Walter's *Alexandreis* encountered great success in the Middle Ages. It became a text of the schools during the thirteenth century (Walter, *Alexandreis*, trans. Pritchard, 7; *Galteri de Castellione Alexandreis*, ed. Colker, xix–xx), and Marvin Colker, the most recent editor, lists over two hundred extant manuscripts (xxxiii–xxxviii). In addition to various Latin imitations, the *Alexandreis* inspired a number of vernacular versions of the Alexander legend (Walter, *Alexandreis*, trans. Pritchard, 6–7). The most interesting of these for the reader of Camoens and Ercilla is the Spanish *Libro de Alexandre*. This is a long poem (2,675 stanzas) in *cuaderna vía* (stanzas of four fourteen-syllable rhymed lines divided into two hemistiches each) that was probably composed sometime in the first half of the thirteenth century.[8] The unknown author of the *Libro de Alexandre* adapted Walter of Châtillon's use of the mapamundi, and found new contexts in which to employ the topos.

In fact, there are four specifically geographical passages in the *Libro de Alexandre*. Of these, the first and most extensive is an imitation of the mapamundi in the *Alexandreis* (*Libro de Alexandre* 276–94), and it fulfills the same basic function in the work (Michael 196–97). The anonymous Spanish poet expands on Walter's comments about individual places, but does not broaden the scope of the treatment overall. Perhaps the most original of the Spanish poet's mapaemundi is the map of the world seen in the form of the human body by Alexander as he flies through the air drawn by two griffins (*Libro de Alexandre*

2508–13).[9] Like the geographical survey that follows Alexander's arrival in Asia, this mapamundi follows the scheme set down by Saint Isidore (*Libro de Alexandre*, ed. Cañas, 550).

The remaining two geographical descriptions in the *Libro de Alexandre* are both examples of ekphrasis in the sense that they purport to describe paintings. There is one brief reprise of the mapamundi that is represented as painted by Apelles on Darius's tomb (*Libro de Alexandre* 1792–98). The poet specifically mentions North Africa, India, Greece, Italy, and Spain, indicating which places are rich and which are poor. By far the most interesting of the ekphrastic mapaemundi of the *Libro de Alexandre*, however, is presented as part of a cosmic icon. Alexander is at the apex of his power, and embassies offering submission stream into Babylon from the lands he has not yet conquered (*Libro de Alexandre* 2515–38). The king sets up his high-seat to receive the tribute brought by the ambassadors beneath a richly worked tent or awning in the marketplace (*Libro de Alexandre* 2538–39). At this point, the poet launches into a detailed description of Alexander's tent (*Libro de Alexandre* 2540–95).[10] The Tent of Alexander, like the Shield of Achilles, is clearly intended to be read as a cosmic icon. The ceiling or crown of the tent is decorated with a portrayal of heaven and the angels that mentions the Fall of Lucifer (*Libro de Alexandre* 2550), followed by a series of biblical scenes including the creation and Fall of humanity, the Tower of Babel, and the drunkeness of Noah (*Libro de Alexandre* 2551–53). This descending order of description corresponds to that of the cosmic icon that begins with the heavens and works on down toward the earth and human history. Below, the four wall panels are described in turn. The first, the flap by the entrance, contains the months of the year (*Libro de Alexandre* 2554–66) and fits neatly into the scheme of the tent as cosmic icon. The second portrays the stories of Hercules and of the Trojan War (*Libro de Alexandre* 2568–75)—which Alexander takes as inspirational (*Libro de Alexandre* 2575)—while the fourth reviews the deeds of Alexander himself (*Libro de Alexandre* 2588–94). The third panel contains the mapamundi (*Libro de Alexandre* 2576–87), rounding off the representation of the universe begun with the portrait of heaven on the ceiling. If seen as the poet intends, the section on the door flap enumerating the months of the year faces the mapamundi at the back, while the historical panels form the sides, thus creating a cruciform structure. This has the effect of ensuring that the reader understands the universality of the context in which the exemplary histories are presented.

The mapamundi on the back panel begins conventionally enough, following the model laid down in Isidore's *Etymologiae* 14. Thus Ocean surrounds the land, and the dry land is insignificant in relation to the waters (*Libro de Alexandre* 2577; *Etymologiae* 14.2.1). Next, following the exact order of Isidore's survey, the poet tells us that the earth is divided into three parts: Asia, Europe, and Africa (*Libro de Alexandre* 2578; *Etymologiae* 14.2.2). Rather than following through with the complete description of each continent, however, the poet here abbreviates, informing the reader that

> Assí fue el maestro sotil e acordado,
> non olvidó çibdat nin castillo ortado,
> nin río nin otero nin yermo nin poblado,
> non olvidó emperio nin ningunt buen condado.
> (*Libro de Alexandre* 2579)

Up to this point, in fact, the anonymous Spanish poet, rather than directly imitating Saint Isidore, has been following another of his immediate subtexts very closely (Willis, *Debt*, 44). As Raymond S. Willis has demonstrated, the Spanish poet elaborates his Tent of Alexander on the basis of the model suggested by the same scene in several versions of the twelfth-century vernacular verse romance known as the *Roman d'Alexandre* (*Debt*, 41–46).

The Venice version of the Old French poem also portrays one wall of the tent as a map:

> En 'autre pan aprés, qui vousist esgarder,
> Veist il mapamondi enseigner e mostrer
> Coment tote la terre est enclose de mer,
> E metre en trois parties que je bien sai nomer,
> Coment li filosofe la voillent deviser.
> C'est Aisa et Europa, et Aufrique sa per,
> Les montagnes, les fluves, les cités a conter;
> Quant que li ciels enclot puet l'om illec trover.
> (*Roman d'Alexandre* 3341–48)

The *Roman d'Alexandre* explicitly invokes the locus of the mapamundi, suggests the whole by reprising the beginning of Saint Isidore's geographical survey, and then rapidly assures the reader that nothing was left out. The tent in the French poem is not fully realized as a cosmic icon. Although the months of the year are present, the description of heaven on the ceiling is absent (Willis, *Debt*, 43). The mapamundi in the *Roman d'Alexandre* really only serves as the pretext for the delivery of a typically medieval moralizing *dictum*.

The Spanish poet of the *Libro de Alexandre*, on the other hand, not only realizes the possibilities of developing the ekphrasis as a cosmic icon; he also takes the opportunity to essay yet another variation on the geographical survey. In this case it is a "medieval schoolman's itinerary" that takes the reader on a tour of the principal university towns of medieval Spain, France, and Italy (*Libro de Alexandre* 2580–84; Michael 218–19). Ian Michael explains this seemingly digressive excursion—with no apparent relevance to Alexander—as an example of the Spanish poet's "medievalization of his source material" (219). Yet there is more than a supposedly medieval didacticism and desire for "well spaced descriptive ornamentation," as Michael would have it, that determines the contents of this particular mapamundi. As the Spanish poet explicitly reminds his reader, it would require considerable space—"otro tamaño livro"—to enumerate the entire Isidorean itinerary (*Libro de Alexandre* 2585). The poet is extremely aware of the dangers of digression, as was Walter of Châtillon in his essay of the topos (*Alexandreis* 1.425–26). In the immediately following stanza, in fact, the poet excuses himself from repeating his description of Asia, although it is more pertinent, because, as he reminds the reader, he has already done so in the imitation of the *Alexandreis* at the outset of the poem (*Libro de Alexandre* 2586). The mapamundi on Darius's tomb has already concentrated on Africa while only briefly touching on Europe (*Libro de Alexandre* 1792–98). Thus in order to complete the coverage, an extensive review of European geography is in order. I find in this mapamundi, not so much a "deliberate medievalization" as a deliberate addition that furthers the construction of a complete cosmic icon. The universality of the image is reinforced in the final stanza of the mapamundi passage where the poet tells us that Alexander could see on this panel all that he had already conquered, as well as all that remained for him to master (*Libro de Alexandre* 2587).

Thus we have seen that the various medieval renditions of the Alexander material make two important contributions to the topos that Camoens and Ercilla will bring to its fullest fruition. The twelfth-century French poets are apparently the first to integrate the medieval schoolman's mapamundi into the fabric of the epic poem. Furthermore, this corresponds precisely with the first major attempt of the Christian West to extend its power beyond its own narrow sphere and dominate its cultural "others." Additionally, at least one Iberian poet saw the possibilities of sculpting this nascent topos into a cosmic icon of prophetic implications. In the case of the Tent of Alexander, of course, the "prophecy" is cautionary. All of the panels speak to some aspect of Alexander's *soberbia*, and thus presage his coming fall. Nonetheless, the ground has been prepared for more exuberantly expansionist exploitations of the mapamundi inscribed in the cosmic icon by later poets.

Unfortunately, however, it is difficult to say if the model suggested by the *Libro de Alexandre* reached Camoens or Ercilla directly. One mid-fifteenth-century manuscript has survived (Faulhaber et al. #2605), but no editions seem to have been printed in the sixteenth century.[11] The poem was known to early seventeenth-century scholars as an object of antiquarian interest (Cañas, ed. 12). The *cuaderna vía* form, unlike Mena's *arte mayor*, was perhaps too outmoded to be viable in the age of Garcilaso. Thus, regardless of how suggestive the innovations of the anonymous Spanish poet may be for our purpose, it is impossible to say with confidence that the *Libro de Alexandre* constitutes a direct model for Camoens or Ercilla. The *Libro de Alexandre* was known to Santillana ("Proemio y carta," 58), however, and so it is quite likely that other poets of the court of John II, especially Juan de Mena, also were acquainted with the work. If this is true, then it can be said with some confidence that the *Libro de Alexandre* played an active, if indirect, role in the genealogy of the mapaemundi of Camoens and Ercilla.

5.2. A Mapamundi for the "New Augustus": Juan de Mena's Geography and the Dream of Empire in the Cosmic Labyrinth

The late-medieval incorporation of the mapamundi into an epic or quasi-epic context that most certainly did serve as a model to Ercilla, and probably to Camoens as well (Lida de Malkiel, *Juan de Mena*, 32, 493), is that effected by Juan de Mena in the opening section of his *Laberinto de Fortuna* (34–53). In a certain sense, Mena's entire poem is an ekphrastic cosmic icon turned inside out, in the sense that the vision of the spheres seen in the wheels of Fortune may be considered an ekphrasis. Although many readers have found an epic quality in the *Laberinto de Fortuna* (Lida de Malkiel, *Juan de Mena*, 491), Mena does not insert a prophetic vision in a heroic narrative; quite the contrary, the poem in its entirety is a cosmic vision that enfolds a sequence of exemplary episodes that are calculated to stimulate the intended reader to heroic action. Mena also inverts the order of the standard medieval cosmic icon. Rather than beginning from the heavens and working down and inward toward the earth at the center as with the Tent of Alexander or Tethys's description of the Neoplatonic Sphere, the *Laberinto de Fortuna* commences with the description of our planet and then proceeds upward and outward through the successive spheres of the heavenly bodies. Mena as poet-protagonist having been swept up by Bellona, and then led to the highest vantage point of Fortune's glass castle by Providence, exclaims:[12]

> Mas preguntadme ya de quan ayna
> Estò en lo más alto de aquella posada
> De donde podía ser bien deuisada
> Toda la parte terrestre y marina:
> Phebo ya aspira pues de tu doctrina
> Módulo canto que cante mi verso
> Lo que allí vimos del orbe vniuerso
> Con toda la otra mundana machina.
>
> (*Laberinto de Fortuna* 32)

It is not quite clear where Mena is standing in relation to the heavenly spheres at this point, but like the protagonist of Cicero's *Somnium Scipionis* (4.1), Mena's attention falls first upon the earth below him.[13] But where Cicero and Dante (*Paradiso* 22.134–35, 151–54), for instance, merely remark upon our planet's relative insignificance, Mena embarks on a lengthy reprise of the set-piece medieval mapamundi before turning his attention to the heavenly spheres.

Faria e Sousa was quick to point out the correspondence between Mena's "mundana machina" and Camoens's "grande máquina do mundo" in Tethys's description of the *globo* (*Lusíadas* 10.80a; 4:col. 456). In fact, Faria e Sousa insists throughout his commentary on the initial stages of Tethys's prophecy on the reminiscences of the *Laberinto de Fortuna*

(4:col. 444–46).[14] The seventeenth-century commentator again refers to Mena as the model in his initial gloss on the beginning of Camoens's mapamundi proper at *Lusíadas* 10.92 (4:col. 487). Yet as Faria e Sousa notes in the same passage, Mena begins his geographical review with Asia, while Camoens commences his with Europe. Indeed, as Lida de Malkiel establishes, Camoens was demonstrably aware of Mena's work (*Juan de Mena*, 491–94). Nonetheless, Camoens certainly does not cleave closely to the content of Mena's mapamundi in his own rendition of the topos. In order to appreciate Ercilla's response to Camoens, it is necessary to briefly review Mena's geographical survey and compare Camoens's rendition of the topos. It will then become clear exactly how Ercilla responds to the challenge of the novel mapamundi in Tethys's globe.

Having announced that he is going to sing of the "orbe universo" and "toda la otra mundana machina" (*Laberinto de Fortuna* 32), Mena begins his survey with a brief reprise of the doctrine of the five zones (*Laberinto de Fortuna* 34). This is the first indication that Mena is not following Isidore of Seville as his direct model. Although Mena does reproduce the general order of the continents established in the *Etymologiae*, it is apparent that he is working from a later elaboration of Isidore's geographical survey. María Rosa Lida de Malkiel has established that the principal model for Mena was some version of the *De imagine mundi* formerly attributed to Saint Anselm (*Juan de Mena*, 41). Where Isidore and the early epic renditions of the mapamundi based on Isidore such as that of the *Alexandreis* and the *Libro de Alexandre* all omit the section on the five zones, the *De imagine mundi* and the various vernacular works based upon it all begin with the description of the five zones (*De imagine mundi* 1.6; *Semeiança del mundo* 3).[15]

Mena then begins the geographical itinerary proper, following the established pattern, with the continent of Asia (*Laberinto de Fortuna* 35). But again, he immediately demonstrates that he has his own agenda by suppressing some of the canonical details of the Isidorean description of Asia. Thus where the standard itinerary based ultimately on Saint Isidore begins the detailed enumeration of the lands of Asia with the terrestrial Paradise (*Etymologiae* 14.3.2; *De imagine mundi* 1.8; *Semeiança del mundo* 7), then describes the fountain from which rise the four rivers that water the earth (*Etymologiae* 14.3.3; *De imagine mundi* 1.9–10; *Semeiança del mundo* 8), then leads into the description of India (*Etymologiae* 14.3.5–7; *De imagine mundi* 1.11–13; *Semeiança del mundo A* 9–23, *B* 9–23), and then takes up a discussion of Persia including Parthia, Media, and Assyria (*Etymologiae* 14.3.8–12; *De imagine mundi* 1.14; *Semeiança del mundo A* 24–28, *B* 24–25), Mena commences with

> La mayor Asia en la zona tercera
> Y tierra de Persia vi entre los ríos
> Tigris y Indus de reynos varios
> Muy espaciosa cada qual ribera:
> Allí la provincia de Susia vi que era
> Iunta con Persia y con Assiria,
> Y tierra de Media, do yo creería
> La mágica auerse hallado primera
>
> (*Laberinto de Fortuna* 35)

It is apparent that Mena has deliberately left out the most "otherworldly" elements of the description, as well as the passages on India—quite extensive in Isidore and the *Semeiança del mundo*—and opened directly with Parthia, the easternmost region of what could be considered the Mediterranean world. This could of course be due to a similar lacuna in his model, but the standard enumeration was so widely diffused that it seems improbable that Mena would have been totally unaware of the canonical sequence.[16]

It is much more likely that Mena is deliberately distancing his mapamundi from the abbreviated but faithful version found in the Alexander poems. The Spanish *Libro de Alexandre*, for example, begins the section on Asia with three stanzas emphasizing the fact that Christ was born and died there, and that the church had its beginnings there (*Libro de Alexandre* 284–86). Then we are given the standard treatment of paradise with its four fountains, as well as India with its gems and elephants, as in the *Alexandreis* (*Libro de Alexandre* 287). Mena does make a perfunctory reference to the baptism of Christ in his treatment of Palestine and Syria (*Laberinto de Fortuna* 37ef), but on the whole avoids biblical references as assiduously as he does mention of India. Both the biblical material and the description of India are characteristic of the medieval Alexander cycle as well as the Isidorean mapamundi.

Mena does systematically expand on his model in the *De imagine mundi* by amplifying the mythological resonances suggested by the toponyms in his itinerary (Lida de Malkiel, *Juan de Mena*, 38). This, of course, accords well with the protohumanist initiative that Lida de Malkiel finds as the underlying program of Mena's work. In addition to highlighting the heritage of classical antiquity, this also implies a distancing from the rude, "barbarous" verses of earlier times. The *cuaderna vía* poetry of the thirteenth and fourteenth centuries was seen as hopelessly antique by the poets of Mena's day, as Santillana makes clear ("Proemio y carta," 58, 61). Mena has borrowed the innovation of the cosmic icon with its attendant mapamundi from the earlier tradition; in fact, he has inverted the scheme so that the cosmic icon embraces the entire poem. He is therefore very careful to underline the differences between his mapamundi and that associated with the antique poems, particularly the *Libro de Alexandre*.

This realization leads us to another significant initiative on Mena's part. Lida de Malkiel defends Mena against the criticism of Menéndez Pelayo and others, who fault Mena for what they take to be the tiresomely lengthy and digressive elaboration of the mapamundi (*Juan de Mena*, 41). Lida de Malkiel correctly notes that Mena has used his geographical sources with independence and a certain economy. She interprets this as an indication of Mena's incipient modernity in the face of the medieval tradition (*Juan de Mena*, 41). Lida de Malkiel is undoubtedly correct on both points, but it is important to bear in mind that while Mena abbreviates and uses the model provided by the geographical treatises selectively and economically, he expands considerably in comparison with the epic poems of the preceding centuries examined above. Walter of Châtillon only permits himself thirty hexameters for his mapamundi, and even then displays anxiety about taxing his reader's patience (*Alexandreis* 1.425–26). The *Roman d'Alexandre* dispenses with the mapamundi in a mere nine lines, while the most extensive of the mapaemundi in the *Libro de Alexandre* expands to eighteen stanzas (72 lines), concluding with the remark that it would be a "luenga ledanía" to render the entire itinerary (*Libro de Alexandre* 294).

Mena, on the other hand, devotes twenty stanzas (160 lines) to his geographical survey (*Laberinto de Fortuna* 34–53). This is more than double the length of the longest passage of the same type in the Alexander poems. Admittedly, Mena has concentrated the entire mapamundi into one continous elaboration, rather than dispersing its various components throughout the structure of his poem as does the poet of the *Libro de Alexandre*. This, of course, is consistent with the architecture of the *Laberinto de Fortuna* as a totalizing cosmic icon. Furthermore, this is precisely the point that needs to be thoroughly understood, for comprehension of both the *Laberinto de Fortuna* and the mapaemundi of the *Araucana* and the *Lusíadas*.

Mena is careful to treat the full geographic itinerary of the earth at some length for two reasons. The first is that he wants to establish the universality of his message. Not only is he constructing an image of the cosmos, in which the earth must take a central, if not necessarily determining, role, but he is also implying potential universality of empire to his intended reader and sovereign. As indicated in Chapter 2, Mena promises John II that he can become the "new Augustus" if only he will consistently foster the program of Alvaro de Luna (Deyermond 159, 163-64; *Laberinto de Fortuna* 230). Late twentieth-century readers may find it incredible that Mena was able to see the germ of worldwide empire in the chaos of John II's reign. Nebrija, an admirer of Mena, had more solid grounds for enthusiasm some fifty years later. Nonetheless, Mena deliberately reprises a much fuller version of the traditional geography than that included in earlier epic poems precisely because he wants to insist on the universality of the potential dominion of the erstwhile "new Caesar."

For the same reason, however, Mena must leave out the earthly paradise and the description of India. The description of Asia that follows Alexander's arrival on that continent (*Alexandreis* 1.396-426; *Libro de Alexandre* 276-94) is already an admonition on the Macedonian's tragic flaw—*soberbia*—as is the entire ekphrasis of the tent that immediately precedes the king's downfall. Although the descriptions of the Holy Land point toward crusade, the earthly paradise indicates the overweening ambition that will bring about the crusader's destruction. Mena does not wish to caution his monarch on the dangers of aspiring to universal monarchy; on the contrary, his poem is meant to be a spur toward precisely that goal. Mena deliberately excludes the description of India—which forms such an important part of both the epic and the Isidorean tradition—both because it is so closely associated with the Alexander poems, with their implication of *soberbia*, and because he wants to focus on the Mediterranean world, a plausible rather than a fantastic field of action for Castilian ambitions in the 1440s.

The second reason for punctiliously describing Asia Major (*Laber-*

into de Fortuna 35–40), Asia Minor (*Laberinto de Fortuna* 41), Europe (*Laberinto de Fortuna* 42–48), Africa (*Laberinto de Fortuna* 49–50), and the islands of the Mediterranean (*Laberinto de Fortuna* 51–53) in such comparatively exhaustive detail is that Mena must establish the full extent of the earth as a counterweight to the heavens before beginning his ascent through the spheres. Mena is not interested in proposing spiritual remedies for the problems of Castile. On the contrary, he is championing an explicitly secular, political program of consolidation of power. The Reconquest is an important element of this program—its most overt justification in fact—but Mena does not want to divert attention from the earthly means of bringing this goal about. In the tradition of the *Somnium Scipionis*, and above all, the *Divina commedia*, the earth is seen as insignificant, and the protagonist's full attention is directed to the heavens. Dante, for instance, is clearly not disinterested in contemporary Italian and European politics, as so much of the episodic content of his journey confirms, but the Italian poet sincerely believes that spiritual realization is a precondition for the proper ordering of earthly affairs. Mena, on the other hand, does not want to confuse the issue.[17] He is going to lead his sovereign upward through the spheres in order to demonstrate the superiority of the constable and his program; at the same time the earthly, mundane nature of both the real field of action and of the solutions proposed must be kept in clear focus.

Thus we see that Mena's mapamundi, far from being digressive or merely ornamental, plays a constitutive role in both the structure and meaning of the *Laberinto de Fortuna*. Furthermore, this meaning is inextricably intertwined with the protoimperialist ambitions of both Mena and his hero, Alvaro de Luna. It is hardly unnatural, therefore, that Iberian poets of the great age of empire should have found an irresistible model for the poetic celebration of imperialist expansion in Mena's mapamundi. As I have indicated, Faria e Sousa saw many aspects of Camoens's mapamundi as imitations of Mena (4:col. 487). In a like vein, Lida de Malkiel affirms: "El mapa poético, tal como se lee en *Os Lusíadas*, . . . era inherente al poema del Descubrimiento, y no mero episodio dentro de su bien trazada contextura. Sin embargo, es claro que Camoens ha tenido presente la visión geográfica del *Laberinto*, y su propio éxito, unido al influjo de Mena, contribuye a imponer el tema en la epopeya española del Siglo de Oro" (*Juan de Mena*, 492).

The Argentine scholar makes three fundamental points here. The first, that the map passage is constitutive rather than digressive in the poem of discovery, may be extended to the poem of empire as it was conceived in the fifteenth and sixteenth centuries, as been explained above. The third and final point, that Camoens's use of the mapamundi, added to that of Mena, exercises a powerful influence in Spanish Golden Age epic, is of course, at the heart of my thesis. Before elucidating that point, however, it is necessary to briefly examine Lida de Malkiel's second observation that Camoens's mapamundi was conceived in the light of Mena's. This is particularly cogent for understanding Ercilla's response to the mapamundi in Tethys's globe, because discerning the ways in which Camoens does, and does not, follow the model presented by Mena, provides the key to comprehending Ercilla's rendition of the topos.

5.3. The Geography of Empire Achieved: The Mapamundi of the *Lusíadas*

Like the author of the *Libro de Alexandre*, Camoens distributes relevant components of his geographical survey among appropriate narrative sections of the *Lusíadas*. Where Mena concentrates the mapamundi into one continuous passage that reinforces the sense of universality of potential dominion, Camoens separates his description of Asia and Africa from that of Europe. Thus the Portuguese poet places his review of European geography at the beginning of Gama's recitation of Portuguese history to the king of Melinde (*Lusíadas* 3.6–20). This responds to both internal and external factors. On the one hand, within the fiction of the poem, it is perfectly logical that Gama should explain the geography of Europe to the non-European ruler. On the other hand, because Camoens does not claim universal empire for Portugal, but only dominion of the seas, and the rich lands of the East Indies in particular, a long description of Europe would have been out of place in Tethys's globe. Nonetheless, we can be sure that Ercilla would have had both of Camoens's geographical passages in mind as he wrote his response to the challenge posed by the vast success of the Portuguese poem.

As far as the summary of European lands is concerned, Camoens begins with the most remote, Scythia (*Lusíadas* 3.9), as in the traditional itinerary (*Etymologiae* 14.4.3; *De imagine mundi* 1.23; *Semeiança del mundo* A 81–82, B 64–65; *Laberinto de Fortuna* 42), but then adds details on the Far North—Lapland and Scandinavia (*Os Lusíadas* 3.10)—that were unknown to Saint Isidore, the medieval treatises and Juan de Mena. This is indicative of Camoens's approach throughout his geographical material. Many details of the lands and conditions of the Far North only became available to Mediterranean learning in the sixteenth century with the publication of the works of Olaus Magnus, Bishop of Uppsala, who spent the better part of the 1530s in Italy.[18] Camoens is thus engaging in the same type of competitive *aggiornaménto* of the topos that we have seen in Ercilla's emulation of Lucan and Mena, and Camoens's own rendition of the cosmic icon or aleph. In fact, Camoens's survey of the geography of Europe may properly be seen as a necromantic imitation of Mena's review of European geography in the mapamundi of the *Laberinto de Fortuna*. The target subtext is signaled at the outset by commencing with the traditional scheme invoked by Mena.[19] Once this has been established, however, Camoens's proceeds with an *aggiornaménto* of the locus that corresponds to his own agenda.

Camoens continues on in the same spirit, following the traditional itinerary with a certain fidelity, but always adding his own embellishments. Thus Venice, Portugal's rival in the spice trade and sub rosa opponent in the Indian Ocean, is given grudging credit with backhanded compliments (*Lusíadas* 3.14), and the drastic decline in the military fortunes of Rome is highlighted (*Lusíadas* 3.15). All of this is of a piece with the overall thrust of the encomium of the Portuguese Empire in the *Lusíadas*, but Camoens most clearly reveals his agenda at the end of the enumeration of the geography of Europe.

Fortuitously enough for the Iberian poets, Saint Isidore ended his description of Europe with the Iberian Peninsula (*Etymologiae* 14.4.28–30). Both Mena (*Laberinto de Fortuna* 48) and the anonymous compilers of the various versions of the *Semeiança del mundo* (A 126–28, B 108–9) follow Isidore on this point.[20] Mena, in fact, does not particularly insist on Hispania here, following the rather parsimonious mention of the various provinces of the peninsula established by Isidore (*Etymologiae* 14.4.29), and adhered to without elaboration by "St. Anselm" (*De imagine mundi* 1.30) and the *Semeiança del mundo* (A 128, B 109).[21] Camoens, happily in keeping with the tradition, saves

Iberia for last. Not surprisingly, however, he expands his treatment of the Peninsula to four full stanzas. He lauds the indomitable, warlike spirit of the "cabeça de Europa" (*Lusíadas* 3.17), and praises each of the peoples of the peninsula in turn. As the penultimate of these groups, Camoens expands on the Castilians, absent completely from the Isidorean itinerary:

> . . . & o grande & raro
> Castelhano, a quem fez o seu Planeta,
> Restituidor de Espanha, & senhor della,
> Betis, Lião, Granada, com Castella.
>
> (*Lusíadas* 3.19e–g)

This seemingly generous treament of Portugal's ancient rival, of course, prepares the ground for the final stroke. In the Isidorean tradition, Lusitania is mentioned among the provinces of the peninsula as the third of the six (*Etymologiae* 14.4.29), and Mena, expanding the list to seven, places Lusitania fourth, with no special enthusiasm (*Laberinto de Fortuna* 48f). Camoens, of course, reserves the place of honor for his homeland:

> Eis aqui, quasi cume da cabeça,
> De Europa toda, o Reino Lusitano,
> Onde a Terra se acaba, & o Mar começa,
> E onde Febo repousa no Oceano:
> Este quis o Ceu justo, que floreça
> Nas armas, contra o torpe Mauritano,
> Deitando-o de si fora, & lá na ardente
> Africa estar quieto o nam consente.
>
> (*Lusíadas* 3.20)

Portugal is portrayed as the "summit" or "apex" of the "head" of Europe, and as the leading light of the crusade against the Moor, taking the battle across to Africa. Furthermore, the reader notes an implicit contrast. Castile is the "restituidor" of Hispania by virtue of its "planeta," which is to say by a mutable astrological influence. Faria e Sousa glosses this as Fortune (2:col. 26). Portugal, on the other hand, flourishes in arms by the will of "o Ceu justo."[22] Thus Camoens prepares the reader for the rivalry between Portugal and Castile that dominates the following section on the history of Portugal.

Indeed, winding up the partial mapamundi with Lusitania provides Camoens with the perfect transition into the real substance of this section of the *Lusíadas*: the history of Portugal from its mythical beginnings to the reign of Manuel I and the dispatch of Gama's expedition (3.21–4.77). This narrative, beginning with the strife between the first king of Portugual, Afonso Henriques, and his mother Teresa of Castile (*Lusíadas* 3.25–35), is in large part the story of Portugal's long-running struggle for independence from its aggressive Christian neighbor. Clearly the tale is punctuated by wars with the Moors, and even cooperation with the Castilians against the common enemy (for instance, the Battle of Salado, *Lusíadas* 3.107–17). Against this can be balanced, however, the Battle of Aljubarrota (*Lusíadas* 4.28–47), one of the most developed of the historical episodes, and the one that dominates the final part of the section leading up to King Manuel's prophetic dream and the dispatch of Gama's expedition. This definitive and crushing defeat of the Castilians in 1385 put the seal of permanence on Portuguese independence. At the end of the passage on Aljubarrota, Camoens makes it clear that it is the Portuguese victors who generously concede peace to the vanquished Castilians (*Lusíadas* 4.47a–d).

The rivalry between Portugal and Castile that Camoens traces in cantos 3 and 4 of the *Lusíadas* is clearly not of the same nature as the struggle against the Muslims. It is more like a family struggle between brothers who love each other all the while they wrestle for dominance. Nonetheless, Camoens's triumphant celebration of Portuguese victories over the Castilians, especially in the political climate of the late 1570s, could only have been read as a poetic gauntlet flung down in challenge to a Castilian courtier, knight, and poet such as Ercilla. I will return to details of this theme in the conclusion of this chapter. For the moment, it is necessary to return to the second section of Camoens's mapamundi, that seen in Tethys's globe.

When the nymph has finished describing the various celestial spheres in descending order, she finally arrives at the center of the entire *machina*: the earth—composed, as in Isidore, of sea and land (*Lusíadas* 10.90). Camoens naturally omits the doctrine of the five zones that precedes Mena's description of the earth (*Laberinto de Fortuna* 34). Portuguese navigations down the coast of Africa during the fifteenth century had put the lie once and for all to the ancient belief in the uninhabitable torrid zone that was supposed to have separated the Mediterranean world from the Antipodes.[23] Camoens, in his review of Gama's voyage down the west coast of Africa, has already taken pride in surpassing the knowledge of antiquity (*Lusíadas* 5.13d). Tethys, therefore, goes directly to the surface of the earth, and she makes it clear that more than with purely geographical features, her survey is concerned with human matters, particularly power and its distribution:

> Neste centro pousada dos humanos,
> Que não somente ousados se contentão
> De soffrerem da terra firme os danos
> Mas inda o mar instabil esprimentão,
> Verâs as varias partes, que os insanos
> Mares diuidem, onde se apousentão
> Varias nações, que mandão varios Reis,
> Varios costumes seus, & varias leis.
>
> (*Lusíadas* 10.91)

Thus it is logical, although he has already dealt at length with European geography at the outset of Gama's historical narration to the king of Melinde, to begin his terrestrial description with:

> Ves Europa Christaã mais alta & clara
> Que as outras em policia, & fortaleza:
>
> (*Lusíadas* 10.92ab)

Europe is placed in the center, as the source of power and organization. Although the rest of the itinerary will deal with the extension of colonial dominion to the periphery of empire, the relationship to the metropolitan ambit is fixed at the outset.

The nature of this relationship is not left ambiguous. In the following lines of the same stanza, Tethys moves quickly on from Europe to Africa:

> Ves Africa dos bens do mundo auara,
> Inculta, & toda chea de bruteza,
> Co cabo que ate qui se vos negara,

> Que assentou pera o Austro a natureza:
> Olha essa terra toda, que se habita
> Dessa gente sem ley, quasi infinita.
>
> (*Lusíadas* 10.92c–h)

In addition to postulating the superiority of Europe, and by extension, of Portugal, Camoens also here lays the groundwork of a justification for empire similar to that being advanced in Spanish America by the opponents of Vitoria and Las Casas. Africa is portrayed as "dos bens do mundo avara," and its peoples as "sem ley." The implication of the entire prophecy is, of course, that the Portuguese will remedy these conditions.

The following stanza, the first to treat a discrete geographical unit within the section on Africa, reveals that although the continent may be "dos bens do mundo avara," the "civilizing" mission is not without its compensations. Thus we read:

> Vé do Benomotapa o grande império,
> De seluatica gente, negra & nua:
> . . . .
> Nace por aste incógnito Hemispério
> O metal, por que mais a gente sua,
> Vé que do lago, donde se derrama
> O Nilo, tambem vindo está Cuama.
>
> (*Lusíadas* 10.93ab, e–h)

Camoens refers here to the state known by the title of its ruler, Monomotapa, situated in what are today Mozambique, Zambia, and Zimbabwe. This was one of the largest, most well-organized, and richest states encountered by the Portuguese in sub-Saharan Africa. The realms of the Monomotapa had been, from time immemorial, a center of gold-panning (Braudel, *Perspective*, 430) and supplied the gold trade with a product that was often attributed to the legendary King Solomon's mines when it reached the Mediterranean world.[24] The Portuguese quickly wrested this rich commerce from the Arab and Gujerati merchants who had preceded them, making the most of this direct source of the "metal for which people sweat the most." Thus Tethys's prophecy not only invokes the pride of defeating the ancestral enemy—the Muslims—and the exercise of dominion over lands and seas unknown to the ancients, but also the phenomenal increase in the wealth of Portugal that was the direct result of her navigations.[25]

By beginning his survey of Africa with the realms of the Monomotapa, far south on the coast of the Indian Ocean and unknown to Europe's ancient geographers, Camoens also announces that he is no longer concerned with following the traditional poetic mapamundi. The Isidorean itinerary is primarily concerned with the Mediterranean littoral of North Africa (*Etymologiae* 14.5), and only refers to the Saharan regions in a vague way as Aethiopia (*Etymologiae* 14.5.14). Isidore, of course, was a firm believer in the uninhabitable Torrid Zone, and thus states that the sub-Saharan regions peopled by the Antipodes were unknowable (*Etymologiae* 14.5.17).[26] Mena reverses the order established by Isidore, commencing his section on Africa with a brief mention of Ethiopia (*Laberinto de Fortuna* 49a), which here must be taken in the Isidorean sense of the great, unknown Saharan interior of Africa down to the Torrid Zone. He devotes only one line to Ethiopia, however, before moving on to the more familiar regions of Mediterranean North Africa (*Laberinto de Fortuna* 49–50). In fact, although Camoens does touch upon a few places in Africa and the East mentioned by Mena, such as the Red Sea (*Lusíadas* 10.97d; *Laberinto de Fortuna* 38), Egypt and the Nile (*Lusíadas* 10.95, 98; *Laberinto de Fortuna* 38), and Arabia (*Lusíadas* 10.100; *Laberinto de Fortuna* 36), the contexts are completely different. There is no effort, unlike in Camoens's map of Europe, to establish an allusion connecting this geographical survey with that of the *Laberinto de Fortuna*. Indeed, the only way to read the geographical prophecy in *Lusíadas* 10 as an imitation or emulation of the mapamundi of the *Laberinto de Fortuna* is to consider it an extension of the description of Europe undertaken in Gama's narration to the king of Melinde (*Lusíadas* 3.6–20).

Thus Tethys begins her geographic revelations, appropriately, with the regions opened up by Gama's voyage. The exploitation of the kingdom of the Monomotapa, with which the prophecy begins, indeed lay in the near future relative to the fictive time of the nymph's prediction. Leaving the region of the Zambezi basin behind, Tethys proceeds on up the eastern coast of Africa to the true Ethiopia, which Gama's son Cristóvão would give his life to save from the local Muslims and their Turkish allies in the 1540s (*Lusíadas* 10.96; Whiteway 275–76), thereby initiating a close relationship between this remote Christian state and Portugal that would endure for at least a century. Tethys goes on up through the Red Sea to Suez (*Lusíadas* 10.98), alluding to the Mamluk fleets based there that would constitute the principal naval opposition to the Portuguese in both the Red Sea and the Indian Ocean during the early decades of the sixteenth century (Guilmartin 9–15).[27] From the head of the Red Sea, Tethys continues on down the coast of Arabia and on around to the straits of Hormuz (*Lusíadas* 10.99–102). At every turn the names recall famous deeds of the Portuguese and their enemies, although Camoens only pauses to point out the most illustrious (cf. *Lusíadas* 10.101gh).

Having arrived at the head of the Persian Gulf (*Lusíadas* 10.102–3), Camoens reenters the ambit of the traditional mapamundi description of Asia, but makes no attempt to invoke the antique tradition. Indeed, this is precisely the part of the Isidorean itinerary that Mena suppressed in the *Laberinto de Fortuna* (35–40), and so Camoens would not have had a subtext against which to write here even if he had not already dispensed with his necromantic emulation of Mena in the section on Europe. In any case, the Portuguese poet's purpose here is not to call on the poetic tradition, but to revel in the newly opened expanses of the East. It is in this spirit that Camoens continues his description of Asia, following down the west coast of India, then up past Ceylon to the Bay of Bengal (*Lusíadas* 10.104–7), where he pauses at Mylapore (Madras) to recount the legendary tale of the preaching of Saint Thomas the Apostle in these distant lands (*Lusíadas* 10.108–19).[28] From the Madras area, Camoens resumes his geographical survey, continuing on up and around the Bay of Bengal only to turn up on the coast of Southeast Asia past Singapore to the mouth of the Mekong where he recalls his own shipwreck (*Lusíadas* 10.120–28)— one of the few autobiographical details found in the poem, and one that has given rise to varied speculation (Camões, *Os Lusíadas*, ed. Pierce, xi). Next, Tethys briefly points out Vietnam and China, including the Great Wall, and Japan, stressing the great riches of these until recently semifabulous regions (*Lusíadas* 10.129–31).

Tethys then turns her gaze on the spice islands of Indonesia, the true fountain of wealth for the Portuguese Empire of the second half of the sixteenth century (*Lusíadas* 10.132–35). The demigoddess explicitly celebrates each in turn for its highly sought-after treasures. Thus of Tidore she says:

> As árvores verás do cravo ardente,
> Co sangue português inda compradas.
>
> (*Lusíadas* 10.132ef)

To the valuable cloves of Tidore she adds the nutmeg of Banda, the camphor of Borneo, the sandalwood of Timor, the naptha oil, silk, and gold of Sumatra (*Lusíadas* 10.131–32). These are the fabled lands from which flowed for centuries the sources of the wealth of Cairo, Antioch, Constantinople, Venice, and Genoa; all now "bought with Portuguese blood" and securely in Portuguese hands. But in the midst of this celebration of colonial riches, there is something else that the reader schooled in the *Laberinto de Fortuna* would surely have noticed.

This tour of the islands appears as if it were the closing section of the mapamundi as seen in Tethys's globe. Camoens, having gone as far north and east as Japan and the Great Wall of China, announces this section in the following manner:

> Olha cá pelos mares do Oriente
> As infinitas ilhas espalhadas:
> (*Lusíadas* 10.132ab)

Thus, we are to be given a specific itinerary of the islands. Where the movement up until this point has been from west to east, Camoens now reverses direction. Tidore is the furthest east of the group described, and by the time Tethys has reached Sumatra the reader has been brought back due south of Singapore, described back at *Lusíadas* 10.125. Nor does Camoens have Tethys halt here, but continues on back toward the west through the major strategic islands of the Indian Ocean: Ceylon, the Maldives, Socotra, and Madagascar (*Lusíadas* 10.136–37). Camoens has brought his geographical survey full circle; at Madagascar we are just off the mouth of the Zambezi where the itinerary began with the kingdom of the Monomotapa and Sofala. The poet then has Tethys confirm that we have reached some sort of a conclusion:

> Eis aqui as novas partes do Oriente
> Que vós outros agora ao mundo dais,
> Abrindo a porta ao vasto mar patente,
> Que com tão forte peito navegais.
> (*Lusíadas* 10.138a–d)

To a careful reader of the *Laberinto de Fortuna*, as we know Ercilla to have been, this concluding section on the islands recalls the traditional closing section of the Isidorean mapamundi as filtered through the *De imagine mundi* (1.34–36) and rendered by Juan de Mena: the "Insulae" (*Etymologiae* 14.6), or as Fernán Núñez titles it in his editions, "Islas" (*Laberinto de Fortuna* 51–53). By returning to this organizational principal, Camoens is signaling that the entire excursion through the East, although it is separated from the section on Europe, is to be read as a continuation of that geographical survey; that the two taken together are to be taken as a single mapamundi that itself is an emulation of Mena's protoimperialist essay of the topos in the *Laberinto de Fortuna*. As I have pointed out, the content of the mapamundi that Tethys displays in her globe does not itself allude textually to Mena's mapamundi in any discernible way. This is equally true of the islands. Mena limits himself to the islands of the Mediterranean, excluding both those of the Atlantic and those of India that are present in his sources.[29] Nonetheless, the reader who is familiar with the traditional Isidorean arrangement of the material, and particularly with Mena's elaboration of the mapamundi, will recognize the subtle allusion that Camoens establishes with his reversal of direction and sweep back toward Africa, touching only upon the islands.[30] That this section is to be read as a distinct unit, corresponding to the section titled "Islas" in Fernán Núñez's editions of the *Laberinto de Fortuna*, is made unmistakable by the introductory statement at *Lusíadas* 10.132*ab* (quoted above) that announces the shift of focus to the islands of the eastern seas. Camoens reinforces this sense of a discrete chapter or division dedicated to islands that closes the overall mapamundi by having Tethys proclaim, just after having dealt with Madagascar, the last of the islands (*Lusíadas* 10.137*h*), that her interlocutor has now seen the new parts of the Orient that he and his companions have "given to the world" (*Lusíadas* 10.138*a–d* quoted above).

In this discussion of the opening of Tethys's description of Africa and the Indian Ocean, I stated that the only way that this second vision in the *globo* could be considered an emulation of Mena's mapamundi would be to read it as a continuation of the description of Europe that opens Gama's historical oration in canto 3. The placing of the section on the islands in the overall itinerary fulfills this requirement and establishes the emulative allusion. Thus Camoens's entire mapamundi up to this point could be taken as a challenge to Portugal's ancient rival Castile. As indicated above, Mena's mapamundi serves as an emblem of the universal scope of authority that would correspond to a "new

Augustus." Camoens has carefully presented a geography of Europe that recalls Mena's, only to demonstrate the superiority of Portugal. This itself serves as a springboard to launch into a historical review of Portuguese triumphs over Castilian attempts to limit or extinguish Lusitanian independence. By reading the mapamundi of *Lusíadas* 10 as an extension of the emulation of Mena in *Lusíadas* 3, we are also reading the two together as a celebration of Portugal's greatness that claims to have far surpassed the Castilian pretensions to universal hegemony expressed in the *Laberinto de Fortuna*. It is my thesis that Ercilla, in fact, read this section of the *Lusíadas* in precisely this manner.

Indeed, if a reader steeped in the rivalry between Portugal and Castile, as well as the poetic tradition exemplified by the *Laberinto de Fortuna*, has read Camoens's mapamundi up to this point as an expression of that rivalry and, concomitantly, as a claim to have outdone both Castile's poets and imperialists, the verses of the *Lusíadas* that follow Tethys's wrapping up of the new parts of the Orient given to the world by the Portuguese only confirm the supposition. Tethys has fulfilled the program announced on the Island of Love (*Lusíadas* 9.86e–g). She has shown Gama all the secrets of the seas that were to be revealed by the Portuguese as a consequence of his voyage. But this is not enough for Camoens, and he has Tethys inform Gama that

> "Mas hé tambem razão, que no Ponente
> Dhum Lusitano hum feito inda vejais,
> Que de seu Rey mostrando se agrauado
> Caminho há de fazer nunca cuidado."

> "Vedes a grande terra que contina
> Vay de Calisto ao seu contrario polo,
> Que soberba a farâ a luzente mina
> Do metal, que a cor tem do louro Apolo,
> Castella vossa amiga ferà dina
> de lançarlhe o colar ao rudo colo,
> Varias prouincias tem de varias gentes
> Em ritos & custumes differentes."

> "Mas cá onde mais se alarga, ali tereis
> Parte tambem co pao vermelho nota,
> De Sancta Cruz o nome lhe poreis,

Descobrila há a primeira vossa frota:
Ao longo desta costa que tereis
Yrá buscando a parte mais remota
O Magalhães, no feito com verdade
Português, porém não na lealdade."
(Lusíadas 10.138c 140)

The Lusitanian, at odds with his own monarch, who is to take the way never before dreamt of, is, of course, Magellan. The great land that stretches from pole to pole is the Americas, rich with gold and silver, and Santa Cruz is Brazil.

What is most curious about this insinuation of the Castilian Empire in America into Tethys's prophecy is that it is bracketed in references to the Portuguese, Magellan. The circumnavigation was certainly a momentous achievement, one with repercussions in many directions. The historian López de Gómara, for instance, refers to it as the ultimate refutation of the doctrine of the uninhabitable Torrid Zone sustained by the ancients (*Historia general*, cap. 6).[31] Although López de Gómara, himself an ardent Castilian chauvinist, explains in his chapters on the circumnavigation itself that Magellan came from Portugal to seek the support of the Castilians for his voyage because of problems with King Manuel (*Historia general*, caps. 91–93), in his early chapter on the refutation of the ancients, he represents the circumnavigation as the achievement of the Crown of Castile and the Castilians (*Historia general*, cap. 6).[32] Furthermore, López de Gómara insists that the Council of the Indies only backed Magellan's voyage after the Portuguese adventurer had convinced them that the spice islands of the Orient fell within the Castilian zone of conquest as defined by the treaty of Tordesillas in 1494, which had shifted the line fixed by the papal bull of 1493 some three hundred and sixty leagues further to the west (*Historia general*, caps. 91, 101).

This is a crucial point for understanding the effect that reading Camoens's references to Magellan at the end of the mapamundi glorifying the Portuguese possession of the spice islands would have had on Castilian courtiers in the 1570s. López de Gómara recounts that the Spaniards who continued on in the *Vitoria* and the *Trinidad* after Magellan's death on the island of Cebu in 1521 finally arrived at their long-sought destination of the Moluccas. According to López de Gómara's account, the local rulers all swore allegiance to Charles V and to

Castile (*Historia general*, cap. 96).³³ López de Gómara says that this occurred on the island of Tidore, precisely the first of the islands mentioned by Camoens in his final, triumphant review of the spice islands in Tethys's mapamundi (*Lusíadas* 10.132). It should be borne in mind that the Moluccas, also known, in fact, as the Spice Islands, were a major part of what Columbus had promised to Ferdinand and Isabel, but had failed to deliver. Juan Sebastián del Cano, who brought the *Vitoria*—the only surviving ship of Magellan's original flotilla—loaded with spices into San Lúcar de Barrameda in September 1522, assured the emperor that his title to the islands was sound, and that the Portuguese had not yet reached Tidore (*Historia general*, cap. 99). López de Gómara tells us that when King John of Portugal came to hear of this, "bufaba de coraje y pesar, y todos sus portugueses querían (como dicen) tomar el cielo con las manos, pensando que tenían de perder el trato de las buenas especias si castellanos se pusiesen en ello" (*Historia general*, cap. 99).

The Portuguese monarch lost no time in arranging for a conference to be held between representatives of the two crowns, and a great reunion of cosmographers and lawyers was duly held in 1524, but each side left claiming the Spice Islands as its own at the conclusion (*Historia general*, cap. 100). The emperor sent out another expedition, but it was brought to a bad end by the Portuguese and their Moluccan allies (*Historia general*, cap. 102). Charles V, supported by his cosmographers, continued to claim the Spice Islands for Castile and protested the Portuguese maltreatment of the Castilian expeditionaries. Matters were smoothed over with the emperor, however, by mutually convenient dynastic marriages. King John of Portugal, now the emperor's brother-in-law, eventually agreed to pay Charles 350,000 ducats for the rights to the spice trade and control of the islands in 1529. As López de Gómara makes clear, this arrangement did not sit well with the emperor's Castilian subjects. López de Gómara notes that the Cortes of Castile were still trying to regain the rights to the trade in 1548. The Castilian historian makes it very explicit that the emperor's arrangement of the matter was still causing considerable resentment in Castile at midcentury (*Historia general*, cap. 105).

On the other hand, the marriage of the Portuguese princess to Charles V that had helped secure the spice trade for the Lusitanians had produced a king of Castile, Philip II, with an undisputable claim on the throne of Portugal (Braudel, *Mediterranean*, 1180). The accession of the unstable young Sebastian as king of Portugal made the bringing of the Lusitanian realm back under the control of the Castilian monarchy appear a feasible project (Pi Corrales 208–9). Also, by the mid-1570s, German businessmen were applying pressure on Philip because they wished to take direct control of the spice trade (Braudel, *Mediterranean*, 557). In this political climate, Camoens's celebration of Portugal at the expense of Castile, of the history of Portuguese independence, of the glories and riches of her empire, especially the Spice Islands, and finally the repeated, underlined as it were, references to the voyage of Magellan would certainly have had an electrifying effect on a Castilian courtier such as Ercilla. Indeed, the shape of his response becomes very clear when we gaze with him for the second time into the globe of the Araucanian wizard Fitón.

5.4. The Mapping of Empire in the Enchanter's *Aleph*: The Mapamundi of the *Araucana*

Unlike the Alexander poets and Camoens, Ercilla constructs a true, complete mapamundi and presents it all together in the same section of his poem. This, of course, is precisely the procedure followed by Juan de Mena in the mapamundi of the *Laberinto de Fortuna*. Mena adheres to the traditional scheme established by Isidore of Seville and the anonymous author of the *De imagine mundi* that commences with Asia Major (*Laberinto de Fortuna* 35–40) and proceeds through Asia Minor (*Laberinto de Fortuna* 41), Europe (*Laberinto de Fortuna* 42–48), Africa (*Laberinto de Fortuna* 49–50), and the islands (*Laberinto de Fortuna* 51–53). As has been demonstrated above, Camoens does not follow this pattern, but alludes subtly to recognizable elements at critical junctures of his mapaemundi. The reminiscences are just sufficient to alert the competent reader that the Portuguese poet is engaged in an exercise in emulation that is designed not only to outshine, but virtually to obliterate the model in the brilliance of its novelty and the splendor of the wealth, power, and achievement that it enshrines. Furthermore, as has been made clear in the previous chapters, Ercilla was both a highly competitive poet—driven by an emulative initiative in the face of his contemporaries and near contemporaries—and a close reader of the

Laberinto de Fortuna. As such, Ercilla could not have failed to recognize the emulation of Mena's mapamundi that is implicit in the mapaemundi of the *Lusíadas*. Thus we would expect Ercilla to both establish an allusion to Mena's as well as Camoens's geographical surveys, and then spare no effort in the attempt to surpass both the common model and the rival subtext in his own rendition of the topos. In fact, this is exactly what we find unfolding before us in Fitón's optical aleph.

Like Mena, and the exponents of the Isidorean itinerary in general, Ercilla begins with Asia. Immediately, however, within this traditional scheme, Ercilla reverses the established order of presentation, and instead of saving Asia Minor for the last of the parts of Asia, he begins his survey at the Bosphorus, from whence he runs through the various provinces to arrive with the flowing Euphrates at the borders of Cappadocia and Syria at the end of the first stanza (*Araucana* 27.6). Passing down into Syria, Ercilla pauses to emphasize the New Testament, Christian resonances of the Holy Land (*Araucana* 27.7).[34] Mena had only made one brief biblical reference, mentioning the baptism of Christ in the Jordan (*Laberinto de Fortuna* 37*ef*), submerged as it were in a sea of classical allusions. Ercilla, in contrast, mentions that Judea was the Promised Land, singles out Nazareth as the favored place of the Annunciation, and points out Jerusalem—so often subjected to fire and the sword—where Christ was crucified (*Araucana* 27.7).

These, and the following stanzas on Asia, reveal that Ercilla is not so much constructing a close textual emulation of Mena, as in the list of alchemical substances, as he is essaying an improvement, an *aggiornaménto* of the topos as a whole. In this way, Ercilla continues on down the Arabian Peninsula to the Indian Ocean and across to China, touching on Ceylon and the Moluccas on his way (*Araucana* 27.8–10). In this Ercilla can be seen to be correcting Mena, and possibly making a sly allusion to Camoens. Mena has left India and the Far East completely out of his vision of Asia, and Camoens has suggested the movement of the eye first northeast to China, then southeast to the Moluccas, and finally back westward to Ceylon. This is not, however, where Ercilla will fully engage Camoens on the issue of the Spice Islands.

Ercilla next brings his reader back across the great landmass of Asia to the shores of the Black Sea, and then back down into Mesopotamia (*Araucana* 27.11–15). Along the way, amid the cascade of exotic toponyms, he has occasion to intersperse references to personages as diverse as Jason and Medea (*Araucana* 27.12), Tamerlane (*Araucana* 27.13), Semiramis, and Alexander the Great (*Araucana* 27.15). Throughout, Ercilla gives a far more complete and up-to-date geography of Asia than Mena, adorned with well-developed biblical, classical, and historical references, and richly redolent with the exoticism of far-off place-names from both classical geography and sixteenth-century exploration. This survey of Asia is also designed to be superior to that of Camoens, in that it is not limited to the sea routes connecting the trading centers of the East. This probably explains the particular emphasis that Ercilla gives to the accumulation of place-names from landlocked central Asia and the regions of the Caucasus. It is curious, in the light of the diachronic development of the mapamundi in the epic that I have outlined in section 5.1 of this chapter, that Ercilla should close his overview of Asia with the death of Alexander in Babylon (*Araucana* 27.15).

Ercilla again modifies the traditional order of the survey by moving his gaze from Asia to Africa. Mena had followed the Isidorean trajectory from Asia Minor to Europe, saving Africa for just before the islands at the conclusion of his mapamundi. Camoens avoids the issue by treating Europe separately, and then following the route of Portuguese exploration rather than the traditional itinerary. Ercilla, however, insists on including the three continents of the Old World, and establishes his links with the tradition by beginning with Asia, but must reserve Europe for the last in order to achieve his purpose of setting up Spain as the fountainhead of a New World empire.

Mena, as I have pointed out, cleaves very closely to the Isidorean model in his treatment of Africa, confining his gaze to the Mediterranean littoral, with only the vaguest of references to the Saharan regions (*Laberinto de Fortuna* 49–50). Camoens, on the other hand, begins the mapamundi in Tethys's globe by leaping directly from Europe to the kingdom of the Monomotapa along the Zambezi in southeastern Africa (*Lusíadas* 10.93). It is also in Africa that Camoens begins both his celebration of the Portuguese overseas empire and his demonstration of the superiority of the knowledge of the Age of Navigations over that of the medieval tradition. Thus it is here in Africa that we would expect Ercilla to enter into a more intense, and discernible, rivalry with both of his predecessor texts.

Ercilla begins his review of Africa with "Mira en Africa al Sur los estendidos / Reynos del Preste Iua*n*" (*Araucana* 27.16).³⁵ This opening signals that we have entered the regions of semifabulous geography. Furthermore, from the exhortation to "look in the south," combined with the observations that there are three harvests a year and that the area in question lies at twenty-two degrees south, the reader comes to the realization that Ercilla is opening his survey, indeed, back in the widespread realms of the Monomotopa, or somewhere very near. Against Camoens's matter-of-fact toponymy, and attendant references to historically accurate incidents of the Portuguese penetration of the region (*Lusíadas* 10.93), Ercilla musters the arms of the marvelous and of poetry itself.

Thus where Camoens puts forward the "grande Imperio" of the Monomotapa (*Lusíadas* 10.93*a*), the largest and most highly organized state to be encountered by Europeans in southern Africa, Ercilla counters with all of the mystery and literary enchantment of "los estendidos Reynos del Preste Iua*n*" (*Araucana* 27.16*ab*). Camoens cites relatively sober, if disparaging, ethnographic information—"selvática gente, negra e nua"—and the martyrdom of a Jesuit of Portuguese origin (*Lusíadas* 10.93*b–d*); Ercilla responds with exotic and fabulous animal life, including "tigres, panteras, grifos y dragones" (*Araucana* 27.17*h*). The Portuguese poet takes pride in the "metal for which people sweat the most"—the very real gold of the Monomotapa region that came under the control of his countrymen—while Ercilla invokes all the legendary associations of the Mountains of the Moon, fabled source of King Solomon's wealth (*Araucana* 27.18*ab*).

Camoens makes two references to the East African lake that was supposed to be the source of Nile. The question of the sources of the river of Egypt had been, throughout antiquity, one of the most intriguing mysteries of geography.³⁶ Camoens first has Tethys point out that "do lago, donde se derrama / O Nilo, também vindo está Cuama" (*Lusíadas* 10.93*gh*). As Faria e Sousa observes, it was believed that the Nile, the Zambezi (Cuama), and the Congo all rose in the same great lake (4:cols. 489–90). Ptolemy's geography placed the sources of the Nile at the foot of the legendary Mountains of the Moon, at approximately the same latitude as the Zambezi.³⁷ The idea that the Portuguese had perhaps come close to the long-sought origin of the Nile was obviously a matter of pride for Camoens. After making references to

Pedro de Naia's defense of Sofala at the mouth of the Zambezi in 1505 (*Lusíadas* 10.94), the Portuguese poet returns to the theme:

> "Olha lá as alagoas donde o Nilo
> Nasce, que não souberam os antigos"
> (*Lusíadas* 10.95ab)

Once again, Camoens insists on making the most of how the Portuguese navigators had surpassed the knowledge of the ancients as he recounts the wonders they have discovered.

To this Ercilla has Fitón counter with

> "Destos peñascos ásperos pendientes,
> llamados hoy el monte de la Luna,
> nacen del Nilo las famosas fuentes,
> y dellos ríos sin nombre y fama alguna,
> que aunque tuercen y apartan sus corrientes
> se vienen a juntar a una laguna
> tan grande, que sus senos y laderas
> baten de tres provincias las riberas:"
>
> "a Gogia y Beguemedros al oriente
> y a Dambaya al poniente; del cual lado
> hay islas donde habita mucha gente
> y todo el ancho círculo es poblado:
> de aquí el famoso Nilo mansamente
> nace, y después más grande y reforzado
> parte a Gogia de Amara y va tendido
> sin ser de las riberas restringido."
> (*Araucana* 27.18–19)

Again, Ercilla responds to Camoens's relative sobriety with all of the resources of the marvelous. The overall conception that the Nile rises from the Mountains of the Moon is essentially taken from Ptolemy.[38] The description of the densely populated lake region perhaps owes something to sixteenth-century travelers' reports, and the names of the provinces are real enough—belonging to actual places in Abyssinia— although their placement is fantastic. Notions of the exact lay of the land in sub-Saharan Africa were vague at best, and Ercilla could rely on arousing the admiration of his audience with both the authentic and the fabulous elements of his description. What is even more evident is the purely poetic dimension of his competition with his rival. Where Camoens has merely mentioned the lakes, albeit twice, Ercilla has dedicated virtually two stanzas to the evocation of their circumstances.

Camoens briefly follows the course of the Nile down as far as ancient Meroë, taking the opportunity to mention both the exotic fauna—crocodiles—and the Christian Ethiopian allies of the Portuguese, before turning back to the coast and the itinerary of empire (*Lusíadas* 10.95–96). Ercilla also proceeds down from the highlands of the lake region, confused here with Abyssinia, to Meroë. The Castilian poet, however, takes pains to include an energetic description of the cataracts (*Araucana* 27.20). Again, Camoens has stressed the difference between ancient and present knowledge:

"Vê Méroe, que ilha foi de antiga fama,
Que ora dos naturais Nobá se chama."

(*Lusíadas* 10.95gh)

Ercilla, on the other hand, has Fitón say that the Nile, once having thundered down the cataracts,

"después más ancho, grave y espacioso
llega a Meroe, gran isla, costeando,
que contiene tres reinos eminentes,
en leyes y costumbres diferentes."

(*Araucana* 27.21e–h)

The Meroë described by both Camoens and Ercilla should not be confused too closely with the ancient cities that bore the name (cf. Camões, *Os Lusíadas*, ed. Pierce, 245 n. 3). Pliny refers to Meroë as a great island in the Nile after the river leaves the highlands of "Ethiopia" (*Naturalis historia* 5.10.52),[39] and this is apparently how both Camoens and Ercilla wish it to be taken here.[40] Maps, particularly cartographic mapaemundi, typically showed Meroë as a very large island, deep in sub-Saharan Africa, that split the course of the Nile.[41] Camoens emphasizes this aspect when he says that Meroë is now called Nubia. Ercilla counters by saying that the area contains "three kingdoms, different in laws and customs." This is either a recognition of the fact that Nubia was inhabited by Christians, Muslims, and animists, or perhaps a reference to the Christian, Muslim, and Jewish communities of Abyssinia.

After Meroë, Ercilla's description of Africa takes leave of that of the *Lusíadas*. From Meroë, and the prediction of the sacrifice of Dom Cristóvão da Gama in Abyssinia, Tethys turns her glance back to the coast and the sea routes followed by the Portuguese, and the closest that she comes to Egypt is Suez at the head of the Red Sea (*Lusíadas* 10.96–98). Ercilla, on the other hand, has Fitón continue straight on down the Nile to Cairo, with appropriate references to the wonders, both ancient and modern, of that great metropolis (*Araucana* 27.21). Here Ercilla is once again outdoing both Camoens and Mena. In regard to Camoens, Ercilla's description of Africa is more complete, being replete with the renowned attractions of traditional itineraries, such as the pyramids (*Araucana* 27.21e–h), than that of his Portuguese rival. In the case of Mena, the Cordovan poet had placed Egypt in his description of Asia (*Laberinto de Fortuna* 38), following the ancient definition of Libya (Africa) as the lands west of Egypt and the model of the *De imagine mundi* (1.18).[42] By linking Egypt to Africa and the Nile, Ercilla is thus updating or correcting his Castilian predecessor.[43]

Ercilla does tip his hat to Mena, and the traditional geographies in general, when he mentions the Troglodytes among the "bruta y negra gente" of the sub-Saharan lands west of the Nile (*Araucana* 27.22de). This antique, fabulous note, however, is more than balanced by the rapid-fire list of "mandingos, monicongos y los feos / zapes, biafras, gelofos y guineos" (*Araucana* 27.22gh), with all of its terrible reminiscences of the classificatory system of the Atlantic *trata de negros* and the slave pens of Cartagena de Indias.

Veering back into the traditional ambit of the locus, Ercilla quickly reprises the standard itinerary of Libya, which is to say the Mediterranean littoral of North Africa from the mouths of the Nile to ancient Carthage (*Araucana* 27.23). This is an opportune vantage point from which to sweep north into Italy, and the third of the continental divisions of the mapamundi (*Araucana* 27.24–29). In Europe, Ercilla simply overwhelms his rivals with details, mostly toponyms. Camoens's strategy in the face of Mena's abbreviated treatment of Europe was to expand; Ercilla follows the same course, cramming even more place names into five stanzas than Camoens does into ten. Thus to compare only the treatment of the Far North (see section 5.3 above):

"Agora nestas partes se nomeia
A Lápia fria, a inculta Noruega,
Escandinávia ilha, que se arreia
Das vitórias que Itália não lhe nega:
Aqui, enquanto as águas não refreia
O congelado Inverno, se navega
Um braço do Sarmático Oceano
Pelo Brúsio, Suécio e frio Dano."
(*Lusíadas* 3.10)

"A Dinamarca, Dacia y a Noruega
hacia el mar de Dantisco y costa helada,
y a Suecia, que al confín de Gocia llega
que está en torno del mar fortificada,
de donde a la Zelandia se navega:
y mira allá a Grolandia desviada
del solar curso y la zodiaca vía,
do hay seis meses de noche y seis de día."
(*Araucana* 27.27)

Ercilla's gloss on Greenland, with its six months of night and six of day, clearly surpasses Camoens's mention of the frozen seas. The inclusion of Greenland itself, in fact, outdoes the Portuguese poet's mention of Lapland as an exotic and only recently accounted-for region of the North. Other of Ercilla's stanzas in this section are nothing more than dense lists of toponyms (for example, *Araucana* 27.29).

In the same way that Camoens found occasion to insinuate politically loaded comments into his survey of Europe, Ercilla exploits two opportunities to comment on political and historical affairs. In fact, when it comes to speaking of Rome, Ercilla contraposes a clever conceit of his own to Camoens's dry observations on the decline in Roman military glories:

"Pelo meio o divide o Apenino,
Que tão ilustre fez o pátrio Marte;
Mas, despois que o porteiro tem divino,
Perdendo o esforço veio a bélica arte:
Pobre está já de antiga potestade.
Tanto Deus se contenta de humildade!"
(*Lusíadas* 3.15c–h)

"mira la ilustre Nápoles famosa
y a Roma, que gran tiempo altivamente
se vio del universo apoderada,
y de cada nación después hollada."
(*Araucana* 27.24e–h)

The Portuguese poet's set of juxtapositions is perhaps more effective, but it also requires the better part of the stanza to work itself out. Ercilla counters with an extremely concise antithesis that has the advantage of brevity, always considered admirable in this type of conceit.

It is here in the description of Europe that Ercilla makes his first reference to a contemporary historical and political reality. Throughout his survey of Asia and Africa, in total contrast to Camoens, Ercilla makes no mention of the contemporary political situation. The closest that he comes to confronting the fact of Turkish domination in western Asia is his reference to Tamerlane's swath of destruction in the fifteenth century (*Araucana* 27.13).[44] The vague reference to Prester John at the outset of the survey of Africa is likewise an evasion of contemporary political realities. So is the insistence on classical toponyms in much of Asia. The overall effect is to create a sense of timeless universality that is unsullied by uncomfortable political realities. It is also a means of evading Camoens's celebration of Portuguese successes in much of Southeast Asia. Thus when Ercilla mentions that Charles V captured Francis I at Pavia (*Araucana* 27.25f–h), it is the first signal that the Castilian poet's mapamundi is entering a new phase of its articulation. This is most appropriate, of course, because Ercilla is fast approaching the metropolitan center of empire.

Juan de Mena dispenses with Hispania in a single stanza (*Laberinto de Fortuna* 48). Camoens dedicates four stanzas to the Iberian Peninsula, reserving the final one for Lusitania (*Lusíadas* 3.17–20). Ercilla doubles Camoens's effort, devoting no less than eight stanzas to "España" (*Araucana* 27.30–37). Where Camoens, in his opening stanza on the peninsula, calls "a nobre Espanha" the head of Europe, and takes pride in how her warlike sons had endured the rotations of Fortune's wheel (*Lusíadas* 3.17), Ercilla has Fitón announce the arrival of his itinerary at the head of empire in the following terms:

"Mira al Poniente a España, y la aspereza
de la antigua Vizcaya, de do es fama
que depende y procede la nobleza,

> que en aquellas prouincias se derrama,
> Ves a Bermeo cercado de maleza,
> cabeça y primer tronco desta rama,
> y tu Torre de Ercilla sobre el puerto
> de las montañas altas encubierto."
>
> (*Araucana* 27.30)

Ercilla subjected the entire mapamundi to intensive corrections when preparing the first complete edition of 1589–90, even adding an additional stanza. The stanza above introducing the reader to Spain, however, was one of the most radically revised (Ercilla, *Araucana*, ed. Medina, 4:163). Among the revisions, Ercilla replaced "que en aquellas prouincias se derrama" (*Araucana* 27.30*d*) with "por todo lo que vemos descubierto." The change clearly shows the intent to universalize the sense of the stanza. The nobility of "la montaña" extends not just over Spain, but the entire world. Both Camoens and Ercilla begin their treatment of the peninsula with references to the noble qualities of the inhabitants, but only Ercilla draws such immediate and foregrounded attention to his own personal roots.

Ercilla does not lose sight of his encomiastic project, however, and devotes two full stanzas to the Escorial (*Araucana* 27.33–34). Without ever mentioning the name, Ercilla evokes the magnificence of the edifice, explicitly connecting its construction to the victory of Saint Quentin that has already played such a large role in his prophetic machinery.[45] In the second of these stanzas dedicated to Philip II, Ercilla places his sovereign squarely in the center of the metropolitan seat of power, singing of his "tan larga y poderosa mano" (*Araucana* 27.34*gh*).

Camoens, as we have seen, reserved the place of honor at the end of his sweep over the Iberian Peninsula for Portugal (*Lusíadas* 3.20). Ercilla, in contrast, does not delineate a separate space for Lusitania as a province, much less as a nation. On the contrary, the Castilian poet, after devoting the first four lines of a stanza to various cities of the peninsula as diverse in location as Burgos, Pamplona, Zaragoza, Valencia, and Barcelona, as well as the province of Galicia, has Fitón say:

> "Ves la ciudad famosa de Lisbona,
> Coymbra, y Salamanca que se muestra,

felice en todas ciencias, do solía
enseñarse también Nigromancia."
                                    (*Araucana* 27.31*e–h*)

Thus Lisbon, although famous, is only one among many cities of "España." Furthermore, Coimbra—site of Portugal's university—is not only balanced, but outshone, by Salamanca. The most important point, of course, is that no mention is made of Portugal's political independence. Lisbon and Coimbra are treated as just two more cities of Spain. This of course, corresponds to the political initiative of the 1570s that was preparing for the takeover of Portugal that was to occur in 1580. The negation of Portugal's statehood in the *Araucana* is particularly significant, however, if read in the light of the celebration of Lusitanian independence in the first mapamundi and the following historical sections of the *Lusíadas*.

The direction that the *Araucana*'s response will take to the encomium of the Portuguese empire in the *Lusíadas* becomes clearly apparent in the final stanzas of Ercilla's description of Spain. Passing swiftly down through Madrid and Toledo to Andalusia with Cordova and Granada, Fitón arrives at the great port city, spider at the center of the web of colonial exploitation:

"Mira a Seuilla, ves la Realeza
de templos, edificios, y moradas,
el concurso de gente, y la grandeza
del trato de las Indias apartadas,
Que de Oro, plata, perlas, y riqueza,
dos flotas en vn año entran cargadas,
y salen otras dos de mercancía
con gente, munición, y artillería."
                                    (*Araucana* 27.36)

Seville itself is awesome as an urban center—one of the largest European cities of the sixteenth century—but even more impressive is its role as unique metropolitan emporium of the far-flung colonial economies. Camoens could vaunt the gold of the Monomotapa, or the spices of the Moluccas, but none of that could compete with the spectacle of the treasure fleets making port at San Lúcar de Barrameda every year, loaded with an unprecedented avalanche of precious metals. If the Portuguese could take pride in the seven hundred kilos of African gold their fleets brought to Lisbon, Ercilla could counter with the more than four tons of American gold that officially landed in Seville—not to mention the contraband—every year (Braudel, *Mediterranean*, 470). Ercilla is also careful to point out the flexing muscles of empire. Not only does wealth stream in, but great fleets carrying arms and men sail forth with regularity. Seville resembles a great beating heart in the body of colonial empire.

It is a natural step from the commercial and administrative heart of the colonial system to the vast reaches of the colonies themselves. Camoens placed Lusitania at the crest of Europe (*Lusíadas* 3.20), and then grounded his survey of Portugal's overseas empire in Christian Europe (*Lusíadas* 10.92ab). Ercilla concludes his survey of Spain in a similar, although rival, spirit. Fitón directs the poet's gaze:

> "Mira a Cáliz donde Hércules famoso
> sobre sus hados prósperos corriendo
> fixó las dos Colunas vitorioso,
> Nichil Vltra, en el Mármol escriuiendo,
> Mas Carlos Quinto Máximo glorioso
> los mojonados términos rompiendo
> del ancho y nueuo mundo abrió la vía
> porque en vn mundo solo no cauía."
>
> (*Araucana* 27.37)

If Camoens could glory in his countrymen's discovery of the "secrets of the seas" (*Lusíadas* 9.86e–g), and their daring in sailing beyond the ken of antique authority (*Lusíadas* 5.13d), Ercilla can invoke the discovery of an entire "new world." Significantly, the Castilian poet ascribes this feat to Charles V, in keeping with his encomium of the emperor's son. Columbus receives some limited credit in the description of the Antilles in the following section.[46] The glory of initiating the enterprise as a whole, the breaking of the bounds set by the *nihil ultra* of ancient authority inscribed in the Pillars of Hercules, the great achievement, is reserved for the dynasty that the poet serves. Ercilla modifies "Carlos Quinto Máximo" in his revision of 1589–90 to "Fernando católico" (ed. Medina, 4:163). This accords better with historical fact, and distances the accomplishment somewhat from Philip II, but does not break with the basic attribution of, to use López de Gómara's words, "la mayor cosa después de la creación del mundo, sacando la encarnación y muerte del que lo crió" (*Historia general*, 7) to the dynasty of his king.

Ercilla devotes twelve stanzas to the New World in the version published in 1578, adding one more for a total of thirteen in 1589–90 (Ercilla, *Araucana*, ed. Medina, 4:163). This section of the mapamundi is clearly a key element in Ercilla's response to the mapamundi of the *Lusíadas*, where the Spanish Empire in America is summarily dealt with in a single stanza (*Lusíadas* 10.139). Ercilla begins logically enough, as did Camoens in the case of the Portuguese overseas empire, by following the route of exploration and conquest to the newly opened territories. Thus he commences with the Canary Islands, but briefly veers northward to have Fitón point out the Azores, specifically mentioning that they are occupied by the Portuguese. These possesions of the rival empire are quickly contrasted with Columbus's discoveries in the Antilles, "populated by strange peoples, never before seen" (*Araucana* 27.39), which receive six of the eight verses.

Ercilla procedes on through the Bahamas to Florida, and from there to New Spain. Mexico receives almost two stanzas, and Cortés is given credit for vastly expanding the realms of the Spanish Crown (*Araucana* 27.40). Cortés is the only *conquistador* to be specifically mentioned in the manner in which Camoens cited the deeds of individual Portuguese captains in his survey of Africa and Asia.[47] If Ercilla avoids the celebration of individual conquerors, he certainly does not soft-pedal the riches of the lands they conquered. He insists on the vast populations involved, for instance those of Mexico and Central America (*Araucana* 27.41). The emeralds of what is now Ecuador (*Araucana* 27.43e), the incredible concentration of silver in the ore of Potosí (*Araucana* 27.47 [1578 27.46]), more than surpass the riches of the East trumpeted by Camoens. Ercilla also pays tribute to the political pomp and circumstance of empire: both the Spanish colonial government of the present (*Araucana* 27.45gh [1589–90]) and the Incas of the indigenous past (*Araucana* 27.46 [1578 27.45]).

Following the north-to-south sweep of his survey, Fitón brings his interlocutor's gaze naturally down the spine of the Andes to Chile (*Araucana* 27.49–50 [1578 27.48–49]). Ercilla and his wizard have finally arrived upon the scene of the war that forms the central action of the poem, and Ercilla does insert a brief but poignant reference to the indigenous protagonists of his epic, referring to "Arauco, estado libre y poderoso" (*Araucana* 27.50*b* [1578 27.49*b*]). Indeed, this would have been a logical place to have brought the geographical survey to a conclusion, tying the universality of the mapamundi and the far-flung empire into the obscure war at the extreme colonial periphery. It is clear, however, that there is another project driving Ercilla's selection and disposition of his material here. Fitón's itinerary continues swiftly down to the southernmost regions of Chile—explored by Ercilla himself, and treated at length in the canto posthumously inserted in Part III of the poem in the edition of 1597—and the old enchanter only pauses to elaborate when he reaches the straits (*Araucana* 27.50 [1578 27.49]):

> "por donde Magallanes con su gente
> al mar del Sur salió desembocando,
> y tomando la buelta del poniente
> al Maluco guió Noruesteando,
> Ves las Islas de Acaca, y Zabú, en frente
> Y a Matán do murió al fin peleando,
> Bruney, Bohol, Gilolo, Terranate,
> Machián, Mutir Badan, Tidore, y Mate."
> (*Araucana* 27.51 [1578 27.50])

Thus Ercilla, like Camoens before him, brings his mapamundi to a conclusion with Magellan and the Spice Islands.[48] There are, however, fundamental contrasts. Ercilla, unlike Camoens, makes no mention of Magellan's nationality. Camoens assigns credit for Magellan's daring and discovery to the fact that he was "no feito, com verdade, / Português, porém não na lealdade" (*Lusíadas* 10.140*gh*). Ercilla, on the other hand, allows his silence on the question to point to Magellan as an Iberian and a servant of the Emperor, the glory of whose deeds accrues naturally to the dynasty and crown that sponsored them. Furthermore, Ercilla democratizes the feat, insisting on "Magallanes con su gente" (*Araucana* 27.51 [1578 27.50]). The reader, of course, recalls that most of Magellan's company were Castilians, such as Sebastián del Cano, who completed the circumnavigation and brought the *Vitoria* back to San Lúcar de Barrameda (the port of Seville) loaded with the coveted spices (López de Gómara, *Historia general*, cap. 99).

Camoens chooses to expand on Magellan's navigations down the coast of Patagonia on his way to the straits (*Lusíadas* 10.141), after having singled him out for the discovery of the long-sought passage

(*Lusíadas* 10.138*gh*). The Portuguese poet says nothing explicitly either of the voyage to the Moluccas or of Magellan's death. In contrast, Ercilla, having accorded Magellan appropriate honor for the navigation of the straits (*Araucana* 27.50*h*–51*ab* [1578 27.49*h*–50*ab*]), strikes directly to the heart of the dispute that so vexed Castilian-Portuguese relations. Not only does Ercilla have Fitón explicitly state the true destination of Magellan's voyage—the Moluccas (*Araucana* 27.51*d* [1578 27.50*d*])—but he continues on to the long-sought islands after recounting Magellan's death. Thus the same islands that Camoens catalogs with such pride in the exotic products they contribute to Portuguese trade, are implicitly included in the Castilian Empire. Speaking of Tidore and Ternate, Camoens has insisted that they were "bought with Portuguese blood" (*Lusíadas* 10.132). Ercilla, who had said quite freely of the Azores that they were "de Portugueses ocupadas" (*Araucana* 27.39*ab*), significantly says nothing at all about the political status of these distant but coveted islands. The implication, clearly, is that they fall within the purview of the universal Christian, Catholic empire headed by his fellow Iberians, especially the Castilians, and their sovereign.

Indeed, the underlying principle of Ercilla's response to the challenge of Camoens's mapamundi with its energetic encomium of Portuguese independence, achievement, wealth, and empire, is superior universality. Thus Ercilla has constructed a complete mapamundi to counter Tethys's very partial description of the earthly globe within her cosmic sphere. Not only has Ercilla covered the three continents of the Old World in something similar to the traditional scheme of the mapamundi, the Castilian poet has elaborated at length on the vast and exotic expanses of the New World, reveling in the names of peoples and places charged with all of the potency of the genuine marvelous. Ercilla underlines the importance of this earthly universality by closing the mapamundi with a stanza dedicated to the vague shadows of lands that cannot quite be made out. Fitón assures his pupil that these are the yet-to-be-discovered territories that will remain mysterious until God sees fit to reveal them (*Araucana* 27.52 [1578 27.51]). If Camoens has excelled in his portrait of the celestial machinery of the cosmos, which Fitón here declines to describe, pleading the lateness of the hour (*Araucana* 27.53 [1578 27.52]), Ercilla has countered with a significantly more complete vision of the earth. Furthermore, it is a vision that stresses the vast expanses of the Castilian Empire that Camoens deals with so summarily, and still more, the universality of scope implicit in the dynasty founded upon the union of the nation forged by the Catholic kings with the far-reaching pretensions of the House of Austria.

In section 5.2 of this chapter, I have explained that Juan de Mena deliberately expanded the length and scope of his mapamundi beyond that found in the Alexander poems in order to achieve two goals. The first was to underline the universality of the empire that, he implied, lies within his sovereign's grasp if only he will adopt the program of Alvaro de Luna. The second purpose propelling Mena to devote so much effort to the description of the earth before ascending the spheres was the necessity of stressing the secular, mundane nature of the project that he championed. It is apparent that Ercilla, when confronted with the polished imitative practice of Camoens's verses, the sophisticated Neoplatonic conception underlying their articulation, and the challenge to Castilian pride that they encapsulated, looked to Mena's mapamundi for a model not so much of a textual nature, but rather of a strategy. Thus Ercilla strives for totalization on the earthly plane, and lets his descriptions of Fitón's globe—his aleph—imply the celestial dimension that he omits from his explicit description of the universe. The vision—taking the aleph and the mapamundi together—remains a cosmic icon, but one that stresses the earthly in contrast with the unworldly. This, of course, is very much to the point, because Ercilla's sovereign was, in fact, laying the groundwork for taking the crown of Portugal, along with its overseas empire, as the Castilian poet was publishing his encomium of his master's empire.

5.5. Conclusion: The Brotherly Rivalry and the Sea Change in the *Araucana*

At this point it should be clear that Ercilla wrote not only his mapamundi, but also the underlying structure and approach of Parts II and III of the *Araucana*, in a direct spirit of rivalry with Camoens. The nature of this rivalry should not be misunderstood, however. There are two dimensions to the question: one nationalistic or dynastic; the other poetic. It is necessary to understand correctly the first before examining the second. Antonio José Saraiva has observed that after the annexation of Portugal in 1580, the *Lusíadas* came to be read as an anti-Castilian tract, a celebration of Lusitania's lost independence. The Portuguese critic cautions against retrospectively applying this reading to Camoens's "authorial intention" in 1570 (Saraiva 381-82). Saraiva points out that Camoens uses the appellation "Espanha" in the sense of Hispania, of the entire peninsula, and that sixteenth-century Portuguese would refer to themselves, when overseas, as being from "Espanha" (382-83). Saraiva indicates that when Philip II took the crown of Portugal, he became, in fact, king of all Spain, unifying the cultural and the political implications of the term (383). Furthermore, Saraiva disputes the notion that Camoens's celebration of Portuguese independence in the historical passages of the *Lusíadas* makes of the poet an "anti-Castilian." The Portuguese critic points out (383-84) that Camoens has called Castile the "restituidor de Espanha e senhor dela" (*Lusíadas* 3.19g) and has Tethys refer to Castile as "vossa amiga" in the description of the Castilian Empire in the New World (*Lusíadas* 10.139e). It is significant that both of these examples come from the geographical passages that I have discussed at length above. Saraiva, of course, must admit that there is a dimension of rivalry in the overseas empires, but asserts that for Camoens the most important element is the common crusade against the Moor. Saraiva concludes that Camoens wishes to celebrate the glory of Hispania in her crusade and overseas enterprise (384-85).

Nonetheless, to refer only to the two examples offered by Saraiva, when Camoens calls Castile the "senhor" of Hispania and leader of the Reconquest, he cannot refrain from saying it is by the will of mutable Fortune, in contrast with the glory of Portugal, which is due to the immutable will of God, as explained above in section 5.3. When Camoens mentions the wide and wealthy lands of Spanish America and has Tethys say that they belong to "your friend," Castile, this generosity is bracketed between references to Magellan, whose accomplishments are attributed to the Portuguese nature of his deeds, if not his loyalty. The triumph of Portuguese independence is worth no less if Camoens can be generous to the losers. There is no mistake about the rivalry that Camoens expresses in reference to his Castilian cousins, especially when referring to the Castilian state, rather than to individuals.

To be sure, this is not the same kind of rivalry as that which exists between all Christian Iberians and Moors or Turks. Camoens does not propose that Portugal destroy or dominate Castile. Saraiva is absolutely correct in reading the *Lusíadas* as primarily a celebration of the Iberian crusade against the ancestral, and common, enemy. Nonetheless, it is important to Camoens that this crusade be carried out on terms of equality. Portugal's independence, and the wealth of her overseas empire, as well as something of her unique glory, are to be jealously maintained. Where the struggle against the Turk, for instance, is to be fought to the death, with no quarter given or asked, the rivalry between Portuguese and Castilians is to be played out as between brothers, indeed brothers who often enough fight shoulder to shoulder in the same ranks. This camaraderie, however, does nothing to diminish the keenness of the competition; on the contrary, the family relationship, all of the affinities, only serve to invigorate the rivalry.

Ercilla, not surprisingly, displays a very similar attitude, with, of course, one major difference. As far as individuals are concerned, Ercilla will give credit to a stalwart Portuguese as easily as to a valiant Castilian, or for that matter, Araucanian. Thus Ercilla sings of "Don Simón Pereira, Lusytano" among the heroic companions of Don García who, badly outnumbered, resist a furious Araucanian assault (*Araucana* 19.48c). Don Simón, of course, like Magellan, was exercising his heroism in the service of the king of Spain; nonetheless, his nationality is no cause for shame—on the contrary, Ercilla glories in it.[49] Indeed, Ercilla, at least before 1580, seems willing enough to give his Portuguese brethren their due, as long as it does not infringe too closely on the rights or prerogatives of the Castilians, as in the case of the Spice Islands. Even in that context, Ercilla's response to Camoens's challenge is stated fairly subtly. After all, in the 1570s various possibilities still existed for reincorporating Lusitania into the "family" of provincial nationalities that all swore fealty to the wearer of the crown of Castile. Philip II, in fact, was still involved in negotiations concerning yet another dynastic marriage that would almost surely result in the prompt return of Portugal to the fold right up to the eve of King Sebastian's disastrous expedition to Morroco in 1578, the year that Part II of the *Araucana* was published. It was widely believed that Sebastian would not live long, and if the young king were to marry Philip's daughter, Portugal might soon fall to the lot of the King of Castile in a natural enough fashion (Rodríguez Moñino 16–22).[50] In 1589, when Philip's taking of the Portuguese crown was long since an accomplished fact, Ercilla was to open the final canto of Part III of the

Araucana, dedicated to the "just war" of reclamation, with the following ringing exordium:

> Canto el furor del pueblo castellano
> con ira justa y pretensión movido,
> y el derecho del reino lusitano
> a las sangrientas armas remitido:
> la paz, la unión, el vínculo cristiano
> en rabiosa discordia convertido,
> las lanzas de una parte y otra airadas
> a los parientes pechos arrojadas.
>
> (*Araucana* 37.1)

The cause is just, as is the ire of the Castilians. Nonetheless, peace and Christian unity are to be preferred to war, especially a war in which cousin must kill cousin. Ercilla, too, sees all of Hispania as a family, united against the ancient enemies of the Faith. But there is an important distinction in Ercilla's view of this family from that of Camoens. For Ercilla, the undisputed paterfamilias is the king of Castile, and his will is not to be flouted, even by respected cousins.

It is precisely the family nature of the rivalry that Ercilla feels with the Portuguese that conditions his poetic rivalry with Camoens. Both men are Iberian soldier/poets of the same age who write in the shadow of Garcilaso. Both have been enthusiastic readers and assimilators of Ariosto, and ultimately, of Petrarch. Camoens here clearly has the advantage; his collection of lyric poems, modeled after the *Canzoniere*, is perhaps the finest expression of Iberian Petrarchism of the generation after Garcilaso. The same mastery of the Petrarchist/Garcilasist idiom, particularly in terms of the sophisticated approach to *imitatio*, moreover, is manifestly evident in the *Lusíadas*. Herrera, for example, the most outstanding Castilian Garcilasist of the day, and not always generous in his appreciations of the work of contemporaries, accords the highest praise to the *Lusíadas*, calling it "aquella hermosa i elegante obra" (quoted by Asensio 6).[51] Both Ercilla and Camoens are also thoroughly conversant with the native Iberian tradition; for instance, the poetry of the age of Juan de Mena. Above all, both have undertaken the composition of an epic poem, the one important genre that Garcilaso failed to cover.

The enthusiasm with which the appearance of Part I of the *Araucana* was received in 1569 is well attested. Courtiers and soldiers of a poetic bent are said to have hailed Ercilla as the Spanish Ariosto (Medina, *Vida*, 99–100). Ercilla showed promise to become the poet so long awaited who would wield the pen as dextrously as the sword and celebrate the military accomplishments of his countrymen with literary skill commensurate with the perceived grandeur of their feats of arms. This reception must surely have stimulated Ercilla to a more ambitious effort in Part II. It is obvious, however, that the publication of the *Lusíadas* in 1572, three years after Part I of the *Araucana*, would have put considerable pressure on Ercilla to expand the scope of his epic. Camoens was a formidable rival, and the *Lusíadas* successfully intertwines the metropolitan with the peripheral spheres of empire in a way that Ercilla had not attempted in Part I of the *Araucana*. Furthermore, where Ercilla had dissimulated his imitations and was being compared to Ariosto, Camoens dazzled his readers with an extremely sophisticated and loudly announced mastery of both classical and modern models and was being hailed in Spanish erudite circles as the new Virgil (Asensio 6–7). Camoens's success was such that imitators sprang up among the courtier poets of the bilingual literary circles of the peninsula close upon the heels of the publication of the *Lusíadas*. One of these was Jerónimo Corte Real, a relative of Ercilla's wife, who incorporated imitations of passages from the *Lusíadas* into his epic poem on Lepanto that he dedicated to Philip II in 1575 (Asensio 13–15).

Ercilla, a rival of Corte Real's for the attention and approbation of King Philip, was obviously not supinely content to recognize Camoens's greatness with mere textual imitations. On the contrary, he organized Part II of the *Araucana* in such a way as to compete seriously with the Portuguese bard, a far more worthy rival than his fellow courtier Corte Real. It is thus apparent that much of the impetus for the sea change in the course of the *Araucana* between Parts I and II can be traced to the stimulus of the *Lusíadas*. Ercilla carefully balances the incidents of the war in Arauco with both amorous and supernatural episodes in Part II. Furthermore, the web of prophecy that elevates the argument of the *Araucana* from rhymed chronicle or *romanzo* to the genuine plane of epic radiates from the visits to Fitón's cave. The emulation of Camoens thus pulsates textually behind the winds that drive the true change of direction in Part II of the *Araucana*. It is my thesis that this same spirit of rivalry with the masterful Portuguese poet also permeates Ercilla's entire redefinition of his project in Part II of the *Araucana*.

Once again, as a closing note, I would like to draw attention to the importance of a coherent theoretical understanding of the practices of *imitatio* to an informed reading of these seminal literary expressions of sixteenth-century imperialist endeavor. If we are truly to approach an accurate comprehension of the discursive practices of imperialism and colonialism in the sixteenth century, we cannot continue to cling to the aesthetic prejudices of Romanticism and reject the issue of *imitatio* as digressive or irrelevant to the historical and ideological dimensions of these literary works. Hopefully, we will be able to bring a more sophisticated reading to these poems of exploration and conquest, one that will permit us to understand how sixteenth-century Europeans employed the traditional practices of *imitatio* as a means of mediating their interactions with the otherness of the peoples and places they were bringing under their sway. Nor should we forget the role, so apparent, for instance, in Fitón's cave or in Proteus's *globo*, of *imitatio* in forging the discursive authority and legitimacy of overseas empire.

Notes

Introduction

1. For the basic concept of *translatio*, see Curtius 28–29. Jean-Claude Carron explicates the implications for the Renaissance poetics of imitation (565–71); Ignacio Navarrete explores the role of this trope in the development of sixteenth-century Iberian poetic practice (*Orphans*, 15–31).

2. Although Pastor does not insist on the point, it is clear that this supposedly medieval model is that which had been articulated in the *libros de caballerías* and the Italian *romanzi*—which is to say that it is a literary model.

3. In all fairness, it should be added that Quint does not fail to recognize the importance of Ariosto to Ercilla's poem. What is unique about his argument is the way in which he frames the relationship: "Epic form and romance formlessness can alternately be seen to win out in Ercilla's poem, whose representation of the Araucanian war, by turns pro-Spanish and pro-Indian, may once again be construed as a war of poetic and generic models, but now as a three-way, if still two-sided battle: Lucan meets and overlaps with Ariosto in the *Araucana*, and together they put up a fight against Virgil" (182).

4. In Quint's terms, this would be to say that Virgil will always win out over Lucan, despite the individual poet's predelictions or sympathies, simply as a consequence of the epic form and genre.

5. A notable exception is the work of Elizabeth B. Davis. Davis explores the construction of authority through imitation in its Old World contexts, especially in the work of Juan Rufo. Of particular interest are her analyses of Rufo's imitations of and poetic rivalry with Ercilla. See especially chapter 2 of her forthcoming book, *Epic Imagination: The Construction of Identity in Imperial Spain*, and her article "Escribir después de Ercilla: la codicia en *La Austriada* de Juan Rufo."

6. As J. Jorge Klor de Alva has made clear, the use of the terms "colonialism" and "imperialism" when applied to the sixteenth-century Iberian enterprise in America must be understood in the context of that undertaking and not confused with nineteenth-century French and British experiences in India and Africa (3). The Portuguese empire created during the sixteenth century, and celebrated by Camoens, must also be understood as distinct in many ways from both the Castilian conquest of America and the nineteenth-century colonization of the Old World.

7. Morínigo breaks down the contents of Part II of the *Araucana* as follows: amorous and marvelous episodes as well as the Old World battles and the mapamundi, 5,058 vv.; treatment of actions occurring among the Araucanians that Ercilla could not have witnessed—many of which are also of literary inspiration, corresponding to established epic topoi—1,298 vv.; historically verifiable events, for the most part witnessed by Ercilla, 1,386 (Ercilla, *La Araucana*, ed. Morínigo and Lerner, 1:53).

8. Quint would read a great deal more into the Dido episode. He posits it not only as a rejection of Virgilian, triumphalist epic from the perspective of the "epic of the losers," but also as the postulation of an alternate, more just and humane, model of conquest (*Epic and Empire*, 182–85).

9. Angel Alvarez Vilela makes the intriguing assertion that the episode of the expedition to Ancud was included in some copies of the 1589 edition, but only those destined for export to the New World. Unfortunately, Alvarez Vilela gives no indication of how he arrives at this conclusion (116–17).

10. I refer here, of course, to the prophecy of Puchecalco (*Araucana* 8.39–43) and the subsequent apparitions of the indigenous deity, Eponamón, and the Virgin Mary (*Araucana* 9.1–21).

11. Due to the addition of a stanza to the mapamundi in the edition of 1589–90, the second visit to Fitón's cave actually ends at 27.53 in the 1578 edition. See Ercilla, *Araucana*, ed. Medina, 4:163.

12. Frank Pierce gives the date of the Lisbon edition, dated 1582 by Medina, as 1588. The total of six editions before the appearance of Part III in 1589 remains the same, however, because Pierce counts two in Zaragoza in 1578 (*La poesía*, 331). As Pierce points out, the fact that four editions appeared in the first year indicates a considerable demand for the poem (Pierce, "Fame," 230).

13. Morínigo offers a concise summary of the criticism of the *Araucana* in the introduction to his Castalia edition (1:61–92), which as Morínigo acknowledges (1:61 n. 14), owes a great deal to Pierce's detailed, thoughtful study of the question in his *La poesía épica del Siglo de Oro*, especially the second edition of 1968. Additionally, Maxime Chevalier dedicates pages of great value to the criticism of the *Araucana* in his *L'Arioste en Espagne* (144–60). Fernando Alegría's essay "Ercilla y sus críticos" remains a useful review from a Spanish American, and specifically Chilean, perspective. Finally, August J. Aquila's annotated bibliography, which follows most of the published criticism up to the early 1970s, can be a useful tool for the study of the panorama of the reception of Ercilla if used with caution.

14. Quintana, to be fair, does not feel that such defects should impede appreciation of the work as whole, which he finds quite admirable. He expresses the opinion, so often repeated, that the elements borrowed from the epic and the *romanzi* are entirely ornamental and secondary to the real matter of the poem (162–63). This, of course, flies in the face of Morínigo's analysis of the relative number of verses dedicated to the fictitious and marvelous, of purely literary inspiration, in comparison with the historical material cited above.

15. Menéndez Pelayo defends the intrinsic quality of the episodes in question, however, and criticizes the Chilean editor König for deleting them from his edition of 1888 (2:222).

16. See Chapter 3 of the present book for an analysis of Ercilla's imitation of Lucan in Fitón's cave in the light of Thomas Greene's theories of "necromantic" imitation and an array of specialist studies on Lucan. The reader will find there a perhaps less ingenuous view of Lucan's approach to the supernatural than that expressed by Menéndez Pidal.

17. Quint argues that by bringing Part I to a close with the storm, and with the reference to Aeolus (mythical king of the winds), Ercilla is making a "pointedly anti-

Virgilian" statement. Quint notes that "the presence of Aeolus alludes to the *opening* of the *Aeneid* and to the storm unleashed by the winds of the god upon the Trojan fleet," and that "the nonnarratable confusion from which the *Aeneid* had started is thus where the first installment of the *Araucana* arrives" (*Epic and Empire*, 162). While this may well be a sustainable argument, close comparison of the texts in question demonstrates that Ercilla does not go out of his way to draw attention to the Virgilian subtext, even in the description of Aeolus's cavern (*Araucana* 15.58–59; *Aeneid* 1.51–63).

18. For examples, see my forthcoming articles "Reading and Responding to the Amorous Episodes of the *Araucana* in Colonial Peru" and "Pedro de Oña and Bernardo de Balbuena Read Ercilla's Fitón."

Chapter 1

1. For Part I of the *Araucana* I rely on the facsimile edition of the princeps of 1569 published by the Hispanic Society of America. For Part II, I rely on the first edition of Part II, printed in 8° by Pierres Cosin in Madrid in 1578 and published as the second part of the *Primera y segunda parte de la Araucana*. For a description of this edition, see Medina (Ercilla, *La Araucana*, ed. Medina, 4:9–10). I also make occasional reference to the edition prepared by Morínigo and Lerner and first published by Castalia in 1979, as well as Isaías Lerner's 1993 Cátedra edition.

2. It is significant that one of the first to note the incongruity of this device was Luis Zapata (Lida de Malkiel, *Juan de Mena*, 64–65), Ercilla's predecessor as a page of the future Philip II (Medina and Reynolds 10). Ercilla and Zapata—both subsequently to celebrate the Spanish Empire in *verista* epic—traveled together in the company of Prince Philip in 1548 (Medina and Reynolds 11; Medina, *Vida*, 27). It is prudent to note, however, that Zapata's *Miscelánea*, where he makes his observation about Mena, was written in the 1590s (Medina and Reynolds 16–17), long after Ercilla had written the *Araucana*. As I demonstrate in Chapters 2 and 3, Ercilla's relationship with Mena is always very complex, but central to the poet of the *Araucana*'s conception of the "Spanish" epic tradition. It is very probable that Ercilla avoids the otherwise tempting locus of the storm portents, at least in part to distance his own poem as much as possible from this "defective" passage of the *Laberinto de Fortuna*. This only reinforces my thesis that the principal reason for leaving out the omens is to dissimulate the literary, imitative provenance of the storm in keeping with the *verista* program announced at the outset of Part I.

3. José Toribio Medina, still Ercilla's most influential biographer, does not give the poet of the *Araucana* much credit for direct contact with classical literature in general, and he omits any mention of Homer among the authors Ercilla may have known. Medina, in fact, seems to doubt that Ercilla could read much Latin, not to mention Greek (*Vida*, 23). As I demonstrate in Chapter 3, Ercilla undoubtedly was intimately familiar with Latin authors for whom no convenient translation was available. On the other hand, there are no grounds to suggest that Ercilla was conversant with Greek. While this probably precluded any close acquaintance with the *Iliad*, there can be little doubt that Ercilla had read at least the first thirteen books of the *Odyssey*. Gonçalo Pérez, like Ercilla a member of the court, published his Castilian translation in 1550. At least six editions had appeared by 1562 (Pierce, *La poesía*, 363). The 1556 and 1562 editions contain all twenty-four books of Homer's poem (Beardsley 48). Given Ercilla's interest in epic and his proximity to Pérez, it is safe to assume that Ercilla would have been familiar with this

translation of the *Odyssey*. Like Ercilla, Pérez addressed his work to Philip (fol. A2), and this at a time when Ercilla was part of Philip's retinue.

4. Almost all of the other literary storms in the tradition, both classical and Renaissance, begin at nightfall of the first day of sailing.

5. I have reproduced Miller's translation from the Loeb edition here.

6. Ovid's journey by sea, so vividly recalled in the *Tristia*, came a year after his finishing the *Metamorphoses* (Miller, ed. and trans., viii–ix).

7. This stanza is one of many that Ercilla polished and altered in subsequent editions (cf. Morínigo and Lerner). The version given above is that of 1578 Cosin and 1578 Soler.

8. The pages of the 1569 edition that bear the prologue and other front matter are without numeration. The 1569 text, in modernized form, is reproduced faithfully in Morínigo and Lerner's Castalia edition (1:121–22) and in Lerner's Cátedra edition (69–70).

9. All translations from the *Orlando furioso* are mine unless otherwise indicated.

10. This is the same narrative technique that Ercilla uses to create suspense between Parts I and II with the storm. In an expansion of the motif of a ferocious duel frozen with weapons in midswing, Ercilla uses the same device to divide Part II from Part III. Again, Rengo is involved, this time with a rival Araucanian, the protean Tucapel. Part II ends with Tucapel's sword slicing down toward Rengo with a surely mortal stroke (*Araucana* 29.53). The original readers had to wait nearly ten years to find out how Tucapel's mighty blow cleaved through Rengo's shield and helmet (*Araucana* 30.9–10) with the publication of Part III in 1589. Critics have long seen Ercilla's masterful use of this narrative trick, learned in the school of the Italian *romanzi*, as one of the principal inspirations for Cervantes's unforgettable duel between the Vizcayan and the "fevered" Manchegan *hidalgo*, which divides Part I from Part II of the first book of the *Quijote* (1:139–40 n. 2). Ercilla obviously felt that such narrative sleight of hand was especially called for given the admittedly monotonous succession of feats of arms that forms the principal matter of his poem.

11. All references to the text of *Orlando furioso* are to Bigi's edition unless otherwise indicated.

12. I have adapted the English translations from Miller's Loeb edition of the *Metamorphoses*.

13. See Ronsard, *Franciade*, ed. Laumonier, 103. Particularily salient is Ronsard's use of Ovid's simile of the first soldier to storm a city's walls to describe the onslaught of the waves that breach the hull (*Franciade* 2.272–82; *Metamorphoses* 11.524–28). This is such an unmistakable point of contact between the two poems that the prudent investigator should have no trouble identifying the other, less obvious aspects of the imitation. Ronsard, of course, throws critics somewhat off the track by his constant references to Homer and Virgil.

14. Ariosto introduces four storms at sea into *Orlando furioso*. Two are brief: 2.28–30 and 13.15–16. The other two are more ambitious: 18.141–45, 19.43–53 and 41.8–24 (Ponte 195). The two longer storm descriptions, especially, are rich in exact, up-to-date nautical terminology. Although Ariosto's nautical vocabulary is often specific to Mediterranean seafaring—many terms refer to galleys and many are of Venetian origin—there are plenty of coincidences with Ercilla's—and Camoens's—shipboard jargon.

15. In both this quotation from the *Lusíadas* and the following quotation from the *Araucana* I have supplied quotation marks not present in the orginals in order to set off the direct speech. Because of the importance for my thesis of Ercilla's reading of Camoens, I have been careful to consult and quote from the facsimile edition prepared by José Maria Rodrigues and published by the Biblioteca Nacional in 1921. This reproduces

the princeps of 1572, the only printed version of *Os Lusíadas* that Ercilla would have been able to consult before the appearance of Part II of the *Araucana* in 1578. Hernâni Cidade explains the complicated problem of the two editions that carry the date 1572 on their title pages, only one of which was probably published in that year (Camões, *Obras completas*, ed. Cidade, 4:x–xxv). The facsimile version used here reproduces the text of Ee, which is generally accepted as the authentic first edition of 1572.

16. In the gloss on 6.71, however, it is unclear whether Faria e Sousa is citing the passage from the *Araucana* as a source or an analogue. Due either to a printer's error or a slip on Faria e Sousa's part, the several verses from the storm of the *Araucana* cited in the commentary on Camoens's storm are incorrectly attributed to *Araucana* 16 (Part II) rather than *Araucana* 15 (Part I), where they are actually to be found. If Faria e Sousa really thought that he was citing Part II of the *Araucana*, of course, there could be no question of Camoens taking his cue from Ercilla, but rather the reverse. It is equally unclear whether Faria e Sousa's remarks about the pertinence of the passage to one with experience of the sea applies to Ercilla as well as Camoens.

17. Part I of the *Araucana* achieved considerable literary success (Ercilla, *Araucana*, ed. Morínigo and Lerner 1:61; Medina, *Vida*, 99–100). Ercilla's poem found its most enthusiastic audience among the courtiers and soldiers of noble birth who shared an enthusiasm for literature (Chevalier, *Lectura*, 119–21). The chronicler Esteban de Garibay, for instance, describes the arrival of Part I of the *Araucana* in Brussels, where it was received with great enthusiasm by the pensinsular gentlemen-at-arms resident in the city (Medina, *Vida* 99–100; Chevalier, *Lectura*, 119). Given the bilingual nature of literary circles in sixteenth-century Spain and Portugal (Asensio 4), it is reasonable to assume that Camoens, a member of precisely the social group most keenly interested in such works, would have read Part I of the *Araucana* soon after its publication.

18. It may well be that Ricci's and Barbaro's imagery of "following," "pulling alongside," and "overtaking" or "surpassing" were originally intended for students or apprentice imitators, who would naturally begin their study of the practice by "following" appropriate models, just as was the custom in the acquisition of rhetorical skill.

19. The translation is that of Ralph G. Williams (101). The italics are mine.

20. The author is Lilius Gregorius Giraldus, probably writing 1515–20 (Vida, *De Arte Poetica*, ed. Williams, xviii), in which case Vida could well be responding in 1527. Giraldus is not precise about exactly who accuses Vida. He uses a passive construction, attributing the criticism to the envious (*malevoli*). The choice of words is precise and playful: *sumere* can mean "buy" as well as "select for use" and is thus aptly contrasted with *surripere*, "to steal furtively."

21. Colombí-Monguió refers in this passage to Roland Barthes, "De l'oeuvre au texte," *Revue d'Esthétique* 24 (1971): 229; Paul De Man, *Blindness and Insight* (New York, Oxford University Press: 1971), 165; Harold Bloom, *A Map of Misreading* (New York, Oxford University Press: 1975); she quotes from Julia Kristeva, *La Révolution du langage poètique* (Paris, Editions de Seuil: 1974), 343.

22. Robert Ball's study "Poetic Imitation in Góngora's *Romance de Angélica y Medoro*" is a model of sophisticated reading of imitative practice. Greene briefly discusses parody as one of the limits of what he calls dialectical imitation. He uses Ariosto's parodic renditions of Dante as examples of parody that does no "real damage" to the subtexts. He goes on to mention Quevedo in the same vein, although I am not so sure that Quevedo's parodies are so harmless or well intentioned.

23. It is true that the reflexive form of the Italian verb *accostare* can also simply mean "to resemble." Nonetheless, Barbaro's use of *accostarsi* should be read in light of Poliziano's use of the Latin verb *assequor*. Poliziano is talking about the failure of philologists to overcome completely anachronism. Greene translates *assequor* in its

meaning as "to comprehend" (8–9). Yet, like its root *sequor* it also means "to follow," and like *accostarsi*, it has the additional meaning of "to reach by following, draw near to." All three verbs are perhaps best interpreted in the light of the metaphor of the path.

24. Greene explains the fundamental transformation in the following terms: "Petrarch plays with the ambiguity of the woman's creaturely status which underlies the dramatic interplay of the *Aeneid*, but he reverses of course the direction taken by appearances: Venus is a goddess who looks like a woman, but Laura is a woman who looks like a goddess" (*Light*, 112).

25. Garcilaso clearly invokes Bernardo Tasso's immediate subtext by echoing Bembo's description of the maiden's eyes that "da far giorno seren la notte oscura" (v. 4) with "vuestro mirar ardiente, honesto, / con clara luz la tempestad serena" (2–4). The Spanish poet redoubles the necromantic dialogue with his subtexts here by restoring the burning quality of the beloved's gaze (Pet. "ardea"; Gar. "ardiente") that is lost in Bembo's rendition. But this is not the limit of Garcilaso's audacious disencrypting of his subtext. In the same two lines, he also engages Petrarch himself in a similar, but even more gallant, dialogue by transmuting Bembo's "notte oscuro" into a "tempestad" and transposing his adjective "sereno" into the verb "serenar." By saying that the woman's gaze "calms the storm," Garcilaso is harking back to Petrarch's principal, Virgilian subtext. What Garcilaso has remembered, of course, and wants to remind the discerning reader, is that just before assuming mortal form to reassure her shipwrecked son, Venus has remonstrated wth Jupiter about the storm raised by Juno to ruin Aeneas and the Trojans (*Aeneid* 1.229–53). By recalling the storm, Garcilaso is making sure that even in the full presence of the Petrarchan subtext, Petrarch's own model is not forgotten.

26. For a concise but cogent exposition of Garcilaso's approach to the imitation of Petrarch in a variety of contexts, see Navarrete, *Orphans*, 90–125.

27. In his translation, Boscán suppresses Castiglione's neologism—*sprezzatura*—but goes on to follow the original text in identifying it with "gracia" (73). Juan María Corominas places Ercilla very accurately in the courtier model proposed by Castiglione and embodied by Garcilaso. For reasons that he does not explain, Corominas assumes that Ercilla would have known *Il libro del cortegiano* primarily through Boscán's translation (6).

Chapter 2

1. Lerner convincingly makes the case that Ercilla's imitations of Lucan and Ariosto are grounded in an unavoidable Virgilian substratum ("Ercilla y Lucano," 690–91).

2. English verse translations from the *Aeneid* in this section are those of Robert Fitzgerald. Line numbers always refer to the Latin text as edited by R. D. Williams. References to the text of the poem are given by book and line numbers, separated by a period. References to Williams's introduction and notes are given by volume and page number, separated by a full colon.

3. Thomas Greene (*Descent*, 77–85) studies this episode, but he is far more interested in Virgil's imitation of Homer than in how the motif of the divine descent fits into the overall web of prophecy in the poem.

4. Bigi's notes to *Orlando furioso* 3.17a and 36.70a are particularly helpful. Boiardo had also dedicated his poem to the House of Este, and Ariosto only refines what he received from his predecessor in regard to the dynastic pair. For their encomiastic purpose it was especially important that Ruggiero's ancestry be traced through the line of Trojan Hector (*Orlando furioso* 36.70b).

5. According to Bigi's notes to these octaves, the principal direct source is Poliziano.

6. Fichter (74–81), for example, sees a reminiscence of Aeneas's dream of the river god Tiberinus's prophecy (*Aeneid* 8.18-25, 36-65) in Orlando's fretful and sleepless obsession with Angelica (*Orlando furioso* 8.71-72).

7. None of Javitch's specific examples of muddied or misread imitations in the *Furioso* deal directly with the prophetic *machina* or dynastic encomium of the poem, for instance.

8. Dolce's commentary was even translated into Spanish and appended to the Venice 1553 edition of Jerónimo de Urrea's Castilian translation of the *Furioso* (Javitch, "Sixteenth-Century Commentaries," 225). The fact that it was published in Italy would not have affected its dissemination among Castilian readers. The 1549 princeps was published in Antwerp (Chevalier, *L'Arioste*, 74), and by midcentury most literary works in Castilian were being produced for the domestic market outside of the peninsula. Books printed in France, the Low Countries, and Italy for the Spanish market had more prestige, were generally cheaper and after c. 1540-50, often the only editions available (Griffin 37-39).

9. This celebration of the Este is actually found in *Orlando furioso* 46.77-98. The passage from canto 42 would appear to be the description of the statues of famous women that adorned the fountain seen by Rinaldo, octaves 79-96. For a more detailed examination of Ariosto's influence in Garcilaso, see Chevalier, *L'Arioste*, 63-69.

10. Although it is only fair to add that many of Urrea's contemporaries praised him and his work (Chevalier, *L'Arioste*, 75-77). For balanced critical examinations of Urrea's translation of the *Furioso*, see Bertini, and Van Horne, "Urrea Translation."

11. There are also at least four subsequent printings up to 1595 (Pierce, *La poesía*, 367). Nor was Urrea the only Spaniard to translate Ariosto during the sixteenth century. Hernando Alcoçer published a translation in Toledo in 1550, and Diego Vásquez de Contreras another in Madrid in 1585 (Chevalier, *L'Arioste*, 84, 99ff.; Cervantes, *Quijote*, ed. Murillo, 1:114 n. 17). It is interesting that each of Ariosto's Spanish translators engaged in a certain amount of creative emendation: relatively little on the part of Urrea, more with Alcoçer, and a considerable amount with Vásquez de Contreras, whose "translation" can also be described as a "grotesque" deformation of the original (Chevalier, *L'Arioste*, 99-100).

12. Van Horne states: "Of Ariosto's canto III stanzas 1-4, 18, and 24-68 are omitted entirely. Stanzas 19-23 are replaced by one stanza, faintly reminiscent of the verses supplanted. Of the omitted portions, stanzas 1-4 constitute an invocation to the Estes, 18 refers in general terms to their accomplishments, and 24-62 include the genealogy and eulogy of the Este household" (219).

13. One of these is a Doña María de Bazán (Van Horne 223). Medina assures us that this is not Ercilla's future bride, who was between twenty and twenty-five when she married Ercilla in 1570 (Medina, *Vida*, 381-82). Nonetheless, it is possible that Urrea's example helped inspire Ercilla to include homage to his own María de Bazán in Part II of the *Araucana* in 1578.

14. Marten Nuyts Vermeer, known in French and Latin as Nutius, and in Spanish as Nucio, had lived for a number of years in Spain and, upon his return to the Low Countries, became one of the leading printers and publishers of books in Castilian in the period 1540-58. In addition to illustrious literary works, his publications include important editions of *crónicas de Indias* by authors such as López de Gómara, Agustín de Zárate, and Pedro Cieza de León (Peeters Fontainas 11-12, 18).

15. The full title is *El felicísimo viaje del príncipe don Felipe, hijo de Carlos V, a Alemania y Flandes*. This was also published (1552) in Antwerp by Nucio, with whom

Calvete de la Estrella seems to have established close relations during the visit described in the tract (Peeters Fontainas 17; Medina, "El preceptor," 271–72).

16. Since the marriage of these two had been arranged just the year before, Chevalier suspects that Garrido must have written with a certain amount of haste (*L'Arioste*, 116). Be that as it may, Garrido was able to produce thirty-six cantos in octaves (Pierce, *La poesía*, 330).

17. "Digo, en efeto, que este libro [Urrea's translation of the *Furioso*], y todos los que se hallaren que tratan destas cosas de Francia, se echen y depositen en un pozo seco, hasta que con más acuerdo se vea lo que se ha de hacer dellos, ecetuando a un *Bernardo del Carpio* que anda por ahí, y a otro llamado *Roncesvalles* que éstos, en llegando a mis manos, han de estar en las del ama, y dellas en las del fuego, sin remisión alguna" (*Quijote* 1.6).

18. Furthermore, however mediocre a poet Garrido may have been, his translation of the *Innamorato* was published at least three times between 1555 and 1581 (Pierce, *La poesía*, 366).

19. As pointed out in Chapter 1, Ercilla uses the verb *ilustrar* to describe the effect he hopes to produce with the visions seen in the enchanter Fitón's magic sphere in *Araucana* 23. It is often used by Ercilla's contemporaries to describe the practice and goal of imitation. This is made especially explicit by Du Bellay and Ronsard (Py 15, 20), and the concept permeates discussions of imitation among the Sevillan disciples of Herrera (Vilanova 20–21).

20. That El Brocense conceived of Mena's role in Castilian literary history in this light is made even more explicit by a comment in a letter directed to his patron at court, Juan Vásquez de Mármol, who had previously aided the Salmantine scholar with the publication of his edition and commentary on Garcilaso. On 9 September 1579, El Brocense indicated that he had been rereading Mena and felt that his *Laberinto*, with commentary, should be republished in a popular format and bound with the edition of Garcilaso (qtd. in Gallardo 452).

21. There is clearly also a distinct contrast with Camoens's treatment of sexual matters in *Os Lusíadas*, as indicated in Chapter 4. Curiously, Mena was also a defender of Dido against Virgil's "calumnies" (Lida de Malkiel, *Dido*, 70).

22. Lida de Malkiel gives what is still the most complete overview of the reception of Mena in the sixteenth-century (*Juan de Mena*, 335–79).

23. Kerkhof and Le Pair's review of the printed editions of the *Laberinto de Fortuna* is conscientious and conservative. They correct Vasvari and others who count the Seville 1517 edition bound with the *Coronación* of 1520 as a separate printing. They also disallow two reported Flemish reprintings of Nucio's 1552 edition. Including the princeps of c. 1481, Kerkhof and Le Pair give a total of twenty-two printings of the various editions of the *Laberinto de Fortuna* up to the end of the sixteenth century. Unfortunately, Kerkhof and Le Pair's article is plagued with typographical errors, especially in regard to numbers. The date of the princeps, for instance, reads 1841 instead of 1481 ("El Laberinto," 322–24).

24. Julian Weiss points out that Núñez's commentary was by no means the first on Mena's *Laberinto*, nor necessarily on the work of a Castilian poet ("El comentarista," 571–75). Nonetheless, the monumental nature of Núñez's work, in combination with the relatively massive and coordinated program of publicatiion throughout the sixteenth century, mark Núñez's project as the first major initiative of literary canonization in Castilian letters.

25. For a complete list of editions of the *Laberinto de Fortuna* consulted, see the Works Cited. Parenthetical references in the text will always refer to the editor of the edition in question unless the reference is to the text of *Laberinto de Fortuna* itself, where

the numbers always refer to stanzas rather than pages. I take the text as established by Fernán Núñez in 1505 and reproduced in all subsequent sixteenth-century editions up until El Brocense's edition of 1582 as the "standard" rather than any subsequent attempts at critical editions based on manuscript sources because Núñez's text would have been the version known to Ercilla and his contempraries.

26. For the political ramifications of Núñez's commentary and the overall resonances of Mena's poem in the immediate post-1492 political climate, see Weiss, "Political Commentary."

27. Street suggests the most plausible explanation for the perplexing lack of concrete, unmistakable allusions connecting the *Laberinto de Fortuna* with the *Divina commedia*, which has led critics such as Post to deny the existence of any meaningful relation at all. According to Street, Mena avoids ostentatious imitation of Dante because the Italian poet writes in the vernacular and as such, despite his many virtues, is not the type of model that will "illustrate" the Spanish poet's work ("Allegory," 10). The overall inspiration for the visionary journey through the Spheres, notwithstanding Post's objections, is patent to virtually all readers of the *Laberinto de Fortuna*. Carl Ralph Borgia gives a brief, updated summary of the problem and concludes that Mena and the other fifteenth-century Iberian poets imitate the "form rather than . . . the meaning" of Dante in their allegorical poems (8).

28. Significantly, at the very outset of his visionary exploration of ancient and modern history, Mena sets his own enterprise into focus in the light of the prophetic model of the *Aeneid*. Confronting the personification of Divine Providence who will be his Sibyl, he asks her if he will need a golden bough like that used by Aeneas to secure passage through the underworld in *Aeneid* 6. His supernatural guide replies in the negative, thus both linking and distancing Mena's visionary experience from Virgil's (*Laberinto de Fortuna* 28).

29. For a detailed discussion, see Chapter 1, section 1.2.

30. Ercilla follows Bellona between "dos montes, que el Atlante y Apenino / con gran parte no son de tal grandeza" to enter the first *locus amoenus* (*Araucana* 17.43). The great height, on the one hand, reminds the reader that Ercilla is in the Andes. On the other hand, the reader will recall that Garcilaso has the nine muses descend from "dos cumbres" (*Egloga II*, vv. 1284). Herrera explains that "el monte Parnasso tiene dos collados" (Garcilaso, *Obras*, ed. Rivers, 383). Ercilla's *locus amoenus*, then, is located on an Andean Parnassus.

31. The Spanish Hapsburg armies achieved a potentially decisive and certainly humiliating victory over the French at the fortress of Saint Quentin on 10 August 1557. Saint Quentin was the most definitive punishment inflicted by the Spaniards on French arms since Pavia in 1525; many prisoners were taken, including the constable of France, and many more were massacred. Philip II was in the rear of his army, in close communication with the field commanders, and in this sense, the victory could be taken as his personally, although perhaps not to the degree that his father was associated with the triumph over the Turks and Moors at Tunis. Despite the great hopes that were raised in the immediate aftermath, either Philip's excessive prudence or the perennial lack of funds prevented any meaningful follow-up, and in the end very little was changed (Braudel, *Mediterranean*, 943–44). Nonetheless, the Spaniards reinvindicated their military pride in Europe with this victory. Philip erected the Escorial as a memorial to the battle, and this premier architectural statement of the reign of the Prudent King is richly ornamented with paintings recounting the battle (Cabello Lapiedra 85ff.). The full significance of both Saint Quentin and Lepanto for Ercilla is addressed in Chapter 4.

32. In his 1993 edition, Lerner modifies this view somewhat: "Esta es la única aparición maravillosa en el poema no para el servicio o como parte de la actividad bélica,

en la tradición de la poesía épica, sino más bien como mecanismo que permite la unificación temporal y espacial de los hechos del Imperio." Nonetheless, he then refers the reader to Pierce for "la función de lo maravilloso mitológico," thus insisting on the idea of Bellona as a mythological figure (508 n. 81).

33. Here the chariot is not Bellona's, but that of Mars, who also enters into this typically complex, Lucanesque simile. Housman's notes make this quite clear (209).

34. This last is the authority cited by Fernán Núñez in his commentary on the *Laberinto de Fortuna* and, as I have explained, would thus certainly have been available to Ercilla (1552 [Nucio], fol. 14v).

35. Lewis explains that the Romans had a tendency to worship abstract concepts as divine and to reduce mythological deities with considerably more personality to the same status as dry abstractions (48–49).

36. Although as Willis notes, Bellona was suppressed by the anonymous author of the *Libro de Alexandre* (*The Relationship*, 12–13). In the episode to which Willis refers (*Alexandreis* 5.205-55), Bellona is acting as the agent of Mars, a genuine Olympian and not an allegorical abstraction, and clearly that is where the objection lay. The passage is obviously Virgilian in inspiration and recalls Juno inciting Fama to spread scandal about Aeneas and Dido (*Aeneid* 4.173–96), or the same goddess, like Mars a true pagan deity, whipping Allecto—another essentially allegorical personification like Bellona (Virgil, *Aeneid*, ed. Williams, 2:191)—into a frenzy and sending her to the surface world in order to drive the Latins to war (*Aeneid* 7.323ff.).

37. It is not immaterial that by 1584 Portugal found itself under the authority of Philip II.

38. Medina gives the variants, citing the 1578 and 1597 editions (Ercilla, *Araucana*, ed. Medina, 4:148). Ercilla, however, had clearly introduced the modification by 1589, as it is present in the version of Part II published with the combined edition of all three parts in 1590. Consequently, Morínigo and Lerner's Castalia edition gives the revised text, based as it is on 1589-90 (ed. Morínigo and Lerner, 1:111, 2:65). Lerner in his 1993 edition indicates the variants in a note without further commentary (536).

39. This vision of María de Bazán is probably inspired, at least in part, by Garcilaso's presentation of María Enríquez, wife of his patron the duke of Alba, in the ekphrastic vision of the urn (*Egloga II*, vv. 1361–78, 1396–414). The contrast with Mars is present as in Ercilla, and just as the woman in white leads Ercilla to a garden where he sees his future bride identified by an inscription, Venus leads the young Fernando to a garden where he is shown a sleeping nymph. In the second section, she is identified as his future bride, her name embroidered on a pillow (*Egloga II*, vv. 1406–14).

40. The story of Glaura, told in *Araucana* 28, the penultimate canto of Part II, is even more obviously rooted in the *Orlando furioso* (Schwartz Lerner 623–24). The tales of Tegualda and Glaura are the two most fully developed, intercalated amorous episodes in the *Araucana*. The interlude of Guacolda in Part I is far briefer. Part III lacks the balance of Part II, and the only major amorous break in the military monotony is the revisionist version of the story of Dido (*Araucana* 32–33).

41. The brief story of Gualemo's father's rescue of his young wife from a sea monster (*Araucana* 21.34–39) is yet another reminiscence of the *Orlando furioso* that has gone, as far I as I know, unnoticed by critics. Ducamin (158 n. 2) makes a general reference to classical mythology in his note to the passage. Lerner, in his 1993 edition, is more specific, alluding at length to a story of classical origin in Pero Mexía's *Silva de varia lección* as well as a number of classical authors (600 n. 73). While Lerner is certainly correct in identifying the tale of a dolphin that falls in love with a human female as a constitutive element, both he and Ducamin seem to ignore the clear parallels to the two battles with marine monsters in the *Orlando furioso*. These had also been incorporated

by Zapata into his account of Cortés in Cozumel in the *Carlo famoso* (12.29–69). (For an account of Zapata's imitation of Ariosto in this episode, see Nicolopulos, "Cortés's Shark Meets Orlando's Orca" 3–6.) There is a direct, lexical reminiscence of Ariosto's "marin mostro" (*Orlando furioso* 11.28h) in Ercilla's "marino monstruo" (*Araucana* 21.36e).

42. Medina notes that in all of the early editions of the *Araucana* the noun *razón* is uncapitalized. He objects, insisting that it is a personification and that therefore it should be capitalized (Medina, ed., 4:358). This is the reading adopted by most subsequent editions (cf. Morínigo and Lerner, eds., 2:142; Lerner, ed., 634). The circumstance is rather odd, because such nouns are generally capitalized in the early editions of the *Araucana*, especially Madrid 1578.

43. I have adapted Duff's translation from the Loeb edition here.

44. Sebastián de Covarrubias, in his *Tesoro de la lengua* of 1610, derives both "escuro" and "oscuro" from *obscurus, a, um* (545, 841).

45. For a full account of Erictho, her necromancy, and the significance of *Pharsalia* 6 for *Araucana* 23, see Chapter 3.

46. Medina gives the variants (Medina, ed., 4:154). Morínigo and Lerner, following 1589–90 read "perpetua luz" (Moríngo and Lerner, eds., 2:147), as does Lerner (Lerner, ed., 640).

47. Medina also cites some verses from Jerónimo de Urrea's translation of *Orlando furioso* "34" which he proposes as a models for *Araucana* 23.64ab and the anaphoric series of "Mira . . ." in *Araucana* 27.6–47 (Medina, ed. 5:450). It is clear that Medina is following the numbering used by Urrea, who conflates cantos 2 and 3, producing a lag of one canto throughout (Van Horne, 219). Hence when Medina refers to *Orlando furioso* 32, we have to look in *Orlando furioso* 33; likewise, when Medina indicates canto "34," we must take this as *Orlando furioso* 35. Medina seems to assume that Ercilla would have read Ariosto in Urrea's translation, for reasons that he does not explain (*Vida*, 24). Ercilla was himself the author of the *aprobación* of the 1585 prose translation of the *Orlando furioso* by Diego Vázquez de Contreras (Medina, *Vida*, 288). It seems highly improbable that Ercilla would have been responsible for approving the translation if he was not conversant with the original. Nonetheless, to search for the correspondences Medina claims, so imprecisely, to have found, it is necessary to consult the various editions of Urrea's translation rather than any Italian text of the *Orlando furioso*.

48. Although Espinosa's *Segunda parte de Orlando* was the only one commercially viable enough to achieve a respectable number of reprintings, Cervantes seems to have expressed the opinion of informed good taste when he has his village priest single it out for consignment to the bonfire. Likewise, Urrea's translation achieved commercial, but not critical, success. Cervantes's judgement was no less harsh.

49. In this regard, Isaías Lerner remarks: "Es, sobre todo, con el sistema de Garcilaso que conviene relacionar a Ercilla para poder entender los procedimientos que hicieron posible la vitalidad de su poema sobre los numerosos similares, hoy olvidados, de su tiempo. Cuando Ercilla busca la expresión adecuada para una epopeya española con el sentido moderno que proponían Boiardo y Ariosto, la encuentra en la lengua de Garcilaso. No sólo en la imitación directa, sino en el acatamiento a principios de selección léxica, como el del buscado equilibrio del cultismo y los usos de la lengua cotidiana" ("Garcilaso," 202).

50. Ercilla places Garcilaso in the company of Dante, Ariosto, and Petrarch under the epithet of "el Ibero" (*Araucana* 15.2e). Medina took this to mean Lucan, but it is generally accepted that in the context of love poets, it must be understood as a reference to Garcilaso (Lerner, "Garcilaso," 202).

51. In fact, necromancy in Latin poetry is almost the exclusive preserve of women. Only the necromancies of Seneca's *Oedipus* (530–658) and Statius's Tiresias (*Thebaid*

4.406–645) are presided over by men. Morford gives a few additional, minor examples of male magic, most involving lycanthropy (68 n. 1).

52. C. A. Martindale describes "two distinct strands within the tradition" (370). According to Martindale, one is a literary witch who belongs to what he calls the "higher genres: epic, elegy and lyric"; the other is more "realistic," and belongs to the lower genres, such as mime. Horace's Canidia, for instance, belongs to this last type (370). Martindale maintains that Lucan systematically distances Erictho from the standard literary witch: "The long description of Erictho . . . , for all its hyperbolic language, is marked by a grisly realism, and is designed to contrast with the literary fantasy, based largely on Medea in Ovid" (371).

53. Although Inés Azar quite cogently points out that "la 'sabiduría' de Enareto, prolijamente descripta en cinco páginas de prosa, es una especie de compendio de artes mágicas en el que se funden reminiscencias de un buen número de textos clásicos. El escenario y la situación en que aparece Severo evocan, en cambio, la economía verbal, el escenario y la situación del pasaje de las *Geórgicas* [4.507-10] en el que Orfeo, solo a orillas del Estrimón, encanta a la naturaleza con su música y sus palabras" (124). While I think that Azar is on the mark in emphasizing the Orphic character of Severo, the quotation from the *Georgics*, especially when read in context, is no more convincing than the vague, and for the most part inaccurate, assertion that the description of Severo's powers is directly modeled on Sannazaro's description of the prowess of Enareto. In both cases the textual allusions are exceedingly tenuous, but as I discuss below, the general ideas are pertinent.

54. Virgil closely equates Diana and Hecate. The priestess, in her invocation of the infernal powers before Dido's pyre, calls upon "threefold Hecate, the three faces of the virgin Diana" (tergeminamque Hecaten, tria virginis ora Dianae) (*Aeneid* 4.511). The "three faces" refer to the phases of the Moon. The correspondence is quite common. Seneca, for instance, has Medea conjure Hecate, who responds in the form of the Moon (*Medea*, vv. 577, 750-51, 787-92; Seneca, *Medea*, ed. Costa, 136, 139-40). At one point she is called Phoebe (v. 770) and contrasted with her brother Phoebus (v. 768). Phoebe is a synonym for Diana, in her character as the Moon.

55. The verse section that follows, is, in fact, an invocation of Apollo and his powers of inspiration. See especially vv. 147-51 (Sannazaro, *Arcadia*, 149).

56. It should be reiterated that El Brocense says nothing about Enareto one way or the other. He simply quotes the relevant passages from what he takes to be the models or analogues in his notes to the corresponding verses in Garcilaso's text.

57. Azar notes: "Por inspiración divina – 'a aquéste Phebo no le 'scondió nada'— Severo conoce la verdadera naturaleza de piedras, hierbas, animales y hombres. 'Con fuerça de palabras' Severo controla el desorden de los elementos y devuelve el alma a su 'natura'" (125).

58. For convenience, I quote Duff's Loeb translation here. The verses are corrupt in the principal mss (Housman 170). Bourgéry and Ponchont give "Le charme hémonien refoule Téthys poussée par un astre et lui interdit le rivage" (The Thessalian spell drives back star-driven Tethys and forbids her the shore) (2:25), with the following note: "Ici un manuscrit ancien ajoute dans le texte des vers inintelligibles que je traduis d'après la restitution de M. Housman: «Elles arrêtent la fuite de l'Océan; et l'onde, fixée aux terres par le vent, renonce à l'habituelle alternance du reflux; comme si la rage des vents ne trouvait pas d'issue, [la terre] tremble dans toute l'enténdue de son globe»" (Here an early manuscript appends to the text some unintelligible verses that I translate from Housman's restoration: "They check the flight of the Ocean; and the waves, held to the land by the wind, renounce their habitual alternation of the ebb; as if the rage of the winds found no escape, the [earth] trembles over its entire extent." [2:25 n. 1]; see Housman 170 for

Latin original translated by Bourgéry and Ponchont). The Paris 1514 edition of the *Pharsalia* reads: "impulsam sydere Tethym / Reppulit Aemonidum defenso littore carmen" (fol. 153v). All three commentators take "Tethys" to stand for Ocean, and "sidus" for the Moon (fol. 154r–v). Martín Lasso de Oropesa, in his translation of c. 1535, gives: "y dexar con las palabras destas Thessalicas el mar de creçer en las horas que la luna le suele comouer" (118).

59. I quote from Martín Lasso de Oropesa's translation of c. 1535 here because his rendering represents the reading of these difficult lines current in sixteenth-century Spain. Lasso de Oropesa's translation also is closer to the Latin than Duff's English. Duff gives: "The earth too throws the poles of her stable mass out of gear, and the pressure that tends to the centre of the sphere becomes unsteady. Smitten by a spell, that mighty weight parts asunder and reveals to sight the stars revolving around it." Again, Bourgéry and Ponchont's translation is perhaps closer to the original than Duff's: "La terre même ébranle l'équilibre immobile de ses axes et son centre de gravité se déplace. La charge d'une pareille masse, frappée par la voix, recule, et découvre en entier le spectacle de l'Olympe qui roulait alentour" (The earth itself disturbs the changeless balance of its axes and its center of gravity is displaced. The force of such a mass whipped up by the voice retreats, and reveals in its entirety the spectacle of a reeling Olympus) (2:25). They add in a note: "La terre cesse d'occuper le centre de l'univers; elle descend plus bas et laisse ainsi au-dessus d'elle la plus grande partie de la sphère céleste" (The earth ceases to occupy the center of the universe, it descends lower and in this way leaves above it the greater part of the heavenly sphere) (2:25 n. 2). I quote the Latin text from the Paris 1514 edition, as being current in Ercilla's time, rather than Housman's revision of the text, followed by Duff.

60. Ercilla's unmistakable allusions to Camoens in crucial passages of the prophecies in Fitón's cave form a case apart, as I make clear in Chapters 4 and 5.

Chapter 3

1. As I have demonstrated, this can be said to be true not just for the *nekuia*, but for the epic genre as a whole (Pierce, *La poesía*, 12–13; "Some Themes," 95–97). The 1527 treatise of Marco Girolamo Vida is an excellent sixteenth-century exposition of this view (Pierce, *La poesía*, 15). Furthermore, as C. A. Martindale has noted (369), Virgil's *nekuia* is the only one in classical epic that is also a *katabasis*.

2. Pio Rajna demonstrates that the immediate model for the finding of the cave and Pinabello's treachery in *Orlando furioso* 2 is the medieval French romance *Palamedès* (123–29). Nonetheless, the whole episode is closely linked to the *nekuia* of *Aeneid* 6. As Fichter states, "It is clear that Ariosto writes canto 3 with a copy of the *Aeneid* opened at Book 6, consciously attempting to emulate Virgil's style" (85). What Ariosto took from *Palamedès* is really the manner of introducing Bradamante into Merlin's cave, not what transpired there. Fichter rightly observes that Bradamante must arrive in the cave precipitously and not as the result of a long chain of prophesy because "neither Ariosto's conception of epic nor his view of history is Virgilian" (85).

3. I discuss Ercilla's web of prophecy in terms of the Ariostesque model in Chapter 2, section 2.4.2.

4. Frederick M. Ahl makes a convincing case for the acceptance of *Pharsalia* as the title of Lucan's poem despite the fact that it appears on no known manuscript, several of which do carry the title *De bello civile* (326–32).

5. Lucan became part of a conspiracy to assasinate Nero in A.D. 65. Nero, warned in

time, obliged the poet and his fellow plotters to open their veins later that same year. The following year, A.D. 66, Lucan's father and uncle Seneca were also ordered to commit suicide, probably because of the young poet's involvement in the plot (Ahl 37–38). Lucan thus died at the age of twenty-six, leaving the unfinished *Pharsalia* as his only poetic legacy and his once prosperous family in ruin.

6. For this examination of Lucan and his relationship with his various subtexts and subsequent imitators, I have consulted Duff's Loeb edition of the *Pharsalia*, the Latin portion of which is based on A. E. Housman's as yet unsurpassed text, as well as Housman's edition itself, Bourgéry and Ponchont's 1929 edition (markedly different from Housman's), and appropriate sixteenth-century editions. When I come to analyze Ercilla's imitation in detail, I abandon the twentieth-century editions in favor of those that Ercilla himself might have known. The most useful of these is that prepared by G. Versellanus and published by I. Petit in Paris in 1514, which contains three extensive commentaries on the text, and is probably very similar to one that a humanist such as Juan Cristóbal Calvete de la Estrella would have had his noble pupils consult.

7. According to Morford (70), Lucan modeled this passage on Ovid's rendition of Medea's nine-day herb hunt in Thessaly (*Metamorphoses* 7.192–237), which forms part of the principal subtext for the necromancy of *Pharsalia* 6.

8. Various sources for the name Fitón have been put forward, but the most convincing was suggested to Abraham König by Enrique Wood A., who demonstrates that the Greek words "Python, Pythonissa," referring to the oracular serpent of the Delphic Oracle, were often written as "Phiton, Phitonisa" by sixteenth- and seventeenth-century Spaniards, and also used to designate a witch or wizard. Wood goes on to complain that Ercilla failed to use an Araucanian word of similar meaning (König xlv). Ducamin cites König for his own glossary entry on "Fitón" (332). Medina also quotes Wood, although he entertains other possibilities as well (4:456–57). In both of the 1578 editions of Part II of the *Araucana* the mage's name is spelled "Phiton." The marqués de Santillana, in the *Comedieta de Ponça* v. 366 (c. 1435), writes "Fitón" or "Phiton" for the serpent Python and also uses the form "Phiton" in his *Sueño* 7 (ed. Kerkhof, 143).

9. Morford examines the possible sources for the Erictho episode and concludes that "it is clear that Ovid and Seneca are the most important for Lucan's magic; Virgil for his conception of the place of the episode in an epic" (68). The work of Seneca in question is his *Medea*, especially 670–739 and 740–842. Ovid's Medea effectively accomplishes a true necromancy in *Metamorphoses* 7 because, in order to rejuvenate the failing Aeson, she first slits his throat, allows all his own blood to pour out, and then replaces it with her own carefully prepared decoction.

10. Erictho has inspired many a grotesque figure in subsequent literature. Ahl (131 n. 14) mentions her reappearances in Dante's *Inferno* (9.20–30) and Goethe's *Faust*,"where Erichtho acts as the prologue for the *Klassische Walpurgisnacht* (Part 2, 7005ff.)." Her reappearance in Juan de Mena's *Laberinto de Fortuna*, which will be discussed at length below, as well as the witch Fabia in Lope de Vega's *El caballero de Olmedo*, and perhaps, Celestina herself could well be added to Ahl's list.

11. Ovid's Medea performs her magic before altars thrown up under the open sky. Seneca's Medea goes into her "penetrale funestum," which Miller translates as "baleful shrine" (*Medea* 676). Neither involves a cave entrance to the underworld.

12. Another possible model, although much briefer, and containing different ingredients, is Virgil's description of how the Massylian priestess prepares Dido's pyre with magical substances (*Aeneid* 4.512–16). It is more probable that Lucan's uncle Seneca provided an important model with his own variation on Ovid's theme. Medea's nurse describes her mistress's preparation of a poisonous concoction that is very strong on snake venom and that also leads into a verbal conjuration (*Medea* 670–739).

13. Lucan's invocation of the powers of hell is not without possible resonances with Virgil. The Massylian priestess calls on Hecate and the other potentates of the Underworld as she prepares Dido's pyre (*Aeneid* 4.509–11). More apropos of Erictho's incantation is the Sibyl's calling on Hecate and Aeneas's offering to Proserpina in preparation for their descent into the netherworld (*Aeneid* 6.247; 249–51). These are all extremely brief, and mostly paraphrase.

14. The best and most complete analysis of the corpse's prophecy that I have found is provided by Ahl (137–49).

15. Fitón's pleasure at learning of the extent of his fame, and the role that this plays in motivating his cooperation, is clearly modeled on Erictho's reaction to Sextus's petition that she foretell the outcome of the impending battle. Erictho, too, is "proud of her widespread fame" (laetatur vulgato nomine famae) (*Pharsalia* 6.604).

16. The introduction to Martín Lasso de Oropesa's early sixteenth-century (c. 1535) translation of the *Pharsalia* calls Lucan a Spaniard, and says: "y haga V.M. como no afrentan à Lucano porque à cabo de mill y quinientos años torna à hablar en la lengua que nacio" (fol. Aii v).

17. Ramón Menéndez Pidal, on the other hand, attributes the historicism of both Lucan and Ercilla to their innate Iberian sense of *verismo* (*Los españoles*, 203–5; "Poesía e historia," 127), and which he wisely qualifies with the admonition "que ha de incluirse en el concepto etnos no sólo la raza, sino la tradición histórica formativa de un pueblo" (*Los españoles*, 204–5). Menéndez Pidal's theories of Spanish *verismo*, particularly in regard to the *Cantar de mio Cid*, have exerted considerable influence on several generations of scholarship, and are frequently referred to in criticism of the *Araucana*.

18. This is the late fifteenth-century humanist and classical scholar Johannes Sulpitius Verulanus, otherwise known as Giovanni Antonio Sulpizio da Veroli, whose commentary on the *Pharsalia* was well known and highly considered throughout the sixteenth century.

19. The earlier of the two known editions of Lasso de Oropesa's translation of the *Pharsalia* indicates neither place nor date of publication. I am not entirely convinced by Herrero Llorente's argument that Lasso de Oropesa could not have dedicated the work to Doña Mencía de Mendoza, marquesa de Çenete, before 1535 (753–56). Beardsley briefly outlines some of the other hypotheses that have been put forward (33).

20. "Dice León Pinelo en sus *Anales* al hablar de las fiestas celebradas en Madrid con motivo de la entrada de Doña María de Austria, en 15 de noviembre de 1649: 'En bajando del Retiro, antes de llegar a la Torrecilla, al otro lado, se levantó el Monte Parnaso en dos cumbres altas; en la vna estaua Hércules, en la otra el caballo Pegaso, abriendo la fuente castalia, y volando entre los dos peñascos Apolo con su lira y cetro; delante de él las nueve musas y a los dos lados nueve poetas españoles de tres edades. De la antigua Séneca el trágico, Marcial y Lucano; de la edad media Juan de Mena, Garcilaso y Luis de Camoes, y de la moderna don Francisco de Quevedo y Villegas, don Luis de Góngora y Lope Felix de Vega Carpio'" (c).

21. Prete Jacopín, in his *Observaciones* on Herrera's work, indicates that Herrera is probably referring to Quintilian's negative comments about Lucan. Another negative comment of Herrera's is attributed to Julius Caesar Scaliger. Prete Jacopín opines that Scaliger may have been disdainful of Lucan because he was a Spaniard. In both comments, Prete Jacopín insists on Lucan's Spanish nationality. Herrera's response does not directly address the issue (Montero 126, 167, 239–40).

22. As shown in Chapter 2, in spite of the revolution in poetic style introduced by Garcilaso de la Vega in the 1530s and 1540s, Mena's masterpiece of c. 1444 continued to exercise great authority and enjoy a wide readership in Spain throughout the sixteenth century. The reader will have seen in detail how Ercilla spins a web of prophecy, in the

style of Virgil and Ariosto, to foretell his arrival in the Chilean wizard's cave that is a direct imitation of important aspects of Mena's poem. Mena himself links his visionary poem to *Aeneid* 6 in *Laberinto de Fortuna* 28. Furthermore, Mena is the most influential author of a long narrative poem in Spain before Ercilla. Just as Ercilla was obliged to confront Lucan because he was the first "Spanish" epic poet of great renown, Mena (also born in Cordova) is a predecessor with whom Ercilla must deal in order to establish his own place in the unfolding of Spanish letters.

23. Deyermond (164) points out that the *Laberinto de Fortuna* was composed during a period of acute political crisis. The king had been abducted by the constable's opponents in 1443, and was still in their hands when the poem was completed in 1444.

24. For a complete list of editions of the *Laberinto de Fortuna* consulted, see the Works Cited. Parenthetical references in the text will always refer to the editor of the edition in question unless the reference is to the text of *Laberinto de Fortuna* itself, where the numbers always refer to stanzas rather than pages.

25. "De orbes setenos vi toda texida" (*Laberinto de Fortuna* 62b).

26. The only other narrative passage that could be said to approximate the imitative density of the sorceress episode can be found in the story of the count of Niebla told in the fifth sphere of Mars (*Laberinto de Fortuna* 160–86). Significantly, the reprise of the omens of disaster at sea (*Laberinto de Fortuna* 163–73) recalling the episode of Caesar and Amyclas in *Pharsalia* 5.504–677 is also based upon an allusion to Lucan.

27. It is curious that Núñez's reference to the anecdote that he "heard from an old man in Llerena" is found only in the 1505 revision of the commentary on the *Laberinto de Fortuna*. Street (58–59) describes how Núñez revised his 1499 edition of the poem for republication in 1505, removing the "Vida del Autor" and most of the Latin quotations, but adding variously to the commentaries. My examination of the 1499 edition reveals that Núñez, in his gloss on *Laberinto de Fortuna* 238, contented himself with recapitulating the main outlines of the episode as Mena recounts it (fols. 163v–164r). Pérez, in his 1976 edition, quotes the substance of this part of Núñez's gloss (153). There is no mention of the old man in Llerena, etc. The anecdote was apparently added in 1505 and appears in all the subsequent reprintings of that edition that I have consulted (i.e., 1528, 1552 [Steelsio], 1552 [Nucio], 1566). Blecua quotes the gist of this segment in his 1943 edition (123). Maxim Kerkhof, in his article "El *Laberinto de Fortuna* de Juan de Mena: las ediciones en relación con la tradición manuscrita," gives the best account of the filiation of the various early editions.

28. This information is based on a team project realized by the students of the Spanish 285 seminar, fall 1988, under the direction of Professor Charles Faulhaber at the University of California, Berkeley. The principal printed sources consulted were Dutton and Faulhaber et al. The relatively high number of surviving mss would appear to make the *Laberinto de Fortuna* one of the poetic bestsellers of the fifteenth century.

29. Allegations of recourse to forbidden arts seem to have formed part of the standard idiom of political slander in the Spain of John II. For instance, chapter 263 of the so-called *Crónica del halconero*, probably written by the king's falconer, Pero Carrillo de Huete, reproduces most of a letter denouncing Alvaro de Luna sent to John II by his enemies King Juan of Navarre, the infante don Enrique and the admiral don Fadrique in 1440. Along with accusations of poisoning and sexual impropriety, they assert "que el dicho condestable tiene ligadas e atadas todas vuestras potencias corporales e animales por mágicas e deavólicas encantaciones, para que vuestra señoría non faga sino lo que él quisiere" (332). Given the fact that this type of aspersion was included in the established vocabulary of libelous propaganda, it is even more significant that neither the *Crónica del halconero* nor the *Crónica de don Alvaro de Luna*, also written by a contemporary with

access to intimate details of court intrigue, mentions anything about any supposed séance with a "maga" or a "fraile nigromántico."

30. Nucio's 1552 text actually reads: "siguiendo *en todas* las pisadas de Lucano," but the 1552 edition published by Steelsio reads "siguiendo *en todo* las pisadas de Lucano" (482), which seems to me to be the better reading (italics are mine). This is supported by the 1499 edition (fol. 163v).

31. Angel Gómez Moreno and Teresa Jiménez Calvente in their 1994 edition follow a similar line of reasoning, although due to considerations of space, they chose to reproduce El Brocense's 1582 edition complete with commentary rather than Núñez's more extensive version. They remark that one of its advantages is that "éstas son *Las Trescientas* leídas por nuestros antepasados, desde los años de los Reyes Católicos hasta fecha reciente" (Mena, *Obra completa*, ed. Gómez Moreno and Jiménez Calvente, xxxix–xl). Clearly in the case of Ercilla, however, whose seminal reading of Mena predates 1582, Núñez's text and commentaries must take precedence.

32. Francisco Sánchez de las Brozas ("El Brocense"), an eminent humanist scholar who produced his own edition of the *Laberinto de Fortuna* in Salamanca in 1582, for instance, possessed copies of both Núñez's 1499 edition and some printing of his 1505 edition (Street 63). Furthermore, it is possible that Calvete de la Estrella, like El Brocense, had been a student of Núñez's at one time (Medina, "El preceptor," 270; Bell 10).

33. Kerkhof notes that the colophon of the Toledo edition gives the date 1547. The Belgian scholar concludes that printing began in mid-December 1547, and that the edition was completed early in 1548 ("El *Laberinto*," 323 n. 10).

34. Kerkhof is very conservative in his listing of the editions. See my note 23 to chapter 2. Kerkhof also believes that the 1586 edition is a reprint of Alcalá 1566 and not of El Brocense's revision ("El *Laberinto*," 328).

35. "*Aemulatio* includes the attempt to surpass the model, . . . *Aemulatio* calls attention to itself and deliberately challenges comparison with its model. The relation between text and model becomes an important element in the text itself" (Pigman 26).

36. According to Sebastiano Broccia, the snake, the stag, and the crow were all associated with longevity and were included in Medea's decoction because its purpose was to rejuvenate the aged Aeson and give him long life (226 n. 124).

37. Cf. *Aeneid* 4.512–16; Horace, *Epode* 5.17–24; Seneca, *Medea* 731–36. For some examples from Greek literature, see Morford 67–68.

38. The power of incantations to draw down the Moon is mentioned by Virgil, *Ecloga* 8.69–71; Horace, *Epodes* 5.45–46; and Tibullus 1.8.21. Ovid tells how the witch Dipsas can make the Moon and stars drip blood (*Amores* 1.8.11–12), and there are frequent references to this lunar dew or foam in the context of witchcraft in Latin literature subsequent to Lucan, cf. "spumis lunaribus" (Statius, *Thebaid* 2.284); "Atracio lunam spumare veneno" (Valerius Flaccus, *Argonautica* 6.447); "magico susurramine . . . lunam despumari" (Apuleius, *Metamorphoses* 1.3). Lucan's uncle Seneca refers to the allegedly poisonous properties of dew "Creditum est quasdam aquas scabiem afferre corporibus . . . quod vitium dicunt habere aquam ex rore collectam" (*Naturales quaestiones* 3.25.11).

39. "Huc quidquid fetu genuit natura sinistro / miscetur." Housman (178) makes it clear that *huc* refers back to the blood and poison in the corpse's chest cavity described in *Pharsalia* 6.667–69.

40. The italics are mine.

41. Housman (178) explains that *quo*, just like the *huc* of 6.670, refers to the blood and "lunar poison" mixed together in the corpse's chest cavity, described in 6.667–69.

42. Bourgéry and Ponchont translate this as "après avoir mélangé les fléaux vulgaires

avec ceux qui on un nom, elle y ajouta" (2:34). They go on to observe in n. 4, "C'est-à-dire ces poisons réputés dont il vient d'etre question; on pourrait comprendre au contraire qu'à ces poisons connus et par conséquent banals Erictho en ajoute d'autres de son invention." Following Housman, I prefer this latter reading.

43. They total sixteen, if the "quidquid fetu genuit natura sinistro" of *Pharsalia* 6.670 is not counted apart from the things "not absent" that are enumerated in *Pharsalia* 6.671-80 and if 6.681 ("viles et habentes nomina pestes") is likewise excluded from the total, as it should be if Housman's reading of the line is correct.

44. Fernán Núñez perhaps fails to effectively translate "squamea tenuis membrana" because he has just rendered Lucan's "membrana" as "el cuero sotil" and does not want to repeat "cuero." Alonso Fernández de Palencia, in his *Universal vocabulario en latín y romance* (Sevilla, 1490), considers "membrana" to be a strictly Latin word, although Nebrija uses it to mean "pergamino" (Corominas, *Diccionario*, 3:369). I cannot explain why Núñez neglects to translate "squamea."

45. Broccia (226 n. 124) does not explain why the *chelydrus* was associated with long life or rejuvenation. For a possible reference to the longevity of the *chelydrus*, see Mynors's commentary *Georigics* 2.214 (Virgil, *Georgics*, ed. Mynors, 129). It is apparent, however, that one of the principal subtexts here is *Georgics* 3.414-39. The passage deals with venomous water snakes at some length. Virgil names the *chelydrus* at the beginning of the section (3.415), then uses the more general terms "vipera" (3.417) and "coluber" (3.418) in the same context, and finally describes in detail the habits and terrors of the Calabrian water snake (3.425-39) without using any noun more specific than "anguis" (3.425). Mynors, basing his assertion on the assumption that the model is Nicander, *Theriaca* 366-71, says that Virgil's Calabrian serpent must be the *chersydrus* and seeks to correct Servius (on *Georgics* 3.415) for equating the *chelydrus* with the *chersydrus* (Virgil, *Georgics*, ed. Mynors, 245). Nonetheless, as both are amphibious snakes, and "chelydrus" is the only really specific term in the complete passage in Virgil, both Servius and Ovid may be pardoned for confusing the two. The adjective "squamea" is applied in 3.426. The image of rejuvenation is most clear in 3.437, where Virgil describes the Calabrian snake as "renewed and shining with youth when it has shed its old skin" (cum positis novus exuuiis nitidusque iuuenta). Probably both Virgil and Ovid had Nicander, *Theriaca* 137-38 in mind for this image; Thomas gives the passage as "when the viper, having doffed his shrivelled old age, again proceeds exulting in his new youth" (Virgil, *Georgics*, ed. Thomas, 2:123).

46. According to Mynors, the first known use of *Cinyphius* as an adjective in Latin is found in Virgil (*Georgics* 3.312), and it "became a convenient equivalent for 'Libyan'" (Virgil, *Georgics*, ed. Mynors, 229).

47. This seems to become standard in poetry after Lucan, for instance: Statius, describing Tisiphone, "centum illi stantes umbrabant ora cerastae, / turba minax diri capitis" (*Thebaid* 1.103-4); "crinalem attollit longo stridore cerasten: / caeruleae dux ille comae" (*Thebaid* 11.65-66); Claudian having Megaera describe how she raised Rufinus, "linguisque trisulcis / mollia lambentes finxerunt membra cerastae" (*In Rufinum* 1.95-96); Claudian describing the three Furies literally "letting their hair down" and celebrating the wedding of Proserpina and Pluto by allowing their festooned manes of horned vipers to drink generously from the wine bowl (*De Raptu Proserpinae* 2.343-47).

48. According to Pliny (8.35), the *cerastes* hides its body beneath the earth leaving the horns exposed, and by moving them, attracts the birds on which it supposedly feeds. Thus it is possible to see a connection with the third, avian, symbol of longevity as well as with the stag.

49. Núñez quotes Pliny's passage on stags at length. The two relevant items concern stags rooting snakes out of their holes and the stags' longevity, which are not linked

causally, but by proximity in the passage (Pliny 8.50.118-19). Núñez attributes the belief that stags feed on snakes in order to rejuvenate to the *glossa ordinaria*, apparently on the *Song of Songs*, and to Solinus. Núñez: "es propio de los ciervos cuando son viejos comer las culebras con lo qual se tornan a la mocedad y cobran su primero vigor" ([1499], fol. 166r).

50. Is it coincidence that Pliny (9.56) speaks censoriously of the joy pampered Roman women took in the sound of pearls rattling together?

51. Fernán Núñez and El Brocense both read "suele," while Blecua, Cummins, Pérez Priego, Vasvari Fainberg, and Kerkhof all give "sabe" without indicating what they base this reading on, or, for that matter, with the exception of Kerkhof (409), that an alternate exists.

52. This is the marginal gloss to *Laberinto de Fortuna* 241*gh* found in MS. 229 of the Bibliothèque Nationale in Paris. Florence Street and most post-1968 editors of the *Laberinto de Fortuna* consider this manuscript to be a copy of one prepared in Mena's lifetime under the author's direction; several of the glosses are first-person statements perhaps made by Mena himself (Street, "The Text," 67-71; Cummins 44; Pérez Priego 44-45; Vasvari Fainberg 72). As I have noted, Kerkhof disputes Street's assessment of the importance of MS. 229 ("Hacia una nueva edición," 181-89; "El *Laberinto*," 337-38), but Kerkhof does not analyze the section of the poem in question, and none of the objections he raises diminish the importance of these early glosses. From the information in Street's article, it is impossible to tell if the gloss on 241*gh* originated with Mena or with "Commentator A" (Street, "The Text," 67-71). Even if this particular gloss did not originate with Mena himself, it represents the very first stage of reception of the poem. Kerkhof speculates that "Commentator A" must have been an Italian scholar associated with the Aragonese court at Naples sometime between 1458 and 1494 (Mena, *Laberinto de Fortuna*, ed. Kerkhof, 50).

53. El Brocense, in his much abbreviated commentary, makes sure to bring out this very point: "Llámase la piedra Aetites, y suena, si la bullen, como que tiene algo dentro" (Mena, *Las obras del famoso poeta*, ed. Sánchez, 293).

54. The three emblematic creatures of rejuvenation that Medea stirs into her cauldron can be seen as corresponding to three of the elements, hence the water snake represents water, the stag earth, and the crow air. Seen in another way, the snake represents the underworld, the stag the world of humans and beasts, and the crow the upper air or heavens. It is likely that Lucan is not only playing on Ovid's avian emblem here, but that he is also recalling the "sands" of *Metamorphoses* 7.267 with the "ash" of the phoenix.

55. Lida de Malkiel uses these verses as an example of how Mena felt obliged to explain his Latinisms (*Juan de Mena*, 252). This is, of course, another indicator of the nascent recognition of the problem of anachronism on Mena's part.

56. Fernán Núñez includes the wolf's glance in his recapitulation of Pliny in the following terms: "la vista de ellos es . . . empecible, quitan la habla al hombre si lo veen primero que ellos sean vistos" ([1552 Nucio], fol. 204r). It is easy to miss the significance for Mena's reference, however, as Núñez reproduces virtually everything Pliny had to say about wolves with little regard for its possible relevance to Mena's text. Thus what is probably the key to unraveling the enigma of this element of Mena's imitation is buried in Núñez's tireless erudition. Significantly, however, Pliny speaks about werewolves in the same paragraph and, in the immediately preceding paragraph, describes the deadly vision of the serpent known as the basilisk (8.33). Mena may well have been moved to combine the "eyes of serpents" (oculi draconum) and the "deadly vision of wolves" by such a coincidence much as Ercilla was to coalesce the eyes of the lynx and the basilisk based on another, similar set of textual coincidences in Pliny (see below).

57. The horned or screech owl (*strix*) is so intimately associated with witchcraft that *strega*, Italian for "witch," is derived from its name (Broccia 225 n. 120).

58. Although not entirely compelling as making sense of "después que formada de espina de muerto," it is true that the *nodus* of the hyena is one of its spinal vertebrae, as Pliny makes clear (28.27). Pliny also tags the hyena as a grave robber (8.44). Núñez, however, cites both of these references to the hyena in his commentary to *Laberinto de Fortuna* 241*ab* that immediately precedes his perplexity over "después que formada," and apparently saw no relationship ([1499], fol. 164v–165r). On the other hand, in the notes to his edition Kerkhof conjectures that Mena might have confused the hyena with some kind of serpent. In support of this reading, he quotes from the commentary on MS. 229 (Kerkhof's PN7) to the effect that: "hiena es un serpente tan venenoso que con su flato mata los ombres" (Mena, *Laberinto*, ed. Kerkhof, 225).

59. See the opening paragraph of section 3.4 of this chapter, and section 1.3.2 of Chapter 1. In the development of the theoretical framework for the study of imitation in section 1.3.2, I refer to how Thomas Greene, in *The Light In Troy* (40), uses Petrarch's sonnet 90, "Erano i capei d'oro a l'aura sparsi," as a prime example of what he calls "necromantic, heuristic" imitation. I then demonstrate how Garcilaso, while imitating sonnet 90 of the *Canzoniere* in the quartets of "En tanto que de rosa y d'açucena," invokes Petrarch's Virgilian subtext in the final lines of the first quartet. I propose this as a paradigm for Castilian Renaissance poetry of what Greene (*Light*, 43) calls "dialectical" imitation. In this type of imitative practice, there is not only "necromantic" resuscitation of the subtext, there is also competitive emulation, or what Greene calls "Oedipal agression" (*Light*, 46).

60. In the 1505 edition, Núñez cut out the Latin, but retained his translations. The subsequent reprintings based on 1505, however, do not all agree in this passage. That of 1528, for example, simply retails the "standard" reading of *Pharsalia* 6.681: "estas ponçoñas *et* otras muchas que tienen no*m*bre" (fol. 86v), while 1552 [Nucio] asserts Núñez's "correction" by translating the emendation "estas ponçoñas y otras muchas que no tienen nombre" (fol. 209v) without any explanation, and 1566 restores the reading found in 1528. Lida de Malkiel was apparently not aware of the alternative reading of Lucan. She could not have found it in Núñez, because in the 1552 edition printed by Juan Steelsio that she consulted (*Juan de Mena*, 32), the commentary on *copla* 243 ends with Núñez's remarks on "otras vípereas sierpes" (*Laberinto de Fortuna* 243*ef*, and omits all reference to 243*gh* (1552 [Steelsio] 498). Professor Arthur L-F. Askins of the Department of Spanish and Portuguese at the University of California, Berkeley, has confirmed my suspicion that Lida de Malkiel relied upon the copy of Steelsio's 1552 printing of Núñez's edition in the Bancroft Library at Berkeley for the preparation of her book on Mena.

61. All quotations from the text of the *Araucana* in this section, unless otherwise indicated, are from the first edition of Part II, printed in 8° by Pierres Cosin in Madrid in 1578 and published as the second part of the *Primera y segunda parte de la Araucana*. For a description of this edition, see Ercilla, *La Araucana*, ed. Medina, 4:9–10. I have modernized the accents but left the capitalization as in the original.

62. The possibility of an even closer linkage exists. Pliny, for instance, compares the shape of the spotted lynx (chama) to that of the wolf (8.28), and refers to the same animal as a "stag wolf" (cervarius) closely following his discussion of werewolves (8.34). The same author relates that the hyena impersonates humans in order to entrap dogs (8.44). According to Virgil (*Georgics* 3.264) and Ovid (*Metamorphoses* 4.24–25) the chariot of the god Bacchus was drawn by lynxes. Of these, *Georgics* 3.264–65 is probably the more important, because of the association with wolves and dogs ("quid lynces Bacchi uariae et genus acre luporum atque canum?"). The context is the madness experienced by beasts in rut, and the passage closes appropriately with the observation of how "wicked

stepmothers" gather the *hippomanes* and mix it with herbs and spells (*Georgics* 3.280–83). The reference to this type of witchcraft would certainly have attracted Lucan's interest.

63. Núñez is referring to Pliny's remark "Lynxes are foreign animals, which see more clearly than any other four-legged animal" (Peregrinae sunt et lynces, quae clarissime quadripedum omnium cernunt) (28.32).

64. Thorndike (1:620) is of the opinion that Boethius is mistaken in his attribution of this remark to Aristotle, and says that it is typical of the attribution of "entire spurious treatises" to the celebrated Greek philosopher in the Middle Ages. Stewart, the editor of the Loeb edition, speculates that it is from a "lost" work (254 n. 1). Aristotles's name had clearly become associated with compendiums of lore such as this by the sixteenth century. Núñez includes Aristotle along with Pliny, Solinus, and Albertus Magnus as sources for his lynx lore ([1552 Nucio], fol. 203v). Typical for Ercilla's time would have been works such as Juan de Jarava's *La philosophia natural copilada de Aristóteles, Plinio, Platón y otros graves autores*, Anvers: 1546 (Beardsley 5, 37–38). Doubtless due to a printer's error, the reference to Boethius in Morínigo and Lerner's edition of the *Araucana* is given incorrectly as "III, 18, 21" (2:147 n. 25).

65. Boethius's *De consolatione philosophiae* was one of the most consistently read works of the Middle Ages (Thorndike 1:618–19). According to Lida de Malkiel, the *De consolatione*, more than any of the other major medieval works on Fortune, helped inform Juan de Mena's approach to his theme (*Juan de Mena*, 24). There can be little doubt that Ercilla, given his preoccupation with Fortune and Providence, knew the work quite well. A number of Castilian translations circulated in manuscript during the fifteenth century, and at least three printed editions in translation are known to have been published before 1500 (Faulhaber et al.). As demonstrated by his enthusiasm for Mena, Ercilla's sensibility is in many ways very "medieval," and a close acquaintaince with Boethius accords well with this side of Ercilla's intellectual profile.

66. Covarrubias explains that the noun *draco* is derived from the Greek verb for *videre* "porque según escriven los naturales es de perfetissima vista" (485).

67. Curiously, the basilisk is also mentioned in fairly close proximity to the lynx in Pliny 8. Additionally, the account of the wolf's "noxious" gaze immediately follows the paragraph dedicated to the basilisk (Pliny 8.34). It is, in fact, very easy to imagine Mena, as well as Ercilla, thumbing through the *Naturalis historia* and being prompted by the proximity of one similar theme to another in its pages. There is presently no way of knowing for sure exactly in what form knowledge of Pliny reached either Mena or Ercilla. One thing is certain: the same coincidences are not present in any text of Solinus that I have consulted. The question requires further research, however, before I feel justified in asserting that Ercilla must have consulted an edition of Pliny rather than some intermediary compendium. Similar problems exist for resolving the issue of whether Ercilla would have read his Pliny in Latin. Printed editions of the complete Latin text of the *Naturalis historia* were common by the mid-sixteenth century; the first is as early as 1469 (Thorndike 1:53), and Beardsley lists no complete Spanish translation prior to 1599 (154). This is hardly conclusive, however, because printed Italian translations were also in circulation (Thorndike 1:53), and it is extremely likely that Ercilla did not need to rely on translations for works in Italian.

68. "Qui hominem, vel si aspiciat tantum, dicitur interimere" (Pliny 29.19).

69. As I have indicated in Chapter 2, including the edition first prepared by Fernán Núñez in 1505 and that readied by Francisco Sánchez in 1582, in all of their various reprintings, the complete text of the *Laberinto de Fortuna* is known to have appeared at least sixteen times between 1505 and 1586; seven of these after 1540 (Kerkhof, "El Laberinto," 322–24). The only conclusion that can be drawn is that, despite the revolution

in taste introduced by the publication of *Las obras de Boscán y algunas de Garcilaso de la Vega* in 1543, as well as Jerónimo de Urrea's widely disseminated 1549 translation of the *Orlando furioso* in *octava rima*, Mena's *Laberinto de Fortuna* continued to be widely read and to enjoy considerable literary prestige. For a work written in a style that conventional literary history assumes to have been hopelessly out of fashion, the sixteen printings of the *Laberinto de Fortuna* do not compare unfavorably with the twelve to eighteen printings registered for Urrea's translation of *Orlando furioso* up to c. 1583–88 (Chevalier, *L'Arioste*, 74–75).

70. "Es muy bien que este poeta sea tenido en mucha estima, aunque no fuera tan bueno como es, por ser el primero que sepamos que haya ilustrado tanto la lengua castellana." As noted in Chapter 2, El Brocense goes on to set up a simile that has Mena in the role of Ennius or Lucretius compared with Garcilaso and the other Italianizers as Virgil or Horace.

71. The Renaissance theory of imitation articulated by Bartolomeo Ricci and Daniel Barbaro in the sixteenth century, and various twentieth-century approaches to the problem—particularly those of Alicia de Colombí Monguió, George Pigman, and Thomas Greene—are all discussed at length in Chapter 1, section 1.3.

72. Both Fernán Núñez and Lasso de Oropesa are more literal and translate *dira* as "cruel" (Núñez 1552 [Nucio], fol. 203v; Lasso de Oropesa 123).

73. Pliny uses both *nodus* and *articulus* to describe the first joint in the hyena's spine (28.27). Fernán Núñez renders these as closely as he can, as "Este nudo o artejo" (1552 [Nucio], fol. 203v). By Covarrubias's time, *nudo* had become *ñudo* and was not principally used in anatomy in this way; *artexo* seems to be reserved for "miembro pequeño" (154, 831), while *coyuntura*, as used by Ercilla, seems to have become the preferred term (Covarrubias 334). A curiosity no editor of Mena, with the exception of Kerkhof (409), deigns to mention: in all of the Núñez editions that I have consulted the text of *Laberinto de Fortuna* 241b reads "mundo" in place of "nodo," although the correct reading is always given in the accompanying commentary.

74. Ducamin remarks, somewhat dryly, that Ercilla "est tellement absorbé par le texte de Lucain qu'il oublie que ce poisson a un nom espagnol: *rémora*" (is so absorbed by Lucan's text that he forgets that this fish has a Spanish name: remora) (175 n. 1). This, however, is to miss the point. Ercilla would have had to look no further than his copy of Fernán Núñez's edition of the *Laberinto de Fortuna* to find "rémora," "echineis," and "echino," where the indefatigable commentator pulls together every conceivable ancient reference to this creature (1552 [Nucio], fols. 206r–207r). Perhaps the most revealing for the pertinence of this fabulous fish to the alchemical decoction is Núñez's observation that "los hechizeros segun dizen usan del en los veneficios amatorios y para detener los juyzios y pleytos, los quales daños compensa con vn prouecho que detiene el fluxo de las mugeres preñadas y detiene los partos hasta el tiempo conueniente del parir" (fol. 206r).

75. "E. mêle ici ce qui est dit du cenchris. Luc. 9, 712–4" (172 n. 9). The passage in *Pharsalia* 9 reads: "Natus et ambiguae coleret qui Syrtidos arva / Chersydros, tractique via fumante chelydri, / Et semper recto lapsurus limite cenchris: / Pluribus ille notis variatam tinguitur alvum / Quam parvis pictus maculis Thebanus ophites" (*Pharsalia* 9.710–14). Lasso de Oropesa translates, somewhat awkwardly: "Tambien nacio la Chersydros inconstante en su habitacion, por*que* unas vezes mora enlos campos, y otras vezes enlas aguas. Y los Chelydros *que* van por el camino hazie*n*do poluareda. Y la Cencris resualando siempre por rastro derecho: *que* tiene mas lauores pintadas por la barriga, que el marmor Ophites de Thebas con sus espessas pecas" (198). This passage may indeed have drawn Ercilla's attention to the possiblities presented by the traditional identification of the *chelydrus* with the *chersydrus*, but the specific allusion is still to the snake's skin, something that does not enter into play here at all, but is central to

of magic mirrors, including examples from Italian literature, can be found in Campbell (xcvi, xcvi n. 2).

4. These *libros de cordel* were published in Latin America as well as Europe over the centuries (Campbell xxi). Another, oriental version of the *Siete sabios* was current in medieval Muslim Spain, and was translated from Arabic into Castilian by order of Prince Fadrique, the brother of King Alfonso X, in 1253. This version, however, does not contain the story of Virgil's Mirror (Keller ix).

5. Douglas composed the *Palice of Honour* in 1501, and the poem was published in 1553 [London], followed by another edition in 1579 [Edinburgh] (Douglas, *The Poetical Works*, ed. Small, 1:viii, clxviii–ix). It should be remembered that Ercilla was in England in 1554.

6. Libavius's *Alchemia* was first published in 1597 at Frankfurt (Thorndike 6:242).

7. The very first verse—"As armas, & os baroes assinalados"—is the unmistakable signal that stanzas 1–2 are an expanded version of Virgil's "Arma virumque cano." The crucial difference, of course, is that Camoens's hero is a collective one—"os barões." Just as Ercilla celebrates the "esforçados españoles" rather than any single captain, Camoens seeks to sing the deeds of the Portuguese national enterprise. To seek an Aeneas figure in Vasco da Gama has been the fundamental mistake of all too many critics (cf. Camões, *Os Lusíadas*, ed. Pierce, xxiv).

8. Camoens, of course, does offer a palinode to his mythological apparatus in Tethys's description of the Sphere, where the nymph explains that the pagan deities are but allegorical personifications proper to the realm of literature, or as Camoens puts it, *Poesia* (*Lusíadas* 10.82–84).

9. Lida de Malkiel links this glass castle with Fortune's house in Mena's *Laberinto de Fortuna* (*Juan de Mena*, 492). The sumptous, supernatural hilltop palace is, of course, an established topos in medieval allegory. As Patch points out (*Goddess Fortuna*, 123–24), one of the first and most memorable of these is the abode of Venus in Claudian's fifth-century *Epithalamium de nuptiis Honorii Agusti et Mariae* (86–96).

10. Thus Garcilaso describes Severo's song:

> Este nuestro Severo pudo tanto
> con el süave canto y dulce lira
> que, rebueltos en ira y torvellino,
> en medio del camino se pararon
> los vientos y escucharon muy atentos
> la boz y los acentos, muy bastantes
> a que los repugnantes y contrarios
> hiziessen voluntarios y conformes.
>
> (*Egloga II*, vv. 1161–68)

Inés Azar convincingly delineates the Orphic qualities and provenience of Severo's song (124-25).

11. I discuss this in some detail in Chapter 2.

12. As Thomas Greene indicates, so-called neo-Latin poetry is not now held in great esteem and is for the most part neglected in favor of the vernacular works that begin to flourish with such energy during the Renaissance (*Descent*, 152–53). Yet as Greene also points out, Sannazaro was highly regarded in the sixteenth century, perhaps more so than today (*Descent*, 145). The first printed edition of Sannazaro's *De partu Virginis* appeared in Naples in 1526, and was followed by a host of further editions published in Italy, France, and Germany throughout the sixteenth century (Sannazaro, *De partu Virginis*, ed. Fantazzi and Perosa, xcvii–civ). Vernacular versions and reworkings also

Lucan's emulation of Ovid in *Pharsalia* 6 and the underlying metaphor of rejuvenation in *Georgics* 3.

76. It is, in fact, quite possible that Pigman is taking Vida somewhat out of context to make his point here. Vida says, "Often I enjoy playing with phrases from the ancients and, while using precisely the same words, expressing another meaning. Nor shall anyone, (however wise) prove my self-betrayed thefts guilty ones, for soon my borrowings will be obvious to all, and our son's sons and their descendants will approve them. Heaven forbid that I should wish to conceal my thefts or hide my spoils because I feared the punishment of disrepute!" (103). As Ralph G. Williams points out (Vida 103 n. 35), Vida deliberately uses the verb *alludere*, himself "playing" with the possibilities of "play" and "allude" that it simultaneously suggests. As Vida goes on to make clear, his "thefts" are meant to be recognized, and "approved." Nor will they bring him "disrepute." Nonetheless, the process is the opposite of that employed by Ercilla, who cleaves to the meaning while changing the words.

77. Morínigo and Lerner in their note on this stanza (1:261 n. 19), base their commentary on Highet's 1947 article elucidating the Lucanian inspiration of the verses in question. Following Highet (331), Morínigo and Lerner fault Ercilla for "erroneously" attributing wings to the "jáculo, a diferencia de Lucano, su fuente." Nothing, of course, could be further from the truth. Housman cites various authorities, including Solinus and Saint Isidore of Seville, to support the reading of "volucer" as "winged" (178). If Ercilla had had any doubts on this point, both Sulpitius and Beroaldus in the 1514 edition would have made it clear that the "Arabum volucer serpens" of *Pharsalia* 6.677 was the "winged" *iaculus*, both insisting on glossing "volucer" as "alatus" (fol. 159v). Furthermore, Fernán Núñez explicitly states that the *iaculus* "tiene alas" (1552 [Nucio], fol. 209r). Ercilla is on very solid ground indeed when he refers to the "wings" of the "iáculo."

78. I have reproduced Duff's translation from the Loeb edition here.

Chapter 4

1. Borges, like Ercilla, is himself a master of dissimulation. Many critics have found reasons to see a ludic, parodic, teasing correspondence between Borges's story and Dante's *Divina commedia* in spite of the fact that Borges himself explicitly rejects the possibility (Monterroso 229). Although Monterroso professes to find the idea ludicrous in the face of Borges's negation (230), many other critics have made a convincing case for the hypothesis (Paoli 44; Stefanini 54–57). Borges's own enumeration of his "sources" is to be read as part of his fictive creation, not as something external, the mere archaeology of criticism.

2. Gower's *Confessio amantis* is of potential interest to Hispanists. A Castilian prose translation of a lost Portuguese translation still exists in a mid-fifteenth-century manuscript (Gower, *The English Works*, ed. Macaulay, 1:clxvii–viii; Faulhaber et al., #251). Three printed editions of the English text appeared between 1483 and 1554 (1:clxix). According to Macaulay, Gower was held in equal esteem with Chaucer by English readers of the fifteenth and sixteenth centuries (1:vii).

3. The diligent reader will find at least four more in H. S. V. Jones's article on the "Squire's Tale" (357–60). The mirrors in Adenès li Rois's *Cléomadès* (vv. 1690–98) and Froissart's *L'Espinette* (vv. 2382ff.) are clearly Virgil's Mirror from the *Siete sabios*. The mirror of Prester John, although of the same type, is perhaps more interesting given its context in one of the seminal works on the extra-European marvelous. Further instances

appeared throughout the sixteenth century in Italy (cvi–cviii). Spanish translations, indicating an especial interest in Sannazaro, were published in Spain (cviii). The first Spanish translation of the *De partu Virginis*, "en octava rima castellana" by Gregorio Hernández de Velasco (also translator of Virgil), was published in Toledo in 1554 (ed. Fantazzi and Perosa, cviii; Pierce, *La poesía*, 366). Fantazzi and Perosa remark: "La versione del *De partu* è alquanto libera, anche perché il traduttore si è concesso frequenti digressioni, inserendo ad es. un ampio *parergon* in lode dei Grandi di Toledo. La versione dello Hernandez fu ristampata nel 1569 a Salamanca da Mathias Marés, e poi più volte in altre città della Spagna; una seconda versione, limitatamente al primo libro, del «capitan» Francisco de Aldana vide la luce a Madrid nel 1591, tra le opere dell'Aldana, pubblicate dal fratello Cosimo presso P. Madrigal" (cviii–cix). Another Spanish translation, by Francisco de Herrera Maldonado appeared in Madrid 1620 (Pierce, *La poesía*, 366). Pierce gives more dates for editions of the Hernández de Velasco translation: Salamanca 1569; Madrid 1569; Salamanca 1580; Zaragoza 1583 (Pierce, *La poesía*, 366). Fantazzi and Perosa note that the *De partu* seemed to lend itself to liberal adaptation and reworking in vernacular versions, and even in otherwise dissimilar works (cix).

13. Proteus is, of course, the original "Old Man of the Sea." Sannazaro invokes the mythological tradition of Proteus's unreliability here by saying of the sea god "sea blue Proteus; a liar about everything else Proteus, but in this matter he poured forth true words in his song" (caeruleus Proteus; mendax si caetera Proteus, / non tamen hoc vanas effudit carmine voces) (*De partu* 3.336–37). Sannazaro again returns to Proteus's reputation for unreliability in general, and the unique veracity of this prophecy, with "siqua fides, siqua est veri prudentia Proteo" (*De partu* 3.420). Interestingly, Sannazaro also applies the adjective *caeruleus* to his personification of the river Jordan (*De partu* 3.283). This epithet is perhaps first applied to Proteus by Virgil (*Georgics* 4.388); in the same passage Virgil refers to Proteus as *vates* (*Georgics* 4.387). Of course, Proteus's reputation for prophecy goes back at least to Homer (*Odyssey* 4.351–570). Sannazaro is also doubtlessly recalling Ovid, who has Proteus prophesy to Thetis that she will bear Achilles (*Metamorphoses* 11.221–23). Ovid goes on to play with the tradition by having Proteus counsel Peleus to seize Thetis and not let go despite her changes in form if he wants to have his way with her (*Metamorphoses* 11.229–56), precisely the advice given to Menelaus relative to Proteus himself (*Odyssey* 4.385–424). Proteus is a particularly apt prophet for a quasi-pastoral epic, as Homer establishes his character as shepherd of the creatures of the sea (*Odyssey* 4.413). Virgil and other later writers develop this point (cf. *Georgics* 4.394–95). Sannazaro, in a letter of 13 April 1521, explains that "E dire che Proteo sempre avesse detto il vero, non mi parea consono con la religione. Cosi, per temperare la fizzione poetica et ornare le cose sacre con le profane, mi parse provederci con dire: *mendax ad caetera Proteus, Hoc uno veras effudit tempore (carmine) voces*. Tanto più che Iordane dice esserli stato predetto molto tempo avanti, e sempre che reservo che in questo disse il vero, non importa che nel resto sia stato mendace. Virgilio fa il contrario: *Namque mihi fallax haud ante repertus, Hoc uno responso animum delusit Apollo*" (quoted by Quint, *Origin*, 234–35). Quint's discussion of Proteus's function in the *De partu* is particularly cogent (*Origin*, 69–80).

14. All translations from *De partu Virginis* are mine.

15. In his gloss on these verses, Faria e Sousa refers to the *De partu Virginis*, remarking: "en lo ultimo con el canto del Iordan, de que dize que lo cantava lo oyo primero a Proteo. . . . Al fin Proteo en la mente destos misteriosos Autores viene a ser lo mismo que la providencia divina" (4:col. 310). Faria e Sousa continues in this vein: "Mas porque ya por todo el c. 9 enseñamos lo mucho que el P. imitó la docta, i rara invención de Sanaz. en lib. 3 de part. Virgin.i prosigue la imitacion en este c. claro es, que tambien imitó aqui con esta Ninfa, cantando lo que oyó a Proteo, lo que allá canta el

Iordan oido al mismo Proteo, de lo que avia de suceder al Nacimiento de Christo" (4:col. 311).

16. The English translation is Fairclough's from the Loeb edition. The italics are mine.

17. Shanzer quotes Ammianus Marc. 14.11.25–26 at length (142). She also indicates *Aeneid* 6.432, Propertius 4.11.19, and Statius *Silvae* 2.1.219 (142).

18. For the English I have quoted from Danuta Shanzer's translation found in appendix 2 of her commentary on Martianus. The Latin text is from the Teubner edition by J. Willis.

19. Shanzer elaborates on this theme: "Plato's *Republic* 10.616 C-617 E contains the unforgettable picture of Ananke holding the cosmic spindle while the three Fates sing and spin the thread of life and Lachesis carries the lots of life on her knees. Plato clearly intended the spindle to be interpreted as a symbol of the heavenly spheres, and Proclus follows the intention [*In Remp*. 2.203.3–204.22]. Martianus has virtually the same ingredients, but makes some slight alterations: Adrastia for Ananke, a heavenly urn for the heavenly spindle, Heimarmene instead of the *prophetes* [*Rep*. 617 D3] of the *Republic* collecting the falling lots. In the *Republic* the lots govern the soul's choice of reincarnation. It is not completely clear what they represent here. Since Heimarmene in Gnostic and Hermetic thought . . . can represent the inexorable time mechanism of the planets, it seems conceivable that the *decidentes sphaerae* [one notes that they are not *drawn* from the urn] represent souls falling into incarnation on earth. The other possibility is that the lots represent the moment of death. The figure of Heimarmene does not clarify the ambiguity, since *inflexi pectoris* can refer to the goddess's inflexibility in either situation" (143).

20. Quint's elucidation of the Jordan's prophecy in *De partu Virginis* 3 supports this interpretation. Quint demonstrates that in medieval Christian exegesis the Jordan was identified with Oceanus, the source of all rivers. Furthermore, the Jordan's waters were also pictured as flowing upward into the heavens (*Origin*, 72–73). As Quint observes: "The description of the baptism depicted on the urn of Sannazaro's Jordan concludes with image of the river's waters flowing back upon their source: 'et fluvias refugas ad fontem convocat undas.' If the Jordan flowing upstream symbolizes the spiritual ascent of man towards God, the downward flow of the river becomes a figure for the Incarnation, the descent of God into humanity" (*Origin*, 73). As Quint goes on to remark, the idea of the Jordan as Oceanus "makes the Jordan the center of a world river system," while a related interpretation "conceives of the Jordan as a heavenly river, flowing out of Paradise" (*Origin*, 74). Quint continues: "Sannazaro's Jordan represents a Christianized version of the oceanic source myth of the *Fourth Georgic*. Virgil posited a divine intelligibility operating through the processes of creation which originate in Cyrene's cave. The significance which resides at the cave of the Jordan, the source of the world's rivers, is constituted by the Word that dwells within nature and history. The presence of the prophetic urn at the headwaters of the Jordan indicates, moreover, that the Word has been present from the beginning. The Judaeo-Christian god created by the Word and its intelligibility is built into the cosmos" (75). This concept then, is germane to the image of the rivers flowing out of the sky, which is to say the "cosmic urn" of the spheres, presented by Martianus Capella (*De nuptiis* 1.14). Shanzer's commentary makes clear the Neoplatonic origin of this image (187–201, 206–7).

21. "Neoplatonism" is a notoriously broad term that in different contexts can cover even contradictory ideas. Nonetheless its influence is undeniable in the main currents of European cultural history throughout the Middle Ages and the Renaissance (Wallis 160). R. T. Wallis defines Neoplatonism as "a term coined in modern times to distinguish the form of the Platonic tradition inaugurated by Plotinus (A.D. 204–70) and lasting in its

pagan form down to the sixth century A.D. from the teaching of Plato's immediate disciples (the 'Old Academy') and from the Platonism of the earlier Roman Empire ('Middle Platonism')" (1).

22. I have used Armstrong's translation for the English, and Ficino's for the Latin.

23. According to Wallis, this passage is a prime example of Plotinus's mystical inclination. The exercise of imagining the visible universe, and then "thinking it away," is linked to theurgic practices of spiritual purification (Wallis 42). The image of the spherical universe held in the mind, and the idea behind it, is based as much on mystical experience as it is on philosophical speculation. Plotinus urges his reader to attempt to attain the same intuitive vision and understanding himself (Wallis 55–56).

24. Cidade observes, in his note on *Lusíadas* 10.7, "Camões é platonizante e por isso concebe, como Platão, que os homens não são mais do que as realizações concretas, na *esfera sensível*, das *ideias* da *esfera inteligível*, o seja dos *tipos gerais*, libertos das limitações do tempo e do espaço, que nos indivíduos transitòriamente se corporizam" (Camões, *Obras*, ed. Cidade, 5:187).

25. The English translation is Wetherbee's.

26. Wetherbee, in the introduction to his translation, remarks: "The Mirror contains the wisdom of Noys, 'mens aeterna,' the vision of life in its cosmic and temporal totality which man enjoyed in his original condition and the abiding capacity for which is hailed by Urania and Noys as the sign of his destiny" (42).

27. Although I quote Alan not as a "source" for Camoens, but rather as a particularly lucid exposition of widely held ideas, Alan's works were present in late-medieval Spanish libraries (Post 226 n. 7).

28. The English translation is Sheridan's.

29. As Ovid relates, Perseus guided himself by the reflected image on his polished bronze shield, and thus avoided being turned to stone by the Gorgon's gaze (*Metamorphoses* 4.782–83).

30. As Wallis points out, the final vision of the *Divina commedia* (*Paradiso* 33) is "wholly Neoplatonic" (169).

31. Faria e Sousa, in his commentary, insists on the similarities between the guide function of Tethys and the nymph who shows Sannazaro's Sincero the rivers of Italy in "Prosa 12" of the *Arcadia*, and on the model provided by Juan de Mena's Providencia in the opening stanzas of the *Laberinto de Fortuna*. Faria e Sousa also foregrounds Mena in his gloss on the *locus amoenus* at the "erguido cume" (4:cols. 444–46). Lida de Malkiel insists on the presence of Mena in the preparations for the prophetic revelations, especially Tethys leading Gama to a glass castle on a hilltop on the Isle of Love (*Lusíadas* 9.86–87; *Juan de Mena* 492). The common use of Mena as a subtext for the prophetic elements in their respective poems forms an important link in the rivalry that I posit between Ercilla and Camoens.

32. Ercilla's representation of Fitón's chamber as paved with "cristalinas losas" and roofed over with a bejewelled simulacrum of the heavens could just as well recall Ariosto's description of Merlin's tomb, made of "pietra dura, / lucida e tersa, e come fiamma rosa," glowing with light that would eclipse the sun, and decorated with "segni impressi all'osservate stelle" (*Orlando furioso* 3.14–15). Other details, such as the sculpted columns, also coincide (*Araucana* 23.67; *Orlando furioso* 3.7).

33. Faria e Sousa writes, in his gloss on *Lusíadas* 10.77e, "Vieron un globo, que pinta casi como en la estanc. 7 el de Proteo. Ercilla imitando esta invencion, finge que tambien delante de aquel Mago Fiton estava otro globo asi. [He quotes *Araucana* 23.68c–e.] I alli le enseño la tierra toda, como acá Tetis al Gama."

34. Camoens, born c. 1524–25, is presumed to have pursued some studies at Coim-

bra, although little is known for certain. Camoens left Portugal for the East in 1553 (Camões, *Os Lusíadas*, ed. Pierce, ix, xvi–xvii).

35. For the philosophical and cosmological scope of Aeneas's encounter with the shade of Anchises, see Habinek.

36. Spenser compares Merlin's Mirror to a tower that "Great *Ptolomaee* it for his lemans sake / Ybuilded all of glasse, by Magicke powre" (*Faerie Queene* 3.2.20). According to Warton, Arab philosophers "invented a story of a magical steel-glass, placed by Ptolemy on the summit of a lofty pillar near the city of Alexandria, for burning ships at a distance. . . . Ptolemy, who seems to have been confounded with Ptolemy the Egyptian astrologer and geographer was famous among the Eastern writers and their followers for his skill in operations of glass" (quoted in Spenser 216). We are reminded that Homer places Menelaus's encounter with Proteus on the island of Pharos, site of Ptolemy's Mirror, off Alexandria (*Odyssey* 4.351ss). Homer specifically calls Proteus "Egyptian" (*Odyssey* 4.385). This becomes a permanent feature of the tradition. Claudian, for instance, refers to "Pharos, the home of Proteus and the seven mouths of the Nile" (Phariumque cubile / Proteos et septem despectat cornua Nili) (*Epithalamium de Nuptiis Honorii Augusti et Mariae* 49–50). Is Spenser making a sly allusion to Camoens's rendition of Proteus's globe? When Spenser says of Merlin's Mirror that "It vertue had, to shew in perfect sight, / What euer thing was in the world contaynd, / Betwixt the lowest earth and heauens hight" (*Faerie Queene* 3.2.19abc), and "For thy it round and hollow shaped was, / Like to the world it selfe, and seem'd a world of glas" (*Faerie Queene* 3.2.19hi), the poet is certainly stretching the limits of the Virgil's Mirror model that is his central subtext, and recalling some of the most salient features of Camoens's *globos*.

37. The exact dates of Martianus and the composition of his work are the subjects of continuing debate, but most scholars agree that Martianus must have written some time during the fifth century A.D. (Shanzer 5–17). Composed during the transition from paganism to Christianity in the West, Martianus's work preserves much of the pagan and Neoplatonic learning that, while widespread in his day, was becoming lost during the early Middle Ages. In fact, the *De nuptiis* became something of a classic for medieval scholars, achieving the status of textbook of ancient learning (Lewis, *Allegory* 81). Martianus, in particular, was a fundamental model and *auctor* for the great writers of the twelfth-century renaissance such as Bernardus Silvestris and Alan of Lille (Lewis 89). Nonetheless, despite the supposed rejection of all things medieval by the humanists of a later day, the *De nuptiis* continued to exert a powerful influence on through the end of the sixteenth century (Lewis 81). Martianus's work found its way into print at least as early as 1499 (see Works Cited), and continued to be edited and read throughout the sixteenth century. Grotius published an edition with commentary in 1599 (Martinius Capella, *Martianus*, ed. J. Willis, xx). I believe that one evidence of that influence, previously unremarked, can be found in the mantic globes of both the *Lusíadas* and the *Araucana*.

38. Danuta Shanzer glosses *in suggestu sidereo* as "The model actually rests on the sphere of the fixed stars" (151).

39. Shanzer comments on *imago quaedam videbatur ideaque mundi*: "The two terms do not form a hendiadys. The *sphaera* is an *imago* in that (from the human point of view) it imitates the form of the sensible world, but is also its *idea* or Platonic form, and consequently prior. *Quaedam* alerts the reader to the reference to the Neoplatonic *kosmos noetos*" (152).

40. As Shanzer points out, what she and Willis read as "Pthyei reformantis speculo" is only one solution of a *locus monstrosus*. A perhaps more plausible reading is "idem in reformanti speculo" (Shanzer 152).

41. For instance, Ercilla's appropriation of the death of Paulus, transfixed by the

flying serpent (*Pharsalia* 9.822–27), to describe the effect of Doña Mencía de Nidos's words on the terrified inhabitants of La Concepción (*Araucana* 7.30).

42. Nonetheless, many preferred to avoid entering into detailed discussions of the higher spheres. For example, Pierre d'Ailly (1350–1420), in whose *Ymago mundi* Columbus was to study geography and cosmology, states that there are said to be nine, ten, eleven, or even twelve heavenly spheres above the earth's orb, depending on the authority consulted. He himself declares that there are nine: the seven planetary spheres, that of the fixed stars, and the Primum Mobile. D'Ailly adds, however, that "above this one (the Primum Mobile) some philosphers put a tenth fixed heaven. Above which it is said that there is a crystalline heaven. And higher than all others there is the Empyrean where is the throne of God and the dwelling-place of the saints. But these last two are not pertinent to the contemplations of the philosophers and astronomers, speaking of nature. Thus few astrologers take into account the tenth fixed heaven. The others (the nine below) most occupy their speculations" (vltra quod ponunt quidam philosophi celum decimum immobile. Super que iterum esse dicutur celum cristallinum. & deinde omnium supremum celum empyreum vbi est dei sedes habitatioque sanctorum. Sed hec duo vltima ad considerationem philosophorum & astronomorumm naturaliter loquentium non pertinent. Pauci etiam astrologi considerant de celo decimo immobili. Sed reliqua magis sunt de eorum speculatione) (*Ymago Mundi* 1:164–65). Although d'Ailly is speaking here specifically about the interests of astrologers (1:166–67), it is also clear that he prefers to leave the delicate matter of the highest spheres to the theologians.

43. Ercilla added a stanza to his description of Peru in the 1589–90 edition. In all subsequent editions, this added stanza is *Araucana* 27.45, and all succeeding stanzas are one number higher. Thus *Araucana* 27.52 in 1578 is 27.53 in editions based on 1589–90.

44. In his prologue to Part II, Ercilla justifies the inclusion of Saint Quentin, in part, by asserting that the great battle in northern France occurred the same day as an action the poet himself participated in against the Araucanians at La Concepción, Chile.

45. I quote the relevant passage from the text of the prologue to Part II in Chapter 1, section 1.2.

46. Hardie remarks that "as cosmic icon the Shield of Aeneas is the true climax and final encapsulation of the imperialist themes of the *Aeneid*, and is thus qualitatively different from the review of individual Roman heroes in book six (although the *encomium* of Augustus there does indeed foreshadow the universalizing of the Shield)" (339).

47. If we read the Shield as a type of aleph, Hardie's interpretation of the miraculous defense of the capitol against the Gauls and the Battle of Actium in terms of Gigantomachy is very suggestive. Hardie writes that "Gigantomachy is in essence a cosmogonic myth, but its emphasis may fall on one of two aspects, corresponding to two senses of the word *kosmos*: firstly, on the assertion of moral and theological order against the anarchy of evil; and, secondly, on the spatial extension of the resulting order to fill the universe. The Virgilian account of Actium and its aftermath corresponds to the second of these emphases, the episode of the Gauls to the first; it is this duality at the heart of the Gigantomachic myth that allows the preservation of the Capitol, the centre of Rome, to stand as a prefiguration of the Battle of Actium, the successful conquest of the periphery" (351).

48. The historian López de Gómara opens his entry for the year 1532 with the remark "Llega sobre Viena el gran Turco Soliman, con el mayor exército de n*u*estros años, ni que ningun otomano tuuo, sabiendo como el Emperador estaua en Alemania; trayó trecientos mil conbatientes y mas de cien mil a cauallo, bien 120 tiros grandes. Otros ponen docientos, y otros quinientos, y Pedro Mexia 600,000, que deuia ser en toda suerte de gentes" (*Annales*, 224).

49. López de Gómara declares: "Juntó el Emp*er*ador 120 M. soldados y mas de 30 M.

de cauallo á su costa, y del Rey su hermano, y del Papa Clemente, que fué sin duda el mayor exército christiano de nu*estros* dias, y no quiso luteranos porque no inficionasen los catholicos ó no ayudasen al Turco. Auia 12 M. españoles con el marques del Basto, y Ant*onio* de Leiua era el gran consejero de la guerra" (*Annales*, 224–25).

50. López de Gómara concludes his summary of the affair: "Afrentosa retirada del gran Turco, los senseros, como dicen, atapados, dexando perdidos 60 M. hombres, y quebrando las puentes de miedo que no le siguiesen, y quando el Emper*ador* llegó á Viena estava ya el quarenta leguas de allí. Dixeron que no esperó batalla por auiso y consejo de christianos sus amigos" (*Annales*, 225).

51. The Turkish admiral Sulaiman Pasha captured Aden and assaulted the Portuguese fortress at Diu in 1538. All of the Muslim potentates of the region repeatedly sent ambassadors laden with gifts and grandiose plans beseeching the aid of the Ottoman sultan against the Portuguese. Turkish naval expeditions continued to be sent into the Red Sea and beyond on up through midcentury (Braudel, *Mediterranean*, 547).

52. Jerónimo Corte Real published a poem that expands Camoens's five stanzas into an entire epic in 1574 titled *Sucesso do segundo cêrco de Diu*. Interestingly enough, Corte Real also authored a heroic verse treatment of Lepanto that, like Part II of the *Araucana*, was published in 1578 (Camões, *Os Lusíadas*, ed. Pierce, xix).

Chapter 5

1. The Hellenistic cosmographer and poet Eratosthenes is said to have combined Platonic cosmology with geographical description in his *Hermes*, an epic poem written in Greek that now exists only in fragments (Hardie 10). Although Eratosthenes's theory of the five zones continued to play an important role up through the sixteenth century—Mena affirms it (*Laberinto de Fortuna* 34) and chroniclers of the Indies such as López de Gómara (*Historia general*, 1:12–17) and the Inca Garcilaso (*Comentarios reales*, caps. 1, 2) still felt it necessary to deal with the subject over a century later—the Greek poet's *Hermes* hardly can be said to have served as a model for either Camoens or Ercilla.

2. Considerable ink has been spilled over the question of the authorship of the *De imagine mundi*. The curious reader should consult Lida de Malkiel, *Juan de Mena*, 34; Wright 403; Bull and Williams 3; Kinkade 263, 268 n. 9; Mena, *Laberinto de Fortuna*, ed. Kerkhof, 113 n. 265.

3. According to Kerkhof, the earliest identification of Mena's mapamundi passage with "Saint Anselm's" work is found in the commentary on a manuscript copy of the *Laberinto* produced between 1460 and 1480 (Mena, *Laberinto de Fortuna*, ed. Kerkhof, 42, 113 n. 265). Early editions of *De imagine mundi* also reflect this attribution, for instance, that of 1491 (Bull and Williams 3). Both Fernán Núñez and El Brocense, as well, attribute the work to "San Anselmo" (Lida de Malkiel, *Juan de Mena*, 32–33).

4. As Marvin Colker, Walter's most recent editor, remarks: "Walter of Châtillon captures in his work the flavour of ancient epic by use of relatively pure prosody and diction, by classical allusions and epic language, and by the avoidance of rhyme" (xix). One of Walter's most notable Virgilian imitations is his portrayal of the ekphrastic Shield of Darius at the end of Book 2 (*Alexandreis* 2.496–539).

5. Pritchard's translation runs: "and the sublime content of the material, which none of the ancient poets, on the evidence of Servius, dared to tackle as a subject" (34). The text in Colker's edition reads: "et altitudinem materiae, / quam nullus ueterum poetarum teste Seruio / ausus fuit aggredi perscribendam" (5).

6. There is some debate over the precise date of composition of the *Alexandreis*.

Pritchard gives a summary of the problem, and opts for some time in the period 1178–82. The poem was apparently already well known by 1189 (Walter, *The Alexandreis*, ed. Pritchard, 4–5).

7. The English translation is Pritchard's. The Latin text is from Colker's edition.

8. The date of the *Libro de Alexandre*, along with the possible identity of the author, have provoked continuing critical controversy. For a relatively recent review of the questions involved, see the *Libro de Alexandre*, ed. Cañas, 15–31. Cañas concludes his discussion with the remark: "Como la cuestión del autor que lo compuso, la fecha en que se escribió sigue siendo en la actualidad una auténtica incógnita, un misterio que la crítica todavía no ha logrado desvelar" (31).

9. This episode is ultimately based on the ascent of Alexander as recounted in the Hellenistic romance that goes under the name of Pseudo-Callisthenes, where it is said that Alexander undertakes the flight in order to determine the boundaries of the earth (Willis, *Debt*, 40). As Willis points out, "The comparison between the structure of the earth and the figure of a man is a conceit which enjoyed considerable vogue in the literature of the middle ages" (*Debt*, 40–41). The prose Pseudo-Callisthenes was mainly known in the medieval West in Latin translations such as the *Res gestae Alexandri Macedonis* of Julius Valerius (c. A.D. 350), the ninth-century *Epitomi Julii Valerii*, and the tenth-century *Historia de Proeliis* (Michael 14). The Pseudo-Callisthenes, in one form or another, is held to be the principal inspiration for the twelfth-century *Roman d'Alexandre* (Michael 22).

10. Willis gives a detailed analysis of the entire passage, comparing the Spanish version with various antecedents and analogues, in particular pointing out the correspondences with several versions of the Old French *Roman d'Alexandre* (*Debt*, 41–46). Michael adds to Willis's remarks, emphasizing the Spanish poet's transformations of and divergences from his French models (216–19).

11. Only two complete manuscripts are known to have survived of the *Libro de Alexandre*. One was produced in the fourteenth century (Faulhaber et al., #1925); the other sometime between 1440 and 1460 (Faulhaber et al., #2605). Additionally there are three fragments. Indications are, however, that more manuscripts were in existence in the sixteenth and early seventeenth centuries (*Libro de Alexandre*, ed. Cañas, 83–84). The first complete printed edition of the poem was that prepared by Tomás Antonio Sánchez and published in his *Colección de poesías castellanas anteriores al siglo XV*, Madrid: 1779–90 (*Libro de Alexandre*, ed. Cañas, 99).

12. All quotes from the *Laberinto de Fortuna* in this section are from the Fernán Núñez edition printed in 1552 by Martín Nuçio. As I have pointed out in Chapters 2 and 3, it would have been most improbable that Ercilla, or Camoens for that matter, would have read Mena in any other than some printing of Núñez's edition.

13. Mena directly recalls the *Somnium Scipionis* at the close of the mapamundi passage where Providence upbraids him for fixing his gaze on the earth when he should be concentrating on the heavens (*Laberinto de Fortuna* 55). It is then that Mena is shown the three wheels representing the cosmic spheres—past, present, and future; these are represented as being *within* Fortune's glass castle (*Laberinto de Fortuna* 56).

14. In his gloss on *Lusíadas* 10.76f–h, Faria e Sousa states: "Tambien en la introducion desta Diosa por esta montaña, por subir a mostrarle los orbes, i sus movimientos, i figuras, i las tierras Orientales, i personas que en ellas huvo, i avia de aver, imitô a Mena, que introduxo en la cop. 23 la Provincia que le mostro todo lo contiene aquel Poema, i en la copla 26 . . . Que es lo mismo que dize acâ Tetis al Gama; con la diferencia de que el Mena dize, *que* la Diosa le queria mostrar lo que podian ver los ojos, o entendimiento humano. I nuestro Poeta haziendo mayor el favor hecho a los Portugueses, dize *que* les

fue mostrado lo que no pueden ver ojos mortales. . . . Ercilla cat. 17 tambien imitó todo esto, quando se fingio llevado de Bellona a un alto monte" (4:col. 444–45).

15. A number of vernacular verse versions of the mapamundi as elaborated in the *De imagine mundi* were widely read in the late Middle Ages. Among the most important of these were the *Mappemonde* composed by Pierre de Beauvais c. 1217–18 and *L'Image du Monde* by Gossuin de Metz c. 1246 (Langlois 123–24, 135–97). Santillana owned a fifteenth-century copy of the *Mappemonde* de Pierre (Schiff 366–67). Of even more immediate interest for the development of Mena's mapamundi is the Castilian *Semeiança del mundo*. This work was probably composed c. 1223 (Bull and Williams 10–11), and at least two mid-fifteenth-century manuscripts are known to have survived. One of these is edited by Bull and Williams as MS. *B*. The other is Ms. 3369 of the Biblioteca Nacional de Madrid (Kinkade 261–63). There are a number of intriguing correspondences between the treatment of the *De imagine mundi* material in the *Semeiança* and the *Laberinto de Fortuna*. This appears to be especially true in the case of MS. 3369 on the basis of Kinkade's description. Unfortunately, the text of MS. 3369 has not been published, and I received a microfilm copy too late for inclusion in this study of the results of a careful comparison.

16. Kinkade, in his description of MS. 3369 of the Biblioteca Nacional, indicates that the text skips from the equivalent of *Semeiança del mundo MS. B* 6 to MS. *B* 20 (264–65), which corresponds closely to what Mena has omitted. Nonetheless, *B* 6 does briefly mention Paradise and the fountain. It is suggestive, however, that in *B* 24, the first paragraph after the details of India, we read, "E de aqueste rrio que dizen Yndus fasta el rrio que dizen Tigris es la tierra que dizen Parchia," which corresponds to Mena's "Y tierra de Persia vi entre los ríos / Tigris y Indus de reynos varios" (*Laberinto de Fortuna* 35*bc*).

17. David William Foster accuses Mena of misunderstanding Dante (345). It is perhaps more likely that Mena understood Dante all too well. Mena is clearly more interested in the political reform of Castile and the furthering of the Reconquest than he is in a "faithful" imitation of the Italian poet.

18. López de Gómara refers especially to his conversations with Olaus Magnus for authority on northern matters (*Historia general* 11, 21). It is to Olaus Magnus that Faria e Sousa refers in his gloss on *Lusíadas* 3.10 (2:col. 13).

19. Camoens is certainly not following the antique, Isidorean scheme because it was current in his day. López de Gómara, whose *Historia general* is a good example of a mid-sixteenth-century "popular science" approach to the subject, relies primarily on Strabo and Pomponius Mela for ancient authority on geographical matters. His references to Isidore are incidental at best, and he makes no mention whatsoever of medieval works such as the *De imagine mundi*. In any case, López de Gómara's references to ancient authors frequently are made in order to refute them in the face of practical experience (cf. *Historia general* [cap. 3] 12–14). Fernán Núñez, writing some fifty years after Mena, and as many before López de Gómara, refers frequently to Isidore and "Saint Anselm," but almost as often to Strabo and Mela (1552 [Nucio] 34–53 passim).

20. Inexplicably, at least in the version published by Migne, the author (thought by the editor to be Honorius of Autun) interpolates the Isle of Britain at the end of Europe, between Hispania and the beginning of Africa (*De imagine mundi* 1.31).

21. With one exception, all give six provinces, including Lusitania. *Semeiança del mundo B*, however, only gives five, omitting Lusitania (Bull and Williams 109).

22. Faria e Sousa's comment bears witness to the importance of this difference: "Mirad el cuidado. Dixo en la e. passada que el Planeta de Castilla la hizo restauradora de Espana: aca de Portugal dize, que el cielo justo: i la causa desta diferencia, es, porque a esta gloria Portuguesa precedio el aparecer el mismo Christo a don Alonso en el capo de

Orique, i prometerle que venceria aquella multitud de infieles, haziendole Rey primero de Portugal, i dandole despues otras muchas vitorias estupendas dellos, i a sus sucessores. De manera que con gran cuidado hablo el Poeta con esta diferencia" (2:col. 27).

23. In an example of precisely the kind of rivalry between Castilians and Portuguese that I have posited for Ercilla, López de Gómara refutes the doctrine of the uninhabitable Torrid Zone by referring to the "muchas naos que ordinariamente van de España a las Indias," and goes on to mention the circumnavigation achieved by Magellan. The voyage is represented as the work of Spain, however; López de Gómara uses the name of the ship, and not that of the commander, and makes sure to mention that it returned to "España" after three years. Magellan's name only enters the passage as the name of the Straits (*Historia general* [cap. 6] 17).

24. The Portuguese took Sofala on the coast in 1505 (Randles, *L'empire*, 16), and by the decade of the 1530s they had established their trading posts of Sena and Tete hundreds of kilometers up the Zambezi. These Portuguese emporia soon dominated the export trade of the whole Zimbabwean plateau (Randles, *L'empire*, 42).

25. According to W. G. L. Randles, the Arabs of Sofala, which was the main center of gold export for the realms of the Monomotapa before the arrival of the Portuguese, claimed to have shipped between 5,500 and 8,500 kg of the precious metal a year (*L'empire*, 16). Although export at Sofala fell off after the Portuguese occupation, they were able to tap the source by penetrating up the valley of the Zambezi. This level of production compares very favorably with the 700 kg, which according to Braudel (*Mediterranean*, 469–70), the Portuguese exported yearly from the fortress of São Jorge da Mina in West Africa during the same period of 1500–20.

26. "Saint Anselm" only adds that in the eastern part of Aethiopia is found the city of Saba, from whence came the queen who visited Solomon (*De imagine mundi* 1.33). The *Semeiança del mundo* follows the *De imagine mundi* here (*A* 140–43, *B* 125–28).

27. Guilmartin indicates that the Mamluks were probably being aided by their enemies the Ottomans in this effort against the Portuguese even before Selim's conquest of Egypt (10).

28. This is the same legend of the "predicación de santo Tomás en Indias" that was used to explain the myths of Quetzalcóatl in Mexico and Viracocha in Peru. Writers as diverse in time, place, and outlook as the Andean chronicler Juan de Santa Cruz Pachacuti Yamqui Salcamayhua (Adorno, *Guamán Poma*, 150–51) and Fray Servando Teresa de Mier were to seize upon the legendary preaching of Saint Thomas to further a variety of programs. Fray Servando, for example, revives the legend in order to justify Spanish American independence from the Spaniards (Lafaye 279–97). Another Andean writer, Felipe Guamán Poma de Ayala, was to use the legend of a similar early evangelization by Saint Bartholomew to establish the injustice of the Spanish conquest (Adorno, *Guamán Poma*, 27–29). For the evangelization of Saint Thomas in both the East Indies and America, see Lafaye (especially 260–87).

29. Isidore includes Ceylon among the "Insulae" (*Etymologiae* 14.6.12), while the anonymous author of the *De imagine mundi* mentions it in the first section on India near the beginning of Asia (1.11). The *Semeiança del mundo* follows "Saint Anselm" (*A* 9, *B* 9). As Mena eliminates all of the material on India, there is no mention of Ceylon or Taprobana in either the section on Asia or on the islands in the *Laberinto de Fortuna*.

30. It is prudent to recall here that any reader who came to know the *Laberinto de Fortuna* through the editions prepared by Fernán Núñez, as both Camoens and Ercilla almost certainly did, would have been well aware of the entire tradition, including Isidore and "Saint Anselm," that underlies Mena's mapamundi.

31. Curiously enough, the Jesuit José de Acosta, writing some forty years after López de Gómara, was to use Magellan's circumnavigation as part of his proof of the geocentric

nature of the universe, in accordance with Ptolemaic cosmology (*Historia natural y moral de las Indias*, cap. 2).

32. López de Gómara's *Historia general de las Indias*, first published in 1552, is of special interest here and can help us understand the significance Camoens's references to Magellan, the Castilian conquests in America, and, in fact, the entire closing section of the mapamundi of *Lusíadas* 10 would have had for Ercilla. López de Gómara's *Historia general* was the first overall survey of Castile's explorations and conquests in what were known as the Indies, both of the New World and the Old, to be printed and widely diffused. First published only a few years before Ercilla embarked for America, and a year before Camoens left Portugal for India, the *Historia general* caused an immediate stir. Quickly going into multiple editions, the work was banned by Prince Philip in 1553. Ercilla was, in fact, in attendance on the prince during this period. Nonetheless, numerous editions continued to be printed outside of Castile, and the *Historia general* was translated into a number of other European languages. As Bernal Díaz, Bartolomé de las Casas, and the Inca Garcilaso all attest, López de Gómara's history was virtually required reading for the conquerors as well as their critics, both in Europe and America (Iglesia 97, 132).

33. López de Gómara states: "Otros muchos señores de aquellas isletas vinieron a Tidore, por ruego de Almanzor, a ofrecerse por amigos y tributarios del rey de Castilla, Carlos, emperador, que no los cuento" (*Historia general*, cap. 96). Notice how carefully López de Gómara insists that this allegiance was given to Charles in his capacity as king of Castile. In the same chapter, López de Gómara comments on how the ruler of Tidore, Almanzor, was said to have claimed to have had foreknowledge of the Spaniards' coming by means of astrology, or, in an alternate version, to have seen it in a dream. López de Gómara appears to be following his source very closely here, even transcribing entire sentences virtually unretouched. The premonitory dream or prophecy seems to have become a standard recourse of the Castilian reportage of first contacts after the publication in 1522 of Cortés's *Segunda carta de relación*.

34. In Morínigo and Lerner's edition, *Araucana* 27.7a repeats *Araucana* 27.8a, clearly a printing error. The edition of 1578 Madrid reads "Mira la Siria, la Iudea, la indina," while 1589–90 reads "Mira la Siria, vees allá la indina" (Ercilla, *La Araucana*, ed. Medina, 4:162). Lerner, in his 1993 edition, rectifies the error, restoring the 1589–90 reading.

35. In the 1597 edition, published posthumously, perhaps under the direction of Ercilla's widow, *Araucana* 27.16a reads "el sur" in place of "al sur" (Ercilla, *La Araucana*, ed. Medina, 4:163). The meaning, that we are looking at the southern reaches of the continent, remains the same in either case. As Le Goff points out, Prester John had originally been conceived of as an Asian potentate, only to be transferred to Africa during the fourteenth and fifteenth centuries (196). A figure titled "Preste Juã" appears in Juan de la Cosa's cartographic representation of Africa from 1500, located west of the Nile in what is present-day Nubia (Randles, "South East Africa," appendix A).

36. Pliny discusses the problem and says that King Juba's investigations revealed that the great river arose somewhere in a great lake. Nonetheless, Pliny is careful to state that the true sources of the Nile were not not known with any real certainty (*Naturalis historia* 5.10).

37. This was still the case in the highly influential and widely diffused 1561 Venice edition of the *Geografia* attributed to Ptolemy. According to Sanz, this is the first edition to present a reasonably scientific map of the world divided into two hemispheres. Nonetheless, the Nile is shown arising from the "Monti da Luna" somewhere between ten and fifteen degrees south of the Equator. Sanz reproduces the map of *Africa meridional* from this edition (216). As confirmed by a perusal of sixteenth-century maps of Africa published under the name of Ptolemy reproduced by Sanz, this is a standard feature.

This continues to be the case in Gerhard Mercator's 1569 world map (Randles, "South East Africa," appendix A), which would seem to represent the best state of European knowledge on the eve of the composition of both the *Araucana* and the *Lusíadas*. This is also true of the Agnese 1555 world map, which Walter Mignolo calls the first published map to resemble our present conception of the contours of world geography ("Putting the Americas," 40), a map which was presented to Philip II by his father Charles V, and which Ercilla almost certainly saw. Randles observes that certain features of Ptolemian geography, such as the Mountains of the Moon, survived as decorations for the uncharted interior of Africa long after detailed information about the coastline became standard on European maps ("South East Africa," 104). For the development of the idea of the Mountains of the Moon, see Randles ("South East Africa," 126–31).

38. Randles notes that Ptolemy's geography only became known in the West in the early fifteenth century (*L'image*, 2). Thus it should be remembered that the Ptolemaean picture of the interior of Africa represented a "modern," humanist, and more authoritative geographical vision in comparison with the medieval Isidorean itinerary.

39. Pliny, of course, uses "Ethiopia" in the ancient sense of all sub-Saharan Africa, not particularly Abyssinia. Fernán Núñez, in his gloss on *Laberinto de Fortuna* 38, also mentions that the Nile, after rushing violently through rough country, spreads out around a large island called Meroë (1552 [Nucio], fol. 30v). Ercilla's description recalls that of Núñez, which the latter attributes to Pomponius Mela.

40. Faria e Sousa cites Herodotus on the history of the city Meroë, capital of a powerful state for many centuries (4:col. 494). Nonetheless, it is plain that Camoens, and Ercilla after him, are referring to the vast island believed by the ancient geographers to have divided the Nile in the unknowable wastes of sub-saharan Africa. The ancient city of Meroë was located approximately one hundred kilometers south of the present-day city of Khartoum, capital of Sudan, along the White Nile.

41. I refer to a reproduction of the *Mappamondo* of Fra Mauro Camaldolese, a famous fifteenth-century Italian cosmographer, found in Longhena (72–73). The 1561 Venice edition of the *Geografia*, attributed to Ptolemy, still has Meroë as a large island embraced by two arms of the Nile, although the placement within the continent has been improved considerably to correspond more closely to the actual lay of the land (Sanz 216).

42. Fernán Núñez comments on Mena's, and his model's, placement of Egypt in Asia at some length (1552 [Nucio], fol. 30r), so Ercilla would have been well aware of the rationale for Mena's choice in this matter. Pliny, too, has Asia begin at the Canopic mouth of the Nile (*Naturalis historia* 5.9.47).

43. Nonetheless, Ercilla does not address one of Mena's most commented-on "noddings" here. As Fernán Núñez points out (1552 [Nucio], fol. 32r), Mena confuses Egyptian Thebes with Boeotian Thebes (*Laberinto de Fortuna* 38*h*). Ercilla passes over the whole issue by describing the bustling city of Cairo, one of the great metropolitan centers of the modern age, in contrast with the classical emphasis of Mena's itinerary.

44. Tamerlane was most famous in the West for having captured the Ottoman sultan Bayazid (López de Gómara, *Crónica de los Barbarrojas*, 312–13).

45. See the discussion of the prophetic vision of Saint Quentin in Chapter 2.

46. The fact that Columbus was not a Spaniard made it inconvenient for Castilian chauvinists to accept that the Genoese could have been entirely responsible for the discovery. Thus arose the tale of the anonymous Spanish pilot who first made the voyage, only to return and die in Columbus's house, leaving his logs and charts in the possesion of the foreigner who would reap the credit. A good example is the version offered by the fiercely Castilian López de Gómara (*Historia general*, cap. 13); another is the Inca Garcilaso de la Vega, who had every motive to stress the accomplishments of his father's

countrymen in this context, if only to avoid accusations of disloyalty or partiality (*Comentarios reales*, cap. 3).

47. Many of the *conquistadores* were controversial figures, to say the least, by the 1570s. In light of the civil wars and revolts in Peru, it is not surprising that Ercilla fails to mention Almagro or Pizarro. Even giving credit to Cortés could not have been calculated to win the poet favor with Philip II. The emperor had banned the publication of Cortés's letters in 1527, and Philip himself had prohibited the publication of López de Gómara's generally laudatory *Historia de la conquista de México* in 1553, and again in 1566 (Bataillon, "Hernán Cortés," 78–79). In a key article, which unfortunately seems to have gone unread by a number of recent critics of the *Araucana*, José Durand explains Ercilla's attitude toward the *conquistadores* of the initial phase of conquest in terms of the widespread distrust and rivalry between the first arrivals—often of fairly humble origin, and often suspected of disloyalty to the crown—and the highborn king's men such as the poet himself who came later to establish order under the authority of the metropolitan government ("El Chapetón Ercilla," 113–17).

48. José Toribio Medina noted the similarities between the two passages on Magellan, and gives the text of *Lusíadas* 10.140e–41 in his note to *Araucana* 27.51a–d. Medina makes no comment on the possible significance of this apparent coincidence, however (Ercilla, *La Araucana*, ed. Medina, 4:383).

49. Camoens, of course, did no less. For instance, he celebrates the heroic defense of Sofala led by the Castilian Pedro de Anaya (Nhaia in Camoens) (*Lusíadas* 10.94h; Asensio 6).

50. It will be recalled that Philip II already had a claim on the throne of Portugal through his mother, daughter of John III. Philip was Sebastian's cousin.

51. Dámaso Alonso ("Recepción," 11) gives the references in Gallego Morell (p. 324 [H-33], pp. 259-60 [H-244]).

Works Cited

Acosta, José de. *Historia natural y moral de las Indias*. Ed. José Alcina Franch. Madrid: Historia 16, 1987.
Adorno, Rolena. *Guaman Poma: Writing and Resistance in Colonial Peru*. Austin: University of Texas Press, 1986.
———. "Literary Production and Suppression: Reading and Writing About Amerindians in Colonial Spanish America." *Dispositio* 11, 28–29 (1986): 1–25.
Ahl, Frederick M. *Lucan: An Introduction*. Ithaca: Cornell University Press, 1976.
Alain de Lille. *Anticlaudianus*. Ed. R. Bossuat. Paris: J. Vrin, 1955.
Alan of Lille. *Anticlaudianus or the Good and Perfect Man*. Trans. James J. Sheridan. Toronto: Pontifical Institute of Medieval Studies, 1973.
Alegría, Fernando. "Ercilla y sus críticos." In *La poesía chilena: orígenes y desarrollo del siglo xvi–xix*, 1–55. México: Fondo de Cultura Económica, 1954.
Alonso, Dámaso. "La recepción de *Os Lusíadas* en España (1579–1650)." In *Obras completas*, 3:9–40. Madrid: Editorial Gredos, 1972.
———. *Romance de Angélica y Medoro*. Madrid: Ediciones Acies, 1962.
Alvarez Vilela, Angel. "L'Expédition à Ancud de Don García Hurtado de Mendoza dans *La Araucana*." *Etudes de Lettres* 3 (1992): 101–20.
Apuleius. *Metamorphoses (Books I–VI)*. Ed. and trans. J. Arthur Hanson. Cambridge: Harvard University Press, 1989.
Ariosto, Ludovico. *Orlando furioso*. Ed. Emilio Bigi. 2 vols. Milano: Rusconi, 1982.
Aristotle. *Poetics*. Trans. Gerald F. Else. Ann Arbor: University of Michigan Press, 1970.
Asensio, Eugenio. *La fortuna de* Os Lusíadas *en España (1572–1672)*. Madrid: Fundación Universitaria Española, 1973.
Aubrun, Charles V. "Poesía épica y novela: El episodio de Glaura en *La Araucana* de Ercilla." *Revista Iberoamericana* 21, 41–42 (1956): 261–73.
Azar, Inés. *Discurso retórico y mundo pastoral en la "Égloga segunda" de Garcilaso*. Amsterdam: John Benjamins, 1981.

Ball, Robert. "Poetic Imitation in Góngora's *Romance de Angélica y Medoro*." *Bulletin of Hispanic Studies* 57, 1 (1980): 33–54.
Barnard, Mary E. "Garcilaso's Poetics of Subversion and the Orpheus Tapestry." *PMLA* 102 (1987): 316–25.
Bataillon, Marcel. "*La desdicha por la honra*: Génesis y sentido de una novela de Lope." In *Varia lección de clásicos españoles*, 373–418. Biblioteca Románica Hispánica 77. Madrid: Gredos, 1964.
———. "L'èdition princeps du Laberinto de Juan de Mena." In *Estudios dedicados a Menéndez Pidal*, 2:325–34. Madrid: CSIC, 1951.
———. "Hernán Cortés, autor prohibido." In *Libro jubilar de Alfonso Reyes*, 77–82. México: Dirección General de Difusión Cultural, 1956.
Beardsley, Theodore S. *Hispano-Classical Translations Printed Between 1482 and 1699*. Pittsburgh: Duquesne University Press, 1970.
Bell, Aubrey F. G. *Francisco Sánchez El Brocense*. London: Oxford University Press, 1925.
Bello, Andrés. "La Araucana, por don Alonso de Ercilla i Zúñiga." In *Temas de crítica literaria*. Ed. Rafael Calderón, 349–62. Vol. 9 of *Obras completas de Andrés Bello*. Caracas: Editorial Nascimento, 1956.
Bernardus Silvestris. *The Cosmographia of Bernardus Silvestris*. Trans. Winthrop Wetherbee. New York; London: Columbia University Press, 1973.
———. *De Mundi Universitate libri duo, sive Megacosmus et Microcosmus*. Ed. Carl Sigmund Barach and Johann Wrobel. Innsbruck, 1876.
Bertini, Giovanni Maria. "*L'Orlando furioso* nella sua prima traduzione ed imitazione spagnuola." *Aevum* 8 (1934): 357–402.
Boethius. *The Theological Tractates; The Consolation of Philosophy*. Ed. and trans. H. F. Stewart. Cambridge: Harvard University Press, 1962.
Boiardo, Matteo Maria. *Orlando innamorato*. Ed. Giuseppe Anceschi. 2 vols. Milano: Garzanti, 1978.
Borges, Jorge Luis. *El aleph*. Madrid: Alianza Editorial; Buenos Aires: Emecé, 1971.
Borgia, Carl Ralph. "Notes on Dante in the Spanish Allegorical Poetry of Imperial, Santillana, and Mena." *Hispanófila* 81 (1984): 1–10.
Braudel, Fernand. *The Mediterranean and the Mediterranean World in the Age of Philip II*. Trans. Siân Reynolds. 2 vols. New York: Harpers, 1976.
———. *The Perspective of the World*. Trans. Siân Reynolds. Vol. 3. New York: Harper & Row, 1984.
Broccia, Sebastiano. "L'Aparato Magico del VIo libro della *Farsaglia*." *Annali della Facoltà di Lettere, Filosofía e Magisterio della Università di Cagliari* 15 (1948): 203–35.
Bull, William E., and Harry F. Williams. Semciança del mundo: *A Medieval Description of the World*. Berkeley and Los Angeles: University of California Press, 1959.
Cabello Lapiedra, Luis María. *La batalla de San Quintín y su influencia en las artes españolas*. Madrid: Voluntad, 1927.
Camões, Luis de. *Obras completas*. Ed. Hernâni Cidade. 5 vols. Lisboa: Livraria Sá da Costa, 1985.
———. *Os Lusíadas*. Ed. Manuel de Faria e Sousa. Introduction by Jorge de Sena. 2 vols. Lisboa: Imprensa Nacional-Casa da Moeda, 1972.
———. *Os Lusíadas*. Ed. José Maria Rodrigues. Lisboa: Biblioteca Nacional, 1921.
———. *Os Lusíadas*. Ed. Frank Pierce. London: Oxford University Press, 1973.

Campbell, Killis. *The Seven Sages of Rome*. Boston: Ginn, 1907.
Carriazo, Juan de Mata, ed. *Crónica de don Alvaro de Luna*. Madrid: Espasa-Calpe, 1940.
———, ed. *Crónica del halconero de Juan II, Pedro Carillo de Huete*. Madrid: Espasa-Calpe, 1946.
Carron, Jean-Claude. "Imitation and Intertextuality in the Renaissance." *New Literary History* 19, 3 (1988): 565–79.
Cascales, Francisco. *Tablas poéticas*. Ed. Benito Brancaforte. Madrid: Espasa-Calpe, 1975.
Castellón, Baltasar. *Los cuatro libros del Cortesano*. Ed. Antonio María Fabié. Trans. Juan Boscán. Libros de Antaño 3. Madrid: Manuel Rivadeneyra, 1873.
Castiglione, Baldassar. *Il Libro del Cortegiano*. Ed. Amedeo Quondam and Nicola Longo. Milano: Garzanti, 1981.
Celsus. *De Medicina*. Ed. and trans. W. G. Spencer. Cambridge: Harvard University Press, 1953.
Cervantes Saavedra, Miguel de. *La Galatea*. Ed. Juan Bautista Avalle-Arce. 2 vols. Madrid: Espasa-Calpe, 1968.
———. *El ingenioso hidalgo don Quijote de la Mancha*. Ed. Luis Andrés Murillo. 2 vols. Madrid: Castalia, 1982.
Cevallos, Francisco Javier. "Don Alonso de Ercilla and the American Indian: History and Myth." *Revista de Estudios Hispánicos* 23, 3 (1989): 1–20.
Chaucer, Geoffrey. *The Complete Works of Geoffrey Chaucer*. Ed. F. N. Robinson. Boston: Houghton Mifflin, 1933.
Chevalier, Maxime. *L'Arioste en Espagne (1530–1650): Recherches sur l'influence du "Roland furieux."* Bordeaux: Institut d'Études Ibériques et Ibéro-Américaines de l'Université de Bordeaux, 1966.
———. *Lectura y lectores en la España de los siglos XVI y XVII*. Madrid: Ediciones Turner, 1976.
———. *Los temas ariostescos en el romancero y la poesía española del Siglo de Oro*. Madrid: Castalia, 1968.
Cicero. *Somnium Scipionis*. Ed. J. F. Stout. London: University Tutorial Press, 1921.
Clarke, Dorothy Clotelle. *Juan de Mena's* Laberinto de Fortuna: *Classic Epic and Mester de Clerecía*. University: University of Mississipi, 1973.
Claudian. *Epithalamium De Nuptiis Honorii Agusti et Mariae*. In *Claudian*. Ed. and trans. Maurice Platnauer, 1:240–67. 2 vols. Cambridge: Harvard University Press, 1922.
Colombí-Monguió, Alicia de. *Petrarquismo peruano: Diego Dávalos y Figueroa y la poesía de la* Miscelánea Austral. London: Tamesis, 1985.
Concha, Jaime. "El otro nuevo mundo." In *Homenaje a Ercilla*, 31–82. Concepción, Chile: Universidad de Concepción, Instituto Central de Lenguas, 1969.
Corominas, J. *Diccionario crítico etimológico de la lengua castellana*. 3 vols. Madrid: Gredos, 1954.
Corominas, Juan María. *Castiglione y* La Araucana: *estudio de una influencia*. Madrid: José Porrúa Turanzas, 1980.
Covarrubias, Sebastián de. *Tesoro de la lengua castellana o española*. Madrid: Ediciones Turner, 1977.
Cruz, Anne J. *Imitación y transformación: el petrarquismo en la poesía de*

Boscán y Garcilaso de la Vega. Amsterdam and Philadelphia: John Benjamins, 1988.

———. "Spanish Petrarchism and the Poetics of Appropriation: Boscán and Garcilaso de la Vega." In *Renaissance Rereadings: Intertext and Context*. Ed. Maryanne Cline Horowitz, 80–95. Urbana: University of Illinois Press, 1988.

Cruz, Sor Juana Inés de la. *Obras completas*. Ed. Alfonso Méndez Plancarte. 4 vols. México: Fondo de Cultura Económica, 1951–57.

Curtius, Ernst Robert. *European Literature and the Latin Middle Ages*. Trans. Willard R. Trask. New York: Harper, 1953.

d'Ailly, Pierre. *Ymago mundi*. Ed. and trans. Edmond Buron. 3 vols. Paris: Maisonneuve Frères, 1930.

Dante Alighieri. *La divina commedia*. Ed. C. H. Grandgent and Charles S. Singleton. Cambridge: Harvard University Press, 1972.

Davis, Elizabeth B. *Epic Imagination: The Construction of Identity in Imperial Spain:* Columbia: University of Missouri Press, forthcoming.

———. "Escribir después de Ercilla: La codicia en *La Austriada* de Juan Rufo." In *Actas del XII Congreso de la Asociación Internacional de Hispanistas: 21–26 de agosto de 1995*. Ed. Jules Whicker, 2:162–68. Birmingham: Department of Hispanic Studies, University of Birmingham, 1998.

Deyermond, Alan. "Structure and Style as Instruments of Propaganda in Juan de Mena's *Laberinto de Fortuna*." *Proceedings of the PMR Conference: Annual Publication of the Patristic, Medieval, and Renaissance Conference* 5 (1980): 159–67.

Dobin, Howard. *Merlin's Disciples: Prophecy, Poetry, and Power in Renaissance England*. Stanford: Stanford University Press, 1990.

Douglas, Gavin. *The Poetical Works of Gavin Douglas*. Ed. John Small. 4 vols. Edinburgh: William Paterson, 1874.

Ducamin, Jean. *L'Araucana. Poème épique par D. Alonso de Ercilla i Zúñiga. Morceaux choisis*. Paris: Garnier, 1900.

Duggan, Joseph J. "The Generation of the Episode of Baligant: Charlemagne's Dream and the Normans at Mantzikert." *Romance Philology* 30 (1976): 59–82.

Durand, José. "El chapetón Ercilla y la honra araucana." *Filología* 10 (1964): 113–34.

Dutton, Brian, et al. *Catálogo/índice de la poesía cancioneril del siglo XV*. Madison: Hispanic Seminary of Medieval Studies, 1982.

Ercilla, Alonso de. *La Araucana*. Ed. Marcos A. Morínigo y Isaías Lerner. 2d ed. Madrid: Castalia, 1979.

———. *La Araucana*. Ed. Isaías Lerner. Madrid: Cátedra, 1993.

———. *Primera y segunda parte de la Araucana*. Madrid: Pierres Cosin, 1578.

———. *Segunda parte de La Araucana*. Zaragoza: Juan Soler, 1578.

Ercilla y Çúñiga, Alonso de. *La Araucana*. Madrid: Pierres Cosin, 1569.

Ercilla y Zúñiga, Alonso de. *La Araucana*. Ed. José Toribio Medina. 5 vols. Santiago de Chile: Elzeviriana, 1910–18.

Farrell, Anthony J. "Late Spanish Survival of the Seven Sages: *Historia de los siete sabios de Roma*, Madrid, 1859." In *Studies on the Seven Sages of Rome and Other Essays in Medieval Literature*. Ed. H. Niedzielski, H. R. Runte, and W. L. Hendrickson, 91–102. Honolulu: Educational Research Association, 1978.

Faulhaber, Charles B., et al. *Bibliography of Old Spanish Texts*. 3d ed. Madison: Hispanic Seminary of Medieval Studies, 1984.
Fichter, Andrew. *Poets Historical: Dynastic Epic in the Renaissance*. New Haven and London: Yale University Press, 1982.
Florit, Eugenio. "Los momentos líricos de *La Araucana*." *Revista Iberoamericana* 33, 63 (1967): 45–54.
Foster, David William. "The Misunderstanding of Dante in Fifteenth-Century Spanish Poetry." *Comparative Literature* 16 (1964): 338–47.
Fucilla, Joseph G. "Ecos de Sannazaro y de Tasso en *Don Quijote*." In *Relaciones hispanoitalianas. Revista de Filología Española*—Anejo 59, 27–37. Madrid: Consejo Superior de Investigaciones Científicas, 1953.
Gallardo, Bartolomé José. *Ensayo de una biblioteca española de libros raros y curiosos*. 4 vols. Madrid: Manuel Tello, 1889.
Gallego Morell, Antonio. *Garcilaso de la Vega y sus comentaristas*. Madrid: Gredos, 1972.
Garcilaso de la Vega. *Obras completas con comentario*. Ed. Elías L. Rivers. Madrid: Castalia, 1981.
Garcilaso de la Vega, Inca. *Comentarios reales de los incas*. Ed. Angel Rosenblat. 2 vols. Buenos Aires: Emecé Editores, 1943.
Gericke, Philip O. "The Narrative Structure of the *Laberinto de Fortuna*." *Romance Philology* 21 (1968): 512–22.
Gower, John. *The English Works of John Gower*. Ed. G. C. Macaulay. 2 vols. London: Oxford University Press, 1900.
Graves, Robert. Introduction to *Pharsalia: Dramatic Episodes of the Civil Wars*, by Lucan. Trans. Robert Graves. Harmondsworth, Middlesex: Penguin, 1956.
Greenblatt, Stephen. *Marvelous Possessions: The Wonder of the New World*. Chicago: University of Chicago Press, 1991.
Greene, Thomas. *The Descent from Heaven: A Study in Epic Continuity*. New Haven: Yale University Press, 1963.
———. *The Light In Troy: Imitation and Discovery in Renaissance Poetry*. New Haven: Yale University Press, 1982.
Grenade, Pierre. "Le mythe de Pompée et les Pompéiens sous les Césars." *Revue des Études Anciennes* 52, 1–2 (1950): 28–63.
Griffin, Clive. *Los Cromberger: la historia de una imprenta del siglo XVI en Sevilla y Méjico*. Madrid: Ediciones de Cultura Hispánica, 1991.
Guilmartin, John Francis, Jr. *Gunpowder and Galleys: Changing Technology and Mediterranean Warfare at Sea in the Sixteenth Century*. London: Cambridge University Press, 1974.
Habinek, Thomas N. "Science and Tradition in *Aeneid* 6." *Harvard Studies in Classical Philology* 92 (1989): 223–55.
Hardie, P. R. *Virgil's Aeneid: Cosmos and Imperium*. London: Oxford University Press, 1986.
Hayes, Aden W. "Fitón's Aleph, Ercilla's World." *Revista de estudios hispánicos* 15, 3 (1981): 349–63.
Herrero Llorente, Víctor-José. "Laso de Oropesa y su traducción de la *Farsalia*." *Revista de Archivos, Bibliotecas y Museos* 69 (1961): 751–73.
Highet, Gilbert. "Classical Echoes in *La Araucana*." *Modern Language Notes* 62, 5 (1947): 329–31.
Homero. *De la Ulyxea de Homero XIII libros, traduzidos de griego en romance castellano*. Trans. Gonçalo Pérez. Anvers: Juan Steelsio, 1550.

Honorius Augustodunensis. *De Imagine Mundi Libri Tres*. In *Honorii Agustodunensis Opera Omnia*. Ed. J. P. Migne. Patrologiae Cursus Completus. Series Latina 172. Paris: Garnier, 1895.

Horace. *The Odes and Epodes*. Ed. and trans. C. E. Bennett. 2d ed. London: Heinemann, 1930.

Housman, A. E., ed. *M. Annaei Lucani belli civilis: libri decem*, by Lucan. Oxford: Blackwell, 1926.

Iglesia, Ramón. *Cronistas e historiadores de la conquista de México: el ciclo de Hernán Cortés*. México: Colegio de México, 1942.

Isidorus Hispalensis. *Etymologiarum sive originum*. Ed. W. M. Lindsay. 2 vols. Oxford: Clarendon Press, 1911.

Janik, Dieter. "Ercilla, lector de Lucano." In *Homenaje a Ercilla*, 83–109. Concepción, Chile: Universidad de Concepción, Instituto Central de Lenguas, 1969.

Jáuregui, Juan de, trans. *La Farsalia por Marco Anneo Lucano*. Ed. Emilio Castelar. 2 vols. Madrid: Viuda de Hernando, 1888.

Javitch, Daniel. "The Imitation of Imitations in *Orlando furioso*." *Renaissance Quarterly* 38, 2 (1985): 215–39.

———. "The Shaping of Poetic Genealogies in the Late Renaissance." In *Comparative Literary History as Discourse: In Honor of Anna Balakian*. Ed. Mario J. Valdés, Daniel Javitch, and A. Owen Aldridge, 265–83. Bern: Peter Lang, 1992.

———. "Sixteenth-Century Commentaries on Imitations in the *Orlando furioso*." *Harvard Library Bulletin* 34, 3 (1986): 221–50.

Johnson, W. R. *Momentary Monsters: Lucan and His Heroes*. Ithaca: Cornell University Press, 1987.

Jones, H. S. V. "The Squire's Tale." In *Sources and Analogues of Chaucer's Canterbury Tales*. Ed. W. F. Bryan and Germaine Dempster, 357–76. Chicago: University of Chicago Press, 1941.

Keller, John Esten, ed. *El libro de los engaños*. Valencia: Castalia, 1959.

Kerkhof, Maxim P. A. M. "Hacia una nueva edición crítica del *Laberinto de Fortuna* de Juan de Mena." *Journal of Hispanic Philology* 7, 3 (1983): 179–89.

Kerkhof, Maxim P. A. M., and Rob Le Pair. "El *Laberinto de Fortuna* de Juan de Mena: las ediciones en relación con la tradición manuscrita." In *Homenaje al profesor Antonio Vilanova*. Ed. Adolfo Sotelo Vásquez and Marta Cristina Carbonell, 1:321–39. 2 vols. Barcelona: Universidad de Barcelona, 1989.

Kinkade, Richard P. "Un nuevo manuscrito de la *Semeiança del mundo*." *Hispanic Review* 39 (1971): 261–70.

Klor de Alva, J. Jorge. "Colonialism and Postcolonialism as (Latin) American Mirages." *Colonial Latin American Review* 1, 1–2 (1992): 3–23.

König, Abraham, ed. *La Araucana: para uso de los chilenos*. Santiago de Chile: Imprenta Cervantes, 1888.

La Du, Milan S., ed. *Text of the Arsenal and Venice Versions*. 6 vols. Princeton: Princeton University Press, 1937.

Lafaye, Jacques. *Quetzalcóatl y Guadalupe: la formación de la conciencia nacional en México*. Trans. Ida Vitale and Fulgencio López Vidarte. 2d ed. México: Fondo de Cultura Económica, 1985.

Lagos, Ramona. "El Incumplimiento de la programación épica en *La Araucana*." *Cuadernos Americanos* 238 (1981): 157–91.

Langlois, Ch. V. *La Connaissance de la Nature et du Monde d'après des écrits français á l'usage des laïcs*. Vol. 3. Paris: Librairie Hachette, 1927.
Lapesa, Rafael. *La trayectoria poética de Garcilaso*. Madrid: Alianza, 1985.
Lasso de Oropesa, Martín, trans. *La historia que escrivio en latin el poeta Lucano: trasladada en castellano*. N.p., 1530.
———, trans. *La historia que escrivio en latin el poeta Lucano: trasladada en castellano*. N.p., n.d. [c. 1535].
Le Goff, Jacques. "The Medieval West and the Indian Ocean: An Oneiric Horizon." In *Time, Work, and Culture in the Middle Ages*. Trans. Arthur Goldhammer, 189–200. Chicago: University of Chicago Press, 1980.
Leonard, Irving A. *Books of the Brave*. 2d ed. New York: Gordian Press, 1964.
Lerner, Isaías. "Ercilla y Lucano." In *Hommage à Robert Jammes*. Ed. Francis Cerdan, 683–91. Vol. 2 of *Anejos de Criticón 1*. 3 vols. Toulouse: Presses Universitaires du Mirail, 1994.
———. "Garcilaso en Ercilla." *Lexis* 2, 2 (1978): 201–21.
Lewis, C. S. *The Allegory of Love: A Study in Medieval Tradition*. New York: Oxford University Press, 1958.
Libro de Alexandre. Ed. Jesús Cañas. Madrid: Cátedra, 1988.
Lida de Malkiel, María Rosa. *Dido en la literatura española: su retrato y defensa*. London: Tamesis Books, 1974.
———. *Juan de Mena: poeta del prerrenacimiento español*. México: Colegio de México, 1950.
Longhena, Mario. *Viaggi in Persia, India e Giava di Nicolò De' Conti, Girolamo Adorno e Girolamo Da Santo Stefano*. Milano: Alpes, 1929.
López de Gómara, Francisco. *Annals of the Emperor Charles V*. Ed. and trans. Roger Bigelow Merriman. Oxford: Clarendon Press, 1912.
———. *Crónica de los Barbarrojas*. In *Memorial histórico español*, 6:331–439. Madrid, 1853.
———. *Historia general de las Indias y vida de Hernán Cortés*. Ed. Jorge Gurría Lacroix. Caracas: Ayacucho, 1979.
López de Toro, José. *Los poetas de Lepanto*. Madrid: Instituto Histórico de Marina, 1950.
Lorris, Guillaume de, and Jean de Meun. *Le Roman de la Rose*. Ed. Daniel Poirion. Paris: Garnier-Flammarion, 1974.
Lucan. *The Civil War: Books I–X*. Ed. and trans. J. D. Duff. Cambridge: Harvard University Press, 1928.
———. *La Guerre Civile (La Pharsale)*. Ed. and trans. A. Bourgéry and Max Ponchont. 2 vols. Paris: Société d'Édition Les Belles-Lettres, 1929.
———. *M. Annei Lucani Cordubensis Pharsalia diligentissime per G. Versellanum recognita. Cum commentariis: Ioannis Sulpitii Verulani; Philippi Beroaldi Bononieñ etc*. Paris: Iehan Petit, 1514.
Macrobius. *Commentary of the Dream of Scipio*. Trans. William Harris Stahl. New York: Columbia University Press, 1952.
Márquez Villanueva, Francisco. "Sobre Ercilla y su épica." *Archivo Hispalense (Seville)* 23 (segunda época), 72–73 (1955): 117–20.
Martianus Capella. *De nuptiis Philologiae et Mercurii*. Vicenza: Henricus de Sancto Ursio, 1499.
———. *Martianus Capella*. Ed. James Willis. Leipzig: Teubner, 1983.
Martindale, C. A. "Lucan's Nekuia." In *Studies in Latin Literature and Roman History*. Ed. Carl Deroux, 367–77. Vol. 2 of Collection Latomus 168. Brussels, 1980.

Mas, Albert. *Les turcs dans la littérature espagnole du Siècle d'Or (Recherches sur l'évolution d'un thème littéraire)*. 2 vols. Paris: Centre de Recherches Hispaniques, Institut d'Études Hispaniques, 1967.

Mazzotta, Giuseppe. "The *Canzoniere* and the Language of the Self." *Studies in Philology* 75 (1978): 271–96.

Medina, José Toribio. "El preceptor de Ercilla." *Boletín de la Academia Chilena* 2, 7 (1919): 265–86.

———. *Vida de Ercilla*. Ed. Ricardo Donoso. México; Buenos Aires: Fondo de Cultura Económica, 1948.

Medina, José Toribio, and Winston A. Reynolds. *El primer poema que trata del descubrimiento y conquista del Nuevo Mundo: reimpresión de las partes correspondientes del* Carlo famoso *de Luis Zapata*. Madrid: José Porrúa Torranzas, 1984.

Mena, Juan de. *El laberinto de Fortuna o las trescientas*. Ed. José Manuel Blecua. Madrid: Espasa-Calpe, 1943.

———. *Laberinto de Fortuna*. Ed. John G. Cummins. Madrid: Cátedra, 1979.

———. *Laberinto de Fortuna*. Ed. Louise Vasvari Fainberg. Madrid: Alhambra, 1976.

———. *Laberinto de Fortuna*. Ed. Maxim P. A. M. Kerkhof. Madrid: Castalia, 1995.

———. *Laberinto de Fortuna/poemas menores*. Ed. Miguel Angel Pérez. Madrid: Editora Nacional, 1976.

———. *Las obras del famoso poeta Juan de Mena*. Ed. Francisco Sánchez [El Brocense]. Madrid: Repullés, 1804.

———. *Obra completa*. Eds. Angel Gómez Moreno and Teresa Jiménez Calvente. Madrid: Turner, 1994.

Menéndez Pidal, Ramón. *Los españoles en la historia y en la literatura*. Buenos Aires: Espasa-Calpe Argentina, 1951.

———. "Poesía e historia en el *Mio Cid*: el problema de la épica española." *Nueva Revista de Filología Hispánica* 3, 2 (1949): 113–29.

Menéndez y Pelayo, Marcelino. *Historia de la poesía hispanomericana*. Ed. Enrique Sánchez Reyes. Vol. 2. Madrid: Consejo Superior de Investigaciones Científicas, 1948.

Michael, Ian. *The Treatment of Classical Material in the* Libro de Alexandre. Manchester, England: University of Manchester Press, 1970.

Mignolo, Walter D. "Putting the Americas on the Map (Geography and the Colonization of Space)." *Colonial Latin American Review* 1 (1992): 25–63.

Montero, Juan. *La controversia sobre las* Anotaciones *herrerianas*. Sevilla: Ediciones ALFAR, 1987.

Monterroso, Augusto. "El Aleph de Ercilla." *Nuevo Texto Crítico* 2 (1988): 229–32.

Morford, M. P. O. *The Poet Lucan: Studies in Rhetorical Epic*. Oxford: Blackwell, 1967.

Murrin, Michael. *History and Warfare in Renaissance Epic*. Chicago: University of Chicago Press, 1994.

Navarrete, Ignacio. "Decentering Garcilaso: Herrera's Attack on the Canon." *PMLA* 106 (1991): 21–33.

———. *Orphans of Petrarch: Poetry and Theory in the Spanish Renaissance*. Berkeley and Los Angeles: University of California Press, 1994.

Nicolopulos, Jaime. "Cortés's Shark Meets Orlando's Orca: The Transformation of History and Poetic Imitation in the First Golden Age Epic Treatment of the New World." *Lucero* 1 (1990): 1–9.

Nicolopulos, James. "Pedro de Oña and Bernardo de Balbuena Read Ercilla's Fitón." *Latin American Literary Review* 26, 52(1998): 100–119.

———. "Reading and Responding to the Amorous Episodes of the *Araucana* in Colonial Peru." *Calíope* 4, 1–2 (1998): 227–47.

Núñez, Fernán, ed. *Copilación de todas las obras del famosissimo poeta Juan de Mena:* Sevilla: Juan Varela, 1528.

———. *Las trezientas d'el famosissimo poeta Iuan de Mena, glosadas por Fernan Nuñez, comendador de la orden de Sanctiago*. Anvers: Iuan Steelsio, 1552.

———, ed. *Las trezientas del famosissimo poeta Iuan de Mena, con su glosa: y las cinquenta con su glosa, y otras obras*. Alcalá: Iuan de Villanueva y Pedro de Robles, 1566.

———, ed. *Todas las obras del famosissimo poeta Iuan de Mena con la glosa del Comendador Fernan Nuñez sobre las trezientas*. Anvers: Martín Nucio, 1552.

Núñez, Hernand, ed. *Las trezientas del famosissimo poeta Juan de Mena glosadas por Hernand Nuñez de Toledo, cauallero de la orden de Sanctiago*. Sevilla: Tres Compañeros Alemanes, 1499.

Ovid. *Heroides and Amores*. Ed. Grant Showerman and J. P. Gould. Trans. Grant Showerman. 2d ed. Cambridge: Harvard University Press, 1977.

———. *Metamorphoses*. Ed. and trans. Frank Justus Miller. 2 vols. Cambridge: Harvard University Press, 1921.

Paoli, Roberto. *Borges: Percorsi di significato*. Messina: D'Anna, 1977.

Patch, Howard R. "Chaucer's Desert." *Modern Language Notes* 34, 6 (1919): 321–28.

———. *The Goddess Fortuna in Medieval Literature*. Cambridge: Harvard University Press, 1927.

Pastor, Beatriz. *Discursos narrativos de la conquista: mitificación y emergencia*. 2d ed. Hanover, N.H.: Ediciones del Norte, 1988.

———. "Silence and Writing: The History of the Conquest." In *1492–1992: Re/Discovering Colonial Writing*. Ed. René Jara and Nicholas Spadacini. Trans. Jason Wood, 121–63. Hispanic Issues 4. Minneapolis: Prisma Institute, 1989.

Peeters Fontainas, J. F. *L'Officine Espagnole de Martin Nutius*. Anvers: Société des Bibliophiles Anversois, 1956.

Pereira da Silva, Luciano. *A astronomia de* Os Lusíadas. Lisboa: Junta de Investigações do Ultramar, 1972.

Pérez de Guzmán, Fernán. *Generaciones y semblanzas*. Ed. J. Domínguez Bordona. Madrid: Espasa-Calpe, 1979.

Pi Corrales, Pazzis. *Felipe II y la lucha por el dominio del mar*. Madrid: San Martín, 1989.

Pierce, Frank. "The fame of the Araucana." *Bulletin of Hispanic Studies* 59, 3 (1982): 230–36.

———. *La poesía épica del Siglo de Oro*. Trans. J. C. Cayol de Bethencourt. 2d ed. Madrid: Gredos, 1968.

———. "Some Themes and their Sources in the Heroic Poem of the Golden Age." *Hispanic Review* 14, 2 (1946): 95–103.

Pigman, G. W. III. "Versions of Imitation in the Renaissance." *Renaissance Quarterly* 33, 1 (1980): 1–32.

Pittarello, Elide. "*Arauco domado* de Pedro de Oña o la vía erótica de la conquista." *Dispositio* 14, 36–38 (1989): 247–70.
Pliny. *Natural History: Libri III–VII*. Ed. and trans. H. Rackham. Vol. 2. Cambridge: Harvard University Press, 1962.
Plotinus. *Opera*. Ed. and trans. Marsilius Ficinus. Florentiae: Antonius Miscominus, 1492.
———. *Plotinus*. Ed. and trans. A. H. Armstrong. 7 vols. Cambridge: Harvard University Press, 1984.
Ponte, Giovanni. "Un esercizio stilistico dell'Ariosto: la tempesta di mare nel canto XLI del *Furioso*." In *Ludovico Ariosto: lingua, stile e tradizione*. Ed. Cesare Segre, 195–206. Milano: Feltrinelli, 1976.
Post, C. R. "The Sources of Juan de Mena." *Romanic Review* 3 (1912): 223–79.
Py, Albert. *Imitation et renaissance dans la poésie de Ronsard*. Geneva: Droz, 1984.
Quint, David. *Epic and Empire: Politics and Generic Form from Virgil to Milton*. Princeton: Princeton University Press, 1993.
———. *Origin and Originality in Renaissance Literature: Versions of the Source*. New Haven: Yale University Press, 1983.
Quintana, Manuel José. *Obras completas*. Madrid: Rivadeneyra, 1852.
Rajna, Pio. *Le fonti dell'* Orlando Furioso. 2d ed. Firenze: G. C. Sansoni, 1900.
Randles, W. G. L. *L'empire du Monomotapa du XVe au XIXe siècle*. Paris: Mouton, 1975.
———. *L'image du Sud-Est africain dans la littérature européene aux XVIe siècle*. Lisboa: Centro de Estudos Históricos Ultramarinos, 1959.
———. "South East Africa and the Empire of Monomotapa as Shown on Selected Printed Maps of the Sixteenth Century." *Studia* 2 (1958): 103–63.
Rigolot, François. "Between Homer and Virgil: Mimesis and Imitatio in Ronsard's Epic Theory." In *Renaissance Rereadings: Intertext and Context*. Ed. Maryanne Cline Horowitz et al., 67–79. Urbana: University of Illinois Press, 1988.
Rodríguez Moñino, Antonio. *Viaje a España del rey don Sebastián de Portugal (1576–1577)*. Valencia: Castalia, 1956.
Ronsard, Pierre de. *La Franciade (1572)*. Ed. Paul Lamonier. 2d ed. Vol. 16 of *Oeuvres complètes*. Paris: Nizet, 1983.
Sabat de Rivers, Georgina. "*La Araucana* bajo el lente actual: el noble bárbaro humillado." In *La cultura literaria en la América virreinal: concurrencias y diferencias*. Ed. José Pascual Buxó, 107–23. Estudios de Cultura Literaria Novohispana 7. México: UNAM, 1996.
Sánchez, Francisco [El Brocense]. *Obras del excelente poeta Garci-Lasso de la Vega*. In *Francisci Sanctii Brocensis Opera Omnia*. Ed. Gregorio Mayans, 4:33–216. 4 vols. Geneviae: Fratres de Tournes, 1766.
Sannazaro, Iacopo. *Arcadia*. In *Opere*. Ed. Enrico Carrara, 49–220. Classici Italiani 25. Torino: UTET, 1952.
———. *De partu Virginis*. Ed. Charles Fantazzi and Alessandro Perosa. Firenze: Leo S. Olschki, 1988.
Santillana, Iñigo López de Mendoza, Marqués de. *Comedieta de Ponça*. Ed. Maxim P. A. Kerkhof. Madrid: Espasa-Calpe, 1987.
———. "Proemio y carta." In *Las poéticas castellanas de la Edad Media*. Ed. Francisco López Estrada, 41–63. Madrid: Taurus, 1984.
Sanz, Carlos. *La geographia de Ptolomeo: ampliada con los primeros mapas*

impresos de América (desde 1507). Madrid: Librería General Victoriano Suárez, 1939.
Saraiva, Antonio José. "Camões e a Espanha." In *Homenaje a Camoens: estudios y ensayos hispano-portugueses*. Ed. Nicolás Extremera Tapia, Manuel Correia Fernández, and Antonio Gallego Morell, 381–85. Granada: Universidad de Granada, 1980.
Scarpa, Luigi, Ed. and trans. *Commentariorum in Somnium Scipionis libri duo*, by Macrobii Ambrosii Theodosii. Padua: Liviana Editrice, 1981.
Schiff, Mario. *La bibliothèque du Marquis de Santillane*. Paris: Librairie Émile Bouillon, 1905.
Schwartz Lerner, Lía. "Tradición literaria y heroinas indias en *La Araucana*." *Revista Iberoamericana* 38, 81 (1972): 615–26.
Seneca. *Medea*. Ed. C. D. N. Costa. London: Oxford University Press, 1973.
———. *Naturales Quaestiones*. Ed. and trans. Thomas H. Corcoran. Cambridge: Harvard University Press, 1971.
Servius Gramaticus. *In Vergilii Bucolica et Georgica Comentarii*. Ed. Georgius Thilo. Lipsiae: Teubner, 1887.
Shanzer, Danuta. *A Philosophical and Literary Commentary on Martianus Capella's* De Nuptiis Philologiae et Mercurii *Book 1*. Berkeley and Los Angeles: University of California Press, 1986.
Spenser, Edmund. *The Faerie Queene: A Variorum Edition*. Ed. Frederick Morgan Padelford. Baltimore: Johns Hopkins Press, 1932–49.
Statius. *Silvae; Thebaid; Achilleid*. Ed. and trans. J. H. Mozley. London: Heinemann, 1928.
Stefanini, Ruggero. "Dante In Borges: L'Aleph, Beatriz e Il Sud." *Italica* 57, 1 (1980): 53–65.
Street, Florence. "The Allegory of Fortune and the Imitation of Dante in the *Laberinto* and *Coronación* of Juan de Mena." *Hispanic Review* 23 (1955): 1–11.
———. "Hernán Núñez and the Earliest Printed Editions of Mena's *El Laberinto de Fortuna*." *Modern Language Review* 61 (1966): 51–63.
———. "The Text of Mena's *Laberinto* in the *Cancionero de Ixar* and its Relationship to Some Other Fifteenth-Century Mss." *Bulletin of Hispanic Studies* 35 (1958): 63–71.
Suárez Fernández, Luis. "Los Trastámaras de Castilla y Aragón en el siglo XV." In *Historia de España*. Ed. Ramón Menéndez Pidal. Vol. 15. Madrid: Espasa-Calpe, 1964.
Thorndike, Lynn. *A History of Magic and Expermental Science*. 8 vols. New York; London: Columbia University Press, 1923–58.
Tibullus. "Tibullus." In *Catullus, Tibullus, and Pervigilium Veneris*. Ed. and trans. J. P. Postgate, 185–339. 2d ed. London: Heinemann, 1924.
Tupet, Anne-Marie. "La scène de magie dans la Pharsale: essai de problématique." In *Hommages à Henri Le Bonniec*. Collection Latomus 201. Ed. D. Porte and J.-P. Néraudau, 419–27. Brussels: Latomus, 1988.
Valerius Flaccus. *Argonautica*. Ed. and trans. J. H. Mozley. Cambridge: Harvard University Press, 1936.
Van Horne, John. "The Urrea Translation of the *Orlando Furioso*." In *Todd Memorial Volumes: Philological Studies*. Ed. John D. Fitz-Gerald and Pauline Taylor, 2:217–29. New York: Columbia University Press, 1930.
Vida, Marco Girolamo. *The De Arte Poetica of Marco Girolamo Vida: Translated*

with Commentary, and with the Text of c. 1517 Edited. Ed. and trans. Ralph G. Williams. New York: Columbia University Press, 1976.

Vidal, Hernán. *Socio-historia de la literatura colonial hispanoamericana: tres lecturas orgánicas*. Minneapolis: Institute for the Study of Ideologies and Literature, 1985.

Vilanova, Antonio. *Las fuentes y los temas del "Polifemo" de Góngora*. Madrid: Consejo Superior de Investigaciones Científicas, 1957.

Virgil. *The Aeneid of Virgil*. Ed. R. D. Williams. 2 vols. New York: St. Martin's Press, 1972–73.

———. *The Aeneid*. Trans. Robert Fitzgerald. New York: Random House, 1984.

———. *Georgics*. Ed. R. A. B. Mynors. Oxford: Clarendon Press, 1990.

———. *Georgics*. Ed. Richard F. Thomas. Cambridge: Cambridge University Press, 1988.

———. *The Pastoral Poems*. Ed. E. V. Rieu. Trans. E. V. Rieu. Hammondsworth, Middlesex: Penguin, 1954.

———. *Virgil, with an English Translation by H. Rushton Fairclough*. Ed. and trans. H. Rushton Fairclough. 2d ed. Cambridge: Harvard University Press, 1935.

Wallis, R. T. *Neo-Platonism*. London: Duckworth, 1972.

Walter of Châtillon. *The Alexandreis*. Trans. R. Telfryn Pritchard. Toronto: Pontifical Institute of Medieval Studies, 1986.

———. *Galteri de Castellione Alexandreis*. Ed. Marvin L. Colker. Padova: Antenore, 1978.

Weinberg, Bernard. *A History of Literary Criticism in the Italian Renaissance*. 2 vols. Chicago: University of Chicago Press, 1961.

Weiss, Julian. "El comentarista en su *Laberinto*: Hernán Núñez y su edición de Juan de Mena." In *Actas del X Congreso de la Associación Internacional de Hispanistas: Barcelona, 21–26 de agosto de 1989*. Ed. Antonio Vilanova, 571–77. Barcelona: Promociones y Publicaciones Universitarias, 1992.

———. "Political Commentary: Hernán Núñez's Glosa a 'Las trescientas.'" In *Letters and Society in Fifteenth-Century Spain: Studies Presented to P. E. Russell on his Eightieth Birthday*. Ed. Alan Deyermond and Jeremy Lawrance, 205–16. Llangrannog: Dolphin Book, 1993.

Whiteway, R. S. *The Rise of Portuguese Power in India 1497–1550*. Westminster: Constable, 1899.

Willis, Raymond S., Jr. *The Debt of the Spanish* Libro de Alexandre *to the French* Roman d'Alexandre. Princeton, New Jersey; Paris: Princeton University Press, 1935.

———. *The Relationship of the Spanish* Libro de Alexandre *to the* Alexandreis *of Gautier de Châtillon*. Princeton: Princeton University Press, 1934.

Wright, John Kirtland. *The Geographical Lore of the Time of the Crusades: A Study in the History of Medieval Science and Tradition in Western Europe*. New York: American Geographical Society, 1925.

Zapata, Luis. *Carlo famoso*. Valencia: Joan Mey, 1566.

Index

Abyssinia, 253–55, 305 n. 39
Achilles, 295 n. 13
  shield of, 214, 218, 226
Acosta, José de, 303 n. 31
Actium, 121, 214–18, 299 n. 47
Adamastor, 187
Aden, 300 n. 51
Adorno, Rolena, 6–7
Adrastia, 192, 296 n. 19
Adriatic, 14, 122
Aeneas, 66–76, 78, 83, 92, 119, 121–23,
  126–27, 186–87, 191, 276 n. 25, 277
  n. 6, 279 n. 28, 280 n. 36, 285 n. 13,
  294 n. 7, 298 n. 35
  shield of, 214, 216, 217–18, 299
  nn. 46–47
Aeolus, 272 n. 17
Aeson, 137, 139, 151, 284 n. 9, 287 n. 36
aëtitae, 147–48, 164, 289 n. 53
Afonso I, king of Portugal, 239, 302 n. 22
Africa, 144, 187, 224, 227–28, 235–36,
  238–42, 245, 249, 251–55, 257, 261,
  271 n. 6, 302 n. 20, 304 nn. 35, 37,
  305 nn. 38–40
African priestess, 107, 109, 112, 282
  n. 54, 284 n. 12, 285 n. 13
Agnese, Battista (map), 304 n. 37
Agrippa, Cornelius, 182–84
Ahl, Frederick M., 134, 283 n. 4, 284
  n. 10, 285 n. 14
Alan of Lille, 177–78, 201, 204–5, 223,
  297 n. 27, 298 n. 37
  Anticlaudianus, 94, 196–99

Alba, dukes of, 79, 190
  Alvarez de Toledo, Fernando [Duke of
  Alba b. 1508–d. 1582], 112, 280 n. 39
Albert, protagonist of Garrido de
  Villena's *Verdadero suceso de la
  famosa batalla de Roncesvalles*, 82
Albertus Magnus, 291 n. 64
Alcalá de Henares, 287 n. 34
Alcibiades, 157, 159
Alcina, 76
Alcoçer, Hernando, 277 n. 11
Aldana, Francisco de, 294 n. 12
Alegría, Fernando, 16, 35–36, 272 n. 13
aleph, xi–xiv, 176–79, 181–82, 185, 193,
  198, 200–201, 204, 206–9, 211–13,
  216–19, 237, 250, 264, 299 n. 47
Alexander of Macedon, xv, 53, 223–29,
  234, 249, 251, 264, 301 n. 9
  tent of, 226–27, 229–30
Alexandria, 53, 298 n. 36
Alfonso X, king of Spain, 294 n. 4
Al-Haçen, 180
Alhambra, 59
Aljubarrota, battle of, 239
Allecto, 280 n. 36
Almagro, Diego de, 306 n. 47
Almanzor, 304 n. 33
Alvarez Vilela, Angel, 272 n. 9
Amara, 253
America(s), 247, 261, 304 n. 32
Amyclas, 26–27, 286 n. 26
Ananke, 296 n. 19
Anatolia, 223

Anaya, Pedro de. *See* Naia
Ancud, 272 n. 9
Anchises, 68, 70–73, 121–22, 176, 298 n. 35
Andalusia, 259
Andes, 94, 261, 279 n. 30
Andrea, 33
Angelica, 52, 76, 277 n. 6
Anna, sister of Dido, 107
Antichrist, 160, 215
Antilles, 260–61
Antioch, 244
Antipodes, 240, 242
Antwerp, 79–80, 277 n. 15
Apelles, 226
Apennines, 256, 279 n. 30
Appius Claudius, 123
Apollo, patron god of the Delphic oracle [Phoebus], 67–69, 108, 110–11, 208, 230, 246, 282 nn. 55, 57, 285 n. 20, 295 n. 13
Aquila, August J., 272 n. 13
Arabia, 225, 242–43, 250
Arauco, 14–15, 34, 36, 83, 213, 261, 268
Arica, 23
Ariosto, Ludovico, xvi, 2, 32–33, 36–37, 52, 63, 92, 97–98, 114–17, 160, 176, 179, 185, 211, 267–68, 271 n. 3, 275 n. 22, 276 n. 1, 277 n. 11, 281 nn. 49–50, 285 n. 22, 297 n. 32
 Orlando furioso, xii–xiv, 13, 29, 59–60, 72–83, 85–88, 100–106, 115, 119, 175, 178, 276 n. 4, 277 nn. 8–9, 278 n. 17, 280 n. 40, 281 n. 47, 283 n. 2, 291 n. 69; rescue from sea monster, 280 n. 41; storm description, 37–42, 274 n. 14
Aristarchus of Samothrace, 53
Aristotle, 43, 53, 157, 291 n. 64
Arle, 75
Armendáriz, Sebastián de, 127
Asia, 223–25, 227–28, 231–32, 234, 236, 243, 250–51, 255, 257, 261, 303 n. 29, 305 n. 42
Asia Major, 234, 249
Asia Minor, 235, 249–51
Askins, Arthur L-F., 290 n. 60
Assyria, 232
Atlante, sage enchanter, 74–76, 114, 160
Atlante, Atlas mountains in N. Africa, 279 n. 30

Atlantic, ocean, 245
Aubrun, Charles, 35
Augustus Caesar, 54–55, 60, 72–73, 78, 88, 121, 130, 214–15, 234, 245, 299 n. 46
aurea saecula (golden age), 72–73, 121
Austria, María de, 285 n. 20
Avernus, 70–71
Azar, Inés, 111–12, 282 nn. 53, 57, 294 n. 10
Azores, 261, 263

Babel, tower of, 226
Babylon, 226, 251
Bacchus, 186–87, 290 n. 62
Bacon, Roger, 181
Bahamas, 261
Bakhtin, M. M., 8,
Balbuena, Bernardo de, *El Bernardo*, 16
Balkans, 216
Ball, Robert, 275 n. 22
Bancroft Library, 290 n. 60
Banda, 244
Barbaro, Daniel, 44–45, 52–53, 55, 161, 275 nn. 18, 23, 292 n. 71
Barcelona, 258
Barnard, Mary, 8–9
Barthe, Roland, 8, 48–51
basilisk, 156, 158–59, 164, 171, 291 n. 67
Bayazid, Ottoman sultan, 305 n. 44
Bazán, Doña María de, 98, 199, 277 n. 13, 280 n. 39
Beardsley, Theodore S., 285 n. 19, 291 n. 67
Bello, Andrés, 16
Bellona, allegorical goddess of war, 2–4, 14, 85, 88–96, 99–100, 104, 128, 199, 230, 279 nn. 30, 32, 280 nn. 33, 36, 301 n. 14
Bembo, Pietro, 44, 58, 137, 276 n. 25
Bengal, bay of, 243
Berkeley, 286 n. 28, 290 n. 60
Bermeo, 258
Bernardus Silvestris, 194, 196, 198–99, 201, 204, 223, 298 n. 37
Beroaldus Bononiensus, Filippo, 162, 171, 293 n. 77
Bigi, Emilio, 276 n. 4, 277 n. 5
Black Sea, 250
Blecua, José Manuel, 286 n. 27, 289 n. 51
Bloom, Harold, 8–9

Boccaccio, Giovanni, 37
Boethius, 48, 159, 291 n. 64
  Consolatione, 94, 157–58, 291 n. 65
Boiardo, Matteo Maria, 29, 33, 37, 73, 81–82, 175, 276 n. 4, 281 n. 49
books of chivalry, 30
Borges, Jorge Luis, 176–78, 182, 184, 203, 207, 293 n. 1
Borgia, Carl Ralph, 279 n. 27
Borneo, 244
Boscán, Juan, 8, 59, 276 n. 27, 291 n. 69
Bosphorus, 250
Bourgéry, A., 282 n. 58, 287 n. 42
Bradamante, 72–76, 78, 81, 83, 101–3, 105, 119, 126, 176, 283 n. 2
Brandiamante, 73
Brazil, (Santa Cruz), 246–47
Britain, isle of, 302 n. 20
Britomart, 178, 180, 182
Broccia, Sebastiano, 145, 287 n. 36, 288 n. 45
Brussels, 275 n. 17
Burgos, 258
Burton, Richard, 178, 182, 184, 207

Cadíz, 260
Cairo, 244, 255, 305 n. 43
Calabria, 144
Calvete de la Estrella, Juan Cristóbal, 44, 59, 80, 136, 277 n. 15, 284 n. 6, 287 n. 32
Calypso, 23
Camaldolese, Fra Mauro, 305 n. 41
Cammerstraat, 80
Camoens, Luis Vaz de, 283 n. 60, 285 n. 20, 294 n. 7, 297 nn. 31, 34, 300 n. 52, 301 n. 12
  Lusíadas: erotic elements, 278 n. 21; mapaemundi, 228–31, 234–64, 301 n. 14, 302 n. 19, 303 n. 30, 304 nn. 32, 37, 305 n. 40, 306 nn. 48–49; naval warfare in the Indian Ocean, 217–19; neoplatonic philosophical basis, 193–94, 297 nn. 24, 27; pagan mythological apparatus, 185, 294 n. 8; prophetic *globos*, 175–76, 179, 183–85, 191, 198–207, 210–13, 217–18, 221, 297 n. 33, 298 nn. 36–37; prophetic structure, 185–89; reception of in light of the *Araucana*, 265–68; storm description, 39–42

Campbell, Killis, 180
Canacee's mirror, 179–80
Canary Islands, 261
Cañas, Jesús, 301 n. 8
Canidia, 109, 282 n. 52
Cano, Juan Sebastián del. See Elcano
Cantar de mio Cid, 127 n. 17
Cape of Good Hope, 187
Cappadocia, 250
Carpio, Bernardo del, 81
Carrillo de Huete, Pero, 286 n. 29
Carron, Jean-Claude, 48, 50, 271 n. 1
Cartagena de Indias, 255
Carthage, 75, 255
Cascales, Francisco, 127
Cassandra, 68, 76
Castiglione, Baldassar, 59, 276 n. 27
Castile, xv, 128, 146, 235, 238, 245–49, 265–67, 302 nn. 17, 22, 304 nn. 32, 33
  cortes of, 248
Catholic kings, Ferdinand and Isabel, 59
Cato, 168
Catullus, 43
Caucasus, 251
Cebu, 247, 262
Celaeno, Harpy queen, 68–70, 187
Celestina, 284 n. 10
Celsus, Aulus Cornelius, 145
cenchris, 168, 292 n. 75
Centella, house of (Valencian nobility), 81
Central America, 261
cerastes, 144–45, 149, 159, 165–67, 172, 288 n. 48
Cervantes Saavedra, Miguel de, 281 n. 48
  La Galatea, 15
  Don Quijote, 79, 82, 274 n. 10
Cevallos, Francisco Javier, 6–7
Ceylon, 243–44, 250, 303 n. 29
chanson de geste, 223
Charlemagne, 60, 78, 223
Charles V, 10, 28, 59–60, 78, 82–83, 182, 215–16, 218, 247–48, 257, 260, 262, 299 nn. 48–49, 300 n. 50, 304 nn. 33, 37
Chaucer, 179–80, 293 n. 2
chelydrus, 144–45, 149, 159, 165–66, 288 n. 45, 292 n. 75

chersydrus, 164–67, 172, 288 n. 45, 292 n. 75
Chevalier, Maxime, 36, 79, 92, 104, 272 n. 13, 278 n. 16
Chiaramonte, house of, 72
Chile, 1–2, 10–13, 21–23, 26, 28, 31, 35, 83–84, 90, 99–100, 213, 261–62, 299 n. 44
China, 243, 250
  Great Wall of, 243–44
Cicero, Marcus Tullius, 48
  Somnium Scipionis, 91, 186, 230, 235, 301 n. 13
Cidade, Hernâni, 274 n. 15, 297 n. 24
Cieza de León, Pedro, 277 n 14
Cinyps, (Wadi Khahan), 145
Circe, 107, 110, 123
Clarke, Dorothy Clotelle, 88
Claudian, 288 n. 47
  Epithalamium de nuptiis Honorii Agusti et Mariae, 294 n. 9, 298 n. 36
Clement VII, pope (fr. 1523-34) (Giulio de Medici), 299 n. 49
Cleopatra, 214
Clonico, 111
Coimbra, xv, 202, 258–59, 297 n. 34
Colchis, 123
Colker, Marvin, 225, 300 n. 4
Colombí-Monguió, Alicia de, 9, 45, 50–51, 292 n. 71
Columbus, Christopher, 248, 260–61, 299 n. 42, 305 n. 46
Concepción, 1, 34, 169, 298 n. 41, 299 n. 44
Concha, Jaime, 16–17, 130
concors machina, 160
Congo, river, 252
conquistadores, 261, 306 n. 47
Constantinople, 216, 244
Copernicus, Nicholas, 202
coplas de arte mayor, 85
Coquimbo, 23
Cordova, 16, 127, 259
Corominas, Juan María, 276 n. 27
Corte Real, Jerónimo, 217, 268, 300 n. 52
Cortés, Hernán, 261, 280 n. 41, 304 n. 33, 306 n. 47
Cosa, Juan de la, 304 n. 35
Cotaldo, semi-legendary Burgundian baron, 81

Covarrubias, Sebastián de, 281 n. 44, 292 n. 73
Cozumel, 280 n. 41
Crepino, 100
Crete, 68
Crónica de don Alvaro de Luna, 286 n. 29
Crónica del halconero, 286 n. 29
crusade(s), xv, 185, 217, 223, 225, 234, 265
Cruz, Anne J., xvi, 8–9
Cruz, Sor Juana Inés de la, *Sueño*, 91
crystallomancy, 176, 182, 184
Cuidad de los Reyes. *See* Lima
Cumae, 74
Cummins, John G., 152, 289 n. 51
Curtius, Ernst Robert, 101, 271 n. 1
Cyrene, 296 n. 20

d'Ailly, Pierre, 299 n. 42
Dambaya, 253
Daneri, Carlos Argentino, 177, 203–4
Dante Alighieri, 32, 91, 230, 275 n. 22, 281 n. 50
  Divina commedia, 88, 101–2, 235, 279 n. 27, 284 n. 10, 293 n. 1, 297 n. 30, 302 n. 17
Danube, 216
Darius, shield of, 300 n. 4
Darius, tomb of, 226, 228
Davis, Elizabeth B., xvi, 271 n. 5
Dee, Dr. John, 182–84
De imagine mundi, 222, 231–32, 244–45, 249, 255, 300 nn. 2–3, 302 nn. 15, 19, 303 nn. 26, 29
Delphi, 123
Delos, 67–68
Denmark, 256
Deyermond, Alan, 147, 286 n. 23
Diana, 110–11, 282 n. 54
Díaz del Castillo, Bernal, 1, 304 n. 32
Dido, queen of Carthage, 12, 70, 86, 107, 186, 278 n. 21, 280 nn. 36, 40, 282 n. 54, 284 n. 12, 285 n. 13
Dipsas, 109, 287 n. 38
Dis, 70–71, 102, 124
discordia concors, 112
discors machina, 112–13, 143, 160
Diu, 217, 300 nn. 51–52
Dobin, Howard, 182
Dolce, Ludovico, 77, 115, 277 n. 8

Douglas, Gavin, 180–81
Palice of Honour, 294 n. 5
Du Bellay, Jacques, 35, 49, 278 n. 19
Ducamin, Jean, 36, 164, 170–71, 280 n. 41, 284 n. 8, 292 n. 74
Duff, J. D., 283 n. 59
Duggan, Joseph J., 223
Durand, José, xvi, 13, 306 n. 47

Ecuador, 261
Edward III, king of England, 82
Egypt, 242, 252, 255, 305 n. 42
Elcano, Juan Sebastián de, 248, 262
Elizabeth I, queen of England, 178, 182
Elysian Fields, 71
Empyrean, cosmic sphere, 200, 202, 221, 299 n. 42
Enareto, 110–12, 282 nn. 53, 56
Endelechia, 195
England, 294 n. 5
Ennius, 86, 292 n. 70
Enríquez de Alvarez, María [wife of the Duke of Alba], 280 n. 39
Eponamón, 272 n. 10
Erasmus, 44
Eratosthenes, 300 n. 1
Ercilla y Zúñiga, Alonso de, 222, 283 n. 60, 291 nn. 65, 67, 292 n. 73, 293 n. 1, 294 nn. 5, 7, 297 n. 31, 298 n. 41, 299 n. 44, 301 n. 12, 303 n. 23, 306 n. 47
  La Araucana: battle of Lepanto, 213–19; conjuration of the infernal powers, 128, 139; description of magical substances, 128, 139, 156–73, 289 n. 56, 293 n. 77; description of the powers of the mage, 107–14; Fitón's *globo*, 175–82, 184–85, 189, 199–200, 204–7, 209–13, 215, 221–22, 297 nn. 32–33, 298 n. 37; mapa-mundi, 228–29, 234, 236, 249–64, 301 n. 14, 303 n. 30, 304 nn. 32, 34, 37, 305 nn. 39–40, 42–43, 306 n. 48; reception of in light of the *Lusíadas*, 264–68; rescue from sea monster, 280 n. 41
  trip to Flanders (1548–49), 80–81
Erictho, 101–2, 107, 109, 113–14, 122, 124–26, 130–31, 133–34, 138–44, 147–48, 150, 153–54, 156, 158–60,

162, 164, 169–71, 281 n. 45, 282 n. 52, 284 nn. 9–10, 285 nn. 13, 15, 287 n. 42
Escorial, 213, 258, 279 n. 31
Espinosa, Nicolás, 81–82, 105, 281 n. 48
Este, house of (dukes of Ferrara), 60, 72, 78–79, 81, 105, 177, 276 n. 4, 277 n. 9
  Ippolito d'Este, 76, 105
Ethiopia, 242, 254, 303 n. 26, 305 n. 39
Euphrates, 250
Europe, 35, 95, 183, 185, 202, 216, 224, 227–28, 231, 235–38, 240–42, 245, 249, 251, 255–57, 260, 279 n. 31, 302 n. 20, 304 n. 32

Fabia, 284 n. 10
Fadrique, prince of Spain, 294 n. 4
Faith, allegorical personification, 196, 198
Fame, allegorical demi-goddess, 280 n. 36
Fantazzi, Charles, 294 n. 12
Far East, 250
Faria e Sousa, Manuel de, xiv, 40–41, 183–84, 189, 200, 206, 230–31, 235, 238, 252, 275 n. 16, 295 n. 15, 297 nn. 31, 33, 301 n. 14, 302 nn. 18, 22, 305 n. 40
Fates, the, 70, 192, 197, 296 n. 19
Faulhaber, Charles, 286 n. 28
Ferdinand II of Aragon, the Catholic, 80, 248, 260
Fernández de Palencia, Alonso, 288 n. 44
Ferrara, 78
Fichter, Andrew, 72, 76–77, 277 n. 6, 283 n. 2
Ficino, Marsilio, 111, 193
Fiorentino, Mauro, 203
Fitón, xiii, xiv, xvi, 14, 16–17, 18–19, 22, 35, 96–98, 103–10, 112–14, 119, 122, 126, 128, 159–60, 169, 175–82, 189, 199–200, 205–7, 209–13, 215, 219, 221–22, 250, 253–55, 257–64, 268–69, 272 nn. 11, 16, 278 n. 19, 283 n. 60, 284 n. 8, 285 n. 15, 297 nn. 32–33
Flanders, 80
Florida, 261
Florit, Eugenio, 106

Fortune, allegorical goddess of, 26–28, 75–76, 88, 90, 93, 95–96, 129–30, 138, 230, 238, 257, 265, 291 n. 65, 294 n. 9, 301 n. 13
Foster, David William, 302 n. 17
France, 3, 14, 81, 91, 223, 228, 277 n. 8, 278 n. 17, 294 n. 12, 299 n. 44
Francis I, king of France (1515–47), 59, 257
Frankfort, 294 n. 6
Fucilla, Joseph G., 104

Galicia, 258
Gama, Cristóvão da, 242, 255
Gama, Vasco da, 39, 186–88, 191, 198, 200–201, 205, 207, 217, 221, 236, 239–40, 242, 245–46, 294 n. 7, 297 nn. 31, 33, 301 n. 14
Garcilaso de la Vega, xiii, 8, 18, 32, 46, 51, 55, 60–61, 86–87, 90, 106–7, 120, 176, 206, 210, 212, 218, 267, 276 nn. 26–27, 277 n. 9, 278 n. 20, 281 nn. 49–50, 285 nn. 20, 22, 291 n. 69, 292 n. 70
  Egloga II, 3, 60, 79–80, 105, 115–16, 188–91, 193, 216–18, 279 n. 30, 280 n. 39, 294 n. 10; description of the powers of the mage, 108–14
  Egloga III, 85
  Elegía II, 127
  "En tanto que de rosa y d'açucena," 57–59, 137–38, 154, 172, 276 n. 25, 290 n. 59
Garcilaso de la Vega, Inca, 300 n. 1, 304 n. 32, 305 n. 46
Garibay, Esteban de, 275 n. 17
Garrido de Villena, Francisco, 81–82, 105, 278 nn. 16, 18
Genoa, 244
Gericke, Philip, 129–30
Germany, 294 n. 12, 299 n. 48
gigantomachy, 299 n. 47
Giraldus, Lilius Gregorius, 275 n. 20
Glaura, 36, 105, 280 n. 40
Goethe, Johann Wolfgang von, *Faust*, 284 n. 10
golden bough, 126
Gómez Moreno, Angel, 152, 287 n. 31
Góngora y Argote, Luis de, 52, 211, 285 n. 20
Gossuin de Metz, 302 n. 15

Gower, John, Confessio amantis, 180–81, 293 n. 2
Granada, 59, 238, 259
Graves, Robert, 177
Greece, 226
Greenblatt, Stephen, 171
Greene, Thomas, xii, 8–9, 19, 43, 45, 53, 55–58, 61–63, 66, 120, 137, 144, 150, 154, 161, 172, 176, 272 n. 16, 275 nn. 22–23, 276 n. 24, 276 n. 3, 290 n. 59, 292 n. 71, 294 n. 12
Greenland, 256
Grenade, Pierre, 133–34
Guacol, 280 n. 41
Guacolda, 31–32, 36, 280 n. 40
Guaticolo, 35, 102, 107–8, 114, 126, 213
Guilmartin, John Francis, Jr., 303 n. 27

Habinek, Thomas N., 298 n. 35
Hardie, P. R., 299 nn. 46–47
Hayes, Aden W., 177
Hecate, 107, 109–10, 142–43, 282 n. 54, 285 n. 13
Hector, 66, 276 n. 4
Helenus, 69–70
Hercules, 226, 260, 285 n. 20
  pillars of, 260
Hernández de Velasco, Gregorio, 294 n. 12
Herodotus, 305 n. 40
Herrera, Fernando de, 35, 46, 127, 267, 278 n. 19, 279 n. 30, 285 n. 21
Herrera Maldonado, Francisco de, 294 n. 12
Herrero Llorente, Víctor-José, 285 n. 19
Hesperia, 68
Highet, Gilbert, 293 n. 77
hippomanes, 290 n. 62
Hispania, 237–38, 257, 265, 267, 302 n. 20
Historia de Carlo Magno y los doce pares de Francia, 181
Historia de Proeliis, 301 n. 9
Holy Land, 216, 225, 234, 250
Holy League, 95
Holy Spirit, 191
Homer, 23–24, 26, 42–43, 46, 53–55, 60, 121–22, 218, 274 n. 13, 276 n. 3
  Iliad, 187, 214, 273 n. 3
  Odyssey, 21–22, 25, 47, 119, 187, 273 n. 3, 295 n. 13, 298 n. 36

Honorius of Autun, 222, 302 n. 20
Horace, 48, 56, 86, 109, 282 n. 52, 292 n. 70
Hormuz, straits of, 243
Housman, A. E., 135, 142, 154, 280 n. 33, 282 n. 58, 283 n. 59, 287 nn. 39, 41–42, 288 n. 43, 293 n. 77
Hungary, 216
Hurtado de Mendoza, García, 36, 266

iaculus, 168, 293 n. 77
Iberian Peninsula, 237–38, 257–58
Imarmene, 192, 296 n. 19
imitation, theoretical apects of
 aemulatio, 45, 51–53, 57, 139, 287 n. 35
 anachronism, role of, 53–58, 61
 construction of poetic "genealogy" through, 115–17
 dialectical, 56–57
 dissimulatio, 45–52
 eclectic, 56–57, 62–66
 eristic imitation, 51
 heuristic, 56–57
 intertextuality, 48–51
 "necromantic," 56–58, 61
 parody, 52
 reproductive, 56, 61–62
India, xv, 41, 186–87, 224–26, 231–32, 234, 243, 245, 250, 271 n. 6, 302 n. 16, 303 n. 29, 304 n. 32
Indian Ocean, 217, 237, 242–45, 250
Indies, 259, 303 n. 23, 304 n. 32
 council of the, 247
Indonesia, 243
Indus, river, 232, 302 n. 16
insulae, geographical topic, 245, 303 n. 29
inquisition, 183
Isabel I, queen of Castile, the Catholic, 88, 248
Isabella, 100
Isle of Love, 187, 246, 297 n. 31
Italy, 26, 59, 68, 71, 73–75, 78–79, 81, 105, 121, 226, 228, 237, 255–56, 277 n. 8, 294 n. 12, 297 n. 31

Janik, Dieter, 127, 172
Japan, 243–44
Jáuregui, Juan de, 127
Jarava, Juan de, 291 n. 64
Jason, 251

Javitch, Daniel, 76–77, 87, 115–16, 277 n. 7
Jerusalem, 225, 250
Jesus Christ, 60, 184, 189, 191, 232, 250, 261, 295 n. 15, 302 n. 22
Jiménez Calvente, Teresa, 152, 287 n. 31
John of Austria, 34
John of Holywood [Sacrobosco], 202–3
John II, king of Castile (fr. 1406–54), 128–30, 132, 146, 148, 229, 234, 286 nn. 23, 29
John III, king of Portugal (fr. 1521–57), 248, 306 n. 50
Johnson, W. R., 92, 112, 143
Jordan, river god, 189–91, 250, 295 nn. 13, 15, 296 n. 20
Juan II, king of Navarre (fr. 1425–79) and Aragón (fr. 1458–79), 132, 286 n. 29
Juba, king of Mauritania, 304 n. 36
Judea, 250, 304 n. 34
Julius Caesar, 26–28, 92, 121–22, 134, 286 n. 26
Juno, Roman goddess, 66, 70, 186, 208, 276 n. 25, 280 n. 36
Jupiter, Roman god, 66, 70, 186, 188–89, 197–98, 200, 205, 207–10, 214, 276 n. 25
Jupiter, cosmographic sphere of, 129

katabasis, 66, 72, 83, 102–3, 105–6, 125–26, 204, 283 n. 1
Kerkhof, Maxim P. A. M., 135, 152, 278 n. 23, 286 n. 27, 287 nn. 33–34, 289 nn. 51–52, 290 n. 58, 292 n. 73, 300 n. 3
Khartoum, 305 n. 40
Kinkade, Richard P., 302 nn. 15–16
Klor de Alva, J. Jorge, 271 n. 6
König, Abraham, 16, 272 n. 15, 284 n. 8
Kristeva, Julia, 8, 50

Lachesis, 296 n. 19
Landino, Franciscus, 166
Lapesa, Rafael, 110
Lapland, 237, 256
Las Casas, Bartolomé de, 241, 304 n. 32
Lasso de Oropesa, Martín, 127, 144, 155, 162, 164, 167, 282 n. 58, 283 n. 59, 285 nn. 16, 19, 292 nn. 72, 75
Laura, 58, 276 n. 24

Lautaro, 31–32, 36
Lautréamont, le comte de [Isidore Lucien Ducasse], 50
Le Goff, Jacques, 304 n. 35
León, 237
Leonard, Irving, 20
Le Pair, Rob, 278 n. 23
Lepanto, xiv, 11, 14–17, 22, 34, 37, 95, 104–5, 128, 175, 209, 211, 213, 218–19, 268, 279 n. 31, 300 n. 52
Leptis Magna, 145
Lerner, Isaías, 27, 60, 106, 108, 157, 276 n. 1, 279 n. 32, 280 nn. 38, 41, 281 nn. 46, 49, 293 n. 77, 304 n. 34
Lethe, 71, 176
Lewis, C. S., 280 n. 35
Leyva, Antonio de, 299 n. 49
Libavius, Andreas, 182, 294 n. 6
Libro de Alexandre, 93, 225–29, 231–34, 236, 280 n. 36, 301 nn. 8, 11
libros de cordel, 181, 294 n. 4
Libya, 127, 145, 168, 172, 255
Lida de Malkiel, María Rosa, xvi, 92, 112, 130–35, 149–53, 170, 222, 231, 233, 235–36, 278 n. 22, 289 n. 55, 290 n. 60, 291 n. 65, 294 n. 9, 297 n. 31
Lima, 23
Lisbon, xv, 41, 258–60, 272 n. 12
Llerena, 131, 286 n. 27
locus amoenus, 90–91, 98, 106, 199, 279 n. 30, 297 n. 31
longaevi, 177
Longhena, Mario, 305 n. 41
Longinus, Dionysius Cassius, 51
López de Gómara, Francisco, 60, 215, 247–48, 260, 277 n. 14, 299 nn. 48–49, 300 n. 50, 300 n. 1, 302 nn. 18–19, 303 nn. 23, 31, 304 nn. 32–33, 305 n. 46, 306 n. 47
López de Mendoza, Iñigo (Marqués de Santillana), 147, 229, 233, 302 n. 15
   Comedieta de Ponça, 284 n. 8
   Sueño, 284 n. 8
Low Countries, 80, 277 nn. 8, 14
Lucan, xiii, 16, 19, 23–24, 42, 62, 107, 133–37, 176, 206, 210–11, 223, 237, 271 nn. 3–4, 272 n. 16, 276 n. 1, 281 n. 50, 283 n. 5, 284 n. 9, 285 nn. 17, 20–22, 288 nn. 44, 47, 289 n. 54, 290 n. 62, 292 n. 74

Pharsalia, xii, 6, 22, 26–27, 52, 92, 101–2, 115–17, 120–28, 130, 211, 283 nn. 4–5, 284 nn. 6–7, 12, 285 n. 16, 286 n. 26, 292 n. 75; conjuration of the infernal powers, 285 n. 13; description of magical substances, 139–50, 153–72; description of the powers of the mage, 107, 109, 112–14, 282 n. 52
Lucifer, 181, 226
Lucretius, 86, 292 n. 70
Luna, Alvaro de, 128–33, 138, 234–35, 264, 286 nn. 23, 29
Lusitania, 238–39, 257–58, 260, 265–66, 302 n. 21
lynx, 156–61, 164, 171, 290 n. 62, 291 nn. 64, 67

Macaulay, G. C., 293 n. 2
Madagascar, 244–45
Madras, (Mylapore), 243
Madrid, 36, 127, 259, 277 n. 11, 285 n. 20, 294 n. 12, 304 n. 34
Magellan, xv, xvi, 246–49, 262–63, 265–66, 303 n. 23, 306 n. 48
   straits of, xv, 262–63, 303 nn. 23, 31, 304 n. 32
Maldives, 244
Malta, 215
Manuel I, king of Portugal (b. 1469–d. 1521), 186, 239, 247
mapamundi, xiii, xv–xvi, 11, 16, 19, 22, 37, 130, 175, 185, 205, 212, 222–29, 231–33, 235–39, 242–47, 249–64, 272 nn. 7, 11, 301 n. 13, 302 n. 15, 303 n. 30
Marcellus, 72
Marfisa, 73–76, 81–82
Mark Anthony, 214–15
Márquez Villanueva, Francisco, 60
Mars, cosmographic sphere of, 129, 286 n. 26
Mars, god of war, 85, 92, 99, 180, 256, 280 nn. 33, 36, 39
Martial, Marcus Valerius, 285 n. 20
Martianus Capella, 192, 208–11, 296 nn. 19–20, 298 n. 37
Martindale, C. A., 134, 139, 282 n. 52, 283 n. 1
Medea, 107, 109–10, 112, 123–25, 137–45, 147, 150–51, 153–55, 157, 161,

251, 282 nn. 52, 54, 284 nn. 7, 9, 11, 287 n. 36, 289 n. 54
Media, 232
Medina, José Toribio, xvi, 80, 104, 136, 272 n. 12, 273 nn. 1, 3, 277 n. 13, 280 n. 38, 281 nn. 42, 46–47, 50, 284 n. 8, 306 n. 48
Medina del Campo, 132–33
Mediterranean, 224, 241, 251, 255
  islands of, 235, 245
Medoro, 52
Medusa, 198, 297 n. 29
Megaera, 288 n. 47
Mekong, river delta, 243
Mele, E., 190
Melinde, 187, 236, 240, 242
Melissa, 72–74, 176
Mena, Juan de, xii, xiii, 19, 120, 122, 125, 176, 206, 210, 222, 267, 278 n. 21, 285 n. 20, 287 n. 31, 289 n. 56, 290 n. 60, 291 nn. 65, 67, 292 nn. 70, 73, 300 n. 1, 302 n. 17
  Coronación, 278 n. 23
  Laberinto de Fortuna, 2–3, 23, 62, 85–98, 101, 115–17, 128–39, 273 n. 2, 278 nn. 20, 23–24, 279 nn. 26–28, 280 n. 34, 284 n. 10, 285 n. 22, 286 nn. 23, 28, 289 n. 52, 291 n. 69, 292 n. 74, 294 n. 9, 297 n. 31, 301 n. 12; conjuration of infernal powers, 138–39; description of magical substances, 139, 143–58, 160–64, 166–73, 289 n. 56; mapamundi passage, 229–39, 242–46, 249–51, 255, 257, 264, 300 n. 3, 301 nn. 13–14, 302 nn. 15–16, 19, 303 nn. 29–30, 305 nn. 39, 42–43; sorceress of Valladolid episode, 130–35
Mendoza, Mencía de [marquesa de Çenete], 285 n. 19
Menelaus, 295 n. 13, 298 n. 36
Menéndez Pidal, Ramón, 16, 272 n. 16, 285 n. 17
Menéndez y Pelayo, Marcelino, 16, 134, 233, 272 n. 15
Mercator, Gerhard, 304 n. 37
Mercury, cosmographic sphere of, 129
Mercury, messenger of the gods, 70, 75–76, 186
Merlin, 72–76, 78, 80, 102–3, 105, 112,
114, 119, 126, 160, 175, 177–82, 204, 212, 283 n. 2, 297 n. 32, 298 n. 36
Meroë, xv, 254–55, 305 nn. 39–41
Mesopotamia, 250
Meun, Jean de, 180
Mexía, Pedro, 299 n. 48
  Silva de varia lección, 280 n. 41
Mexico, 261, 303 n. 28
Michael, Ian, 228, 301 n. 10
Migne, J. P., 302 n. 20
Mignolo, Walter, 304 n. 37
mimesis, 43, 53
Minos, 192
Moluccas, xv, 247–48, 250, 259, 262–63
Monomotapa, kingdom of, 241–42, 244, 251–52, 259, 303 n. 25
Monterroso, Augusto, 177, 293 n. 1
Moon, 110, 129, 140, 145, 195, 282 n. 54
  mountains of, 252–53, 304 n. 37
  pulling down of by witches, 109, 111, 140–41, 171, 287 n. 38
Morínigo, Marcos A., 11–12, 15, 35–36, 157, 272 nn. 7, 13–14, 280 n. 38, 281 n. 46, 293 n. 77, 304 n. 34
Morford, M. P. O., 25–26, 121, 123–24, 281 n. 51, 284 nn. 7, 9
Mortlake, 183
Morroco, 266
Mozambique, 241
Muy, tower of, 79
Mynors, R. A. B., 288 nn. 45–46

Naia, Pedro de, 253, 306 n. 49
Naples, 79, 257, 289 n. 52, 294 n. 12
Nature, allegorical personification, 142–43, 153, 155, 160, 169
Navagero, Andrea, 59
Navarrete, Ignacio, xvi, 8–9, 87, 271 n. 1
Nazareth, 250
Nebrija, Antonio de, 234, 288 n. 44
nekuia, 119, 121–24, 126, 128, 134–38, 140, 171, 204, 283 nn. 1–2
Nemoroso, 79, 108
Neoplatonic Intelligible All, xiv, 176, 193, 200–203, 207, 209–10
neoplatonism, 296 n. 21
Neptune, 187
Nero, 120, 148, 283 n. 5
New Spain, 261
Nicander, of Colophon, 144
  Theriaca, 165, 288 n. 45

Nidos, Mencía de, 169, 298 n. 41
Niebla, count of, 23, 286 n. 26
Nile, xv, 241–42, 252–55, 298 n. 36, 304 nn. 35–37, 305 nn. 39–42
  white branch, 305 n. 40
Noah, 226
North Africa, 226, 242, 255
Norway, 256
Noys, 198–99, 203, 205–6, 297 n. 26
Nubia, [Nobá], 254–55, 304 n. 35
Nucio, Martín, 79–81, 277 nn. 14–15, 278 n. 23, 287 n. 30, 301 n. 12
Numa, the lawgiver, 72–73
Nunes, Pedro, 202–3
Núñez Cabeza de Vaca, Alvar, 1
Núñez, Fernán [El commendador griego], 87, 116, 131–36, 144, 146, 148–49, 151–52, 154–57, 162, 166, 168, 245, 278 nn. 24–25, 279 n. 26, 280 n. 34, 286 n. 27, 287 nn. 31–32, 288 nn. 44, 49, 289 nn. 51, 56, 290 nn. 58, 60, 291 nn. 63–64, 69, 292 nn. 72–74, 293 n. 77, 300 n. 3, 301 n. 12, 302 n. 19, 303 n. 30, 305 nn. 39, 42–43

Oceanus, 296 n. 20
Octavian. *See* Augustus Caesar
Odysseus, 23, 25, 122
Olaus Magnus, 237, 302 n. 18
Olmedo, 131–32
Olympus, 196–197
Orlando, 76, 78, 81, 277 n. 6
Orpheus, 282 n. 53
ottava rima, 85, 105
Ovid, xii, 22, 24, 26, 52, 58, 137, 214, 223
  Metamorphoses, 37–42, 123–25, 274 nn. 6, 13, 284 nn. 7, 9, 11–12, 289 n. 54, 290 n. 62, 295 n. 13, 297 n. 29; description of magical substances, 139–57, 159–62, 165–71, 292 n. 75; description of the powers of the mage, 107, 109, 282 n. 52
  Tristia, 274 n. 6

Palamedès, 283 n. 2
Palestine, 232
Pamplona, 258
Parnassus, 2, 14, 127, 279 n. 30, 285 n. 20
Parthenio, Bartholomaeus, 166
Pastor, Beatriz, 5

paradise, 231–32, 234, 296 n. 20, 302 n. 16
Parthia, 232, 302 n. 16
Paris, 284 n. 6
Patagonia, 262
Patch, Howard R., 294 n. 9
Paulus, 169, 298 n. 41
Pavia, 257, 279 n. 31
Peeters Fontanais, J. F., 80
Pegasus, 127 n. 20
Peletier du Mans, Jacque, 54
Peleus, 295 n. 13
Pelias, daughters of, 123
penates, 67–68, 70–71
Penco, 1–3
Pereira, Simón, 266
Pereira da Silva, Luciano, 202–3
Pérez, Gonçalo, 25, 47, 273 n. 3
Pérez Priego, Miguel Angel, 152, 286 n. 27, 289 n. 51
Pérez de Guzmán, Fernán, 146
Perosa, Alessandro, 294 n. 12
Perseus, 198, 297 n. 29
Persia, xv, 232
Persian Gulf, 243
Peru, 36, 303 n. 28, 306 n. 47
Petit, Jehan, 284 n. 6
Petrarch, Francis, xiii, 32, 48–49, 55–58, 115, 137, 154, 172, 267, 276 nn. 24–26, 281 n. 50, 290 n. 59
Pharos, 298 n. 36
Pharsalia, battle of, 27
Philip II, 2, 10, 12, 26–28, 30, 80, 82–83, 117, 160, 205, 213, 248–49, 258, 260, 265–66, 268, 273 nn. 2–3, 279 n. 31, 280 n. 37, 304 nn. 32–37, 306 nn. 47, 50
Phoebe. *See* Diana
Phoebus. *See* Apollo
phoenix, 148, 163, 289 n. 54
Phronesis. *See* Prudence
Pico della Mirandola, Giovanni, 111
Pierce, Frank, 272 nn. 12–13, 279 n. 32, 294 n. 12
Pierre de Beauvais, 302 n. 15
Pigman, George W. III, 8–9, 43–45, 47–52, 55, 139, 161, 166–67, 292 n. 71, 293 n. 76
Pinabello, 73, 101–2, 283 n. 2
Pinelo, León, 127, 285 n. 20
Pittarello, Elide, 36

Index

Pizarro, Francisco de, 306
Plato, 192–93, 198, 291 n. 64, 296 n. 21, 297 n. 24
  Republic, 296 n. 19; "Vision of Er the Armenian," 192
Pléiade, group of French poets, 48
Pliny, 134, 146–49, 151, 157–59, 162, 171, 254, 288 nn. 48–49, 289 nn. 50, 56, 290 nn. 58, 62, 291 nn. 63–64, 67, 292 n. 73, 304 n. 36, 305 nn. 39, 42
Plotinus, 178, 193–94, 198–201, 203–4, 209, 296 n. 21, 297 n. 23
Pluto, god of the underworld, 119, 125, 288 n. 47
Poliziano, Angelo, 275 n. 23, 277 n. 5
Poma de Ayala, Felipe Guamán, 303 n. 28
Pompey the Great, 92, 121, 123, 133–34
Pompey, Sextus, 122–24, 126, 134, 138, 285 n. 15
Pomponius Mela, 302 n. 19, 305 n. 39
Ponchont, Max, 283 n. 58, 287 n. 42
Portugal, 12, 19, 41, 237, 241–42, 258–60, 275 n. 17, 280 n. 37, 297 n. 34, 302 n. 22, 304 n. 32
  independence from Castile, xv, 238–39, 245–49, 264–66, 306 n. 50
Porphyry, 192
Post, C. R., 279 n. 27
Potosí, 261
Prester John, 252, 257, 293 n. 3, 304 n. 35
Prete Jacopín, 285 n. 21
Priam, 69
Pritchard, R. Telfryn, 300 n. 6
Proclus, 296 n. 19
Proserpina, 285 n. 13, 288 n. 47
Proteus, 183, 187–89, 193–94, 198, 200–201, 205, 207, 217, 269, 295 nn. 13, 15, 297 n. 33, 298 n. 36
Provence, 79
Providence, Divine (allegorical figure), 90–91, 93–96, 129–30, 160, 207, 230, 279 n. 28, 291 n. 65, 295 n. 15, 297 n. 31, 301 n. 13
Providence, mirror of, 194–96, 297 n. 26
Prudence, allegorical figure, 196–98, 205
Pseudo-Callisthenes, 301 n. 9
Ptolemy, Claudius, 202, 252–53, 304 n. 37, 305 nn. 38, 41
Ptolemy II, king of Egypt, 298 n. 36
Puchecalco, 272 n. 10
Pulci, Luigi, 37

Py, Albert, 49
Python, 123, 284 n. 8
Pythonissa, 284 n. 8

Quetzalcóatl, 303 n. 28
Quevedo y Villegas, Francisco de, 52, 211, 275 n. 22, 285 n. 20
Quint, David, 5–6, 26–27, 271 n. 3, 272 nn. 8, 17, 295 n. 13, 296 n. 20
Quintana, Manuel José, 15–16, 272 n. 14
Quintilian, Marcus Fabius, 285 n. 21

Rajna, Pio, 283 n. 2
Randles, W. G. L., 303 n. 25, 304 n. 37, 305 n. 38
Rauco, river in Chile, 96, 98, 100
Reason, allegorical goddess of, 14, 94, 98, 101, 159
Red Sea, 149, 242–43, 255, 300 n. 51
remora, 148, 163, 292 n. 74
Rengo, 33, 274 n. 10
Ricci, Bartolomeo, 43–45, 52–53, 55, 61, 154, 161, 275 n. 18, 292 n. 71
Rigolot, François, 54
Rinaldo, 277 n. 9
Rivers, Elias, 79
Rodomonte, 99
Rodrigues, José Maria, 274 n. 15
Roland. *See* Orlando
Roman d'Alexandre, 227–28, 233, 301 nn. 9–10
Romanticism, xiv, xvi, 5, 15, 269
Rome, xv, 43, 54–55, 60, 72, 78, 86, 121–22, 148, 180, 186, 214, 218, 237, 256–57, 299 n. 47
Roncesvalles, 81
Ronsard, Pierre de, 35, 56, 60, 278 n. 19
  Franciade, 39, 46–47
Rufinus, 288 n. 47
Rufo, Juan, 271 n. 5
Ruggiero, 72–76, 78, 81, 276 n. 4
Ryence, king, 180–81

Saba, 303 n. 26
Sabat-Rivers, Georgina, 31, 36
Saint Anselm, 222, 231, 237, 300 n. 3, 302 n. 19, 303 nn. 26, 29–30
Saint Bartholomew, 303 n. 28
Saint Isidore, of Seville, 222–24, 226–27, 231–32, 237, 239, 242, 249, 293 n. 77, 302 n. 19, 303 nn. 29–30

Saint Thomas, the apostle, 243, 303 n. 28
Saint Quentin, battle of, 2–3, 11, 14–17, 22, 34, 37, 91, 94–95, 104, 213, 258, 279 n. 31, 299 n. 44
Salado, battle of, 239
Salamanca, 151, 258–59, 287 n. 32, 294 n. 12
Sánchez de las Brozas, Francisco [El Brocense], 46, 86–87, 110–11, 115–16, 134–35, 149, 155, 161, 278 nn. 20, 25, 282 n. 56, 287 nn. 31–32, 34, 289 nn. 51, 53, 291 n. 69, 292 n. 70, 300 n. 3
San Lúcar de Barrameda, 248, 259, 262
Sannazaro, Jacopo, 115, 210
  Arcadia, 297 n. 31; description of the powers of the mage, 110–12, 189, 282 n. 53
  De partu Virginis, 184, 189–91, 193, 294 n. 12, 295 nn. 13, 15, 296 n. 20
Santa Cruz Pachacuti Yamqui Salcamayhua, Juan de, 303 n. 28
São Jorge da Mina, 303 n. 25
Saraiva, José Antonio, 265–66
Saturn, cosmographic sphere of, 129–30
Sanz, Carlos, 304 n. 37
Scaliger, Julius Caesar, 54, 285 n. 21
Schwartz Lerner, Lía, 100
Scandinavia, 237, 256
Scotland, 181
Scythia, 237
Sebastian, king of Portugal (fr. 1557–78), 248, 266, 306 n. 50
Selim I, Ottoman sultan (fr. 1512–20), 303 n. 27
Semeiança del mundo, 232, 237, 302 nn. 15–16, 21, 303 nn. 26, 29
Semiramis, 251
Sempere, Jerónimo, *La Carolea*, 82, 105
Sena, 303 n. 24
Seneca, Lucius Annaeus [The Philosopher], 22, 24, 120, 283 n. 5
  Medea, 124–25, 284 nn. 9, 11–12; conjuration of infernal powers, 282 n. 54; description of the powers of the mage, 107, 109
  Oedipus, 281 n. 51
Servius Gramaticus, 165, 288 n. 45, 300 n. 5
Seven Sages of Rome, xiv, 180–82, 293 n. 3

Severo, 108–14, 188–90, 212, 282 nn. 53, 57, 294 n. 10
Seville, 151–52, 238, 259–60, 262
Shanzer, Danuta, 192, 210–11, 296 nn. 17, 19, 298 nn. 38–40
Sibyl, of Cumae, 70–72, 74, 101, 126–27, 191, 279 n. 28, 285 n. 13
sibyl, prophetic guide figure, 94, 122, 124, 138
Sicily, 70–71, 134
Silius Italicus, 121
Silva, 195
Sincero, 297 n. 31
slave trade, [trata de negros], 255
Singapore, 243–44
Socotra, 244
Sofala, 244, 253, 303 nn. 24–25, 306 n. 49
Solinus, 146, 288 n. 49, 291 nn. 64, 67, 293 n. 77
Solomon, king, 303 n. 26
  mines of, 241, 252
Song of Songs, 288 n. 49
Sophia, 196–97, 199
Southeast Asia, 243, 257
Spain, 11, 13, 78, 81–82, 105, 129, 131, 148, 181, 183, 216, 226, 228, 238, 251, 257–60, 265–66, 275 n. 17, 277 n. 14, 285 n. 22, 294 nn. 4, 12, 303 n. 23
  reconquest of, 59, 81, 88, 128–30, 235, 265, 302 nn. 17, 22
Spanish America, 241, 265
Spanish pilot, legend of, 305 n. 46
Spenser, Edmund, 63, 182, 184, 204, 207
  Fairie Queene, 178–80, 298 n. 36
sprezzatura, 48, 59, 85, 276 n. 27
Spice Islands, xv, 243, 247–50, 262, 266
Statius, 2, 121, 223
  Thebaid, 281 n. 51, 288 n. 47
Steelsio, Juan, 287 n. 30, 290 n. 60
Stewart, H. F., 291 n. 64
Strabo, 302 n. 19
Street, Florence, 151, 279 n. 27, 286 n. 27, 289 n. 52
Strymon, 282 n. 53
Sturm, Johannes, 166
Styx, 125–26
Suez, 242, 255
Sudan, 305 n. 40
Sulaiman Pasha, 300 n. 51

Suleiman II, [the Magnificent] (Ottoman emperor fr. 1520–66), 60, 215–16, 299 n. 48, 300 n. 50
Sulpitius Verulanus, Johannes (Giovanni Antonio Sulpizio da Veroli), 127, 162, 171, 285 n. 18, 293 n. 77
Sumatra, 244
Sun, 110, 129, 195
Susa, 232
Sweden, 25
Syria, 232, 250, 304 n. 34

Tamerlane, 251, 257, 305 n. 44
Taprobana. *See* Ceylon
Tartarus, 70–71, 125, 208
Tasso, Bernardo, 58, 137, 276 n. 25
Tasso, Torquato, 63
   Gerusalemne liberata, 16
Tegualda, 36, 100, 105, 280 n. 40
Teresa de Mier, Fray Servando, 303 n. 28
Teresa of Castile, 239
Ternate, 262–63
Tete, 303 n. 24
Tethys, 187–88, 191, 198, 200, 205–7, 221–22, 230–31, 236, 239–48, 251–52, 255, 263, 265, 294 n. 8, 297 nn. 31, 33, 301 n. 14
Thebes, 292 n. 75
   Boeotian, 305 n. 43
   Egyptian, 305 n. 43
Thessaly, 123, 127, 140, 284 n. 7
   witches of, 107, 112–14, 123–24, 140–42, 160
Thetis, 295 n. 13
Thorndike, Lynn, 171, 291 n. 64
Thomas, Richard F., 288 n. 45
Thrace, 67
Tiberinus, river god, 277 n. 6
Tidore, 243–44, 248, 262–63, 304 n. 33
Tigris, river, 232, 302 n. 16
Timor, 244
Tiresias, 122, 281 n. 51
Tisiphone, 288 n. 47
Toledo, 87, 136, 259, 277 n. 11, 287 n. 33, 294 n. 12
Tordesillas, treaty of (1494), 247
Tormes, river god, 190, 212
torrid zone, 239–40, 242, 247, 303 n. 23
translatio, 4, 53, 60
Trent, council of, 81
Trinidad, 247

Tristano, 74, 105
Trojan War, 226
Troy, 67–68
Tucapel, 2, 99–100, 274 n. 10
Tudor, Mary, 82
Tunis, 279 n. 31
Turnus, 71

Urania, 198, 297 n. 26
Urrea, Jerónimo de, 79–81, 87, 98, 104–5, 277 nn. 8, 10–11, 13, 278 n. 17, 281 nn. 47–48, 291 n. 69

Valencia, 258
Valerius, Julius, 301 n. 9
Valladolid, 131–33, 144, 150, 152–53, 156, 160, 162
Van Horne, John, 277 n. 12
Vásquez de Contreras, Diego, 277 n. 11, 281 n. 47
Vásquez de Mármol, Juan, 278 n. 20
Vasvari, Louise, 152, 278 n. 23, 289 n. 51
Vega Carpio, Lope Félix de, 31, 285 n. 20
   Caballero de Olmedo, 284 n. 10
Venice, 227, 237, 244, 277 n. 8, 304 n. 37, 305 n. 41
Venus, cosmographic sphere of, 95, 129
Venus, goddess of love, 57–58, 137, 180, 186–87, 276 nn. 24–25, 280 n. 39, 294 n. 9
Venus, mirror of, 180–81
Versellanus, G., 284 n. 6
Vida, Marco Girolamo, 45–46, 49, 167, 275 n. 20, 283 n. 1, 293 n. 76
Vienna, 216, 218, 299 n. 48, 300 n. 50
Vietnam, 243
Vilanova, Antonio, 46
Villena, Enrique de, 131
Vincent of Beauvais, 222
Viracocha, 303 n. 28
Virgil, 2, 16, 22, 26, 37, 40, 42–43, 46, 48, 52, 60, 82–83, 86–87, 106, 112, 114–15, 154, 176, 179, 191, 210, 214, 216–18, 223, 268, 271 nn. 3–4, 274 n. 13, 276 nn. 1, 3, 278 n. 21, 283 n. 1, 292 n. 70, 294 nn. 7, 12:
   Aeneid, ix, xii, xiii, 3, 6, 13, 24–25, 27, 29, 46, 54–55, 57–60, 66–78, 88, 92, 97, 101–2, 107, 119–21, 121–25, 137–38, 181, 185–87, 204, 211, 272 n. 17, 276 nn. 24–25, 279 n. 28, 283

Virgil (*continued*)
    n. 2, 284 nn. 12, 285 n. 22, 299 n. 46; conjuration of infernal powers, 282 n. 54, 285 n. 13; description of the powers of the mage, 107, 109
    Georgics, 23, 144–45, 165–66, 198, 282 n. 53, 288 nn. 45–46, 290 n. 62, 292 n. 75, 295 n. 13, 296 n. 20
Virgil the Mage, 180
Virgil's mirror, 180–81, 194, 293 n. 3, 294 n. 4, 298 n. 36
Virgin Mary, 272 n. 10
Vitoria, Francisco de, 241
Vitoria, la nao, 247–48, 262
Vives, Juan Luis, 27
Vizcaya, 257
Vulcan, smith of the gods, 180

Wallis, R. T., 296 n. 21, 297 nn. 23, 30
Walter of Châtillon, 300 n. 4
    Alexandreis, 92, 223–25, 228, 231–33, 300 n. 6

Warton, Thomas, 179, 298 n. 36
Weiss, Julian, 278 n. 24
Wetherbee, Winthrop, 297 n. 26
Williams, R. D., 70, 72
Williams, Ralph G., 293 n. 76
Willis, Raymond S., 227, 280 n. 36, 298 n. 40, 301 nn. 9, 10
Wood A., Enrique, 284 n. 8

Zambezi, river [Cuama], 241–42, 244, 251–53, 303 nn. 24, 25
Zambia, 241
Zapata, Luis, 273 n. 2
    Carlo famoso, 30, 82, 105; rescue from sea monster, 280 n. 41
Zaragoza, 151, 258, 272 n. 12
Zárate, Agustín de, 277 n. 14
Zeeland, 256
Zerbino, 100
Zeus, 23
Zimbabwe, 241, 303 n. 24

www.ingramcontent.com/pod-product-compliance
Lightning Source LLC
Chambersburg PA
CBHW031544300426
44111CB00006BA/162